WORLD MONETARY REFORM

WORLD MONETARY REFORM

Plans and Issues

Edited by

HERBERT G. GRUBEL

STANFORD UNIVERSITY PRESS
Stanford, California

LONDON: OXFORD UNIVERSITY PRESS

Stanford University Press
Stanford, California
London: Oxford University Press
© 1963 by the Board of Trustees of the
Leland Stanford Junior University
Printed in the United States of America
Original edition 1963
Reprinted 1965

Preface

"Would you tell me, please, which way I ought to go from here?" [asked Alice]
"That depends a good deal on where you want to get to," said the Cat.

The question of how to modify the current organization of the international monetary system so that it can better fulfill the functions assigned to it has been discussed widely and intensively in recent years. This book brings together some of the most important contributions to this discussion made by the world's outstanding authorities in this field.

Most of the articles are reprinted as they appeared in the original source, with some additions or deletions of subheads. Minor stylistic changes have been made throughout, and changes have been made in the wording of some footnotes to attain uniformity and consistency. As indicated in the appropriate place, the contributions by Altman, one by Triffin, and one by Harrod represent condensations of the original writings. I hope, however, that I have succeeded in not letting the process of condensation alter the substantive content of these writings. The last selection of this volume is a contribution by Triffin which amplifies and re-emphasizes some of the points made in selection 1. But it also contains his reactions to the criticisms leveled against his original proposal and to the alternative plans offered. This is the main justification for the inclusion of that article.

There are several references in this book to a plan proposed by Professor S. Posthuma, Director of the Bank of the Netherlands. The details of this plan were presented as an internal document to the Monetary Committee of the EEC in the fall of 1962. Only after production of this book had progressed too far to permit inclusion of any further papers were Posthuma's views made public. Because of the wide interest that the Posthuma plan has attracted, the reader is referred to his two articles: "The International Monetary System," *Banca Nazionale del Lavoro Quarterly Review* (September 1963), and "Wandlungen im internationalen Waehrungssystem," *Kieler Vortraege* (Neue Folge 29, Kiel, 1963). Also, Robert V. Roosa, in "Reforming the International Monetary System," in the October 1963 issue of *Foreign Affairs*, presents a view that differs substantially from the one he held at the time the article reprinted in this book was written. Roosa now believes that a major reform of the international monetary system may be necessary and recommends that a study of the problem be made.

This book would not have materialized without the encouragement which I have received from my teachers Robert Triffin and James Tobin at Yale University and my colleague Lorie Tarshis at Stanford University. I am deeply indebted to them.

H.G.

Contents

Contents

PART II

Improvement of the Gold Exchange Standard System

Contributors

OSCAR L. ALTMAN, Adviser on Research and Statistics, International Monetary Fund

JAMES ANGELL, Professor of Economics, Columbia University, New York

THOMAS BALOGH, Reader, Balliol College, Oxford University

EDWARD M. BERNSTEIN, Consulting Economist; United States Expert at Bretton Woods; for many years Director of Research, International Monetary Fund

BROOKINGS GROUP:

    WALTER S. SALANT, Brookings staff

    EMILE DESPRES, Professor of Economics, Stanford University

    LAWRENCE B. KRAUSE, Yale University

    ALICE M. RIVLIN, Brookings staff

    WILLIAM A. SALANT, Economic Consultant

    LORIE TARSHIS, Professor of Economics, Stanford University

SIR ROY HARROD, Tutor in Economics, Christ Church, Oxford University; Nuffield Reader in International Economics, Oxford University

MICHAEL A. HEILPERIN, Professor at the Graduate Institute of International Studies, Geneva

PER JACOBSSON, Managing Director of the International Monetary Fund until his death in May 1963

HARRY G. JOHNSON, Professor of Economics, University of Chicago

JOHN MAYNARD KEYNES, English economist and monetary expert

FRIEDRICH A. LUTZ, Professor of Economics, University of Zurich

FRITZ MACHLUP, Professor of Economics, Princeton University

JAMES E. MEADE, Professor of Political Economy, Cambridge University

DAVID ROCKEFELLER, President, Chase Manhattan Bank

ROBERT V. ROOSA, Under Secretary for Monetary Affairs, U.S. Treasury

JACQUES RUEFF, Member of the Economic and Social Council of France; honorary Vice Governor of the Bank of France

SIR MAXWELL STAMP, Director of Phillip Hill, Higginson and Co. Ltd.; formerly with the Bank of England and the International Monetary Fund

ROBERT TRIFFIN, Pelatiah Perit Professor of Political and Social Science, Yale University

HENRY C. WALLICH, Professor of Economics, Yale University

LELAND B. YEAGER, Associate Professor of Economics, University of Virginia

XENOPHON ZOLOTAS, Governor of the Bank of Greece; formerly Professor at the University of Athens

Abbreviations

BIS   Bank for International Settlements, Basel, Switzerland

EEC   European Economic Community (Common Market): the Six

EFTA   European Free Trade Association: the Seven

EMA   European Monetary Agreement (successor of EPU)

EPU   European Payments Union (defunct December 1958)

GATT   General Agreement on Tariffs and Trade

IBRD   International Bank for Reconstruction and Development

IDA   International Development Association

IMF   International Monetary Fund

OECD   Organization for Economic Cooperation and Development

OEEC   Organization for European Economic Cooperation

XIMF   Symbol for an International Monetary Fund remodeled according to the Triffin proposals

Introduction:
Plans and Issues

HERBERT G. GRUBEL

This book brings together the most important writings on the various plans that have been advanced for reform of the world monetary system in the past few years. Since the plans are dealt with in detail in the book and are classified in the articles by Johnson and Machlup, it does not appear useful to introduce the reader to them by a detailed analysis of their working mechanism or yet another classification. Instead, this preface seeks to provide the reader with a general analytical framework in which to fit the various issues raised in the essays reprinted in this book.

LIQUIDITY, BALANCE OF PAYMENTS, AND CAPITAL NEEDS

Almost all these essays were written during the period 1958–62, when the United States experienced a serious drain on her gold reserves. Many writers relate these gold losses to two different but interconnected problems facing the United States and the world. One problem is the persistent deficit in the United States balance of payments. Some papers suggest measures to alleviate or eliminate this deficit (see especially Wallich). It was one of Triffin's contributions to demonstrate that the solution of the U.S. balance-of-payments deficit was likely to bring to the fore another, and in the long run perhaps more serious, problem. This problem is the necessary consequence of the growth of the gold exchange standard in the 1950's, when the U.S. balance-of-payments deficits served as a source of world liquidity as long as they were neither too large nor too persistent. Indications at the end of the 1950's were that these deficits may have been both too large and too persistent. The danger inherent in this situation is that elimination of the deficits, by drying up a most important source of liquidity, would threaten to throw the world into a deflationary spiral. The second problem thus becomes how to supply the world with adequate mon-

This introductory note has benefited from comments made by Harry G. Johnson.

etary reserves once the United States succeeds in re-establishing balance in her international payments.

This issue in turn can be distinguished from another problem frequently confused with it. Underdeveloped countries seem to experience chronic shortages of foreign exchange, and therefore appear to suffer from a "liquidity" problem. In fact, however, what these countries require is not "liquidity" but additional foreign capital. The need for liquidity and these needs of underdeveloped countries are logically quite distinct problems. However, Stamp, Triffin (paper 1), and Harrod (paper 10) have some suggestions on how they might be solved together.

In reading this book it is therefore useful to remember that there exist three analytically distinct issues: (1) current U.S. balance-of-payments difficulties; (2) the underdeveloped countries' need for capital; and (3) the ability of the world's monetary system to adjust liquidity creation to the actual requirements of noninflationary economic growth rather than to subject it to the inflationary or deflationary pressures arising from the vagaries of gold production and of the balance of payments of the so-called key-currency countries. The last of these points is the central subject of the essays that follow. But since the three problems can be separated only analytically, and in the real world are interconnected in various ways, all three figure prominently in the discussion of any one.

LIQUIDITY AND THE ADJUSTMENT MECHANISM

Two more issues, in a sense preliminary to the crucial ones involved in the subject of liquidity, need to be pointed out. In the first place, all the writers represented in this book explicitly or implicitly make certain assumptions about the institutional framework of the world. The issue is, Which of these institutions do they take for granted and which do they plan to reform in the effort to develop a more adequate world monetary system? All except Meade assume a regime of fixed exchange rates. All assume that prices and wages are relatively inflexible in the downward direction, and that full employment is the dominant goal of national economic policies. Meade shows that it is these institutional characteristics that underlie the basic need for liquidity.

In the second place, it is important to recall that the provision of liquidity to the world can never be fully adequate if the mechanism of adjustment to disturbances of international equilibrium does not function. The reader may therefore find it helpful to examine each author's comments from two points of view. (1) How far is his analysis consistent with his or the other authors' assumptions about the institutional framework of the world, i.e., fixed exchange rates, inflexible wages and prices, and national full-employment policies? (2) Does he deal with the problem of how to provide more liquidity, or of how to construct a more efficient mechanism of adjustment?

PROBLEMS OF DIAGNOSIS

Proposals for an adequate provision of world liquidity imply that the need for a change in the current status has been recognized. The basis for such a recognition is usually an interpretation of past facts and the projection of trends into the future. The resultant diagnosis of the problem is of great importance, since it determines significantly the content of the reform proposals proper. Yet the interpretation of past facts and the projection of needs are themselves subject to theoretical and practical difficulties, which it may be well to keep in mind when reading the essays in this book.

First, what is meant by the term "liquidity"? Most of the writers relate liquidity to the stock of internationally acceptable means of payment, which must usually possess, or at least be thought to possess, the properties of stable and predictable value. Such assets held by a country constitute its "reserves." What in the past have served as instruments of liquidity in international payments? Triffin (paper 1) provides tables showing the history of the world's supply of gold and acceptable national obligations during the past sixty years. Given that these are the most relevant data available, what do they reveal about the adequacy of future supplies of liquidity?

This question cannot be answered properly without clarification of the term "adequacy," which implies some standard of comparison. Authors do not usually explain explicitly what their adequacy criteria are, and it may be well to search for implicit valuations. Are reserves considered adequate when they are large enough to permit countries to finance seasonal and cyclical deficits in their balances of payments without having to resort to trade and exchange restrictions or to changes in prices, incomes, or exchange rates? Or does "adequacy" require that reserves be large enough to permit countries to make basic adjustments in relative prices and economic structure to correct fundamental disequilibria, without assuming too great a cost in terms of unemployment, trade restrictions, and the like? How great do the authors of the articles in this book consider the costs of accelerated adjustment forced by inadequate liquidity to be? The social costs of unemployment, exchange and trade restrictions, devaluations, and interruptions of government and private plans are nonquantifiable elements entering into the definition of adequacy of reserves. Balogh's contribution deals with these issues in some detail.

Triffin tackles the problem of how actually to measure liquidity requirements with available data, and projects his estimates into the future. While he admits the importance of nonmeasurable elements, he works with ratios of monetary reserves to world trade. He emphasizes how poor aggregate measures are and performs various disaggregations of these ratios. This is important because of the asymmetry of the forces working on deficit and surplus countries. An unsettled issue remains: Has there been a change in the form and intensity of domestic and foreign pressures experienced by surplus countries in recent years?

Stamp suggests an intuitive and appealing approach to judging the adequacy of present reserves. He asks whether we can think of any countries that at this time would be willing to increase their exports if they could be sure to receive gold in return. If there are such countries, and Stamp suggests that there are some, this implies that these countries have lower levels of reserves than they wish. More likely than not, these low levels have prompted domestic restrictions on income and employment, and the demand from foreign countries would presumably be met by drawing idle resources into employment. Such a higher level of domestic income and employment could in turn be expected to lead to increased imports and an over-all higher level of sustainable international trade.

It might be a fruitful exercise for the International Monetary Fund to collect and publish regularly the plans to improve national balances of payments made by all the countries of the world. These plans often add up to amazingly large sums. They are inconsistent with each other because one country's surplus leads of necessity to deficits in some other countries. Yet the mere efforts to put these plans into effect tend to reduce employment, trade, and welfare. Might not an over-all higher level of reserves in the world induce some of the countries to abandon their effort to improve their balances of payments, and so increase the chances of success of those countries that have really low reserve levels? Perhaps nations do have a mercantilist urge to accumulate foreign exchange reserves, which, irrational as it may be for the twentieth century, ought to be taken into account by a rationally designed world payments system.

The data actually available and the narrative of the events underlying them are interpreted differently by each author. Some (Jacobsson, Bernstein, Zolotas, Wallich, Roosa) believe that there is no shortage of liquidity now and that there is unlikely to be one in the near future. But most authors admit that a shortage may develop in the distant future. Most authors also agree that the current gold exchange standard involves many dangers to the key currencies, and that it creates liquidity haphazardly. Some of the authors (Harrod, Rueff, Heilperin, Stamp, Machlup, Balogh, Angell, Yeager) share Triffin's alarm over the dangers of the present system and the possibility that inadequate supplies of liquidity may lead to serious disruptions of world commerce.

REFORM SCHEMES

Central issues with which all reform schemes have to deal are these.

How does the plan overcome the present vulnerability of the key currencies? This vulnerability has its roots in the custom that some national currencies are held as international reserves. Because of the universal acceptability as means of payment of the national obligations issued by the reserve-currency countries, principally the United States and the United Kingdom, these countries have in the past decade been able to run cumulatively large balance-of-payments deficits. The resultant large outstanding obligations are mostly payable in gold on demand or short notice, and are held partly by central banks and partly by private parties. Any crisis of confidence in the ability of the key-currency countries to make good on their obligations, triggered as it may be by real or imagined difficulties in their balances of payments, could lead to massive conversions into gold, devaluations, gold embargoes, or other restrictive actions. Substantial interest arbitrage operations or speculative short-term capital movements are prime causes of such imbalances in receipts and outlays. Does the proposed plan aim at the prevention of such disturbances by going to their basic causes, or does it provide instruments and institutions to remove their harmful effects *after* they have occurred?

What is the provision for increases in reserves immediately and over time? Increases in reserves can be provided by new mining of gold, by revaluations of existing gold stocks, by extensions of credit from countries to each other bilaterally or multilaterally, through regional or world-wide organizations, automatically or on an ad hoc basis, in discrete steps or continuously, etc.

Are there safeguards against excessive and inflationary increases in liquidity? Schemes for creating liquidity involving human judgment could conceivably be used to create too much purchasing power in the world and cause inflation. How important do the authors of the plans consider these dangers either in their own proposals or in those of others, and how do they propose to deal with them?

How much national sovereignty do countries have to give up under the plan? The most prominent rights of national sovereignty in the economic sphere involve issuing domestic currency, regulating the money supply, setting interest rates and fiscal policy, changing the external value of the domestic money, and holding international reserves in forms and quantities as chosen. The only realm of national sovereignty touched by any of the plans is the composition of reserves, which may require the holding of gold only, the holding of certain percentages in foreign currencies, or internationalized reserves in the form of deposits with an international agency. The composition requirement may be in force at all times or only under certain conditions.

What is the role of gold under the specific plan? Gold could be made the ultimate and only means of settlement in international transactions. Alternatively, it could be supplemented by other forms of international payments media while retaining its character as the ultimate standard of value. Other solutions to the liquidity problem could envisage a complete demonetization of gold, gradually or immediately, directly or in a roundabout way.

The issues raised up to this point are common to all plans. But each type of reform proposal is associated with its own and new specific problems, which will be discussed next. The succession in which these problems appear is dictated by the organization of the book.

The book is made up of three parts. Part One contains proposals for the centralization of international reserves and commentaries on these plans. In Part Two the plans for the improvement of the gold-exchange standard system, along with suggestions for the revaluation of gold can be found. Part Three consists of proposals for the introduction of flexible exchange rates and proposals for return to the gold standard. This part contains in addition a number of articles in which experts comment in general on these plans. One of these articles presents Triffin's answers to his critics and his reactions to some prominent alternative plans advanced at the time the article was written (early in 1961).

CENTRALIZATION OF RESERVES

The Keynes plan is of historic interest as an effort to construct a system of world payments that can efficiently meet the needs of a growing world economy. It was conceived when a unique opportunity for improving the international monetary system presented itself at the end of World War II. Why was the Keynes plan never accepted? Was it the lack of safeguards against inflation, the insistence on responsibility for action by surplus countries, the lack of provision for an adjustment mechanism? Did it imply too much loss of sovereignty by participating countries?

The Triffin plan was also designed as a system of world payments capable of supplying the needs of a growing international economy; it therefore resembles the Keynes plan in many respects. But Triffin tried to meet some of the objections that had been raised against the Keynes plan. He provided for institutional limitations on the rate of increase in liquidity, to serve as safeguards against the potential threat of inflation. Are these limitations too mechanistic, as Altman suggests? The emphasis on regional organization might help to overcome the distrust countries have for world-wide associations and lead to greater willingness to give up certain national rights. How much loss of national sovereignty is involved when countries subject their reserve composition to certain rules and commit themselves to holding certain percentages of reserves in the form of deposits with an international organization? Would the existence of such deposits make currency devaluations impossible, or more costly than they are now (see Altman)?

The treatment of gold and the continued but limited convertibility of currencies into gold under the Triffin plan are criticized by Angell and Yeager. The technique of ensuring long-term growth of liquidity by open-market operations comes under fire from Bernstein and Harrod (paper 10). The latter suggests the alternative of using the available funds to set up world-wide price stabilization schemes.

The creation of additional liquidity does not automatically produce an increase in effective demand. Stamp suggests and Triffin endorses a close cooperation between agencies providing capital to underdeveloped countries and a centralized holder of reserves. The Triffin plan raises the further issue of how to carry out the transition, especially what to do with outstanding dollar and sterling obligations.

Furthermore, can countries be expected to consider deposits with the Triffin agency as part of their reserves, to be drawn on freely, or will these deposits be considered inferior in some way and used as sparingly as the gold tranche with the IMF? In the latter event the Triffin plan may actually reduce liquidity, since countries have to give up gold and dollars to obtain these IMF deposits (see Harrod).

Rockefeller raises the point that the Triffin plan would be likely to reduce New York's importance as a financial center of the world. Harrod similarly suggests that the position of London and sterling would be undermined as a result of internationalized reserves under the Triffin plan. Are the losses of New York and London likely to be serious? Do these objections raised by Rockefeller and Harrod merely represent the pleadings of vested interests in the present system, or would it be bad for the world if New York and London lost some of their eminence as world financial centers?

IMPROVEMENT OF THE GOLD EXCHANGE STANDARD SYSTEM

Various techniques designed to improve the current system of the gold exchange standard are proposed by Jacobsson, Bernstein, Zolotas, Roosa, and Wallich. Some of these measures are aimed at reducing the vulnerability of the key currencies through cooperation among central banks. Are these agreements mainly stopgap measures designed to fight undesirable symptoms of a basically irrational system, or do they succeed in altering the basic nature of the system? When do agreements to cooperate under precisely defined circumstances become equivalent to real losses of sovereignty? Are these proposals perhaps more practical than the Triffin plan, since cooperation rather than basic reform may be the only change for which countries are ready in today's world?

The problem of providing an adequate long-run growth of reserves has received attention by Bernstein, Jacobsson, Roosa, and Zolotas. Will periodic but nonautomatic increases in IMF quotas provide increases in reserves in a sufficiently smooth manner to permit steady and continuous growth of world commerce? Countries have in the past been behaving as though they considered their IMF quotas imperfect substitutes for reserves in gold and dollars. Can the IMF members be induced to change their attitudes? Are these quotas logically equivalent to credit creation under the Triffin plan (see Testimony of the Experts)?

Roosa and Zolotas suggest that countries should hold more of each other's currencies; Zolotas, but not Roosa, adds that such holdings should be assured against devaluations by a gold guarantee. Is the U.S. Congress likely to allow the Treasury to hold potentially very large sums of foreign exchange without any gold guarantees? Is it conceivable that the United States could ever be induced to provide a gold guarantee on her outstanding dollar obligations?

CHANGES IN THE PRICE OF GOLD

Among his other suggestions Harrod proposes an increase in the price of gold. What would this solution do to the future willingness of countries to hold foreign currencies, including dollars? What would this in turn do to the over-all amount of world liquidity, i.e., gold plus national obligations? Further issues connected with the revaluation of gold, which the reader may want to keep in mind, are the following. Who would gain by the revaluation of gold at the time it occurs and afterward? Would there be excess liquidity immediately after the revaluation? Would periodic changes in the price of gold be necessary, and if so would each one be accompanied by runs on national currencies and the hoarding of gold?

The problem of gold hoarding has been tackled directly by Machlup, who suggests that if there has to be a revaluation of gold, the price should be changed downward. Would such a step bring gold out of the hoards? It might do so only if downward adjustments occurred at intervals not too far apart. But the addition to liquidity resulting from gold drawn out of hoards would be offset by a series of factors accompanying the decline in the gold price. Under such an arrangement, the total value of the physical gold stock tends to become smaller and smaller. Industrial uses of gold are encouraged and gold production is discouraged. How soon would Machlup's suggestion thus lead to liquidity shortages? Is this proposal Machlup's tongue-in-cheek way of informing us of his opinion about the rationality of building a world monetary system around gold in an age when humanity is reaching for the stars?

FLEXIBLE EXCHANGE RATES AND RETURN TO THE GOLD STANDARD

An intellectually appealing solution to the liquidity problem is that advanced by Meade. Rather than being concerned with how to ensure the adequacy of reserves in the short and long runs, his plan for flexible exchange rates would do away with the need for reserves almost completely. The word "almost" is the key to an issue that arises out of Meade's proposals. The issue is raised by his attempt to meet one of the standard objections to flexible exchange rates, namely, the alleged instability of rates in the short run. In Meade's plan there is an agency that intervenes in the markets to even out these short-run fluctuations.

Would the existence of such an agency deprive this solution of one of its most appealing features, complete freedom of the market? Would this agency face the problems faced by central banks under fixed exchange rates, namely, problems arising from the efforts of speculators to outguess and outmaneuver those responsible for maintaining stable rates? Might not such a system of flexible exchange rates have the worst properties of both worlds, a relatively unpredictable value of the exchange rate and frequent destabilizing speculative runs on the currency?

This issue arises in addition to all the other objections to flexible exchange rates frequently made, such as their effects on domestic price stability, on trade as a result of uncertain prices or expensive forward cover, and on long-term capital flows. Another point, recently brought up by R. A. Mundell,[1] should be kept in mind by the reader. For what geographic or national areas would it be desirable to have one currency and stable exchange rates within the area borders and flexible exchanges rates vis-à-vis the rest of the world? Should the areas be countries as defined by currently existing boundaries? If flexible exchange rates really solve problems as well as their advocates claim, why not have different currencies and flexible exchange rates for each region within a country? Why should the unit not be continents, or hemispheres?

The plan for a modified flexible exchange rate system proposed in the Brookings Report seeks to create two interdependent world blocs. How realistic is the effort to tie the United Kingdom to the United States and turn her away from the European continent? Is the creation of a quasi-dividing line through the Channel and the Atlantic in the interest of a strong West? Which bloc should some of the underdeveloped areas join? There are countries with strong British ties in Africa, and some South American countries have substantial economic relations with Europe.

The return to the gold standard is suggested by Rueff and Heilperin. Countries should give and receive in settlement for external debts only gold. National monetary systems should change the money supply in response to gold losses or gains. In short, Heilperin and Rueff want the world to return to the automaticity of the intellectually appealing regime of complete laissez faire in international economic relations.

---

[1] "A Theory of Optimum Currency Areas," *American Economic Review*, September 1961, pp. 657–64.

Some issues connected with this proposal are: To what extent can the gold standard model be expected to work in the real world? Has it ever worked, as the blueprint suggests? Are countries willing to subject their economic growth and stability to the unmitigated forces of the market? Heilperin also proposes a rise in the price of gold. Is the gold supply price-elastic, and at what price could production be expected to fill the world's long-run demand for liquidity? Ought we perhaps to wait with any decisions on the price of gold until we can find out at what price it could be brought to the earth economically from the moon or one of the planets?

Some of the proposals reprinted in this volume have been described as idealistic, or as idle schemes having no chance of acceptance because they do not take account of the realities of the world. The realities are allegedly the ideas and preconceived notions of central bankers and politicians, who ultimately decide the shape of the world's payments system.

But are bankers and politicians really beyond influence by dreamers and theorists? Quite the contrary: as Keynes has pointed out in a famous passage in his *General Theory*, the dreams and impractical plans of one generation are often the political and economic dogma of the next. The present international monetary system is itself the outcome of plans developed by men who analyzed what was wrong with the system of the 1930's. Resistance to change now makes us the slaves of ideas worked out twenty years ago.

Dahl and Lindblom have said: "Many people think of invention and innovation in technology, but not in social structure; the bias probably accounts for a frequent failure to take account of the increasing possibilities for rational social reform through the improvement in techniques. . . . Rational and responsible reform may consequently suffer from a serious limitation at the hands of those who fail to grasp the fact that alternatives are many, that new ones can be expected to appear, and that they can be created."[2]

In the field of international monetary institutions these alternatives have been formulated for our time by some of the world's first-rate minds. The contributions selected for this book indicate that the discussion of these alternatives has progressed far and well. May the time come soon when negotiations and actions at the official level fully reflect the state which the intellectual work has reached.

[2] Robert Dahl and Charles Lindblom, *Politics, Economics and Welfare* (New York, 1953), pp. 7–8.

Part I

CENTRALIZATION OF
INTERNATIONAL RESERVES

1

Excerpts from
'Gold and the Dollar Crisis'

ROBERT TRIFFIN

DIAGNOSIS

The Changing Role of Monetary Reserves

Radical changes in the international and national monetary and banking systems have fundamentally altered the role of monetary reserves and capital movements in balance-of-payments adjustments from what they used to be during the gold standard era.

Current discussions of reserve requirements stress primarily the role of reserves in the cushioning of balance-of-payments deficits, and rely for an approximate, and admittedly very rough, measurement of reserve adequacy on the ratio of a country's over-all reserves to annual imports or exchange sales. Such a concept would have been largely alien to nineteenth-century writers, and did not indeed play any prominent role in either academic or policy analyses of the problem until World War II.[1] Legal prescriptions on monetary reserves and monetary issues varied widely from country to country, but never made any reference to a country's export or import levels. They were concerned exclusively and directly with the avoidance of excessive currency issues and relied for this purpose either on an over-all ceiling on such issues, or on the limitation of fiduciary issues—

This essay represents a condensation of Mr. Triffin's book *Gold and the Dollar Crisis* (1961), and is reprinted through the courtesy of the publisher, Yale University Press. In the process of condensation the following changes were made: some passages were omitted, the order in which the material is presented was altered slightly and some passages were added to ensure continuity of the text. Mr. Triffin has approved this condensed version of his book and I have made every effort to reproduce Mr. Triffin's ideas and concepts exactly as he had originally presented them.

[1] Its explicit recognition as one of several criteria for central bank management was introduced for the first time in central bank legislation in 1944. See the author's *Monetary and Banking Reform in Paraguay*, Board of Governors of the Federal Reserve System (Washington, 1946), pp. 82–84, and 136–37.

i.e., the amounts that could be issued over and above the metallic reserves held as counterpart by the issuing bank—or on a minimum ratio of reserves to note issues or slight liabilities. This latter criterion was the one that conformed mostly closely to practical bankers' experience as to their own liquidity requirements, and tended more and more to determine legal or customary standards of reserve adequacy. The maintenance of a ratio of about one-third between liquid reserves and sight obligations gradually became the usual minimum benchmark for central bank as well as for commercial bank operations.

It hardly need be said that this could result in extremely disparate ratios between central bank reserves and the level of the country's imports. This ratio can be estimated, for instance, to have been less than 5 per cent for the Bank of England in 1913, as compared with more than 40 per cent for the Bank of France.[2] This contrast was not without significance for monetary management, and complaints were often voiced against the frequency with which the Bank of England had to resort to changes in the discount rate in order to protect its slender level of reserves. The Bank, however, was a private firm, motivated by the search for profits as well as by broader considerations of public service, and showed great reluctance to accumulate nonearning gold assets greatly in excess of liquidity requirements as judged in the light of its own experience in the past. Private capital movements were regarded as the normal source of cushioning for balance-of-payments fluctuations, and could be hastened, whenever necessary, by open-market operations and changes in the discount rate. The main test of this mechanism, from the Bank's point of view, lay in the fact that any substantial drain on its gold reserves could be arrested long before it would endanger the Bank's own liquidity.

The radical changes imparted to monetary institutions and policies by World War I and the world depression have completely revolutionized the role of monetary reserves and have consequently brought about fundamentally different views as to their measurement and adequacy.

First of all, the universal disappearance of gold coin from active monetary circulation has deeply modified the significance of central bank liquidity. Reserves need no longer be held to convert bank deposits and paper

---

[2] Only a minor portion of this striking contrast is due to the difference in the ratio of gold reserves to liabilities for the two banks (approximately 35 per cent for the Bank of England, and 50 per cent for the Bank or France). Most of it can be ascribed to the much greater role played in England by private bank deposits in total money supply and by the much higher ratio of imports, and lower ratio of money, to GNP in England as compared with France.

currency into legal gold tender for purposes of domestic circulation. Reserve drains are now associated exclusively with external deficits in the balance of payments of the country. In a closed economy, central bank liquidity would be fully assured by its mere ability to print notes. Excessive issues would be reflected in inflationary pressures upon prices, but would not affect the bank's liquidity.

Second, international flows of private capital can no longer be relied upon as a major source of cushioning for current account disequilibria. Fears of currency depreciation and exchange restrictions often indeed tend to stimulate private capital flows from deficit countries to surplus countries, and to aggravate, rather than cushion, the impact of current account imbalance.[3] These movements of "hot money" played a particularly large role in the interwar period and continue even today to elude, in many cases, the nets of exchange control legislation. On the other hand, the unprecedented development of official loans and grants provides today vast amounts of cushioning capital, which substitute in part for the private capital flows of the gold standard era. The International Monetary Fund, the International Bank for Reconstruction and Development, the European Payments Union, the European Fund, the European Investment Bank, the Colombo Plan, etc., were specifically set up for that purpose. France and England have also stepped up enormously financial aid to their overseas territories and associated monetary areas. The Marshall Plan and other U.S. foreign aid programs completely dwarfed, in the early postwar years, the rather modest flows of private investments abroad and still account today—even excluding military grants—for about half of the United States total capital exports.

Official grants and loans, however, cannot be regarded as a normal and dependable source of financing for short-run disequilibria. They usually require long and uncertain negotiations whose ultimate success may also be made dependent at times on political or economic conditions unacceptable to the prospective borrower. In spite of the more flexible and automatic procedures recently developed by the International Monetary Fund —and, up to its recent demise, by the European Payments Union—countries must still look today to their own monetary reserves as their first and most important line of defense against temporary deficits in their balance of payments.

---

[3] International political tensions are a further factor of instability which would continue to paralyze or distort capital flows even if full confidence could be restored in the wisdom of economic policies proper.

The main function of monetary reserves is no longer to preserve the over-all liquidity of individual central banks, but to permit the financing of short-run deficits in the country's external transactions. The types of deficits which may appropriately be met in this manner fall into two categories. The first is that of reversible deficits reflecting purely temporary fluctuations in foreign receipts and expenditures on current and capital account. Such deficits should obviously be financed, rather than prevented or immediately corrected by policy action. Basic policy adjustments— such as deflation or devaluation—to temporary factors of imbalance would indeed sow the seeds of more fundamental and lasting imbalance in the country's economy. The shortage of reserves is more likely to induce, in such cases, a recourse to trade or exchange restrictions which would have been perfectly avoidable otherwise.

The second case is that of more fundamental disequilibria, calling for corrective action, but in which the most appropriate and desirable remedies will act relatively slowly and smoothly, and leave residual needs for the financing of tapering off deficits.

In both cases, an insufficient level of reserves will force the deficit country to resort to otherwise unnecessary measures of deflation, devaluation, or restrictions to keep its payments in closer and more continuous balance with its receipts than would be called for by the need to preserve long-run equilibrium in its international transactions.

Adequacy Criteria and Reserve Measurement

Adequacy criteria. These deep-seated changes in the role of monetary reserves entail corresponding changes in their methods of measurement and criteria for adequacy. Neither, however, can be couched in any precise and clear-cut formula, invariant from time to time and from country to country. Reserves have to be higher in an unstable economic and political environment than in a world enjoying a greater degree of economic and political stability. Higher reserves are also needed by underdeveloped countries, with more volatile levels of export proceeds and capital imports, than by the richer and more diversified economies of the industrial countries. The burden of reserve accumulation, however, in relation to national wealth and savings on the one hand, and to competing needs for the financing of developmental imports on the other, will unfortunately be higher for the former countries than for the latter. In this balancing of needs and costs, the underdeveloped countries are likely therefore to assign a lower priority than the more developed countries to a reserve level adequate to eschew or minimize undesirable resort to devaluation or restrictions.

The appraisal of reserve needs for any individual country, at any particular time, would have to take these and other factors into account. The order of magnitude of future deficits calling for reserve financing might first be gauged quantitatively on the basis of past experience. The first approximation should then be revised, upward or downward, in the light of other pertinent evidence about the probable course of external and internal developments.[4]

Such a line of approach, however, cannot be used in a broad survey of world liquidity requirements, such as the one which will now engage our attention. Availability of data and simplicity of calculation inevitably dominate the choice of measurement methods applicable to such comprehensive intertemporal and intercountry comparisons. Their results would admittedly be too crude to determine any precise level of reserve adequacy, but they will prove more than sufficient to indicate whether current and prospective reserve levels are likely to facilitate, or seriously hamper, the smooth functioning of international currency convertibility.

The ratio of gross reserves to annual imports will be retained in all that follows as a first, and admittedly rough, approach to the appraisal of reserve adequacy. The main reason for this choice, I must confess, is the fact that the recent study of the IMF Staff on *International Reserves and Liquidity*[5] conveniently presents such ready-made calculations for eleven prewar and postwar years for all regions of the world and for more than sixty individual countries. The second is that this ratio is the one that has been most popularized in all postwar discussions of the subject, and that monetary authorities in many countries are apt to think today of reserve adequacy in these terms, and to act accordingly.[6]

[4] The ratio of reserves to money and other liquid claims on the banking system may be of particular relevance, for instance, if past "compensatory" policies have pushed the ratio of such liquid claims to GNP to an abnormally high level. The current status of private banks' cash reserves and the strength or weakness of the legal or regulatory controls exercised by the monetary authorities over the banks' credit policy will also influence the speed with which corrective action may be applied in case of need.

[5] Washington, 1958.

[6] My own preference would have gone otherwise to a ratio of reserves to balance-of-payments *receipts*, rather than expenditures, on current, rather than merely merchandise, account, but including also net private unilateral transfers which play an important equilibrating role in several countries' balances of payments. The arguments that may be marshaled for and against this view are not worth retaining the attention of the reader, since the matter is only of academic interest, both methods of measurement leading to similar results in all but very few cases.

Economic students should devote some time, instead, to the closely reasoned and sug-

It should finally be noted that the estimates of monetary reserves used in these calculations give an exaggerated impression of definiteness and of comparability over time and over space. Methods of reporting are not uniform in all countries, and, most of all, the true "reserve" character of the sterling assets reported varied considerably over the period. The usability and acceptability of "transferable," and particularly "bilateral," sterling accounts were severely limited in the early postwar years. This was of minor importance to countries normally in deficit with the United Kingdom or the sterling area, but highly significant for countries whose bilateral deficits with other countries—particularly in the dollar area— could not be settled through the use of such sterling balances.

Moreover, the Fund's attempted breakdown of foreign exchange reserves into their major components (sterling, dollar, EPU, and BIS claims) can only be regarded as a rough approximation. This qualification, once again, applies particularly to *official* holdings of sterling, for which estimates have only recently been made available and only for the end of 1945, 1951, and 1957 (in *Economic Trends,* May 1958, p. viii). The Fund's estimates incorrectly include as official reserves all sterling holdings except those held in the United Kingdom's colonies and in the dollar area.

Important as they would be for a more refined analysis, these qualifications are not too damaging for the broad appraisal of reserve adequacy to which we shall now turn. They will be duly noted again in the few cases in which our conclusions, based on rough orders of magnitude only, could be significantly affected by them.

National reserve requirements under convertibility. The appraisal of desirable and feasible reserve levels in relation to imports varies enormously from country to country. In addition to the structural factors which facilitate or hamper the maintenance of high reserve levels (relative levels of wealth and savings, ratios of bank money to total money, and of money and imports to GNP, etc.), some countries are less able or insistent than others in restraining inflationary pressures and in avoiding recourse to trade and exchange restrictions.

The Fund's study lays great stress on these variations. A series of tables stresses the enormous differences in reserve ratios from country to country as well as from one year to another. In 1957, reserves were only 1 per cent

---

gestive discussion of reserve adequacy by Tibor Scitovsky in *Economic Theory and Western European Integration* (Stanford, Calif.: Stanford University Press, 1958), pp. 101–9. The ratio of monetary reserves to money supply, or to a broader concept of relatively liquid liabilities, also deserves more attention than it receives in the IMF study referred to in the preceding footnote.

of imports in Bolivia, but 137 per cent in Portugal. The number of industrial countries—excluding the United States and the United Kingdom—with reserves below 30 per cent of imports doubled—from one-fourth to one-half of their total number—between 1955 and 1957. In the latter year, 27 per cent of the nonindustrial countries showed reserve ratios inferior to 20 per cent, as against 8 per cent of these countries only four years earlier.

These wide variations conceal, however, some broad trends and regularities duly noted in the Fund's report. Thus, a large number of non-industrialized countries unwillingly accumulated abnormally high reserves in wartime, but drew heavily on them for restocking and development when supplies became again available. The average reserve ratio for this group of countries thus fell from 73 per cent in 1948 to 37 per cent in 1957. Continental Western Europe, on the other hand, suffered heavy reserve losses in wartime and in the early postwar years, but more than doubled its reserves between 1948 and 1957.

Within each group, some countries—such as Switzerland, Portugal, Venezuela, Iraq, and Iran—persistently tend, for a variety of reasons, to maintain relatively high reserve levels, while others—Norway, Denmark, Yugoslavia, Israel, Malaya, Canada, and South Africa, for instance—seem to be satisfied with reserve levels well below 30 or even 20 per cent of imports. See Table 1.[7]

The differences in national conditions and policies reflected in these estimates are not as significant as would seem at first—and as the Fund's study sometimes suggests[8]—for an appraisal of liquidity requirements for the world as a whole, under conditions of monetary convertibility. There are two reasons for this. The first is that few of the countries with persistently low reserves account for a significant proportion of total world trade, while most of the large trading countries traditionally hold reserves well in excess of 30 per cent. The second is that most of the countries with low reserves also maintain much more stringent trade and exchange restrictions than the others. Both of these facts are brought out in Tables 2 and 3. What they suggest is that:

1. Some countries may indeed continue to hold relatively low reserves, but are also likely to have great difficulties in restoring and maintaining convertibility, unless assured of other sources of finance in times of need.[9]

---

[7] See IMF Staff, *International Reserves and Liquidity*, pp. 46–55. Substantial reserve declines in the nonindustrialized areas, however, occurred between the end of the war and 1948 and are not shown in Table 1.

[8] See, for instance, *ibid.*, the comments on p. 73.

[9] The proposals developed on pp. 38–54 would greatly expand the capacity of the International Monetary Fund to provide such assistance.

TABLE 1
VARIATIONS IN REGIONAL RESERVE LEVELS

	1928	1937	1948	1957
In per cent of imports....................	43	109	89	55
Continental OEEC	46	78	40	42
Nonindustrial areas	42	51	73	37
Latin America	47	51	44	41
Outer sterling countries.............	28	46	95	41
Other countries*	50	67	74	30
Canada	7	21	33	29
United Kingdom	13	81	24	21
United States	85	358	303	161
In per cent of world's gross reserves........	100	100	100	100
Continental OEEC	39	24	13	28
Nonindustrial areas	25	14	28	21
Latin America	9	3	6	7
Outer sterling countries.............	6	5	16	8
Other countries*	11	6	7	6
Canada	1	1	2	3
United Kingdom	6	15	4	4
United States	29	46	25	43

Source: IMF, *International Reserves and Liquidity*, Appendix Table 1, pp. 100–101.
* Including Japan.

2. The maintenance of international convertibility, however, depends primarily on the policies of the major trading countries, and the avoidance of trade and exchange restrictions by them is clearly related to their ability to maintain adequate reserve levels.[10]

3. The reserve requirements of the latter countries exercise an overwhelming influence—as compared with those of the smaller trading countries—on the world demand for monetary reserves.

Table 2 classifies the sixty-two countries (other than the United States and the United Kingdom) for which reserves are reported by the Fund into three groups, on the basis of their average ratio of reserves to imports over the three most "normal" years of the postwar period, i.e., 1953–55. The number of countries in each group is approximately the same, but those

---

[10] Bilateralism will remain confined to a very minor portion of world trade at most as long as the United States, Canada, and Western Europe—with which most of the other countries' trade also takes place—refuse to participate in bilateral agreements. The functioning of the nineteenth-century gold standard depended essentially on the policies of the major trading countries, and was never endangered by the exchange rate instability of other countries, particularly in Latin America. The same would hold today for exchange restrictions outside Europe and North America.

TABLE 2

AVERAGE RESERVE LEVELS, 1953–1955

(All countries, excluding the United States and the United Kingdom)

National Ratio of Reserves to Imports	Average Ratio of Reserves to Imports	Number of Countries	Proportion of Total Imports	Proportion of Total Reserves
Reserves below 33% of imports: Yugoslavia (6), Denmark (13), Norway (15), Paraguay (16), Bolivia and Chile (18), Peru and Spain (19), Haiti and Israel (21), Costa Rica (22), Nicaragua and Iceland (23), Taiwan and South Africa (25), Malaya (26), Sweden (27), Syria and Finland (29), Colombia (31).	22%	21	20%	9%
Reserves from 33% to 50% of imports: Dominican Republic and France (33), Mexico, Korea, and New Zealand (34), Philippines (35), Honduras and Ecuador (36), Brazil (37), Indonesia (38), Canada (39), Lebanon (40), Turkey and Belgium (42), Italy (43), Japan and the Netherlands (45), Ireland (46), Vietnam (47), Venezuela (49), Guatemala and Salvador (50).	40%	22	52%	43%
Reserves above 50% of imports: Argentina (51), Ceylon and Austria (52), Germany (54), Panama (56), Greece (60), Australia (61), Burma (76), Cuba (78), Ethiopia (81), Iran (85), Thailand (89), Pakistan (101), Iraq (106), Uruguay (110), India (136), Egypt and Switzerland (137), Portugal (180).	81%	19	28%	48%
Total	48%	62	100%	100%

Source: IMF, *International Reserves and Liquidity*, Appendix Table 1, pp. 100–101.

with reserves lower than 33 per cent of imports accounted for only one fifth of total imports, and for less than one tenth of total reserves. All of them, moreover, were characterized by much tighter trade and exchange restrictions than those applied by most of the countries with higher reserve levels.

The other forty-one countries accounted for 80 per cent of the total imports, and more than 90 per cent of the total monetary reserves, of the sixty-two countries taken together. They included all the European countries outside of Scandinavia and Iceland, and all the other countries with

TABLE 3

EVOLUTION OF TWELVE MAJOR TRADING COUNTRIES' RESERVES, 1950–1957

(Percentage ratio of reserves to imports)

									Number of Cases		
									Below 20%	20–32%	33% and Above
	1950	1951	1952	1953	1954	1955	1956	1957			
Canada	55	44	42	38	43	37	31	29	—	2	6
Germany	10	15	31	52	58	53	65	75	2	1	5
France	44	20	23	24	32	44	24	13	1	5	2
Netherlands	29	24	47	52	45	40	29	26	—	4	4
Belgium	38	40	42	44	41	40	35	33	—	—	8
Italy	59	46	39	39	43	46	41	42	—	—	8
Japan	58	46	54	37	43	54	47	24	—	1	7
Australia	92	47	52	93	61	39	49	68	—	—	8
Brazil	61	26	26	46	30	38	50	32	—	4	4
Switzerland	150	120	138	150	141	124	107	98	—	—	8
India	172	105	102	146	137	127	80	43	—	—	8
Venezuela	56	49	51	52	46	48	75	77	—	—	8
Total									3	17	76

Source: IMF, *International Reserves and Liquidity*, Appendix Table 1, pp. 100–101.

imports in excess of $1 billion a year, except South Africa and Malaya. It is these countries' policies—and, of course, those of the United States and the United Kingdom—that will overwhelmingly determine the fate of the present convertibility experiment. These policies will be very largely influenced, in turn, by these countries' ability to preserve reserve levels sufficient to eschew unnecessary resort to trade and exchange restrictions. And it is the global level of these reserve requirements in relation to available supplies from gold production and other sources—primarily dollar and sterling balances—that will play a crucial role in determining the adequacy or inadequacy of world reserve levels for the maintenance of convertibility tomorrow.

Twelve of these forty-one countries accounted for about 60 per cent of the total imports of the sixty-two countries taken together, and for 65 per cent of their total monetary reserves. Their actual reserve ratios in each of the eight years 1950–57 are shown in Table 3. Only in three cases did they fall below 20 per cent. Two of these refer to Germany in 1950 and 1951, before that country had emerged from the economic and financial prostration in which the war had left it. The third is that of France in the middle of a severe exchange crisis in 1957. In seventeen other cases, reserves were below 33 per cent of imports. Nine of those occurred in

France and Brazil and were accompanied by severe exchange controls. In all seventy-six of the other cases observed, reserves were maintained throughout above 33 per cent of imports.

The over-all record of these eight postwar years strongly suggests that most of the major countries would aim at maintaining a reserve level of not less than 40 per cent in most years, feel impelled to adopt severe readjustment measures if this level fell below, let us say, 30 or 33 per cent, and consider themselves forced to adopt drastic measures of control in the face of any persistent or substantial contraction below that critical range.[11] A 20 per cent level of gross reserves would be widely regarded as an absolute minimum, to be earmarked for rare emergencies such as the outbreak of war, or as necessary collateral for the negotiation of short- or medium-term loans abroad.

Under normal conditions, the actual amount of reserves in excess of 33 per cent held by some countries would far outweigh the deficiencies of other countries' reserves in relation to this level. There can be little doubt, therefore, that the 35 per cent *average* level reached in 1957 by all countries outside the United States and the United Kingdom was on the low side of any reasonable estimate of world liquidity requirements, and that any further contraction below that level would make it very difficult for a number of key countries to adhere firmly to the convertibility policies which they would otherwise be willing and eager to pursue.

If this conclusion is accepted, the further question must be asked: Is the prospective development and supply of reserves over the next few years likely to alleviate or intensify the present reserve shortage for countries other than the United States and the United Kingdom?

Prospective Adequacy of Reserves over the Ten Years 1958–1967

The Fund's study on *International Reserves and Liquidity* calculates the growth of reserves which would appear necessary over the next ten years to prevent a further decline of world reserves in relation to world imports.

The Fund bases these calculations on the assumption of an average growth rate of 3 per cent a year. For the ten years 1957–66, world reserves would have to increase by $19 billion, as against roughly $7 billion expected from the monetization of new gold production and sales of USSR

[11] The Fund's study (p. 48) also remarks that most industrialized countries "appear to have tried to achieve reserve ratios of between 30 and 50 per cent, or perhaps 40 and 50 per cent, in the sense that if reserves were below these levels they tried to increase reserves, and if reserves rose beyond some such level, they saw fit to adopt a more expansionary policy."

TABLE 4

AVERAGE ANNUAL RATES OF GROWTH OF TRADE AND MANUFACTURING, 1876–1957
(In per cent; compound basis)

	Trade		Manu-facturing Activity
	Primary Products	Manufactured Products	
During war years and the 1930's depression:			
From 1913 to 1920			−1
From 1913 to 1921–25	−1.5	−2.6	0.3
From 1926–29 to 1931–35	−1.9	−5.7	−1.5
From 1938 to 1948	0		3.7
During "normal" peacetime years:			
From 1876–80 to 1901–5	3.3	2.8	4.1
From 1901–5 to 1913	3.5	4.7	4.2
From 1921–25 to 1926–29	6.3	7.1	6.8
From 1948 to 1956	7.5		6.1
From 1950 to 1956	6.5		5.7
From 1950 to 1957	6.3		5.1
From 1951 to 1957	5.4		5.0

Sources: Estimates for "normal" years are from the IMF study on *International Reserves and Liquidity*, Table 17, p. 70. Estimates for war years and the 1930's depression have been calculated from the indices given in the original source (League of Nations, *Industrialization and Foreign Trade*, 1945, pp. 130 and 157) and quoted on p. 104 of the IMF study. Average rates of growth for these years are not shown separately in this study (except for 1938–48) but merged into average rates over longer periods.

gold over this period. The Fund then proceeds to lower the required $19 billion to $8 billion by considering as unlikely any increase in the reserves of four high-reserve countries, i.e., the United States, Germany, Switzerland, and Venezuela. The minor gap thus left between the required growth of reserves and the amounts expected from new gold production and USSR sales should not cause any serious worry, as it may easily be bridged, and indeed more than bridged, by a further growth of foreign exchange reserves—primarily dollar balances—and by a possible decline in private gold and dollar holdings.[12]

These optimistic conclusions are open to serious questions. First and foremost is the 3 per cent growth rate assumed as "normal" by the Fund. The data which underlie this assumption are presented on page 70 of the Fund's study, and are condensed here in Table 4. They would hardly suggest a growth rate as low as 3 per cent. The general picture that emerges

[12] See IMF, *International Reserves and Liquidity*, pp. 69–75.

is rather one of an expanding growth rate of roughly 3 to 4 per cent in the rather depressed period of the 1880's and 1890's, of 4 per cent or more in the last decade preceding World War I, and of 6 to 7 per cent a year both in the 1920's and in the post–World War II period. The 3 per cent rate assumed by the Fund becomes plausible only when "normal" peacetime experience is diluted with the abnormally low, and in fact predominantly *negative*, growth rates of wartime years and of the 1930's world depression. An expected adequacy of reserves based upon the assumption of a third world war or of another deep and protracted world depression is hardly encouraging as a guide to policy. The least that should be done, it seems to me, would be to present alternative calculations based on different rates of growth, ranging from, let us say, 3 to 6 per cent a year. This has been done in Table 5.[13]

A second source of underestimation in the Fund's calculations is the exclusion of high-reserve countries—the United States, Switzerland, Germany, and Venezuela—without any parallel upward adjustment for any of the low-reserve countries. On the contrary, the Fund's study comments (p. 72) that "it may be doubted whether all other countries would in fact wish to increase their reserves so much." This statement is formally correct, but also highly misleading. While it is probably true that not *all* of these countries will increase their absolute amount of reserves sufficiently to avoid a further decline in their already low reserve ratios, one would expect such declines to be far more than offset by the reconstitution of adequate reserve levels by *some* at least of the countries which emphatically and rightly proclaim such an increase essential to enable them to achieve and consolidate a satisfactory rate of progress toward full currency convertibility.

Table 5 adjusts the Fund's estimates for such an increase in the reserve levels of two countries only: France and the United Kingdom. The postulated increase in the reserves of these countries is one that would bring them to 40 per cent of imports. This would correspond, as of the end of 1957, to a $4,564 million reserve level for the United Kingdom and a $2,468 million reserve level for France. These figures may be compared with the $5 billion reserve level often mentioned as a target by the British

---

[13] It might also be noted that all these calculations with reference to an assumed rate of *physical* growth leave aside the impact of price rises upon liquidity requirements. This is, of course, reasonable insofar as one should not plan to increase international liquidity in such a way as to facilitate or stimulate inflationary price increases. Yet, if such increases are not avoided in fact by the major trading countries, corresponding liquidity adaptations might be preferable to alternative adjustments such as gold revaluation or, certainly, a tightening of trade or exchange restrictions.

TABLE 5

INCREASES IN WORLD RESERVES CORRESPONDING TO VARIOUS RATES OF GROWTH

(In billions of U.S. dollars)

	At Growth Rate of			
	3%	4%	5%	6%
Over the ten years 1958–67:				
1. All countries	18.5	25.8	33.7	42.3
2. Excluding United States, Germany, Switzerland, and Venezuela	7.5	10.4	13.7	17.2
3. Including reconstitution of 40 per cent reserve level by the U.K. and France	12.7	16.2	20.0	24.1
4. Per cent of (3) covered by assumed supplies from new gold production and USSR sales	55%	43%	35%	29%
In 1967, on basis of assumption (3) above:				
1. In billions of U.S. dollars...........	1.0	1.5	2.0	2.6
2. Per cent covered by assumed supplies from new gold production and USSR sales	70%	48%	35%	27%

Sources: Reserve estimates as of the end of 1957 are taken from the January 1959 issue of *International Financial Statistics* ($53,600 million for all countries, $31,864 million for the United States, Germany, Switzerland, and Venezuela taken together, and $31,149 million for the United Kingdom and France, leaving an initial shortfall of $3,883 million of reserves for these two countries with relation to 40 per cent of their 1957 import levels as estimated in the same publication). The estimated increase in the world's monetary gold over the ten years 1958–67 ($7 billion) is taken from the IMF study on *International Reserves and Liquidity*, p. 72.

in past convertibility discussions, and with the $2.1 billion reserve level actually reached by France in the closing months of 1955.

Even at the 3 per cent growth rate assumed by the Fund's study, prospective gold supplies from new production and USSR sales would cover only 55 per cent of liquidity requirements over the ten years 1958–67. This proportion would drop to 43 per cent at a 4 per cent growth rate, 35 per cent at a 5 per cent growth rate, and 29 per cent at a 6 per cent growth rate. The maintenance of adequate reserve levels, under the above assumptions, would thus require increases of gold production, decreases in gold hoarding, or supplementary reserve supplies in forms other than gold, ranging from roughly $6 billion to $17 billion over the next ten years.

Past and Future Sources of Liquidity

It is possible to estimate the future supply of liquidity in the world whether or not we accept the validity of the computations for the projected needs of liquidity presented in Table 5.

In order to make some predictions about future supply of liquidity it
is useful to examine the record of the past fifteen years. Table 6 summa-
rizes the relevant facts.

Of the $27 billion increase in foreign countries' and international insti-
tutions' gold reserves and foreign dollar holdings—public and private—
from the end of 1949 to the end of September 1960, only $6 billion were
derived from new gold production and Russian gold sales in Western markets. The overwhelming bulk of the increase sprang from U.S. gold losses
($5.8 billion) and increases in short-term liabilities abroad ($15.2 billion).

Tables 7 and 8 analyze the structure of world reserves in general, including official sterling as well as dollar balances, but excluding private
holdings of these currencies.

TABLE 6
WORLD MONETARY GOLD AND DOLLAR HOLDINGS, 1949–1960
(In billions of dollars)

	End of					Change	
	1949	1952	1957	1959	Sept. 1960	1949–Sept. 1960	1957–Sept. 1960
I. Monetary gold	34.7	35.8	38.8	40.2	40.7	+6.0	+1.9
A. International institutions	1.5	1.7	1.2	2.4	2.6	+1.1	+1.4
B. United States	24.6	23.3	22.9	19.5	18.7	−5.8	−4.1
C. Rest of world	8.6	10.9	14.8	18.3	19.4	+10.8	+4.6
II. Foreign dollar holdings	8.2	11.7	16.6	21.6	23.4	+15.2	+6.8
A. International institutions	1.8	1.9	1.7	3.8	4.2	+2.4	+2.5
B. Rest of world	6.4	9.9	14.9	17.7	19.1	+12.7	+4.3
III. Total							
Gross (I + II)	42.9	47.6	55.4	61.7	64.1	+21.2	+8.6
Net (= I)	34.7	35.8	38.8	40.2	40.7	+6.0	+1.9
A. International institutions (IA + IIA)	3.3	3.5	2.9	6.2	6.8	+3.5	+3.9
B. United States (IB − II)	16.3	11.5	6.3	−2.0	−4.7	−21.0	−10.9
C. Rest of world (IC + IIB)	15.0	20.8	29.6	36.0	38.5	+23.5	+8.9

Source: Computed from *Federal Reserve Bulletin* data and estimates. Note that a large portion of
increases of monetary gold in recent years has been derived from USSR sales in Western markets,
rather than from current gold production in the West.

TABLE 7

WORLD MONETARY RESERVES, 1913–1959

	1913	1928	1933	1938	1949	1959
I. In per cent of imports:						
A. World	37	45	110	118	79	56
1. Gold	35	34	*101*	*111*	58	38
2. Foreign exchange	2	11	9	8	21	18
B. World outside U.S. and U.K.	35	44	93	62	48	48
1. Gold	32	29	81	51	21	23
2. Foreign exchange	3	16	12	11	27	24
a) Dollar	1	3	1	3	7	12
b) Sterling and other	3	13	11	8	20	12
II. In per cent of total reserves:						
A. World	100	100	100	100	100	100
1. Gold	94	77	92	94	74	67
2. Foreign exchange	6	23	8	6	26	33
B. World outside U.K. and U.S.	100	100	100	100	100	100
1. Gold	91	64	87	83	43	49
2. Foreign exchange	9	36	13	17	57	51
a) Dollar	2	7	1	5	15	25
b) Sterling and other	7	29	12	12	42	26

Source: These estimates are derived from Federal Reserve and IMF publications. They exclude the Eastern bloc countries throughout and are subject to a larger margin of error for the years before 1938. Reserve figures include gold coin in circulation in 1913 and 1928, IMF gold (but not local currency assets) and BIS, EPU, and European Fund reserves.

The salient facts brought out by Table 7 are:

1. The lowering of the ratio of reserves, and particularly gold reserves, to imports since 1933 (see lines I A, I A1, I B, and I B1). While some of these ratios are still higher than in 1913 or 1928, one should not forget that the fears universally expressed around the latter year about the consequences of a gold scarcity relieved by an exaggerated dependence on an unorganized and nationalistic gold exchange standard were dramatically confirmed by the collapse of the world monetary system in 1931.

2. The spectacular shift in the structure of reserves outside the key currency countries from 91 per cent gold and 9 per cent foreign exchange in 1913 to 49 per cent gold and 51 per cent foreign exchange in 1959. Admittedly, the relative share of foreign exchange reserves in the total was even higher in 1949, but sterling—which then made up the bulk of these foreign exchange holdings—was then, and remained for years, an inconvertible currency.

TABLE 8

SOURCES OF INCREASES IN WORLD RESERVES, 1914–1959

(In per cent of total increases)

	1914–1959	1914–1928	1929–1933	1934–1938	1939–1949	1950–1959	1958–1959
I. World:							
A. Monetary gold	**66**	**68**	**131**	**89**	**47**	**43**	**91**
1. Production	*43*	*38*	*12*	*90*	*46*	*34*	*59*
2. Coin withdrawal	*6*	*30*	*10*	*—*	*—*	*—*	*—*
3. Dollar devaluation	*15*	*—*	*109*	*—*	*—*	*—*	*—*
4. USSR sales	*2*	*—*	*—*	*−1*	*1*	*9*	*32*
B. Foreign exchange	**34**	**32**	**−31**	**11**	**53**	**57**	**9**
1. Dollar	*17*	*6*	*−7*	*5*	*13*	*50*	*70*
2. Sterling and other	*17*	*26*	*−24*	*5*	*41*	*7*	*−60*
II. World outside the United States:							
A. U.S. transactions						**65**	**92**
1. U.S. gold losses						*29*	*67*
2. Increases in official dollar balances						*36*	*24*
B. Other sources						**35**	**8**
1. Foreign gold						*30*	*26*
a) Production						*24*	*17*
b) USSR sales						*6*	*9*
2. Other transactions						*5*	*−18*
a) Official sterling balances							*−2*
b) Other reserve balances							*−16*

Source: See Table 7. The breakdown between gold and foreign exchange—particularly reserve balances other than sterling and dollars—is distorted in 1959 by the exclusion from reserve calculations of the EPU balances, following their consolidation upon the expiration of the EPU Agreement.

Table 8 is even more telling. It brings out the utter dependence of the present world monetary system on totally erratic and haphazard sources of reserve supply in an expanding world economy (see particularly 1914–59 and 1950–59):

1. Gold production in the West (line I A1) has provided less than half of the increases in world reserves in the last half-century, and barely a third in the last ten years. Even this source of supply might be seriously disturbed tomorrow by the threatening eruption of racial warfare in the major gold-producing country, South Africa.

2. The withdrawal of gold coin from circulation, and the 1933 devalu-

ation of the dollar contributed major shares of reserve increases in the 1920's and 1930's (see lines I A2 and 3). The first of these two sources may, of course, be regarded as exhausted for practical purposes, while willful recourse to the second would be an act of folly, for reasons discussed elsewhere.[14] [See below, "Sterling and dollar balances."]

3. USSR sales to the West (line I A4) have become a major source of reserve increases in recent years.

4. The persistent growth of U.S. short-term indebtedness to foreign central banks has contributed half of the world reserve increases of the last decade, and as much as 70 per cent in 1958–59 (line I B1). World reserves outside the United States have been fed—to the extent of two-thirds over the last ten years, and 92 per cent in 1958–59—by U.S. gold losses and the increase in U.S. short-term liabilities to foreign central banks and international institutions (line II A). What do these developments imply for the future? Let us examine what we know about the future supply of the various components which we have seen were the sources of world liquidity during the past fifteen years.

Gold. The Fund's estimate of a $7 billion increase in gold reserves over the next ten years rests on solid ground. It is based on a previous and excellent staff study,[15] whose main conclusions are summarized in the first three columns of Table 9. The estimates of production and nonmonetary gold uses appear reasonable in the light of past experience.

The most vulnerable part of these forecasts is that referring to USSR gold sales to the West. All estimates of USSR gold stocks, gold production, and gold sales are, of course, highly conjectural. Mr. Altman quotes estimates of $7 billion for stocks, and of $600 million for current production in 1957. Even more conjectural is the course of future USSR policy with respect to gold sales in world markets. An aggressive use of Russia's gold resources to serve political or economic objectives would, of course, play havoc with all estimates regarding the prospective supply of future gold reserves.

Sterling and dollar balances. Little reliance should be placed on the future growth of sterling balances to fill world reserve requirements. The main reason for this is that gross British reserves are very low in relation to short-term sterling liabilities. The difficulties repeatedly encountered

---

[14] *Gold and the Dollar Crisis*, pp. 79–82 [not reprinted here].

[15] Oscar L. Altman, "A Note on Gold Production and Additions to the International Gold Reserves," *IMF Staff Papers*, April 1958, pp. 258–88.

TABLE 9

SUPPLIES AND USES OF GOLD: 1890–1957 AND FORECASTS, 1958–1967

(Yearly averages, expressed in millions of U.S. dollars at $35 an ounce)

	Forecast 1958–67			Past Averages						
	Pessimistic	Optimistic	Probable	1952–1957	1945–1951	1939–1944	1934–1938	1929–1933	1914–1928	1890–1913
1. New production*	1,050	1,150	1,100	940	800	1,090	970	780	670	520
2. USSR sales	—†	200†	100	105	10	30	-10	—	—	—
3. Total supplies (1 + 2 = 4 + 5)	1,050	1,350	1,200	1,045	810	1,120	960	780	670	520
4. Nonmonetary uses*	660	330	470	495	440	-70	-310	480	280	220
a. Arts and industry	210	130	170	185	180	100	100	100	140	130
b. Hoarding	450	200	300	310	260	-170	-410	380	140	90
5. Monetary uses*	390†	1,020†	730	550	370	1,190	1,270	300	390	300

Sources: These rough estimates have been pieced together from the following: Oscar L. Altman, "A Note on Gold Production and Additions to the International Gold Reserves," *IMF Staff Papers*, April 1958, pp. 258–88; IMF, *International Reserves and Liquidity*; IMF, *International Financial Statistics*, January 1959; statistical tables regularly published in the *Federal Reserve Bulletin*; "The Private Demand for Gold," *Federal Reserve Bulletin*, September 1954, pp. 935–44; estimates on private demand for gold, regularly published since the war, in Bank for International Settlements, *Annual Reports*, and for 1931–37 in *Eighth Annual Report*, May 1938, p. 45; *Annual Report of the Secretary of the Treasury*, p. 294, for the fiscal year ended June 30, 1954; various reports issued by the Gold Delegation of the Financial Committee of the League of Nations, particularly its *Interim Report*, 1930, pp. 79–84, 90–94, 114–17.

  * USSR included before 1934.

  † Altman's study estimates USSR sales at $100 million throughout, and gives therefore a narrower range—$500 million to $920 million—for forecast additions to monetary gold.

by Britain, for that very reason, in 1931, 1947, 1949, 1951, 1953, and 1957 are likely to induce her to match any increase in sterling balances by equivalent, or more than equivalent, increases in her own reserve assets. Little net additions to world liquidity should, therefore, be expected from this source.

The prospective growth of dollar balances offers, at first view, more promising possibilities. In spite of their enormous increase since the war, dollar balances still do not appear excessive in relation to United States exports. The ratio of the first to the latter (87 per cent) is only slightly larger than in 1938, and still well below the corresponding ratio for the United Kingdom (100 per cent).

It is indeed the persistent decline in the U.S. net reserve position which has been, by far, the major source of supply for the very satisfactory growth of other countries' reserves since 1949. (See Table 10.) This fact received little public notice as long as the drain on our reserves took the form of an increase in our short-term dollar liabilities abroad rather than in a loss of gold from Fort Knox. From 1949 to the end of 1957, the gold stock decreased only by $1.7 billion, or about 7 per cent, while the dollar liabilities more than doubled, from $8.2 billion to $16.6 billion.

This rapid growth of dollar balances during the postwar years reflected, at least in part, the substitution of convertible dollars for inconvertible

TABLE 10

THE RESERVE POSITION OF THE CENTER COUNTRIES, 1928–1958

	1928	1932	1936	1947	1949	1953	1957	1958
I. The United States:								
A. Gold reserves ($billions)	4.1	4.0	14.6	22.9	24.6	22.1	22.9	20.6
B. Dollar balances ($billions)	2.5	0.7	2.2	7.1	8.2	12.7	16.6	17.6
1. International	—	—	—	2.3	1.8	1.9	1.7	2.0
2. Countries	2.5	0.7	2.2	4.9	6.4	10.8	14.9	15.6
a) Official*				0.5	1.8	3.4	6.5	9.1	9.6
b) Private				1.7	3.0	3.1	4.4	5.7	6.0
C. Ratio of dollar balances (excl. international) to U.S. exports (in per cent)	48	44	71	32	53	68	72	87
1. Official*			16	12	28	41	44	54
2. Private			55	19	26	28	27	33
D. Ratio of total dollar balances to U.S. gold reserves (in per cent)	61	17	15	31	33	57	72	86
II. The United Kingdom:								
A. Gold and dollar reserves ($billions)	0.7	0.6	2.9	2.2	1.8	2.5	2.4	3.1
B. Sterling balances ($billions)†	2.4	1.4	2.8	15.7	10.4	11.2	10.9	11.1
1. International	—	—	—	1.6	1.6	1.4	1.8	1.7
2. Countries	2.4	1.4	2.8	14.1	8.8	9.8	9.2	9.4
a) Colonies				1.9	1.5	3.1	2.5	2.5
b) Other sterling area	0.7	1.6	7.2	4.5	4.8	5.1	4.9
c) Nonsterling area	0.7	1.2	5.0	2.7	1.9	1.6	2.0
1) OEEC			1.7	1.0	0.6	0.7	1.0
2) Other			3.3	1.8	1.3	0.9	1.0

TABLE 10 (continued)

	1928	1932	1938	1947	1949	1953	1957	1958
C. Ratio of sterling balances (excl. international) to U.K. exports (in per cent)	69	108	104	288	127	131	94	100
1. Colonies		} 54	59 {	39	22	41	26	26
2. Other sterling area				147	65	64	53	52
3. Nonsterling area		54	44	102	39	25	16	22
a) OEEC				35	14	8	7	11
b) Other				67	25	17	9	11
D. Ratio of total sterling balances to U.K. gold and dollar reserves	320	240	95	705	595	440	460	360

* Official dollar balances include small amounts of "bonds and notes," reported only since 1949 and for which no breakdown is available between official and private holdings.

† Sterling balance estimates for 1928 are from the (Macmillan) *Committee on Finance and Industry Report* (London, 1931), pp. 42, 301. Those for 1932 are from the BIS study on *The Sterling Area* (Basel, 1953) and actually refer to the end of 1931. The 1938 estimate is taken from the *Twenty Second Annual Report* of the BIS (Basel, 1952), p. 172. These are probably fairly rough estimates, not fully comparable with postwar estimates.

sterling in world settlements and world reserves. This throws further doubt on the likelihood of any continued and indefinite accumulation of dollar balances abroad on a scale comparable to that experienced during the last decade. The prediction which I had ventured in this respect in the spring of 1957[16] seemed to find some confirmation in 1958. In the course of that year, foreign countries' short-term dollar holdings—including bonds and notes—rose only by $700 million, while net gold purchases from the United States totaled $2,300 million.

The United States gold losses of 1958 are beginning to create some concern about the continued deterioration in the country's net reserve position. The excess of gold reserves over short-term liabilities to foreign countries—including bonds and notes—has declined continually from $18.2 billion at the end of 1949 to less than $5 billion at the end of 1958, i.e., at an annual rate of more than $1.3 billion over the years 1950–57, and by nearly $3 billion in 1958 alone.

Such a movement obviously could not continue indefinitely without ultimately undermining foreigners' confidence in the dollar as a safe medium for reserve accumulation. The time will certainly come, sooner or

[16] *Europe and the Money Muddle*, p. 297.

later, when further accumulation of short-term foreign liabilities will have to be either slowed down or substantially matched by corresponding increases in our already bloated gold assets. If this were not done on our own initiative, foreign central banks would do it for us by stopping their own accumulation of dollar assets and requiring gold payment instead for their over-all surplus with the United States.

As in the case of sterling balances, therefore, further increases in dollar balances cannot be relied upon to contribute substantially and indefinitely to the solution of the world illiquidity problem.

The Folly of the Present System

The system described in the above paragraphs in which the major portion of world liquidity requirements has been met by the accumulation of short-term obligations of the key-currency countries has become known as that of the gold exchange standard. Its basic absurdity is that it makes the *international* monetary system highly dependent on individual countries' decisions about the continued use of one or a few *national* currencies as monetary reserves. In the absence of any widespread doubts about exchange rate stability, the choice of such currencies as reserves normally falls on the currencies of the countries which play a major role in world trade and finance. Sterling, the dollar and, subsidiarily, the French franc thus became the main reserve currencies in the 1920's. When doubts about the future stability of exchange rates begin to develop, however, the weaker currencies quickly tend to be eliminated from this competition, and the choice of reserve currencies narrows down to the strongest, hardest, and thus safest, currencies in world trade and settlements. When even these begin to be questioned, a further shift to gold may bring the gold exchange standard to an end and move the world back toward the previous gold, or gold bullion, standard.

The gold exchange standard *may*, but *does not necessarily*, help in relieving a shortage of world monetary reserves. It does so only to the extent that the key-currency countries are willing to let their net reserve position decline through increases in their short-term monetary liabilities unmatched by corresponding increases in their own gross reserves. If they allow this to happen, however, and to continue indefinitely, they tend to bring about a collapse of the system itself through the gradual weakening of foreigners' confidence in the key currencies.

This happened to the United Kingdom in 1931. The collapse was then brought about by large shifts of sterling balances into gold and dollars, leading to the devaluation of sterling. It happened again as a consequence of wartime developments and resulted then both in the 1949 devaluation and in the protracted inconvertibility of sterling and recurring balance-of-payments crises of Britain through the postwar years.

The United States authorities are well aware of the problem and determined to tackle it long before the danger point is reached. The real danger which we face is not that of a dollar collapse. It is the fact that such a collapse can ultimately be avoided only through a substantial slowdown of the contributions to world liquidity derived in the last nine years from the persistent weakening of our net reserve position. The solution of the dollar problem will thus involve a reopening or aggravation of the world liquidity program.

The world's normal requirements for monetary reserves appropriate to the maintenance of convertibility by the major trading countries are likely to exceed considerably—by \$5 billion to \$15 billion—over the next ten years the contribution which may be expected for the purpose from current levels of gold production.[17]

This gap is unlikely to be filled by the supplementary contribution to world liquidity that may be derived from the further growth of dollar, sterling, and other national currency balances as media for reserve accumulation.

In the absence of any specific planning and policies, the growing inadequacy of world reserves would be most likely to lead, within a relatively short span of years, to a new cycle of international deflation, devaluation, and restrictions, as it did after 1929. Such a cycle might possibly be triggered by unfavorable economic developments outside the center countries themselves, but its international spread would begin with the difficulties which the United States or the United Kingdom might experience as a result of any considerable slowdown or reversal of the inflow of foreign funds to their markets. The lessons of the 1930's and the radical changes which have taken place since then in governmental attitudes and policies would probably rule out any widespread recourse to, or acceptance of, internal deflation as a method of adjustment. Devaluation and restrictions would be the most likely outcome of such a situation.

[17] Including about \$200 million a year of Russian gold sales to the West. The conclusions of this paper would, I must admit, be thoroughly upset if the USSR decided to use aggressively its vast gold stock in world markets, for economic or political purposes. Depending on the policies adopted on both sides of the famed iron curtain, this could either save or definitely wreck the gold standard as an international monetary mechanism.

PRESCRIPTION

A New Charter for the International Monetary Fund

Devaluations of currencies and restrictions on world trade are undesirable. Yet, as the above analysis suggests, these may be ahead of us if the folly of the current world monetary system is allowed to continue its reign. In what follows I present a set of proposals aimed at removing the weaknesses of the current system.

The keystone of these proposals would be the substitution of IMF balances for balances in national currencies—i.e., mostly dollars and sterling —in all member countries' monetary reserves. Such balances should be made equivalent in all respects to gold itself and as widely usable and acceptable in world payments.

Sources and limits of the Fund's over-all lending capacity. The IMF lending capacity would be based on the accumulation of bancor accounts— in the form of deposits with the IMF—by member countries as part and parcel of their total monetary reserves, alongside of gold itself and fully equivalent to it in international settlements. This basic objective, however, requires neither that the Fund be endowed with an *unlimited*—and potentially inflationary—lending capacity, nor that each member country commit itself in advance to accumulate *unlimited* amounts of bancor in settlement of its surpluses.

The over-all lending capacity of the Fund can properly be limited to the creation of bancor amounts sufficient to preserve an adequate level of international liquidity. Various criteria could be retained for this purpose. The simplest one might be to limit the Fund's net lending, over any twelve-month period, to a total amount which would, together with current increases in the world stock of monetary gold, increase total world reserves by, let us say, 3 to 5 per cent a year.[18] The exact figure could not, of course, be determined scientifically and would, in any case, depend in practice upon the compromise between divergent national viewpoints which would emerge from the negotiation of the new Fund Agreement. A reasonably conservative solution would be to retain a 3 per cent figure as definitely noninflationary, and to require qualified votes (two-thirds, three-fourths, and ultimately four-fifths of the total voting power, or even unanimity) to authorize lending in excess of 3, 4, or 5 per cent a year.[19]

---

[18] See pp. 25–28.

[19] Alternative criteria, more logical but also more difficult to define concretely, might be derived from the current trend of some international price index reflecting inflationary or deflationary pressures on the world economy.

Assuming, for instance, that monetary gold stocks continue to increase by $700 million or $800 million a year, the Fund's annual lending quota based on a 3 per cent rate could be roughly estimated today at about $800 million to $900 million. A 4 per cent rate would raise this to about $1.4 billion, and 5 per cent to about $2 billion a year.[20] These estimates would rise gradually, but slowly, with further increases in world reserves. They could decrease as well as increase, on the other hand, with future fluctuations in the current additions to the world monetary gold stock.

Minimum deposit requirements. What provisions would be necessary to induce member countries to finance such lending by the Fund through the accumulation of an equivalent amount of Fund balances as part of the annual increase in their total monetary reserves?

Most member countries have, for many years past, held a considerable portion of their monetary reserves in the form of foreign exchange—primarily U.S. dollars and pounds sterling—rather than gold. The percentage of foreign exchange reserves to total reserves averaged at the end of 1957 some 30 per cent for the world as a whole, and as much as 55 per cent for countries other than the United States and the United Kingdom. During the five years preceding the Suez crisis, official dollar balances alone increased at an average pace of nearly $1 billion a year.

The major stimuli to such accumulation are, of course, the lower costs incidental to the use of key currencies rather than gold in world settlements, and the earnings derived from the portion of a country's reserves held in the form of foreign exchange. The major deterrents to such accumulation, on the other hand, are the risks of exchange fluctuations, inconvertibility, blocking, or even default, inseparable from holdings in a foreign country's currency.

The shift from national currency balances to balances with the IMF could preserve fully the same incentives and decrease considerably at the same time the weight of the deterrents mentioned above. The Fund's earnings on its own loans and investments[21] should be distributed among members *pro rata* of the balances held by them with the institution. These balances should—as all other Fund accounts—be expressed in a gold unit, and escape therefore the foreign exchange risk always attached to foreign

---

[20] These calculations are based on the IMF estimates of world reserves—excluding international institutions—of about $54 billion at the end of 1958.

[21] See below, pp. 46–49. Since the Fund, however, would hold in nonearning gold a portion of the assets corresponding to its deposit liabilities to members, the rate of earnings on such deposits would be somewhat lower than the rates of earnings on the Fund on its loans and investments. On the other hand, the Fund might attract free deposits by paying a higher rate of interest on these than on minimum, compulsory deposits.

exchange holdings in national currencies. They would similarly remain unaffected by any inconvertibility decision adopted by any individual member of the Fund. They could, at any time, be used by their holders as freely and widely as gold itself to make payments to any other member country, and even to nonmembers.[22] These provisions should make it possible for all countries to count their balances with the Fund as a normal and valuable component of their monetary reserves, and as fully equivalent to gold for the calculation of reserve or gold cover requirements wherever legal provisions still exist in this respect.

These various advantages should ensure a considerable demand for Fund balances on the part of most member countries, and particularly on the part of those which are already holding a large portion of their monetary reserves in the form of foreign exchange rather than gold. Members' voluntary holdings of Fund balances might well exceed after a time the amounts needed to finance the Fund's lending operations, in which case a growing portion of the Fund's assets would take the form of gold.

This is not likely to become true, however, until members have grown fully familiar with the system and with the security, liquidity, and earning power of this new form of reserve assets. In the initial years at least, it will be necessary to require Fund members to hold with the institution balances amply sufficient to finance its lending and to guarantee—through a sufficient accumulation of gold reserves—the full convertibility of Fund balances into any currency, even the "hardest," actually needed in settlements.

Both of these purposes could be achieved most simply by requiring all members to hold in the form of Fund deposits a certain proportion of their gross monetary reserves. All would agree to accept such deposits in settlement of their international claims without limit, but would have the right to convert at any time into gold, if they wished, deposits accrued to their Fund account in excess of this minimum requirement. This obligation would substitute for the present system of Fund quotas, and offer considerable advantages over it from the point of view of individual members as well as from the point of view of the Fund itself.

The first of these advantages would lie in the fact that such balances

[22] The membership of the Fund now includes practically all countries outside the Soviet bloc, except Switzerland and New Zealand. Some further efforts could be made to induce these two countries to join a reformed IMF, and the rest of our discussion will assume that these efforts have been successful. The special arrangements otherwise needed to enable members to draw on their Fund account for settlements to nonmembers would not create any serious financial burden for the Fund.

with the Fund would remain as fully liquid and usable in payments as gold itself, and should therefore—as already noted above—be considered as part of each country's monetary reserves. The maintenance of a portion of a country's reserves in this form would therefore be no burden on it and would not raise the internal financing problems which some countries now find in financing their quota subscription to the Fund.[23]

The second advantage is that deposit obligations would adjust automatically to fluctuations in the over-all reserve position of each country. The Fund's over-all resources would thus increase as the over-all level of world reserves increases. Most of all, however, the increase in Fund minimum deposit requirements would concentrate on the countries which currently develop net surpluses and whose currency is therefore most needed for international settlements. This flexibility should be contrasted with the rigidity, arbitrariness, and wastefulness of the present quota system which can be changed only infrequently and only through a laborious process of international renegotiation and of new national legislation on the part of all Fund members.

In order to satisfy the minimum reserve requirements, all countries would have to transfer to the Fund equivalent amounts of assets. Three types of assets would be eligible for this purpose.

1. Net creditor claims previously accumulated on the Fund; these would automatically be transformed into IMF deposits.

2. Other liquid or semi-liquid foreign exchange holdings, i.e., primarily dollar and sterling balances.

3. Gold.

If we assume that all countries would initially prefer to hold onto their gold assets, most of them would satisfy fully their reserve obligation by transferring to the Fund only part of their present foreign exchange holdings. Only a handful of countries—primarily the United States and the United Kingdom—would have to transfer gold to the Fund in order to fulfill their deposit obligation.

Table 11 shows the new balance sheet of the Fund after all such transfers have taken place. Nearly half of the Fund assets ($4.9 billion) would be in gold, and the rest in various claims on member countries, but very

---

[23] Since such subscriptions cannot now be used freely for payment by the subscriber, but merely give him a right to apply for Fund borrowings, many countries do not regard their creditor position with the Fund as part of their reserves. Subscriptions to, and claims on, the Fund must then be financed by the government itself, either out of accumulated funds or through borrowings from its central bank or from the market.

TABLE 11*

HYPOTHETICAL IMF BALANCE SHEET AT END OF 1958 AFTER PROPOSED REFORM

(In billions of U.S. dollars)

Assets		Liabilities	
Gold	4.9	Members' minimum deposits	
December 31, 1958, holdings.	1.5	on current account.............	11.2
New deposits	3.4	From members' net claims	
Claims on members............	6.3	on December 31, 1958.......	2.6
December 31, 1958........	1.1	From additional gold and	
New deposits	5.1	foreign exchange deposits...	8.7
		Net earnings	0.02
Total	11.2	Total	11.2

* The assumption is that countries maintain only the minimum required deposits with the Fund and transfer gold to the Fund for this purpose only insofar as their foreign exchange reserves are insufficient to feed such required deposits.

largely in U.S. dollars (probably more than $3 billion) and in pounds sterling (probably close to $2 billion). There would be no reason to change the present repayment provisions covering existing Fund claims (about $1 billion) arising from past operations. Provision would have to be made, however, with regard to the new claims acquired by the Fund as a result of the proposed reform. The bulk of these claims would be in the form of bank deposits, acceptances, and treasury bills now held by member countries in New York or London as part of their monetary reserves. The Fund would have no immediate need to modify these investments, but should be empowered to do so, in a smooth and progressive manner, insofar as useful for the conduct of its own operations. This purpose would be served by giving the Fund an option to liquidate such investments at a maximum pace of, let us say, 5 per cent a year. The maximum yearly liability for repayment which this would entail for the United States and the United Kingdom would be of the order of $150 million and $100 million respectively.[24]

This pattern of Fund assets should rule out in practice any real danger of a "currency scarcity" in the Fund and guarantee therefore the full and continued convertibility of Fund deposits into any currencies needed by

[24] If a faster rate of repayment were deemed desirable, the 5 per cent option might be made to apply either to the debt itself—as suggested in the text—or to the excess of the country's gold reserves over a "normal" amount defined by the average ratio of world reserves to world imports. This second criterion would leave the United Kingdom's obligation unchanged, but would raise to about $750 million initially the annual repayment liability of the United States.

members. Currency sales by the Fund would be credited to the deposit accounts of the countries whose currency had been sold, and the large gold holdings of the Fund (nearly $5 billion) would enable it to meet any request by such members to convert into gold the excess of their deposits above their 20 per cent minimum requirement.[25] Moreover, countries which are in debt to the Fund should not have an absolute right to such conversions. The Fund could, in such cases, insist upon extraordinary amortization of their debts to it as an alternative to gold repayments susceptible of jeopardizing its own liquidity. This would also constitute an additional safeguard against any scarcity of the two major currencies in world trade and settlements—the U.S. dollar and the pound sterling—in view of the large initial holdings (more than $5 billion) of these two currencies by the Fund.

Fund absorption of residual foreign exchange reserves. The operations described above would absorb and consolidate a substantial portion (about $5 billion) of the foreign exchange reserves of member countries, but would still leave outstanding about $10 billion of such national currency reserves. In order to eliminate fully from the international monetary system certain absurdities and dangers, these national currency reserves should also be converted into international Fund deposits, and all member countries should undertake to hold henceforth all of their reserves exclusively in gold and Fund deposits, except possibly for small working balances in actively traded currencies. If this were done, the Fund's initial deposit liabilities, estimated above at about $11 billion, would rise to approximately $21 billion, and its foreign exchange holdings to $16 billion. Its gold reserve would initially be left unaffected, at about $5 billion, or a little less than 25 per cent of total liabilities. This might be deemed uncomfortably low and entail a possible danger that the Fund might have insufficient gold to procure for its members a currency in strong demand in the event that the issuing country insisted on converting into gold any Fund deposits accruing to it in excess of its 20 per cent deposit requirement.

Such a danger, however, would be more remote than one might think. First of all, it could hardly materialize as far as the two major currencies in world trade and payments are concerned. The Fund would now hold indeed close to $9 billion in U.S. dollars and more than $5 billion in pounds

---

[25] The minimum deposit requirement itself would, of course, rise by 20 per cent of the amount credited to the member's account since such amounts would increase correspondingly the country's gross monetary reserves.

sterling.[26] A strong world demand for dollars or sterling should be met, in large part, by extraordinary amortization of this indebtedness rather than by equivalent gold settlement by the Fund of the balances accruing to these two countries beyond their 20 per cent deposit requirement.

The danger of an excessive depletion of the Fund's gold resources could thus come only from two other sources:

1. Direct conversion into gold of the Fund balances acquired in exchange for the initial transfer to the Fund of the foreign currency balances now held by members; or alternatively;

2. A similar conversion into gold by the countries—other than the United States and the United Kingdom—whose subsequent over-all surpluses are settled through transfers of Fund balances from the deficit countries' account to the surplus countries' account.

The first of these two dangers could be warded off as far as sterling balances—but not dollar balances—are concerned by providing that the conversion of national currency balances into Fund balances should not entitle their holders to claim gold from the Fund if the balances so transferred did not entitle them to claim gold from the country on which these balances were held. This would not impair in any way the convertibility of these Fund balances into all and any currencies actually needed by their holders in international settlements, nor the gold exchange guarantee and other privileges attaching to Fund balances in general. What it would mean is that the right to claim gold from the Fund would attach only to the Fund balances exceeding the sum of the country's normal 20 per cent requirement *plus* the balances initially acquired in exchange for gold-inconvertible national currency balances. This second limitation, moreover, would be eliminated gradually as the debtors of such balances—primarily the United Kingdom—amortized their corresponding indebtedness to the Fund.

The only residual danger of an excessive depletion of the Fund's gold assets would then arise from the conversion into gold of deposits at the Fund transferred to over-all surplus countries other than the United States and the United Kingdom. Let us note, however, that only 80 per cent, at most, of such transfers would expose the Fund to gold payments since 20

[26] Official dollar balances of foreign countries were reported at $8,665 million at the end of 1958, and total—official and private—U.S. Government bonds and notes at $983 million. Noncolonial sterling balances were estimated at about $6.9 billion. On the basis of the 1957 ratio of official to private sterling balances, this might be broken down roughly into $5.3 billion of official balances and $1.5 billion of private balances.

per cent of them would increase the minimum deposit requirements of the receiving countries. Second, the option of the Fund to claim annual amortization installments from the debtors of the balances could be exercised, whenever necessary, and bring in up to $1 billion a year of additional gold resources to the Fund.[27]

The danger of a gold or currency scarcity in the Fund would thus appear extremely remote, especially as most countries could be expected to hold Fund deposits well in excess of their minimum requirements. Convenience and earning incentives have so far prompted countries other than the United States and the United Kingdom to retain, on the average, more than half—rather than merely 20 per cent—of their gross reserves in foreign exchange rather than gold. They will have, in any case, to retain some working balances in a form other than gold in order to avoid repeated gold sales or purchases each time they wish to sell or buy foreign currencies in the market to stabilize their own exchange rate. These working balances will have to be held either as excess deposits with the Fund or directly in the key currencies actively traded on the exchange markets. Either of these two alternatives would reduce substantially the danger of an excessive gold drain from the Fund. Working balances equal to only 5 per cent of annual imports, for instance, would absorb as much as $5 billion.

All in all, therefore, the absorption and consolidation of all outstanding foreign exchange reserves—with the possible exception of moderate working balances—into Fund deposits would appear feasible, even on the basis of the 20 per cent minimum deposit requirement envisaged up to now. Yet, provision would have to be made to safeguard the Fund's liquidity both against unforeseen conversions of excess deposits into gold and, in the long run, against the increasing gap between the probable level of world gold stocks and the desirable expansion of over-all monetary reserves. Three different techniques might be used—either alternatively, or in combination—to meet both problems. The simplest one would be for the Fund to issue medium-term gold certificates, payable either in gold or in excess Fund deposits, and carrying a higher rate of interest than liquid Fund deposits. Such certificates should be particularly attractive to high reserve holders. The second possibility would be to authorize the Fund to

---

[27] Under the formula described on p. 42 above, this option would normally apply to 5 per cent of the total currency balances (about $15 billion) transferred to the Fund, i.e., $750 million. It could, however, also be applied, alternatively, to 5 per cent of the excess of the debtor's gross reserves over and above the average ratio of world reserves to world imports. This would raise initially by about $300 million the annual repayment liability of the United States.

raise uniformly the 20 per cent deposit requirement to a higher ratio—25 per cent or 30 per cent, for instance—of each country's gross monetary reserves. The third would be to leave the basic 20 per cent requirement unchanged—or to increase it more moderately—but to impose higher deposit requirements upon that portion of each member's reserves which exceeds the average ratio of world monetary gold to world imports.

Any increase in the compulsory deposit obligation initially accepted by members should normally require a qualified majority (two-thirds, three-fourths, or even four-fifths) of the Fund's total voting power. If, however, such a majority could not be reached at a time when a real gold scarcity develops in the Fund, such a "gold scarcity" would have to be declared by the Fund and entail the automatic adoption of either the second or the third of the three solutions discussed above, to the extent necessary to preserve the Fund's ability to meet its gold conversion commitments. If this provision for automatic quota increases in such a case proved unnegotiable, a less satisfactory, but still workable, alternative might be envisaged. Any country would be recognized the right to refuse such an increase in its deposit obligation, but with the proviso that the exercise of this right would automatically entail the "scarcity" of that particular country's currency in the sense of Article VII of the present Fund Agreement, and carry the consequences envisaged in that Article. As different from the present—and politically inapplicable—procedure, such a declaration would be left to the discretion of the country concerned rather than of the Fund. In fact, our previous discussion makes it abundantly clear that such a contingency would be most unlikely to arise, at least for many years to come, and that confidence in Fund deposits should by that time be sufficiently strong to avert any such decision on the part of any country.

Clearing and lending operations of the Fund. As indicated above,[28] the major safeguard against an inflationary level of Fund lending would lie in the over-all limitations placed on the net increase of the Fund's loans during any twelve-month period.

These loans should fall into two broad categories, similar in many respects to those of national central banks' credit operations:

1. Advances or rediscounts, undertaken at the initiative of the borrowing country;

2. Open-market operations, or investments, undertaken at the initiative of the Fund itself.

[28] Pp. 38–39.

The normal procedures for Fund advances need not differ substantially from those gradually developed by the Fund over its twelve years of existence. They should be subordinated to full agreement between the Fund and the member with relation not only to the maturity of the loan, but also the broad economic and financial policies followed by the member to ensure long-run equilibrium in its international transactions without excessive recourse to trade and exchange restrictions. The recent stand-by techniques of lending might, in addition, be supplemented by overdraft agreements, to be renewed at frequent intervals, and guaranteeing all members in good standing rapid and automatic Fund assistance in case of need, but for modest amounts and with short-term repayment provisions. These overdraft agreements would be primarily designed to give time for full consideration of a request for normal, medium-term loans or stand-by agreements, and would be guaranteed by the country's minimum deposit obligation.

The only basic difference between the new lending procedures and the ones now in existence is that the proposed structure of Fund operations would eliminate one of the most puzzling requirements of the present Articles of Agreement. Article V, Section 3, Subsection (a) provides that "A member shall be entitled to buy the *currency of another member* from the Fund in exchange for *its own currency* subject to the following conditions: (i) The member desiring to purchase *the currency* represents that *it* is presently needed for making *in that currency* payments which are consistent with the provisions of the Agreement."[29]

This is very bizarre indeed and raises at least two broad questions. First of all, it is very difficult, under convertibility conditions, to identify *any particular currency* as needed by a member. The settlement of most international transactions takes place through private sales and purchases of foreign exchange in the market and need not involve the member itself, or its monetary authorities. The latter's *need* for foreign exchange arises only when they feel impelled to intervene on the exchange markets to re-purchase excess supplies of their own currency and arrest its depreciation in terms of other currencies. They do not, even then, however, need any *particular* currency for this purpose, although they will presumably tend to operate chiefly in widely traded currencies and to sell preferably those which command the highest market price—in relation to their par value or official buying rate for foreign currencies—at that particular moment.

[29] The italics are mine.

Second, it should be noted that the Fund Agreement allows members to purchase foreign currencies in exchange *for their own currency*—i.e., in exchange for their own I.O.U.'s—but not in exchange for other foreign currencies owned or acquired by them. This means in effect that the Fund could never really fulfill effectively one of the main purposes stated in Article I, Section (iv) of the Agreement, i.e., "to assist in the establishment of a multilateral system of payments in respect of current transactions between members . . ." This was a major gap in the Fund Agreement and made it necessary to set up in 1950 a separate institution, the European Payments Union, to restore a multilateral system of settlements among the European countries and their associated monetary areas.[30]

Both of these shortcomings would be remedied by the Fund reform proposed in this study. Bilateral settlements among central banks would be obviated through the use of the Fund as a clearing house for such settlements. Foreign currency balances acquired by a central bank would be deposited to its Fund account and debited from the account of the debtor of such balances. Any other member's currency could, conversely, be purchased by a member through corresponding debits to its own account and credits to the account of the country whose currency is bought. Finally, any loan granted by the Fund to a member would be credited to its Fund deposit account, and the member could draw on this account in any currency whatsoever without having to make any "representation" that it needs it to make payments in that particular currency.[31]

The second broad category of Fund lending would take place through investments in the financial markets of member countries. These operations would be decided very largely at the initiative of the Fund itself, but always of course in agreement with the monetary authorities of the countries concerned. Such agreement would be necessary in any case to attach to these investments the same guarantees against exchange and inconvertibility risks as those which protect the Fund's own deposit liabilities.

[30] The restoration of convertibility for nonresidents by most major trading countries provides, as long as it lasts, an alternative machinery for the multilateralization of payments. It does not, however, dispense with the need to discourage through international cooperation and agreements later relapses into inconvertibility by a country in difficulty, or with the need to help other countries withstand the impact of such a decision by one of their major trading partners. This is indeed one of the major objectives of the European Monetary Agreement which replaced, at the end of last year, the European Payments Union Agreement. A further discussion of the vital issues involved may be found in my book on *Europe and the Money Muddle*, particularly pp. 113–16, 202, and 223–29.

[31] This would also put an end to the kind of absurdities under which Fund loans have been mostly financed so far by the country—the United States—which suffered the worst loss of reserves, and hardly or not at all by the countries whose reserves were increasing.

The first investments of this character would be imposed upon the Fund by its absorption of the outstanding national currency reserves transferred to it by members in exchange for Fund deposits. They would be overwhelmingly dollar and sterling investments and would be subject to special provisions, already outlined above, to avoid unnecessary disturbances to the monetary and financial markets of the United States and the United Kingdom. The resources derived from their progressive liquidation, however, would normally be re-employed in other markets whose need for international capital is greater than in the United States and the United Kingdom. A portion of such investments might even be channeled into relatively long-term investments for economic development through purchases of IBRD bonds or other securities of a similar character.

A primary consideration in determining the pattern of Fund investments would be the need to preserve the full liquidity of its members' deposits. It should be noted, however, that the Fund would be in a particularly strong position in this respect as the total amount of its required deposits—initially some $11 billion—could hardly decline in practice, but would on the contrary grow year by year with the increase of world reserves. Any withdrawals of deposits by members whose over-all reserves are declining would be more than matched by increases in the required deposits of members whose reserves are increasing.[32] The liquidity problem of the Fund would be very largely confined to the preservation of the convertibility of its excess deposits into any currency needed in payment, and, eventually, into gold if their holders requested it. This problem has already been amply discussed above and need not detain us further.

A number of other interesting suggestions relating to the Fund's lending procedures have recently been presented by Mr. Maxwell Stamp,[33]

[32] The theoretical possibility of a decline in the monetary reserves of all countries taken together should, however, be noted in passing. The only case on record is that of the first years of the great depression when world reserves declined by about $2 billion from 1928 to 1932 as a result of the wholesale liquidation of their foreign exchange assets by central banks. The above proposals are precisely designed to ward off the repetition of a similar collapse of the gold exchange standard. Over-all world reserves could also decline through large-scale sales of official reserves to private holders, reversing the trend of at least the last forty years of monetary history. Article 4 (f) of the European Payments Union Agreement provided that "Each Contracting Party shall use its best endeavors to ensure that abnormal balances in the currencies of other Contracting Parties are not held by banks other than central banks or otherwise placed so that they are excluded from the calculation of bilateral surpluses or deficits." A similar provision should be written in the new Fund Agreement to prevent countries from eluding their minimum deposit requirement by excessive transfers of international reserves to private banks.

[33] Maxwell Stamp, "The Fund and the Future," in *Lloyds Bank Review*, October 1958, pp. 1–20. [See "The Stamp Plan—1962 Version," reprinted as selection 3 in this book.]

former Advisor to the Governors of the Bank of England, British Alternate Executive Director of the Fund from 1951 to 1953, and Director of the Fund's European Department from 1953 to 1954. Mr. Stamp would also favor the channeling of part of the IMF credits through the IBRD, through the International Finance Corporation, and even through private corporations. He also proposes to explore further the possibility of using collateral pledges of commercial bills, treasury bills, tax revenues, etc., as guarantees of the Fund's loans, and favors a more active and flexible use of the interest rates as an instrument of policy.

Regional Cooperation as a Steppingstone toward World Cooperation

The political obstacles standing in the way of the adoption of the reform plans presented above are bound to be much smaller within such regional groupings as the European and Latin American Common Markets. The degree of cooperation, respect, and confidence in the member countries' integrity already achieved makes the adoption of such reform plans much more likely. The creation of such regional organizations does not mean the surrender of efforts toward solution of the liquidity problem on a world-wide basis. To the contrary, it is quite likely that strong regional associations are more willing and able to cooperate in a world organization than are the individual countries by themselves.

The chances for the adoption of such regional schemes for cooperation are greatest in Western Europe, where many of the supranational organizations are in the process of formation. The following pages are devoted to a proposal for the reorganization of the present European Monetary Agreement.

The keystone of such a reform of the present EMA would bear a close similarity to the proposals advanced above for the reform of the IMF. The project would be regional, rather than world-wide in scope, however, and could probably be negotiated and implemented more easily, more rapidly, and more fully within such a framework.

The participating countries would establish jointly a Clearing House centralizing all payments among their separate central banks. These payments would be effected through corresponding debits and credits to the account maintained by each central bank with the Clearing House.

These clearing accounts would be fed, first of all, by the compulsory transfer to each country's account of any and all balances in another member's currency purchased from the market by its central bank or credited to it by another central bank. They could be fed, in addition, by transfers of gold, or convertible currencies of third countries, or even of other currencies specified by the Clearing in the light of its members' current demand for such currencies. The first of these two provisions would be designed both to simplify payments among members and to prevent any relapse into open or concealed bilateralism among them.

The clearing accounts would, of course, be fully convertible and could be freely drawn upon by their holders to make payments to third countries as well as to member countries. They would, moreover, carry an exchange guarantee in terms of a jointly agreed unit of account. This unit might, as in the case of the IMF, be defined merely and simply in terms of gold. A less rigid, and on the whole preferable, procedure might be to revive a unit similar to the former EPU unit of account, i.e., tantamount in effect to an exchange guarantee in terms of whichever European currency will in fact remain stablest in the future with respect to gold itself.[34]

The participating countries might be required, at least initially, to maintain in their clearing account a minimum balance equivalent to, let us say, 10 or 20 per cent of their total gold and foreign exchange reserves. Based on current reserve levels, these required balances would total today as much as $2 billion if a 10 per cent "reserve requirement" were adopted. The resources thus placed at the disposal of the Clearing would be totally unaffected by intra-European disequilibria, since any decrease in some countries' global reserves and minimum deposits would then be exactly offset by corresponding increases in other members' reserves and required deposits. The resources of the Clearing would fall only as a consequence of global deficits of the OEEC area as a whole toward the rest of the world, and even then by only 10 per cent of the amount of such deficits. A cumulative deficit of $10 billion would be necessary, for instance, to reduce by

[34] Such a clause would have the same effect as a gold guarantee unless *all* member currencies modified *in the same direction*—upward or downward—their present parity with respect to gold. The application of a straight gold clause in such an event would probably result in unjustified windfall losses or gains for the debtors and creditors in the Clearing. It might be noted that the elimination of the EPU unit of account by EMA and its substitution by a gold clause for some transactions and a dollar clause for others would open a serious and unsolved question in the improbable event of a change in the United States gold price or gold policy. A whole article (Article 14), entitled "Modification in the United States Price or Policy for Gold," is devoted to this very problem, but its call for an urgent and comprehensive review of the Agreement in such a case is only a thin disguise for a total lack of agreement at this stage as to the way in which the situation should be handled. The needless introduction of such complications and uncertainties in the Agreement is difficult to explain except on the basis of British fears that the EPU unit of account might enjoy greater prestige than the pound sterling, displacing it gradually as a key currency in world trade and payments.

one-half the funds initially placed at the disposal of the Clearing. Such an evolution would be highly improbable, and would in any case call for joint readjustment policies in order to harmonize the European pace of monetary and credit expansion with that of other areas, or for preserving a desirable pace of expansion against the impact of outside deflation through the negotiation of foreign credits or through an increase of restrictions on trade and payments with nonmember countries.

The resources of the Clearing would be held primarily in gold and convertible foreign currencies, so as to enable it to maintain the world-wide convertibility of its members' accounts. The factors of stability underlined above, however, would make it possible for the Clearing—just as for any bank—to reinvest at short or medium term, within or outside the OEEC area, a reasonable portion of its assets without endangering thereby the effective liquidity of its deposits for their individual holders.

The lending procedures of the Clearing would follow the same general pattern outlined above with respect to the IMF. The criteria determining the over-all amount of such lending, however, would be different, and far less automatic in character. The total amount of assistance provided to members would have to be adjusted in the light of the current inflationary or deflationary pressures within the area and of the evolution of the balance of payments and monetary reserves of the group as a whole toward the outside world. This would not, of course, ensure that the policies of the group as a whole would be wiser than those of other countries or than those which would have been independently followed otherwise by its national member states. The group's policies might be more inflationary or more deflationary, as well as less inflationary or less deflationary, more foolish as well as wiser, than those pursued in the rest of the world. The choice of policies open to it would merely be wider and freer than that otherwise available to its individual members. It should certainly be exercised in such a way as to preserve freedom of trade within the area, and strengthen its ability to follow liberal policies toward the rest of the world as well. The latter result could not be guaranteed, however, in the absence of a sufficient coordination of policies and mutual financial assistance between the group and other major trading countries. Important tasks would thus continue to devolve on world-wide organizations such as GATT and the IMF, even though effective performance at that level is likely to develop more slowly and gradually than will prove feasible at the regional level.

As in the case of the IMF the influence and means of action of the

Clearing would be likely to grow at a rapid pace, as experience overcomes initial diffidence toward the system and the inertia of old habits and traditions. Its deposit accounts, particularly, might be expected to exceed largely, after a time, the minimum requirements initially adopted and even, possibly, to make these unnecessary. Those accounts should indeed prove highly attractive to member banks in view of the unique guarantees attached to them. The convertibility and exchange rate guarantees provided would eliminate the risks of unilateral inconvertibility or exchange rate devaluation inseparable from the current investment of monetary reserves in national, so-called "key" currencies. Default risks, moreover, would be practically eliminated by the obligation accepted by all members to channel through the Clearing all payments due by any one of them to another. The overdrafts of a defaulting borrower would thus be automatically amortized by the transfers made to its account by any other member, and this procedure would not be dependent on the good faith of the borrowing country itself, but on the commitments subscribed to by all other members of the Clearing.

Finally—but only as long as the IMF reforms proposed above are not adopted—the Clearing might attract similar accounts even from central banks of nonmember countries whose payments relations are largely with the EPU area. Indeed, nearly 40 per cent of non-EPU countries' merchandise imports originate in the EPU area, and this proportion exceeds 50 per cent for the countries outside the dollar area. The European Clearing, based on a close alliance between sterling and other European currencies, would tend to develop gradually into a powerful monetary center, susceptible to assume an international role comparable to that of London before 1914, but which London alone has become too weak to perform today. Nonmember countries could be expected to transfer gradually into clearing accounts some portion of the national currency balances now held by them as monetary reserves. Insofar as these balances are now held in nonmember currencies—i.e., practically in U.S. dollars—this would strengthen the gross reserve position of the Clearing and result in some further expansion of its lending capacity. Insofar as they are now held in member currencies—practically pounds sterling—it might help smooth out the impact now exercised upon the debtor of such balances—practically the United Kingdom—by fluctuations in their over-all amount. The largest portion of these fluctuations would indeed be associated with the settlement of imbalance between the owners of the balances and the European area itself, and would not cause any drain on the Clearing's gold and dollar reserves, or any change in its other assets, but merely a reshuffling of its net claims or debts vis à vis the United Kingdom on the one hand, and its other members on the other. While persistent movements of this sort in the same direction would obviously require in the end cash settlements among the member countries concerned, a great many of them could properly be cushioned by the Clearing and help avoid or smooth out the undesirable pressures which they would otherwise exercise upon these countries' policies.

A European Clearing House would therefore be able to offer a substantial contribution to the preservation of international liquidity and to the reduction of the dangers attendant to the use of national currencies as international monetary reserves. It could not, however, solve such world-wide problems as fully and effectively as a revised IMF might do. The proposals therefore should not be regarded as a lasting substitute for the IMF reforms discussed in the preceding section. On the other hand, neither should a global IMF approach be regarded as a full substitute, making a European Clearing superfluous and useless. First of all, the setting up and implementation of a fully satisfactory IMF system will probably require several years of negotiation and experimentation. Second, the management of a world-wide monetary clearing system, and particularly the investment of the large funds derived from its operation, will present enormous administrative and political hurdles, which can best be surmounted through some decentralization of the Fund's decision-making process. Finally, the high degree of economic and political interdependence of the European countries and their experience of past cooperation are likely to make feasible far more extensive regional trade liberalization, credit commitments, and policy harmonization among them than could conceivably be negotiated and implemented on a world-wide level.

2

Proposals for an International Clearing Union

Immediately after the war all countries who have been engaged will be concerned with the pressure of relief and urgent reconstruction. The transition out of this into the normal world of the future cannot be wisely effected unless we know into what we are moving. It is therefore not too soon to consider what is to come after. In the field of national activity occupied by production, trade, and finance, both the nature of the problem and the experience of the period between the wars suggest four main lines of approach:

1. The mechanism of currency and exchange;

2. The framework of a commercial policy regulating the conditions for the exchange of goods, tariffs, preferences, subsidies, import regulations, and the like;

3. The orderly conduct of production, distribution, and price of primary products so as to protect both producers and consumers from the loss and risk for which the extravagant fluctuations of market conditions have been responsible in recent times;

4. Investment aid, both medium- and long-term, for the countries whose economic development needs assistance from outside.

If the principles of these measures and the form of the institutions to give effect to them can be settled in advance, in order that they may be in operation when the need arises, it is possible that taken together they may help the world to control the ebb and flow of the tides of economic activity which have, in the past, destroyed security of livelihood and endangered international peace.

Reprinted from the British Government Publication, Cmd. 6437 (London: H.M. Stationery Office, 1943). The paper was presented by the Chancellor of the Exchequer to Parliament by Command of His Majesty, April 1943. It is customarily attributed to John Maynard Keynes, and has become known as the Keynes plan.

All these matters will need to be handled in due course. The proposal that follows relates only to the mechanism of currency and exchange in international trading. It appears on the whole convenient to give it priority, because some general conclusions have to be reached under this head before much progress can be made with the other topics.

In preparing these proposals care has been taken to regard certain conditions, which the groundwork of an international economic system to be set up after the war should satisfy, if it is to prove durable:

(i) There should be the least possible interference with internal national policies, and the plan should not wander from the international terrain. Since such policies may have important repercussions on international relations, they cannot be left out of account. Nevertheless in the realm of internal policy the authority of the governing board of the proposed institution should be limited to recommendations, or at the most to imposing conditions for the more extended enjoyment of the facilities which the institution offers.

(ii) The technique of the plan must be capable of application, irrespective of the type and principle of government and economic policy existing in the prospective member states.

(iii) The management of the institution must be genuinely international without preponderant power of veto or enforcement to any country or group; and the rights and privileges of the smaller countries must be safeguarded.

(iv) Some qualification of the right to act at pleasure is required by any agreement or treaty between nations. But in order that such arrangements may be fully voluntary so long as they last and terminable when they have become irksome, provision must be made for voiding the obligation at due notice. If many member states were to take advantage of this, the plan would have broken down. But if they are free to escape from its provisions if necessary they may be the more willing to go on accepting them.

(v) The plan must operate not only to the general advantage but also to the individual advantage of each of the participants, and must not require a special economic or financial sacrifice from certain countries. No participant must be asked to do or offer anything which is not to his own true long-term interest.

It must be emphasized that it is not for the Clearing Union to assume the burden of long-term lending which is the proper task of some other institution. It is also necessary for it to have means of restraining improvident borrowers. But the Clearing Union must also seek to discourage creditor countries from leaving unused large liquid balances which ought to be devoted to some positive purpose. For excessive credit balances necessarily create excessive debit balances for some other party. In recognizing that the creditor as well as the debtor may be responsible for a want of balance, the proposed institution would be breaking new ground.

I. THE OBJECTS OF THE PLAN

1. About the primary objects of an improved system of international currency there is, today, a wide measure of agreement:

(*a*) We need an instrument of international currency having general acceptability between nations, so that blocked balances and bilateral clearings are unnecessary; that is to say, an instrument of currency used by each nation in its transactions with other nations, operating through whatever national organ, such as a treasury or a central bank, is most appropriate, with private individuals, businesses, and banks other than central banks each continuing to use their own national currency as heretofore.

(*b*) We need an orderly and agreed method of determining the relative exchange values of national currency units, so that unilateral action and competitive exchange depreciations are prevented.

(*c*) We need a *quantum* of international currency, which is neither determined in an unpredictable and irrelevant manner as, for example, by the technical progress of the gold industry, nor subject to large variations depending on the gold reserve policies of individual countries; but is governed by the actual current requirements of world commerce, and is also capable of deliberate expansion and contraction to offset deflationary and inflationary tendencies in effective world demand.

(*d*) We need a system possessed of an internal stabilizing mechanism, by which pressure is exercised on any country whose balance of payments with the rest of the world is departing from equilibrium *in either direction,* so as to prevent movements which must create for its neighbors an equal but opposite want of balance.

(*e*) We need an agreed plan for starting off every country after the war with a stock of reserves appropriate to its importance in world commerce, so that without due anxiety it can set its house in order during the transitional period to full peacetime conditions.

(*f*) We need a central institution, of a purely technical and nonpolitical character, to aid and support other international institutions concerned with the planning and regulation of the world's economic life.

(*g*) More generally, we need a means of reassurance to a troubled world, by which any country whose own affairs are conducted with due prudence is relieved of anxiety for causes which are not of its own making, concerning its ability to meet its international liabilities; and which will, therefore, make unnecessary those methods of restriction and discrimination which countries have adopted hitherto, not on their merits, but as measures of self-protection from disruptive outside forces.

2. There is also a growing measure of agreement about the general character of any solution of the problem likely to be successful. The particular proposals set forth below lay no claim to originality. They are an attempt to reduce to practical shape certain general ideas belonging to the contemporary climate of economic opinion, which have been given publicity in recent months by writers of several different nationalities. It is difficult to see how any plan can be successful which does not use these general ideas, which are born of the spirit of the age. The actual details put forward below are offered, with no dogmatic intention, as the basis of discussion for criticism and improvement. For we cannot make progress without embodying the general underlying idea in a frame of actual working, which will bring out the practical and political difficulties to be faced and met if the breath of life is to inform it.

3. In one respect this particular plan will be found to be more ambitious and yet, at the same time, perhaps more workable than some of the variant versions of the same basic idea, in that it is fully international, being based on one general agreement and not on a multiplicity of bilateral arrangements. Doubtless proposals might be made by which bilateral arrangements could be fitted together so as to obtain some of the advantages of a multilateral scheme. But there will be many difficulties attendant on such adjustments. It may be doubted whether a comprehensive scheme will ever in fact be worked out, unless it can come into existence through a single act of creation made possible by the unity of purpose and energy of hope for better things to come, springing from the victory of the United Nations, when they have attained it, over immediate evil. That these proposals are ambitious is claimed, therefore, to be not a drawback but an advantage.

4. The proposal is to establish a currency union, here designated an *International Clearing Union,* based on international bank-money, called (let us say) *bancor,* fixed (but not unalterably) in terms of gold and accepted as the equivalent of gold by the British Commonwealth and the United States and all the other members of the Union for the purpose of settling international balances. The central banks of all member states

(and also of nonmembers) would keep accounts with the International Clearing Union through which they would be entitled to settle their exchange balances with one another at their par value as defined in terms of bancor. Countries having a favorable balance of payments with the rest of the world as a whole would find themselves in possession of a credit account with the Clearing Union, and those having an unfavorable balance would have a debit account. Measures would be necessary (see below) to prevent the piling up of credit and debit balances without limit, and the system would have failed in the long run if it did not possess sufficient capacity for self-equilibrium to secure this.

5. The idea underlying such a Union is simple, namely, to generalize the essential principle of banking as it is exhibited within any closed system. This principle is the necessary equality of credits and debits. If no credits can be removed outside the clearing system, but only transferred within it, the Union can never be in any difficulty as regards the honoring of checks drawn upon it. It can make what advances it wishes to any of its members with the assurance that the proceeds can only be transferred to the clearing account of another member. Its sole task is to see to it that its members keep the rules and that the advances made to each of them are prudent and advisable for the Union as a whole.

II. THE PROVISIONS OF THE PLAN

6. The provisions proposed (the particular proportions and other details suggested being tentative as a basis of discussion) are the following:

(1) All the United Nations will be invited to become original members of the International Clearing Union. Other states may be invited to join subsequently. If ex-enemy states are invited to join, special conditions may be applied to them.

(2) The governing board of the Clearing Union shall be appointed by the governments of the several member states (as provided in (12) below); the daily business with the Union and the technical arrangements being carried out through their central banks or other appropriate authorities.

(3) The member states will agree between themselves the initial values of their own currencies in terms of bancor. A member state may not subsequently alter the value of its currency in terms of bancor without the permission of the governing board except under the conditions stated below; but during the first five years after the inception of the system the governing board shall give special consideration to appeals for an adjust-

ment in the exchange value of a national currency unit on the ground of unforeseen circumstances.

(4) The value of bancor in terms of gold shall be fixed by the governing board. Member states shall not purchase or acquire gold, directly or indirectly, at a price in terms of their national currencies in excess of the parity which corresponds to the value of their currency in terms of bancor and to the value of bancor in terms of gold. Their sales and purchases of gold shall not be otherwise restricted.

(5) Each member state shall have assigned to it a *quota*, which shall determine the measure of its responsibility in the management of the Union and of its right to enjoy the credit facilities provided by the Union. The initial quotas might be fixed by reference to the sum of each country's exports and imports on the average of (say) the three prewar years, and might be (say) 75 per cent of this amount, a special assessment being substituted in cases (of which there might be several) where this formula would be, for any reason, inappropriate. Subsequently, after the elapse of the transitional period, the quotas should be revised annually in accordance with the running average of each country's actual volume of trade in the three preceding years, rising to a five-year average when figures for five postwar years are available. The determination of a country's quota primarily by reference to the value of its foreign trade seems to offer the criterion most relevant to a plan which is chiefly concerned with the regulation of the foreign exchanges and of a country's international trade balance. It is, however, a matter for discussion whether the formula for fixing quotas should also take account of other factors.

(6) Member states shall agree to accept payment of currency balances, due to them from other members, by a transfer of bancor to their credit in the books of the Clearing Union. They shall be entitled, subject to the conditions set forth below, to make transfers of bancor to other members which have the effect of overdrawing their own accounts with the Union, provided that the maximum debit balances thus created do not exceed their quota. The Clearing Union may, at its discretion, charge a small commission or transfer fee in respect of transactions in its books for the purpose of meeting its current expenses or any other outgoings approved by the governing board.

(7) A member state shall pay to the Reserve Fund of the Clearing Union a charge of 1 per cent per annum on the amount of its average balance in bancor, whether it is a credit or a debit balance, in excess of a quarter of its quota; and a further charge of 1 per cent on its average bal-

ance, whether credit or debit, in excess of a half of its quota. Thus, only a country which keeps as nearly as possible in a state of international balance on the average of the year will escape this contribution. These charges are not absolutely essential to the scheme. But if they are found acceptable, they would be valuable and important inducements toward keeping a level balance, and a significant indication that the system looks on excessive credit balances with as a critical an eye as on excessive debit balances, each being, indeed, the inevitable concomitant of the other. Any member state in debit may, after consultation with the governing board, borrow bancor from the balances of any member state in credit on such terms as may be mutually agreed, by which means each would avoid these contributions. The governing board may, at its discretion, remit the charges on credit balances, and increase correspondingly those on debit balances, if in its opinion unduly expansionist conditions are impending in the world economy.

(8)—(*a*) A member state may not increase its debit balance by more than a *quarter* of its quota within a year without the permission of the governing board. If its debit balance has exceeded a quarter of its quota on the average of at least two years, it shall be entitled to reduce the value of its currency in terms of bancor provided that the reduction shall not exceed 5 per cent without the consent of the governing board; but it shall not be entitled to repeat this procedure unless the board is satisfied that this procedure is appropriate.

(*b*) The governing board may require from a member state having a debit balance reaching a *half* of its quota the deposit of suitable collateral against its debit balance. Such collateral shall, at the discretion of the governing board, take the form of gold, foreign or domestic currency, or government bonds, within the capacity of the member state. As a condition of allowing a member state to increase its debit balance to a figure in excess of a half of its quota, the governing board may require all or any of the following measures:

(i) a stated reduction in the value of the member's currency, if it deems that to be the suitable remedy;

(ii) the control of outward capital transactions if not already in force; and

(iii) the outright surrender of a suitable proportion of any separate gold or other liquid reserve in reduction of its debit balance.

Furthermore, the governing board may recommend to the government of the member state any internal measures affecting its domestic economy which may appear to be appropriate to restore the equilibrium of its international balance.

(*c*) If a member state's debit balance has exceeded *three-quarters* of its quota on the average of at least a year and is excessive in the opinion of the governing board in relation to the total debit balances outstanding on the books of the Clearing Union, or is increasing at an excessive rate, it may, in addition, be asked by the governing board to take measures to improve its position, and, in the event of its failing to reduce its debit balance accordingly within two years, the governing board may declare that it is in default and no longer entitled to draw against its account except with the permission of the governing board.

(*d*) Each member state, on joining the system, shall agree to pay to the Clearing Union any payments due from it to a country in default toward the discharge of the latter's debit balance and to accept this arrangement in the event of falling into default itself. A member state which resigns from the Clearing Union without making approved arrangements for the discharge of any debit balance shall also be treated as in default.

(9) A member state whose credit balance has exceeded a *half* of its quota on the average of at least a year shall discuss with the governing board (but shall retain the ultimate decision in its own hands) what measures would be appropriate to restore the equilibrium of its international balances, including—

(*a*) Measures for the expansion of domestic credit and domestic demand.

(*b*) The appreciation of its local currency in terms of bancor, or, alternatively, the encouragement of an increase in money rates of earnings.

(*c*) The reduction of tariffs and other discouragements against imports.

(*d*) International development loans.

(10) A member state shall be entitled to obtain a credit balance in terms of bancor by paying in gold to the Clearing Union for the credit of its clearing account. But no one is entitled to demand gold from the Union against a balance of bancor, since such balance is available only for transfer to another clearing account. The governing board of the Union shall, however, have the discretion to distribute any gold in the possession of the Union between the members possessing credit balances in excess of a specified proportion of their quotas, proportionately to such balances, in reduction of their amount in excess of that proportion.

(11) The monetary reserves of a member state, viz., the central bank or other bank or treasury deposits in excess of a working balance, shall

not be held in another country except with the approval of the monetary authorities of that country.

(12) The governing board shall be appointed by the governments of the member states, those with the larger quotas being entitled to appoint a member individually, and those with smaller quotas appointing in convenient political or geographical groups, so that the members would not exceed (say) twelve or fifteen in number. Each representative on the governing board shall have a vote in proportion to the quotas of the state (or states) appointing him, except that on a proposal to increase a particular quota, a representative's voting power shall be measured by the quotas of the member states appointing him, increased by their credit balance or decreased by their debit balance, averaged in each case over the past two years. Each member state, which is not individually represented on the governing board, shall be entitled to appoint a permanent delegate to the Union to maintain contact with the board and to act as *liaison* for daily business and for the exchange of information with the executive of the Union. Such delegate shall be entitled to be present at the governing board when any matter is under consideration which specially concerns the state he represents, and to take part in the discussion.

(13) The governing board shall be entitled to reduce the quotas of members, all in the same specified proportion, if it seems necessary to correct in this manner an excess of world purchasing power. In that event, the provisions of 6 (8) shall be held to apply to the quotas as so reduced, provided that no member shall be required to reduce his actual overdraft at the date of the change, or be entitled by reason of this reduction to alter the value of his currency under 6 (8) (*a*), except after the expiry of two years. If the governing board subsequently desires to correct a potential deficiency of world purchasing power, it shall be entitled to restore the general level of quotas toward the original level.

(14) The governing board shall be entitled to ask and receive from each member state any relevant statistical or other information, including a full disclosure of gold, external credit and debit balances, and other external assets and liabilities, both public and private. So far as circumstances permit, it will be desirable that the member states shall consult with the governing board on important matters of policy likely to affect substantially their bancor balances or their financial relations with other members.

(15) Executive offices of the Union shall be situated in London and New York, with the governing board meeting alternately in London and Washington.

(16). Members shall be entitled to withdraw from the Union on a year's notice, subject to their making satisfactory arrangements to discharge any debit balance. They would not, of course, be able to employ any credit balance except by making transfers from it, either before or after their withdrawal, to the clearing accounts of other central banks. Similarly, it should be within the power of the governing board to require the withdrawal of a member, subject to the same notice, if the latter is in breach of agreements relating to the Clearing Union.

(17) The central banks of nonmember states would be allowed to keep credit clearing accounts with the Union; and, indeed, it would be advisable for them to do so for the conduct of their trade with member states. But they would have no right to overdrafts and no say in the management.

(18) The governing board shall make an annual Report and shall convene an annual Assembly at which every member state shall be entitled to be represented individually and to move proposals. The principles and governing rules of the Union shall be the subject of reconsideration after five years' experience, if a majority of the Assembly desire it.

III. WHAT LIABILITIES OUGHT THE PLAN TO PLACE ON CREDITOR COUNTRIES?

7. It is not contemplated that either the debit or the credit balance of an individual country ought to exceed a certain maximum—let us say, its *quota*. In the case of debit balances this maximum has been made a rigid one, and, indeed, countermeasures are called for long before the maximum is reached. In the case of credit balances no rigid maximum has been proposed. For the appropriate provision might be to require the eventual cancellation or compulsory investment of persistent bancor credit balances accumulating in excess of a member's quota; and, however desirable this may be in principle, it might be felt to impose on creditor countries a heavier burden than they can be asked to accept before having had experience of the benefit to them of the working of the plan as a whole. If, on the other hand, the limitation were to take the form of the creditor country not being required to accept bancor in excess of a prescribed figure, this might impair the general acceptability of bancor, while at the same time conferring no real benefit on the creditor country itself. For, if it chose to avail itself of the limitation, it must either restrict its exports or be driven back on some form of bilateral payments agreements outside the Clearing Union, thus substituting a less acceptable asset for bancor bal-

ances which are based on the collective credit of all the member states and are available for payments to any of them, or attempt the probably temporary expedient of refusing to trade except on a gold basis.

8. The absence of a rigid maximum to credit balances does not impose on any member state, as might be supposed at first sight, an unlimited liability outside its own control. The liability of an individual member is determined, not by the quotas of the other members, but by its own policy in controlling its favorable balance of payments. The existence of the Clearing Union does not deprive a member state of any of the facilities which it now possesses for receiving payment for its exports. In the absence of the Clearing Union a creditor country can employ the proceeds of its exports to buy goods or to buy investments, or to make temporary advances and to hold temporary overseas balances, or to buy gold in the market. All these facilities will remain at its disposal. The difference is that in the absence of the Clearing Union, more or less automatic factors come into play to restrict the volume of its exports after the above means of receiving payment for them have been exhausted. Certain countries become unable to buy and, in addition to this, there is an automatic tendency toward a general slump in international trade and, as a result, a reduction in the exports of the creditor country. Thus, the effect of the Clearing Union is to give the creditor country a choice between voluntarily curtailing its exports to the same extent that they would have been involuntarily curtailed in the absence of the Clearing Union, or, alternatively, of allowing its exports to continue and accumulating the excess receipts in the form of bancor balances for the time being. Unless the removal of a factor causing the involuntary reduction of exports is reckoned a disadvantage, a creditor country incurs no burden but is, on the contrary, relieved, by being offered the additional option of receiving payment for its exports through the accumulation of a bancor balance.

9. If, therefore, a member state asks what governs the maximum liability which it incurs by entering the system, the answer is that this lies entirely within its own control. No more is asked of it than that it should hold in bancor such surplus of its favorable balance of payments as it does not itself choose to employ in any other way, and only for so long as it does not so choose.

IV. SOME ADVANTAGES OF THE PLAN

10. The plan aims at the substitution of an expansionist, in place of a contractionist, pressure on world trade.

11. It effects this by allowing to each member state overdraft facilities of a defined amount. Thus each country is allowed a certain margin of resources and a certain interval of time within which to effect a balance in its economic relations with the rest of the world. These facilities are made possible by the constitution of the system itself and do not involve particular indebtedness between one member state and another. A country is in credit or debit with the Clearing Union as a whole. This means that the overdraft facilities, while a relief to some, are not a real burden to others. For the accumulation of a credit balance with the Clearing Union would resemble the importation of gold in signifying that the country holding it is abstaining voluntarily from the immediate use of purchasing power. But it would not involve, as would the importation of gold, the withdrawal of this purchasing power from circulation or the exercise of a deflationary and contractionist pressure on the whole world, including in the end the creditor country itself. Under the proposed plan, therefore, no country suffers injury (but on the contrary) by the fact that the command over resources, which it does not itself choose to employ for the time being, is not withdrawn from use. The accumulation of bancor credit does not curtail in the least its capacity or inducement either to produce or to consume.

12. In short, the analogy with a national banking system is complete. No depositor in a local bank suffers because the balances, which he leaves idle, are employed to finance the business of someone else. Just as the development of national banking systems served to offset a deflationary pressure which would have prevented otherwise the development of modern industry, so by extending the same principle into the international field we may hope to offset the contractionist pressure which might otherwise overwhelm in social disorder and disappointment the good hopes of our modern world. The substitution of a credit mechanism in place of hoarding would have repeated in the international field the same miracle, already performed in the domestic field, of turning a stone into bread.

13. There might be other ways of effecting the same objects temporarily or in part. For example, the United States might redistribute her gold. Or there might be a number of bilateral arrangements having the effect of providing international overdrafts, as, for example, an agreement by the Federal Reserve Board to accumulate, if necessary, a large sterling balance at the Bank of England, accompanied by a great number of similar bilateral arrangements, amounting to some hundreds altogether, between these and all the other banks in the world. The objection to par-

ticular arrangements of this kind, in addition to their greater complexity, is that they are likely to be influenced by extraneous, political reasons; that they put individual countries in a position of particular obligation toward others; and that the distribution of the assistance between different countries may not correspond to need and to the real requirements, which are extremely difficult to foresee.

14. It should be much easier, and surely more satisfactory for all of us, to enter into a general and collective responsibility, applying to all countries alike, that a country finding itself in a creditor position *against the rest of the world as a whole* should enter into an arrangement not to allow this credit balance to exercise a contractionist pressure against world economy and, by repercussion, against the economy of the creditor country itself. This would give everyone the great assistance of multilateral clearing, whereby (for example) Great Britain could offset favorable balances arising out of her exports to Europe against unfavorable balances due to the United States or South America or elsewhere. How, indeed, can any country hope to start up trade with Europe during the relief and reconstruction period on any other terms?

15. The facilities offered will be of particular importance in the transitional period after the war, as soon as the initial shortages of supply have been overcome. Many countries will find a difficulty in paying for their imports, and will need time and resources before they can establish a readjustment. The efforts of each of these debtor countries to preserve its own equilibrium, by forcing its exports and by cutting off all imports which are not strictly necessary, will aggravate the problems of all the others. On the other hand, if each feels free from undue pressure, the volume of international exchange will be increased and everyone will find it easier to re-establish equilibrium without injury to the standard of life anywhere. The creditor countries will benefit, hardly less than the debtors, by being given an interval of *time* in which to adjust their economies, during which they can safely move at their own pace without the result of exercising deflationary pressure on the rest of the world, and, by repercussion, on themselves.

16. It must, however, be emphasized that the provision by which the members of the Clearing Union start with substantial overdraft facilities in hand will be mainly useful, just as the possession of any kind of reserve is useful, to allow time and method for necessary adjustments and a comfortable safeguard behind which the unforeseen and the unexpected can be faced with equanimity. Obviously, it does not by itself provide any

long-term solution against a continuing disequilibrium, for in due course the more improvident and the more impecunious, left to themselves, would have run through their resources. But, if the purpose of the overdraft facilities is mainly to give time for adjustments, we have to make sure, so far as possible, that they *will* be made. We must have, therefore, some rules and some machinery to secure that equilibrium is restored. A tentative attempt to provide for this has been made above. Perhaps it might be strengthened and improved.

17. The provisions suggested differ in one important respect from the prewar system because they aim at putting some part of the responsibility for adjustment on the creditor country as well as on the debtor. This is an attempt to recover one of the advantages which were enjoyed in the nineteenth century, when a flow of gold due to a favorable balance in favor of London and Paris, which were then the main creditor centers, immediately produced an expansionist pressure and increased foreign lending in those markets, but which has been lost since New York succeeded to the position of main creditor, as a result of gold movements failing in their effect, of the breakdown of international borrowing, and of the frequent flight of loose funds from one depository to another. The object is that the creditor should not be allowed to remain entirely passive. For if he is, an intolerably heavy task may be laid on the debtor country, which is already for that very reason in the weaker position.

18. If, indeed, a country lacks the productive capacity to maintain its standard of life, then a reduction in this standard is not avoidable. If its wage and price levels in terms of money are out of line with those elsewhere, a change in the rate of its foreign exchange is inevitable. But if, possessing the productive capacity, it lacks markets because of restrictive policies throughout the world, then the remedy lies in expanding its opportunities for export by removal of the restrictive pressure. We are too ready today to assume the inevitability of unbalanced trade positions, thus making the opposite error to those who assumed the tendency of exports and imports to equality. It used to be supposed, without sufficient reason, that effective demand is always properly adjusted throughout the world; we now tend to assume, equally without sufficient reason, that it never can be. On the contrary, there is great force in the contention that, if active employment and ample purchasing power can be sustained in the main centers of the world trade, the problem of surpluses and unwanted exports will largely disappear, even though, under the most prosperous conditions, there may remain some disturbances of trade and unforeseen situations requiring special remedies.

V. THE DAILY MANAGEMENT OF THE EXCHANGES
UNDER THE PLAN

19. The Clearing Union restores unfettered multilateral clearing between its members. Compare this with the difficulties and complications of a large number of bilateral agreements. Compare, above all, the provisions by which a country, taking improper advantage of a payments agreement (for the system is, in fact, a *generalized payments agreement*), as Germany did before the war, is dealt with not by a single country (which may not be strong enough to act effectively in isolation or cannot afford to incur the diplomatic odium of isolated action), but by the system as a whole. If the argument is used that the Clearing Union may have difficulty in disciplining a misbehaving country and in avoiding consequential loss, with what much greater force can we urge this objection against a multiplicity of separate bilateral payments agreements.

20. Thus not only should we obtain the advantages, without the disadvantages, of an international gold currency, but we might enjoy these advantages more widely than was ever possible in practice with the old system under which at any given time only a minority of countries were actually working with free exchanges. In conditions of multilateral clearing, exchange dealings would be carried on as freely as in the best days of the gold standard, without its being necessary to ask anyone to accept special or onerous conditions.

21. The principles governing transactions are: first, that the Clearing Union is set up, not for the transaction of daily business between individual traders or banks, but for the clearing and settlement of the ultimate outstanding balances between central banks (and certain other supranational institutions), such as would have been settled under the old gold standard by the shipment or the earmarking of gold, and should not trespass unnecessarily beyond this field; and, second, that its purpose is to increase *freedom* in international commerce and not to multiply interferences or compulsions.

22. Many central banks have found great advantage in centralizing with themselves or with an exchange control the supply and demand of all foreign exchange, thus dispensing with an outside exchange market, though continuing to accommodate individuals through the existing banks and not directly. The further extension of such arrangements would be consonant with the general purposes of the Clearing Union, inasmuch as they would promote order and discipline in international exchange transactions in detail as well as in general. The same is true of the control of

capital movements, further described below, which many states are likely to wish to impose on their own nationals. But the structure of the proposed Clearing Union does not *require* such measures of centralization or of control on the part of a member state. It is, for example, consistent alike with the type of exchange control now established in the United Kingdom or with the system now operating in the United States. The Union does not prevent private holdings of foreign currency or private dealings in exchange or international capital movements, if these have been approved or allowed by the member states concerned. Central banks can deal direct with one another as heretofore. No transaction in bancor will take place except when a member state or its central bank is exercising the right to pay in it. In no case is there any direct control of capital movements by the Union, even in the case of 6 (8) (*b*) (ii) above, but only by the member states themselves through their own institutions. Thus the fabric of international banking organization, built up by long experience to satisfy practical needs, would be left as undisturbed as possible.

23. It is not necessary to interfere with the discretion of countries which desire to maintain a special intimacy within a particular group of countries associated by geographical or political ties, such as the existing sterling area, or groups, like the Latin Union of former days, which may come into existence covering, for example, the countries of North America or those of South America, or the groups now under active discussion, including Poland and Czechoslovakia or certain of the Balkan States. There is no reason why such countries should not be allowed a double position, both as members of the Clearing Union in their own right with their proper quota, and also as making use of another financial center along traditional lines, as, for example, Australia and India with London, or certain American countries with New York. In this case, their accounts with the Clearing Union would be in exactly the same position as the independent gold reserves which they now maintain, and they would have no occasion to modify in any way their present practices in the conduct of daily business.

24. There might be other cases, however, in which a dependency or a member of a federal union would merge its currency identity in that of a mother country, with a quota appropriately adjusted to the merged currency area as a whole, and *not* enjoy a separate individual membership of the Clearing Union, as, for example, the states of a federal union, the French colonies, or the British Crown Colonies.

25. At the same time countries, which do not belong to a special geographical or political group, would be expected to keep their reserve bal-

ances with the Clearing Union and not with one another. It has, therefore, been laid down that balances may not be held in another country except with the approval of the monetary authorities of that country; and, in order that sterling and dollars might not appear to compete with bancor for the purpose of reserve balances, the United Kingdom and the United States might agree together that they would not accept the reserve balances of other countries in excess of normal working balances except in the case of banks definitely belonging to a Sterling Area or Dollar Area group.

VI. THE POSITION OF GOLD UNDER THE PLAN

26. Gold still possesses great psychological value which is not being diminished by current events; and the desire to possess a gold reserve against unforeseen contingencies is likely to remain. Gold also has the merit of providing in point of form (whatever the underlying realities may be) an uncontroversial standard of value for international purposes, for which it would not yet be easy to find a serviceable substitute. Moreover, by supplying an automatic means for settling some part of the favorable balances of the creditor countries, the current gold production of the world and the remnant of gold reserves held outside the United States may still have a useful part to play. Nor is it reasonable to ask the United States to demonetize the stock of gold which is the basis of its impregnable liquidity. What, in the long run, the world may decide to do with gold is another matter. The purpose of the Clearing Union is to supplant gold as a governing factor, but not to dispense with it.

27. The international bank-money which we have designated *bancor* is defined in terms of a weight of gold. Since the national currencies of the member states are given a defined exchange value in terms of bancor, it follows that they would each have a defined gold content which would be their official buying price for gold, above which they must not pay. The fact that a member state is entitled to obtain a credit in terms of bancor by paying actual gold to the credit of its clearing account, secures a steady and ascertained purchaser for the output of the gold-producing countries, and for countries holding a large reserve of gold. Thus the position of producers and holders of gold is not affected adversely, and is, indeed, improved.

28. Central banks would be entitled to retain their separate gold reserves and ship gold to one another, provided they did not pay a price

above parity; they could coin gold and put it into circulation, and, generally speaking, do what they liked with it.

29. One limitation only would be, for obvious reasons, essential. No member state would be entitled to demand gold from the Clearing Union against its balance of bancor; for bancor is available only for transfer to another clearing account. Thus between gold and bancor itself there would be a one-way convertibility, such as ruled frequently before the war with national currencies which were on what was called a "gold exchange standard." This need not mean that the Clearing Union would only receive gold and never pay it out. It has been provided above that, if the Clearing Union finds itself in possession of a stock of gold, the governing board shall have discretion to distribute the surplus between those possessing credit balances in bancor, proportionately to such balances in reduction of their amount.

30. The question has been raised whether these arrangements are compatible with the retention by individual member states of a full standard with two-way convertibility, so that, for example, any foreign central bank acquiring dollars could use them to obtain gold for export. It is not evident that a good purpose would be served by this. But it need not be prohibited, and if any member state should prefer to maintain full convertibility for internal purposes it could protect itself from any abuse of the system or inconvenient consequences by providing that gold could only be exported under license.

31. The value of bancor in terms of gold is fixed but not unalterably. The power to vary its value might have to be exercised if the stocks of gold tendered to the Union were to be excessive. No object would be served by attempting further to peer into the future or to prophesy the ultimate outcome.

VII. THE CONTROL OF CAPITAL MOVEMENTS

32. There is no country which can, in future, safely allow the flight of funds for political reasons or to evade domestic taxation or in anticipation of the owner turning refugee. Equally, there is no country that can safely receive fugitive funds, which constitute an unwanted import of capital, yet cannot safely be used for fixed investment.

33. For these reasons it is widely held that control of capital movements, both inward and outward, should be a permanent feature of the postwar system. It is an objection to this that control, if it is to be effective,

probably requires the machinery of exchange control for *all* transactions, even though a general permission is given to all remittances in respect of current trade. Thus those countries which have for the time being no reason to fear, and may indeed welcome, outward capital movements, may be reluctant to impose this machinery, even though a general permission for capital, as well as current, transactions reduces it to being no more than a machinery of record. On the other hand, such control will be more difficult to work by unilateral action on the part of those countries which cannot afford to dispense with it, especially in the absence of a postal censorship, if movements of capital cannot be controlled *at both ends*. It would, therefore, be of great advantage if the United States, as well as other members of the Clearing Union, would adopt machinery similar to that which the British Exchange Control has now gone a long way toward perfecting. Nevertheless, the universal establishment of a control of capital movements cannot be regarded as essential to the operation of the Clearing Union; and the method and degree of such control should therefore be left to the decision of each member state. Some less drastic way might be found by which countries, not themselves controlling outward capital movements, can deter inward movements not approved by the countries from which they originate.

34. The position of abnormal balances in overseas ownership held in various countries at the end of the war presents a problem of considerable importance and special difficulty. A country in which a large volume of such balances is held could not, unless it is in a creditor position, afford the risk of having to redeem them in bancor on a substantial scale, if this would have the effect of depleting its bancor resources at the outset. At the same time, it is very desirable that the countries owning these balances should be able to regard them as liquid, at any rate over and above the amounts which they can afford to lock up under an agreed program of funding or long-term expenditure. Perhaps there should be some special overriding provision for dealing with the transitional period only by which, through the aid of the Clearing Union, such balances would remain liquid and convertible into bancor by the creditor country while there would be no corresponding strain on the bancor resources of the debtor country, or, at any rate, the resulting strain would be spread over a period.

35. The advocacy of a control of capital movements must not be taken to mean that the era of international investment should be brought to an end. On the contrary, the system contemplated should greatly facilitate the restoration of international loans and credits for legitimate purposes. The object, and it is a vital object, is to have a means—

(*a*) of distinguishing long-term loans by creditor countries, which help to maintain equilibrium and develop the world's resources, from movements of funds out of debtor countries which lack the means to finance them; and

(*b*) of controlling short-term speculative movements or flights of currency whether out of debtor countries or from one creditor country to another.

36. It should be emphasized that the purpose of the overdrafts of bancor permitted by the Clearing Union is, not to facilitate long-term, or even medium-term, credits to be made by debtor countries which cannot afford them, but to allow time and a breathing space for adjustments and for averaging one period with another to all member states alike, whether in the long run they are well-placed to develop a forward international loan policy or whether their prospects of profitable new development in excess of their own resources justifies them in long-term borrowing. The machinery and organization of international medium-term and long-term lending is another aspect of postwar economic policy, not less important than the purposes which the Clearing Union seeks to serve, but requiring another, complementary institution.

VIII. RELATION OF THE CLEARING UNION TO COMMERCIAL POLICY

37. The special protective expedients which were developed between the two wars were sometimes due to political, social, or industrial reasons. But frequently they were nothing more than forced and undesired dodges to protect an unbalanced position of a country's overseas payments. The new system, by helping to provide a register of the size and whereabouts of the aggregate debtor and creditor positions respectively, and an indication whether it is reasonable for a particular country to adopt special expedients as a temporary measure to assist in regaining equilibrium in its balance of payments, would make it possible to establish a general rule *not* to adopt them, subject to the indicated exceptions.

38. The existence of the Clearing Union would make it possible for member states contracting commercial agreements to use their respective debit and credit positions with the Clearing Union as a test, though this test by itself would not be complete. Thus, the contracting parties, while agreeing to clauses in a commercial agreement forbidding, in general, the use of certain measures or expedients in their mutual trade relations, might make this agreement subject to special relaxations if the state of their respective clearing accounts satisfied an agreed criterion. For example, an

agreement might provide that, in the event of one of the contracting states having a debit balance with the Clearing Union exceeding a specified proportion of its quota on the average of a period it should be free to resort to import regulation or to barter trade agreements or to higher import duties of a type which was restricted under the agreement in normal circumstances. Protected by the possibility of such temporary indulgences, the members of the Clearing Union should feel much more confidence in moving toward the withdrawal of other and more dislocating forms of protection and discrimination and in accepting the prohibition of the worst of them from the outset. In any case, it should be laid down that members of the Union would not allow or suffer among themselves any restrictions on the disposal of receipts arising out of current trade or "invisible" income.

IX. THE USE OF THE CLEARING UNION FOR OTHER INTERNATIONAL PURPOSES

39. The Clearing Union might become the instrument and the support of international policies in addition to those which it is its primary purpose to promote. This deserves the greatest possible emphasis. The Union might become the pivot of the future economic government of the world. Without it, other more desirable developments will find themselves impeded and unsupported. With it, they will fall into their place as parts of an ordered scheme. No one of the following suggestions is a necessary part of the plan. But they are illustrations of the additional purposes of high importance and value which the Union, once established, might be able to serve:

(1) The Union might set up a clearing account in favor of international bodies charged with postwar relief, rehabilitation, and reconstruction. But it could go much further than this. For it might supplement contributions received from other sources by granting preliminary overdraft facilities in favor of these bodies, the overdraft being discharged over a period of years out of the reserve fund of the Union, or, if necessary, out of a levy on surplus credit balances. So far as this method is adopted it would be possible to avoid asking any country to assume a burdensome commitment for relief and reconstruction, since the resources would be provided in the first instance by those countries having credit clearing accounts for which they have no immediate use and are voluntarily leaving idle, and in the long run by those countries which have a chronic international surplus for which they have no beneficial employment.

(2) The Union might set up an account in favor of any supranational

policing body which may be charged with the duty of preserving the peace and maintaining international order. If any country were to infringe its properly authorized orders, the policing body might be entitled to request the governors of the Clearing Union to hold the clearing account of the delinquent country to its order and permit no further transactions on the account except by its authority. This would provide an excellent machinery for enforcing a financial blockade.

(3) The Union might set up an account in favor of international bodies charged with the management of a Commodity Control, and might finance stocks of commodities held by such bodies, allowing them overdraft facilities on their accounts up to an agreed maximum. By this means the financial problem of buffer stocks and "ever-normal granaries" could be effectively attacked.

(4) The Union might be linked up with a Board for International Investment. It might act on behalf of such a Board and collect for them the annual service of their loans by automatically debiting the clearing account of the country concerned. The statistics of the clearing accounts of the member states would give a reliable indication as to which countries were in a position to finance the Investment Board, with the advantage of shifting the whole system of clearing credits and debits nearer to equilibrium.

(5) There are various methods by which the Clearing Union could use its influence and its power to maintain stability of prices and to control the trade cycle. If an International Economic Board is established, this Board and the Clearing Union might be expected to work in close collaboration to their mutual advantage. If an International Investment or Development Corporation is also set up together with a scheme of Commodity Controls for the control of stocks of the staple primary products, we might come to possess in these three institutions a powerful means of combating the evils of the trade cycle, by exercising contractionist or expansionist influence on the system as a whole or on particular sections. This is a large and important question which cannot be discussed adequately in this paper; and need not be examined at length in this place because it does not raise any important issues affecting the fundamental constitution of the proposed Union. It is mentioned here to complete the picture of the wider purposes which the foundation of the Clearing Union might be made to serve.

40. The facility of applying the Clearing Union plan to these several purposes arises out of a fundamental characteristic which is worth pointing out, since it distinguishes the plan from those proposals which try to develop the same basic principle along bilateral lines and is one of the grounds on

which the plan can claim superior merit. This might be described as its "anonymous" or "impersonal" quality. No particular member states have to engage their own resources as such to the support of other particular states or of any of the international projects or policies adopted. They have only to agree in general that, if they find themselves with surplus resources which for the time being they do not themselves wish to employ, these resources may go into the general pool and be put to work on approved purposes. This costs the surplus country nothing because it is not asked to part permanently, or even for any specified period, with such resources, which it remains free to expend and employ for its own purposes whenever it chooses; in which case the burden of finance is passed on to the next recipient, again for only so long as the recipient has no use for the money. As pointed out above, this merely amounts to extending to the international sphere the methods of any domestic banking system, which are in the same sense "impersonal" inasmuch as there is no call on the particular depositor either to support as such the purposes for which his banker makes advances or to forgo permanently the use of his deposit. There is no countervailing objection except that which applies equally to the technique of domestic banking, namely that it is capable of the abuse of creating excessive purchasing power and hence an inflation of prices. In our efforts to avoid the opposite evil, we must not lose sight of this risk, to which there is an allusion in 39 (5) above. But it is no more reason for refusing the advantages of international banking than the similar risk in the domestic field is a reason to return to the practices of the seventeenth-century goldsmiths (which are what we are still following in the international field) and to forgo the vast expansion of production which banking principles have made possible. Where financial contributions are required for some purpose of general advantage, it is a great facility not to have to ask for specific contributions from any named country, but to depend rather on the anonymous and impersonal aid of the system as a whole. We have here a genuine organ of truly international government.

X. THE TRANSITIONAL ARRANGEMENTS

41. It would be of great advantage to agree on the general principles of the Clearing Union before the end of the war, with a view to bringing it into operation at an early date after the termination of hostilities. Major plans will be more easily brought to birth in the first energy of victory and while the active spirit of united action still persists, than in the days of ex-

haustion and reaction from so much effort which may well follow a little later. Such a proposal presents, however, something of a dilemma. On the one hand, many countries will be in particular need of reserves of overseas resources in the period immediately after the war. On the other hand, goods will be in short supply and the prevention of inflationary international conditions of much more importance for the time being than the opposite. The expansionist tendency of the plan, which is a leading recommendation of it as soon as peacetime output is restored and the productive capacity of the world is in running order, might be a danger in the early days of a sellers' market and an excess of demand over supply.

42. A reconciliation of these divergent purposes is not easily found until we know more than is known at present about the means to be adopted to finance postwar relief and reconstruction. If the intention is to provide resources on liberal and comprehensive lines outside the resources made available by the Clearing Union and additional to them, it might be better for such specific aid to take the place of the proposed overdrafts during the "relief" period of (say) two years. In this case credit clearing balances would be limited to the amount of gold delivered to the Union, and the overdraft facilities created by the Union in favor of the Relief Council, the International Investment Board, or the Commodity Controls. Nevertheless, the immediate establishment of the Clearing Union would not be incompatible with provisional arrangements, which could take alternative forms according to the character of the other "relief" arrangements, qualifying and limiting the overdraft quotas. Overdraft quotas might be allowed on a reduced scale during the transitional period. Or it might be proper to provide that countries in receipt of relief or Lend-Lease assistance should not have access at the same time to overdraft facilities, and that the latter should only become available when the former had come to an end. If, on the other hand, relief from outside sources looks like being inadequate from the outset, the overdraft quotas may be even more necessary at the outset than later on.

43. We must not be overcautious. A rapid economic restoration may lighten the tasks of the diplomatists and the politicians in the resettlement of the world and the restoration of social order. For Great Britain and other countries outside the "relief" areas the possibility of exports sufficient to sustain their standard of life is bound up with good and expanding markets. We cannot afford to wait too long for this, and we must not allow excessive caution to condemn us to perdition. Unless the Union is a going concern, the problem of proper "timing" will be nearly insoluble. It is sufficient at

this stage to point out that the problem of timing must not be overlooked, but that the Union is capable of being used so as to aid rather than impede its solution.

XI. CONCLUSION

44. It has been suggested that so ambitious a proposal is open to criticism on the ground that it requires from the members of the Union a greater surrender of their sovereign rights than they will readily concede. But no greater surrender is required than in a commercial treaty. The obligations will be entered into voluntarily and can be terminated on certain conditions by giving notice.

45. A greater readiness to accept supranational arrangements must be required in the postwar world. If the arrangements proposed can be described as a measure of financial disarmament, there is nothing here which we need be reluctant to accept ourselves or to ask of others. It is an advantage, and not a disadvantage, of the scheme that it invites the member states to abandon that license to promote indiscipline, disorder and bad-neighborliness which, to the general disadvantage, they have been free to exercise hitherto.

46. The plan makes a beginning at the future economic ordering of the world between nations and "the winning of the peace." It might help to create the conditions and the atmosphere in which much else would be made easier.

3

The Stamp Plan–1962 Version

SIR MAXWELL STAMP

THE ORIGINAL STAMP PLAN

Two years ago when I was writing the two articles for the *Manchester Guardian* which contained the ideas which ultimately became known as "the Stamp plan," I felt that because of its unorthodox nature the proposal had at best one chance in ten of being adopted, but it was worth putting forward because, if it were adopted, it could ultimately give us greater control over our economic destinies, enabling us to bring into use productive capacity which would otherwise stand idle and providing additional resources for the development of the poorer parts of the world. Additional probable advantages seemed to be that it would remove any need for raising the price of gold, with all the upsetting consequences that such a rise would entail, and that the need for adjustments in the par values of currencies would be lessened.

Since that time I have watched the ripples caused by that idea, and those from similar suggestions, lapping apparently ineffectively against the dykes of orthodox monetary and banking opinion; the idea has been rejected as wild or unnecessary, as inflationary and unacceptable, but somehow has refused to die. Indeed, I have been encouraged by the way the idea has been accepted, particularly by the economic profession, as a useful contribution which may, in due course, lead to reforms.

Much of the argument has turned on whether there is, or is likely to be, a shortage of international liquidity. I feel that this is a pity, for it is only half the story. In this article I propose to try to emphasize the other half, to clarify the arguments, and to try to set out a modified version of the plan which meets at least some of the objections which have been raised.

My original plan was as follows:

Reprinted from *Moorgate and Wall Street*, Autumn, 1962, a review issued by Philip Hill, Higginson, Erlangers Limited, and Harriman Ripley and Company through the courtesy of the author and publishers.

The Board of Governors of the Fund would authorize the issue of Fund certificates to a value of, say, $3,000 million over the next twelve months. The value of these certificates would be expressed in terms of gold, but they would not be automatically convertible into gold. Each member would agree to accept them when tendered by the Fund or a central bank and to provide its own national currency in exchange. Countries such as the United States which at present undertake to sell gold at a fixed price when their currency is tendered by a central bank could modify that obligation: henceforward, they would have the option of selling gold or tendering any Fund certificates in their possession. The holder of a Fund certificate would be able to exchange it at known rates into the currency of any country which is a member of the Fund.

The Fund would then give the certificates to an aid coordinating agency which would allocate them to the underdeveloped countries under an agreed program. The country receiving the certificates would use them to buy, say, machinery in Germany, the U.S., and the United Kingdom, by tendering them to the central bank and acquiring DM, dollars, or sterling. If Germany were in over-all surplus she would add the certificates to her reserves; if the U.S. were in over-all deficit she could, if she desired, use them to meet that deficit instead of losing gold. The certificates would end up with the countries which are in over-all surplus—which, therefore, would have automatically lent part of that surplus to the rest of the world.

Now it will be observed that this plan attempts to kill two birds with one stone. If one's main object is to get an idea accepted this is, of course, a mistake. "Killing two birds" at once ought to be an advantage, but in practice it smacks of black magic or gimmickry, and anyone who thinks that either of the birds does not need killing will oppose it, without considering the other advantages.

The main opposition to the adoption of the plan has come from two completely opposed groups: those who think that there is no shortage of international liquidity, and those who think that there is a shortage of international liquidity but that there are other and better ways of curing it. The latter have had some success: first of all, Fund quotas were increased; then the suggestions made at Vienna for enabling the Fund to increase its resources by borrowing, if necessary, have now been adopted; and various swap arrangements and the mechanisms for increasing the reserves which individual countries can borrow at need have been entered into. Then, at Washington this year Mr. Maudling made yet another proposal, by which if one country supports another country whose currency is under pressure by acquiring its currency in the market it would pay the resulting balances into the Fund and acquire a gold value guaranteed credit in the Fund books which it could use when it, in turn, needed reserves.

But somehow despite all these measures and proposals, each of which was supposed to solve the problem, the nagging doubt remains that something more needs to be done. And to turn to the other "bird" for a moment, the International Development Association is running out of funds and it is clear that it will be difficult adequately to replenish them. In other words, despite its great unused capacity, the world cannot find the mechanism to produce the goods which the poorer nations so urgently need.

I believe that the possible inadequacy of international liquidity now, or in future, though important, is only a relatively minor reason why improvements in the monetary system are necessary. I think one can admit that there may be no immediate shortage of international liquidity and yet believe that an annual increase in world reserves (beyond the supplies of new gold) is desirable, even essential, if the optimum performance from the world's economic system is to be obtained.

Part of the trouble in arriving at an agreed diagnosis is that there is no figure for the reserves of the world or of an individual country which is indisputably "right," any more than there is a figure for a national money supply which is absolutely "right." In the case of the money supply there is a range in which supply will be adapted to needs by changes in the velocity of circulation: in the case of reserves inadequacy of "owned reserves," i.e., reserves which are the absolute property of the countries owning them, will be partly compensated by more frequent use of "borrowed reserves." Frequent use of the IMF, in fact, is a sign that the level of "owned reserves" is on the low side. But countries do not like going to the Fund to borrow, and I think it would be true to say that most developed countries would like to have higher reserves; i.e., if they could sell the extra exports necessary to pay for an increase in reserves without turning the terms of trade against them by selling at uneconomically low prices they would welcome the opportunity. But if the price of increasing reserves is high—if, for instance, it means cutting down home demand and stultifying industrial growth for years in order to accumulate a large surplus on balance-of-payments account—then they will prefer to get along with what they have got. I suspect that extra orders for a billion dollars' worth of steel, mechanical products, food, and other articles in easy supply in the United States, to be paid for in gold or currencies which could be counted as reserves, would be highly welcome to the American authorities; I know they would make all the difference to Britain's prospects.

Therefore, even if one admits that total reserves—i.e., "owned" reserves, plus lines of credit, are now reasonably adequate, it can still be true that many countries would be willing to pay a reasonable price to see their "owned" reserves increase, and thus to diminish the chance of their having to go through the painful process of borrowing to keep them out of trouble. To put the matter in another way, if Russia were to put a considerable quantity of gold on the world market there is no reason to believe that countries would not be glad to absorb it. Most industrial countries would be glad to export the goods and services necessary to pay for the additional gold. The developing countries are quite another matter: they cannot afford the luxury of keeping more resources, which could be used for development, in the comparatively "idle" form of gold or dollar balances. But, on balance, if more gold were available the world would be glad to absorb it and to pay the price for so doing. Therefore, one can conclude that even if we are in the range in which the supply of "owned" reserves is adequate, we are certainly at the low end of that range.

In my view, there is a very good case for increasing the amount of "owned" reserves until we are nearer the top end of that range—until the majority of countries begin to feel that their reserves are, if anything, on the high side and are unwilling to increase them further. The justification for this somewhat unorthodox view is that, even if a country's reserves are considered just adequate it will still try and run a surplus in its balance of payments "to be on the safe side." Just as an individual will try to live within his income—with a margin for safety—so will a country; but whereas all individuals in principle can achieve this object, all countries in the world cannot, because one country's surplus is another country's deficit. It is like a game of musical chairs, in which a deficit is passed round from player to player—each taking the necessary measures to "put his house in order" and putting the other person's house out of order in the process; and each, even if he is safe for the moment (i.e., is in bare balance), worrying about the future. There is an asymmetry in the attitude of most countries to their balances of payments: each wants to be in surplus; this explains the odd phenomenon that even countries which are in balance-of-payments surplus continue to encourage exports artificially.

The consequences of this asymmetry are not necessarily always bad. If the world is, generally speaking, in a state of overfull employment, or inflation, this worry about balance-of-payments deficit can exercise a salutary braking effect. But if, as Dr. Jacobsson suggests, we are now entering a period in which deflation is a more serious danger than inflation, and in which there is a real danger of the under-utilization of our productive resources, then the effect could be to aggravate these tendencies to a very serious extent.

Now I think that even the most "orthodox" will agree that if the economic machine can be induced to produce more goods and services for people to enjoy, this is a good thing provided that the good is not more than balanced by countervailing disadvantages, such as inflation. Where the under-utilization of resources is severe the onus is clearly on the opponents of expansionist measures to prove the balance of disadvantage; but if there is any under-utilization at all, where it is clear that goods could be produced for people to enjoy which are not being produced, I think the case has to be made against bringing these resources into use. And this is particularly the case where the potential beneficiaries of this extra production are desperately poor and in need.

Consider the present situation. On the "capacity front" there is spare capacity—and a lot of spare capacity—almost everywhere except in continental Europe. Every country, except some of the Six, would welcome an increase in export demand if it were paid for in cash. There is, I think, no question but that production could be expanded by several billion dollars a year in the Western world by bringing into use spare capacity and unemployed labor, and that everybody would think that this would be a good thing.

The extra demand which would call forth this increase in production could be created by the expansion of purchasing power within individual countries—but each country is scared to expand its domestic demand because of balance-of-payments considerations.

It would, I think, be generally agreed that underdeveloped countries could benefit from more aid: even if their "absorptive capacity" for more capital is limited they can still benefit on a pure relief basis, to mitigate the grinding poverty under which the majority of mankind suffers. So, on the one hand, we have urgent need, and, on the other hand, the capacity to produce more: only the mechanism to match the two up is defective.

To put the matter in concrete terms, the International Development Association is running out of money. It can only replenish its funds from grants from the wealthy nations of the West. To raise their contributions to the IDA the developed nations must tax their citizens more or pre-empt a portion of their savings; yet in most countries taxation is already high enough to be a brake on initiative and effort, so governments are reluctant to increase taxes to give more aid to underdeveloped countries. Moreover, those which are in deficit or bare balance are afraid that to give any more will have an adverse effect on their balance of payments. They feel they cannot afford to give any more, and the creditworthiness of the under-developed countries is not such as to enable them to borrow more on economical terms: the result is deadlock—a failure of mechanism. The U.S. and Britain have run out of credit to give; other countries are slow or unable to fill the gap. Hence the advantages of using Fund credit, of the whole Western world, as a source of the additional funds.

The main case for my plan, therefore, does not rest on the argument that there is a shortage of international liquidity in the sense of a shortage of reserves, plus ability to borrow. Rather it rests on three propositions. The first is that there is a constant struggle by all advanced countries to achieve an export surplus, which is understandable but impossible for all countries to achieve simultaneously, and that this causes, or may cause, some or many countries to under-utilize their capacity, or to seek to export their troubles. The second is that the world is capable of producing more, without adverse effects, and that this "more" is urgently needed by the underdeveloped countries. The third is that to call forth this extra production we may need to create extra reserves or create credit on a world scale in a manner analogous to that in which, on a national scale, it is created by national banking systems. It must be emphasized again that the credit must be used to be effective. So by itself merely to increase the resources of the Fund is not enough, whether this is by an increase in quotas, or borrowing, or even, à la Triffin, allowing the Fund to create credit.[1]

The need is not to give the Fund bigger resources to lend to members in trouble, but to create conditions under which the members are less likely to get into trouble and to need to use the resources.

THE NEW STAMP PLAN

My original plan proposed to use the credit created by the Fund to provide additional purchasing power for the underdeveloped countries: they would spend the "credit" in the developed countries who would expand their exports to improve their balance of trade. The corresponding worsening of the balances of trade of the underdeveloped countries would be covered by the newly created funds. This would counterbalance the tendency of all developed countries to seek an export surplus—they could, in fact, achieve it. Of course the fact that the Fund could create credit could be used also, if necessary, to provide additional resources for the Fund to lend to members to cover ordinary balance-of-payments deficits;

---

[1] [Cf. above, pp. 38–42 and 49–52.]

but putting the new purchasing power into the pockets of the underdeveloped countries could mean that fewer advanced countries would run deficits and, therefore, the probable calls on the Fund to cover ordinary balance-of-payments crises would be lessened.

The scheme remains, in theory, a good one. It is, of course, disliked by those who feel that balance-of-payments crises are the only thing which will force governments to do what is necessary to avoid inflation; and suspected by those who are unable to imagine a money which is not issued by a sovereign state or "backed" in some mysterious way by gold or silver. More seriously, it would not, on present form, be accepted by some of the governments whose consent to treat the Fund credit as equivalent to gold would be necessary.

Is it possible, while retaining most of the advantages of the plan, to remove enough of the features to which the opponents object to make the plan acceptable?

Now one of the reasons why the surplus countries have been reluctant to agree to the scheme is a practical one: the fear that it might add to their difficulties in controlling inflation. To create extra purchasing power on an international scale would be fine if the extra exports were called forth only from those countries which are in deficit and which have unused resources. But, it is argued, part of the extra purchasing power will be spent in countries like Germany or France which are fully employed, already earn adequate surpluses, and wish to decrease the rate at which they increase reserves. The price of curing underemployment in some countries may be to increase inflationary pressures in others.

There is some force in this argument. On the other hand if a country is fully employed the delivery dates will lengthen and costs may rise, so that the new purchasing power of the aid-receiving countries will ultimately be diverted to those countries where delivery dates are shorter; this is probably happening now in the case of Germany and the U.S. Moreover, the effect of purchasing power created in this way is hardly different from the effects produced by international bank lending or other untied aid. The surplus countries would hardly claim that these should be curtailed in order to ease their own domestic problems.

Fortunately, the world is now in better balance; Germany's embarrassing surplus, for instance, is now much reduced. There is now comparatively little reason to believe that a disproportionate part of the "burden" represented by the scheme would fall on any particular countries or that the extra pressure would add seriously to their difficulties. Nevertheless the problem remains one which must be taken seriously, and proper provision must be made to protect the interest of those countries which are in surplus or very fully employed by allowing them, in whole, or in part, to "opt out."

The second modification to the original scheme might be that instead of being given away to the underdeveloped countries, the Fund certificates or Fund credit could be lent. We now have an ideal instrument for the purpose in the form of IDA, which is ably staffed with plenty of worthwhile projects which it would like to finance and very little money.

The third modification is that some "backing" might be given to the Fund certificates, and conversely some limits might be put to the extent to which Fund members are automatically obliged to accept them when tendered by another central bank.

Fourth, it would be desirable for the Fund certificates to carry a very modest rate of interest, but this in practice may not be possible.

The scheme—"Stamp plan 1962"—might then be as follows:

1. The Governors agree that the Fund shall be allowed to create credit. I think as a start a modest amount—say, $2 billion—would be appropriate.

2. The Fund issues the certificates, which would be denominated in U.S. dollars, at a par value of $35 per ounce and convertible into other Fund currencies at par value equivalents. (Of course physical certificates are not essential: credit entries in the Fund books could have the same effect.) In the event of a rise in the price of gold or a devaluation of the dollar, the value of the certificates would be written up correspondingly.

3. Member countries would agree to receive these certificates from central banks or monetary authorities in settlement of international obligations, up to a total amount equal to their quotas. (In my original scheme there was no such provision: members would have undertaken an obligation to receive as many Fund certificates as were tendered.) They would hold these certificates as reserves and would undertake to use them in payment only if under pressure and not for the purpose of adding to their gold or dollar reserves.

4. The Fund would lend the certificates for fifty years to IDA. The latter would pay to the Fund interest in such currencies as it receives from its investments. These funds would then, in turn, be credited, as far as practicable, to the members holding the Fund certificates, in proportion to their holdings.

5. IDA would lend in the normal way: as currencies were required

it would present the certificates to the countries concerned, receiving currency in exchange.

6. If any member country, on presenting the certificates to another member, finds that the latter would not honor its obligation to provide its own currency in exchange, or if the latter country already had its full quota of certificates and was unwilling to accept more, the Fund could redeem the certificates out of its own resources—including, if necessary, its gold reserves. In the latter case the country receiving gold would undertake to reverse the transaction as soon as it was in a position to do so, thus replenishing the Fund's gold stock.

7. If any Fund member was suffering from overfull employment and, therefore, was unwilling to accept additional export orders, it could notify IDA that it did not wish the proceeds of the IDA loans to be spent within its economy, or it could limit the purposes for which the funds could be spent. It would, however, still be obligated to receive its quota of Fund certificates when presented by other central banks. If, for instance, India gets $500 million, Germany might notify IDA that it could not accept the onus of providing Deutsche marks direct to the Indians in exchange for the certificates, and that the IDA should make certain that contracts arising out of the loan should not be placed in Germany. Under this provision Germany would not be completely shielded, for if the contracts were placed in the U.S., which would receive the Fund certificates, then Germany would still be obliged to receive these from the U.S. if the latter ultimately required to tender them to obtain foreign exchange to support her currency. Germany would be insulated for the "primary" pressure, but might ultimately feel a "secondary" pressure.

This might not be enough safeguard—though I think it should be. It might be necessary to devise other special rules to protect countries which were suffering from temporary "overheating" from the consequences of the extra demand which would be created by the issue of the certificates.

8. As a less desirable alternative, if the safeguards failed to satisfy any country, it would be possible to work the scheme even if some members of the Fund refused to join it. The certificates would then have limited acceptability and would not be entirely equivalent to gold: but if they were accepted by the U.S. and the U.K. and most other countries as well as backed by the Fund they would be at least sufficiently valuable to be counted as reserves: they would be as good, for instance, as credits with EPU which we had no difficulty about accepting. But clearly the scheme would be much better if accepted by all the major countries.

This new version removes some of the objections to my original plan: it sets limits both to what the Fund can create in the way of credit and to the amount of Fund paper which any individual country can be asked to absorb. And against the Fund liabilities there is an asset on the books, albeit an illiquid one. The scheme could still be worked if one or two countries elected to "opt out," provided that they could agree that the proceeds of the IDA loans should not be spent on their exports. The country holding the certificates would have a real and valuable asset guaranteed by the Fund and not merely depending on the willingness of other countries to accept it. And it would enable countries to contribute to IDA without fearing the adverse effects on the balance of payments.

I believe the scheme would be workable, and that the two birds could, indeed, be "safely" killed. Perhaps if IDA does not in the event find it possible to raise sufficient funds, or if the world does show signs of sliding into a real recession it may stand a chance of being introduced.

4

The Reorganization of the International Monetary System: An Alternative Proposal

JAMES ANGELL

I. INTRODUCTION

In the last several years a number of proposals have been made for reorganizing the international monetary system and for increasing its general "liquidity." Of these the most comprehensive have been the ones advanced by Professor Triffin.[1] Triffin's plan will hence be used as a preliminary framework for the general analysis and the alternative proposals presented below. What will eventually be said, however, is not restricted to the boundaries of Triffin's discussion.

Triffin's own familiar analysis of the inherent instability of the present gold-exchange system standard, and of the difficulties and dangers it can entail when a "key" currency is subjected to severe pressure, is dramatic and to my mind quite persuasive. The events of late 1960 and early 1961 provided a forceful example of the risks involved. His proposed solution, to increase the supply of potentially available international liquidity substantially by transforming the International Monetary Fund into an international central bank, is imaginative and bold. Both analysis and proposed solution have attracted deservedly wide attention.

This article is reprinted from *The Economic Journal*, LXXI (December 1961), through the courtesy of the author and the Royal Economic Society.

[1] See especially R. Triffin, *Gold and the Dollar Crisis* (New Haven: Yale University Press, 1960), and his Statement before the Joint Economic Committee, reprinted in the Committee's Hearings on the Current Economic Situation (December 7 and 8, 1960); also, in those Hearings, Oscar Altman's detailed criticisms of Triffin. Among many other discussions of the general problems in issue, also see the Radcliffe Committee's *Report on the Working of the Monetary System* (Cmd. 827, 1959), Chapter VIII; E. M. Bernstein, *International Effects of U.S. Economic Policy* (Joint Economic Committee, U.S. Congress, Study Paper No. 16 [Washington, 1960]); and Brian Tew, *The International Monetary Fund* (Essays in International Finance, No. 36, Princeton University, 1961). The suggestions made to the Radcliffe Committee by A. C. L. Day (*Report on the Working of the Monetary System*, paras. 660, 678) are in many ways, of course, parallel to Triffin's.

To date, however, few responsible officials have shown much desire to put Triffin's proposals into effect.[2] My impression is that this tacit opposition arises from a feeling, first, that while Triffin's scheme would probably solve certain problems, it would leave others of almost equal importance largely untouched; and second, that it would also create grave new dangers that might be even worse than those inherent in the admittedly unsatisfactory arrangements which now prevail.

In what follows, I shall first describe briefly what seem to me to be the principal actual or alleged defects in Triffin's original proposals, and then outline the major elements of a somewhat different international monetary system which while free of these defects will, I think, effectively solve the problems created by our present arrangements, and in a workable and safe way. What I shall suggest is in large part, except with respect to gold, a series of substantial modifications of a number of Triffin's ideas rather than a departure in some wholly new direction. I believe that these modifications and the gold proposals taken together, however, are sufficiently different from Triffin's to constitute a separate though closely related system. No attempt will be made to comment on the revisions, I think essentially minor, which Triffin has subsequently made in his plan.[3]

II. ANALYSIS OF THE TRIFFIN PLAN

The principal defects in Triffin's scheme, which in combination seem serious enough to bar its adoption in its present form, are as follows:[4]

1. Triffin's principal proposed remedy for serious threats to international monetary stability that are due to severe balance-of-payments pressures against one or more countries is to provide for large increases in the available supply of international "liquidity" (here a quantity), through an expansion of the IMF's proposed new deposit liabilities.[5] I agree that

---

[2] Though Prime Minister Macmillan has recently expressed interest in some new type of arrangement, not specified, which might produce similar end results. See *British Record* (British Information Services, New York), April 19, 1961.

[3] I am indebted to Professors P. B. Kenen and S. W. Rousseas for helpful comments on the relation between Triffin's plan and an earlier draft of the ideas set out below, and on several aspects of these ideas themselves.

[4] See also the numerous other specific criticisms made by Altman (*Current Economic Situation*). But I think no critic would wish to disparage the contributions Triffin has made to a better understanding of the real problems in issue, or the power of his constructive imagination.

[5] The term "liquidity" is used in many senses: sometimes to denote a ratio, sometimes an existing quantity of "liquid" assets, sometimes the ability to obtain or create cash

under proper safeguards such measures can almost certainly solve the problems of seasonal or cyclical deficits in the current-account balance of an economically advanced country which has the means and the will to enforce appropriate internal policies at the same time. Similar measures can presumably also deal satisfactorily with movements of short-term capital from such countries which are undertaken to engage in interest-rate arbitrage—and which in any event are self-limiting. They can likewise cope with most "hot-money" movements arising from profit-motivated speculation against the exchanges (though perhaps not with all: even the reorganized IMF could not buy up the whole of the U.S. short-term foreign liabilities).[6]

There are other important types of balance-of-payments pressure, however, which can also threaten the stability of the international monetary system as a whole, but which cannot be remedied merely by increasing the supply of international liquidity, and which the IMF should not try to handle at all, unless on a very limited scale and temporarily. These types include pressures due to serious "primary" inflation in a country (itself due to defective internal monetary or fiscal policies), or to a persistent inability for other reasons to maintain the costs of exports or of import-substitute home products at fully competitive levels, or to currently excessive programs of aid and investment abroad, or to "secondary" inflation in the countries receiving such foreign funds, or to the collapse (usually cyclical) of a primary-producing country's exports, or to the more enduring imbalance which can result from trying to force through development programs on too large a scale or too rapidly, or finally, to actual or impending political upheavals. If Triffin's IMF were to try to take effective counteraction in any of these latter cases it would merely load itself with burdens which could easily threaten its liquidity and even its solvency. Triffin makes no sharp differentiation between such cases and those with which the re-

---

in the future, sometimes little more than a state of mind. But liquidity on any definition is always potentially inadequate, except when cash held equals total liabilities. It is an especially elusive and variable concept when applied to a "key-currency" country. What is ample liquidity today may, perhaps only in consequence of speculators' whims and the resulting capital movements, be judged tomorrow to be dangerously inadequate. It should also be noted that merely increasing the "quantity" of international liquidity, in the absence of other measures, in the long run solves nothing. In itself, it will not restore international balance, and it may induce inflation.

[6] Hot-money movements due to fear, as of a major internal economic crisis or a political overturn, are borderline cases which must be judged individually with respect to the appropriateness of IMF action.

organized IMF could properly deal, and this failure has aroused a good deal of misgiving. Yet such a differentiation is clearly essential.[7]

2. Triffin also makes no sharp differentiation, in proposing increases in IMF holdings of member currencies to relieve serious balance-of-payments difficulties, between currencies that are convertible and those that are not.[8] If the financial world comes to feel that the IMF's holdings of inconvertible currencies are excessive, however, the result may easily be the creation of doubt (under Triffin's plan) about the IMF's own liquidity and even its solvency, consequent refusals by central banks to accept IMF deposits in payment of international balances due, and hence the effective collapse of the whole new system. Both for these reasons, and still more to prevent IFM operations from becoming a source of inflation, IMF holdings of both types of currency should be specifically limited; and the limits on inconvertible currencies should probably be more severe.

3. Triffin's plan would *require* the members of the IMF to keep a stated minimum proportion of their own monetary reserves, say 20 per cent, in the form of IMF deposits—a requirement which in some cases would also entail payments of gold to the IMF.[9] This proposed requirement seems guaranteed to arouse the hostility of central bankers, however, if only because it would interfere seriously with their own exercise of judgment and discretion and might necessitate frequent adjustments of the IMF portion of their reserves. In any event, it seems to be aimed at the wrong target. The essential thing, as Triffin himself argues, is only that each member should agree to accept IMF deposits in payment from any other member if the latter wishes to pay with such deposits. Triffin really proposes the requirement primarily as a way of providing the IMF with additional financial resources, but this objective is better achieved in other ways.

4. Triffin contemplates the utilization of a substantial and perhaps increasing part of the IMF's total resources in investments designed to promote economic development.[10] Although he suggests that such placements should be confined to IBRD bonds or "other securities of a similar character," this suggestion too has aroused misgivings, and with some justifica-

---

[7] The Radcliffe Committee *Report* (especially paras. 679f.) offers very interesting propositions which I think are at least not inconsistent with the above differentiation.

[8] The term "currency" must be understood throughout to include not only currency in the literal sense plus bank deposits but also any other demand or short-term liabilities of sorts now included in "official" exchange holdings.

[9] *Gold and the Dollar Crisis*, pp. 107–10 [reproduced in part above, pp. 41–43].

[10] *Ibid.*, pp. 117, 118 [reproduced above, pp. 48, 49].

tion. Perhaps some small fraction of the IMF's resources might be so used, if only for political purposes. As a general proposition, however, it seems clear that the assets underlying an international monetary system should not consist of any large quantity of long-term placements, and still less be used directly to promote development. The two functions are irreconcilably separate.

5. Triffin's plan has also been criticized on the ground that it would make the IMF into an engine of potentially disastrous international inflation. This danger has perhaps been exaggerated, but I think it is substantial enough to debar adoption of the plan in its present form. The danger could come from any of at least four sources. First are the consequences of the four defects already examined. The consequences relevant here are the potentially inflationary effects, which do not need to be spelled out, of excessive accumulations of specific types of assets that are or that might become inconvertible, illiquid or salable only at a loss. Second is the fact that the limits Triffin proposes to set on the total volume of IMF deposits are at best loosely defined. Thus at one point he says only that this total is to be "sufficient to preserve an adequate level of international liquidity"; at another, that the IMF's lending is to be restricted so that it will "increase total world reserves by, let us say, 3 to 5 per cent a year."[11] But the term "adequate" has no very precise meaning (and who is to judge?); and in the absence of foreknowledge of what the total real output of the IMF's members will be in the future, it is clearly difficult to assert that these or any other fixed rates will be either stabilizing, inflationary, or even deflationary. Some critics have feared that any such provision would virtually guarantee continuous and perhaps severe international inflation.

Third, even if one had enough faith in the IMF administration to believe that increases in the total of IMF deposits would be kept within sensible limits, this is still only a *total*. If some countries elected to keep their own monetary reserves and effective money supply constant despite current increases in the aggregate of IMF deposits, for example, the expansion of the system as a whole might be concentrated on a few other countries alone, with conceivably disastrous results.

Fourth, except in an extraordinary emergency, the IMF *must* always buy country A's holding of B's currency from A, if A offers them for sale; and in the ordinary case will pay for B's currency by giving A new IMF deposits (or perhaps gold), unless A is already in debt to the IMF. This

---

[11] *Ibid.*, p. 103 [reproduced above, p. 38].

operation is at the very heart of the proposed new central-banking function of the IMF, and is one main way both of maintaining A's liquidity and of temporarily relieving B from pressures that might otherwise imperil B's own currency. But suppose that B had been running a protracted deficit with A and other countries, had not borrowed from the IMF and had hitherto made payment merely by transferring title to some of its own currency to A and the others; and suppose that now A and the others have suddenly become uneasy, and all sell their holdings of B's currency to the IMF in return for new IMF deposits. The total of these deposits will then increase, though the IMF has not made any "direct" loan to B and under Triffin's plan would have no leverage over it. And of course the IMF has no leverage over A or the others. The results could be seriously inflationary. It is true that the nominal total of the reserves of A and the others will not have increased. But these countries may now elect to expand internally on the "safe" basis of their new IMF deposits, whereas they had previously thought B's currency a rather dubious asset, and had hence refrained from such expansion.

The over-all conclusion hence seems clear that to prevent serious and perhaps unforeseen inflationary dangers, quite specific restrictions must be placed not only on the IMF's creation of its own deposits, but also—again—on its total holdings of member currencies, whether acquired by "direct" loans to the member issuing the currency or by purchase from a second member; and that the IMF must have power to enforce the restrictions. Triffin hardly touches on the two latter problems, particularly as concerns inconvertible currencies, except so far as IMF holdings are affected by the granting or repayment of "direct" loans.

6. Finally, what seems to me the most serious defect of all in Triffin's plan is something which others may regard as its saving grace: its treatment of gold. Triffin makes a convincing demonstration of the total inadequacy of the free world's supply of monetary gold, yet he proposes to retain gold as one of the important and normal means for making international settlements; and the adoption of his plan could well increase rather than decrease the demand for gold. Under his plan, some members would have to pay gold to the IMF to cover part of the proposed increases in their subscriptions, and perhaps to meet the requirement that they hold, say, 20 per cent of their own reserves in the form of IMF balances. Thereafter, however, the IMF would have no assurance of ever getting any additional gold except by buying in the open market, or except so far as members might elect to sell gold to it voluntarily. On the other hand, each member would be

free to demand conversion into gold of any IMF deposits it held in excess of the proposed minimum of 20 per cent of its own reserves.[12] Hence nothing would explicitly prevent a member from selling as much as it pleased of its reserves held in the form of foreign exchange—which the IMF ordinarily *must* buy, as remarked earlier—in return for new IMF deposits (net, of course, of any debt from the member to the IMF), and then demanding conversion of the excess above the 20 per cent minimum into gold held by the IMF. If many members did this the process would quickly exhaust the IMF's gold, and would wreck the whole mode of operation which Triffin proposes for it.

Triffin himself recognizes this possibility, of course, and advances reasons for thinking that it would not actually materialize, but I do not find the reasons convincing.[13] Nor do his proposed remedies—an accelerated "amortization" of IMF currency holdings (how is it to be enforced?), and various restrictions on the right to convert—seem likely to be very effective unless other and more specific sanctions are also provided against the members whose currencies the IMF is holding in excessive amounts. This is the more true, since a considerable part of the IMF's currency holdings under the new system would have originated not in "direct" loans to the members issuing the currencies, but in sales of such currencies to the IMF by second parties. Triffin's proposals provide no very specific controls over such sales. Moreover, if a "gold run" on the IMF actually developed, as it easily might in consequence of the process described in the preceding paragraph, under Triffin's plan the IMF might then have no course open except to go into the market itself and buy gold, in order to restore its own gold "reserve" position. But then the IMF's demand would be, in considerable part if not entirely, a net addition to the more or less continuous market demands of its members, and would intensify rather than ease the general shortage.

III. BASIC DEFECT OF THE PRESENT SYSTEM

The difficulties in Triffin's plan which have just been summarized are substantial. Some of them, it is true, could be materially reduced by a series of fairly obvious modifications of the plan itself. I think that even with these modifications, however, neither Triffin's plan nor any of the other proposals for reform that have been advanced to date quite gets to the heart of the matter. A still more fundamental modification of our

---

12 *Ibid.*, pp. 107, 112, 113, 118 [reproduced above, pp. 41, 44, 45, 49].
13 *Ibid.*, especially p. 112 [reproduced above, p. 44].

present arrangements is necessary if the free world's international monetary system is to be put on an enduringly stable basis.

The reason is that the form of gold-exchange system which has been reestablished in recent years rests, I think, on a basic contradiction with respect to the role it assigns to gold itself. We now require gold to serve as part or all of the internal central reserves of many free-world countries, including nearly all the larger industrialized nations; at the same time we treat gold as the last-resort means for making international payments; and we also insist on using our limited monetary stocks to help satisfy the intermittent but sometimes enormous demands of private and governmental gold speculators and hoarders all over the world. Yet as is by now obvious to almost everyone, and as Triffin himself has persuasively argued, the free world's supply of monetary gold is completely inadequate to carry all three of these burdens effectively and at the same time, or even to carry the first two alone, in periods when there are very severe pressures. Nor would the adoption of Triffin's own plan, as shown earlier, really solve the problem with respect to gold; indeed, it might even make the problem worse.

This, then, is the contradiction: we have no way of making the supply equal to the upper reaches of the probable aggregate demand, yet we cling tenaciously to the system. A collapse, in the sense of an enforced devaluation or a suspension of the convertibility of one or more major currencies, is hence always possible. We managed, by a combination of emergency measures and perhaps some good luck, to slide through the crisis of late 1960 and early 1961, but it would be merely self-deluding to regard this crisis as unique. Another one like it, or perhaps something worse, could occur at any time and with little advance warning. Our present system is a moderately good fair-weather craft when managed skillfully, but in storms it leaks badly and could easily founder. No mere patching or caulking will strengthen it sufficiently. It is hence imperative to devise some better set of arrangements, and to do so quickly.

If this basic conclusion is accepted—and I believe it is the only one which is defensible—then we must rebuild part of the system itself. There are, I think, only two major alternatives. First, we can devote all our monetary gold to the effecting of international settlements alone, and deliberately abandon its use as an important internal national reserve. This step, however, would scarify the monetary traditions of the leading countries, hence would probably arouse insuperable opposition, and might not be workable in practical terms. Nor would it alone assure the maintenance of international balance. Or, second, we can do just the opposite. We can devote our monetary gold primarily to the maintenance and expansion of national internal reserves alone, and, for those last-resort international settlements which would otherwise have to be made in gold, use instead something like the new IMF deposit balances which Triffin proposes. These deposit balances, when protected by the additional safeguards described later, will be just as liquid, as generally acceptable, and as "safe" as gold, and in most cases will also pay interest to their holders instead of being a non-earning asset. This is the simplest solution and the only one which seems broadly practicable. Eliminating the use of monetary gold to make international settlements in all ordinary circumstances will likewise reduce short-run fluctuations in national gold reserves, and in countries that orient their internal policies on their gold holdings to any substantial degree will thus increase internal economic stability.

This step alone, of course, will likewise not solve the broader problems of stability and balance at the international level. If the further modifications of our present system and of Triffin's plan which are proposed below are also adopted, however, together with the necessary additional safeguards, I believe a really workable and adequate international monetary system can at last be achieved: that is, a system which can handle every probable future international pressure, of the types which such a system should properly be expected to deal with at all, yet which at the same time need be neither inflationary nor deflationary in its effects. The more important specific provisions required to implement the basic principles here involved are summarized in later sections.

It is true that in the traditional theory of gold-standard central banking international gold flows were assigned a key "barometric" role even when their absolute size was small. If the gold flow was of appreciable size relative to the country's total reserves, an adjustment of the internal currency and banking system was supposed to ensue—especially in the case of gold losses. This adjustment was also supposed to help maintain the "value" of currency. With these considerations in mind, many will now contend that with the recent spread of gold convertibility, these effects of international gold flows are once more an essential part of the process by which over-all international balance is maintained, and hence that the use of gold itself to effect net international settlements must be preserved at all costs.

To these contentions there are three answers, each partial but mutually complementary and in combination complete. First, the experience of the interwar years—the last period of substantial length when any large number of leading countries maintained fairly unrestricted gold convertibility—suggests that the "traditional" rules of positive internal response to gold flows were actually followed less than one-third of the time: the theory does not correspond well to recent practice.[14] Second, however, there is obviously no reason why IMF members should not respond to gains and losses of the proposed new IMF deposits, if they so choose, precisely as traditional theory required them to respond to gold flows. Third, as to the "value" of member currencies, the new IMF deposits will be gold-denominated and kept at par with gold. Hence any member that maintains the stated par value of its currency in terms of IMF deposits (within the permitted limits of variation) will enjoy the same beneficial effects on the *external* value of its currency as those which it now does or could receive from maintaining external convertibility into gold. The *internal* value of any member currency, on the other hand, always has been and will continue to be governed primarily by the actions of the member's own monetary and fiscal authorities alone.

To summarize, in the proposed new system and in all ordinary circumstances the need, and hence the demand, for gold to make international settlements will simply disappear. Its place here will be taken by the new IMF deposits, and the existing monetary gold stocks can be used exclusively for internal reserves.[15]

All this does not mean, however, that the members of the IMF should hereafter use their gold simply to plate their palaces and parliament houses. Gold will continue to serve as a vital internal restraint and regulator for any country that so desires, and as the traditional symbol of financial strength; and each member will be free to increase its stocks by buying from any holder who sells voluntarily. Only what is in effect the present *compulsory* aspect of international gold sales will be removed. Moreover, for a long time to come ordinary prudence will require that the present monetary gold stocks be retained as safety reserves against a possible future liquidation of IMF, some other breakdown of the new system, or a new war.

IV. ALTERNATIVE PROPOSAL

Even if the proposed general principles concerning the international use of gold are accepted, this would obviously not be sufficient to define or to establish an adequate new international monetary system. To permit an

---

[14] See the League of Nations study, *International Currency Experience* (1944), pp. 68, 69. The data used, however, relate only to year-to-year changes.

[15] Nor would the change in the position of gold be revolutionary. Few, if any, major countries today allow the internal circulation of gold coin, or pay out gold on demand to private domestic buyers (except for limited industrial purposes); almost none sells to private buyers in other countries, unless in emergencies like 1960–61.

intelligent appraisal of the probable effects of the adoption of the principles, it is therefore necessary to describe briefly the more important additional provisions which also seem required, in order to ensure the satisfactory operation of the reconstituted international monetary system. So far as these proposed provisions parallel Triffin's, a summary reference will suffice.

1. Reorganization of the IMF

The present IMF should be completely reorganized, along somewhat the same general lines as those proposed by Triffin, though with a good many differences, and should be made into a central bank for its members. The present quota system for regulating loans to members should be abolished. The present guarantee clause protecting IMF holdings of member currencies should be retained.

2. Transactions in Gold

As part of the reorganization, and to implement the general principles proposed in Section III, above, the IMF members should agree that: (*a*) both the members and the IMF itself are free to buy anywhere any gold which the holder wishes to sell; (*b*) no member will request gold in settlement of payments due, either from another member or from the IMF; (*c*) the IMF will not request gold from a member, except in connection with the application of the proposed "sanctions" described below; (*d*) neither the IMF nor any member will sell gold to any private individual (except for limited industrial purposes) or to a nonmember; and (*e*) the IMF may sell or lend gold voluntarily to a member, and a member may lend or sell gold voluntarily to another member or to the IMF. The IMF, in particular, should be free to make limited loans or sales of gold to a member for internal stabilization purposes.[16]

3. Initial Creation of IMF Deposits; Conversion Rights

At the date of the inauguration of the new system the IMF will create its own gold-denominated deposit balances in favor of each member, as Triffin proposes, in an amount equal to the member's subscription at that date minus any existing net debt of the member to the IMF. Each member will be free to sell, lend, or otherwise transfer its IMF deposits to another

---

[16] It would also be desirable that all members require the sale to them of all private gold stocks (other than industrial) already held within their territories, as the United States did in 1933, but this is not essential.

member. Each member may also use its IMF deposits to buy back its own currency from the IMF. No member, however, may demand that the IMF convert any part of its deposits into gold. On the other hand, the IMF *must* always buy a member's holdings of a second member's currency, if requested, in return for IMF deposits (but subject to the limitations on IMF currency holdings described in para. 6, below). The IMF may also convert a member's deposits into the currency of another member, if requested, provided the IMF both holds the second currency and wishes to sell it, but the IMF is not automatically obliged to make such conversions. Should the IMF refuse, the first member is always protected in any event, because each member will have agreed always to accept IMF deposits in payment from another member (para. 4, (*a*) below). The IMF may also serve as an agent for the exchange of currencies and for the clearing of payments between members.[17] Finally, the deposit liabilities of the IMF will carry interest at the current net IMF earnings rate, except in special circumstances described later. Any increases in IMF deposits after the inaugural date should be limited and controlled as proposed below (para. 5).

4. *IMF Deposits and Member Reserves*

If the proposed new system is to work at all, if international transfers of the ownership of IMF deposits are to take the place now filled by international transfers of gold, and especially if the new IMF is to operate as an international central bank—that is, as an international lender of last resort —then it is obviously necessary that as of the date of inauguration of the new plan, each member of the IMF shall agree to: (*a*) acecpt title to IMF deposits, if offered, in *pro tanto* payment of any debt due from another member or from the IMF itself; and (*b*) count IMF deposits it owns as part of its own central monetary reserves, at least to the extent that its aggregate reserve assets would otherwise be insufficient to meet its minimum legal or traditional reserve requirements.[18] If these provisions are agreed to, the IMF, even without any further increase in its subscribed resources,

[17] The problem of the conditions (if any) under which member currencies should be exchangeable for IMF deposits at prices different from par, and the problem of the conversion rights attached to IMF deposits in the event of a subsequent liquidation of the IMF itself, will not be explored here.

[18] The present IMF regulations and procedures permit the IMF to act as a central bank only to the extent that it has gold on hand or obtainable, or other currencies which are acceptable to the creditors, and then only to the extent (often severely limited) that the debtor can obtain the necessary initial loan from the IMF itself.

Note that acceptance of the second condition will require new legislation in some countries, notably the United States.

should be able to deal with any situation likely to occur within the next several years where any substantial use of IMF funds at all is appropriate, short of a general international collapse.

Triffin would go farther with respect to the second provision, and would *require* members to keep a stated proportion (say 20 per cent) of their internal monetary reserves in the form of IMF deposits. As remarked earlier, however (Section II, 2), such a requirement would both be almost certain to arouse profound opposition, and in what follows will be shown to be unnecessary.

5. *The Subsequent Expansion of IMF Deposits*

After the initial creation of IMF deposits, and assuming no increases in subscriptions, a member may nevertheless increase both its own holdings of such deposits and the over-all total in any of three main ways: (*a*) selling gold voluntarily to the IMF; (*b*) selling the currency of another member B to the IMF; or (*c*) selling its own currency to the IMF.

Turning these transactions around, from the point of view of the IMF the purchase of gold is always desirable, other things equal, and creates no problems. Second, an IMF purchase of member A's currency from A itself, when undertaken at A's own request, is in effect a "direct" loan to A, analogous to direct loans by the IMF under the present system. Such loans should be subject to charges that vary with both the relative size and the duration of the loan, much as at present. They should be freed, however, from the present often-crippling restrictions as to purposes, amounts, and timing: subject to the safeguards outlined below, the IMF should have freedom to exercise its own judgment. Here the IMF is in control, and if its management is intelligent, and also follows the guides suggested below, neither overlending nor other major difficulties need arise.[19] Third, however, the situation is quite different when the IMF purchases member B's currency from A. Subject only to the limitations proposed below, the new IMF *must* always make such purchases (see para. 3, above). They are one of the two main processes through which the IMF can and must serve as the international lender of last resort (the other being "direct" loans to A). These purchases will operate both to restore A's liquidity and to relieve the current pressure on B; in effect, they temporarily substitute

---

[19] If the IMF buys A's currency at the initiative of the IMF itself, however, this is clearly not a direct loan to A, and no charges should be imposed. But if IMF deposits become generally accepted by members in payment from other members it is in any event unlikely that such purchases will be important.

the obligations of the IMF to member A for for those of member B. Looked at from the other side, however, by buying B's currency the IMF is in effect making an "indirect" loan to B. But under the provisions thus far considered the IMF has *no* way of bringing any controlling pressure to bear on B. In entirely conceivable circumstances, therefore, continued IMF purchases of B's currency through this procedure could at one extreme threaten a serious and perhaps indefinite inflation of IMF deposits; and at the other extreme might, by loading the IMF with too large a volume of assets of uncertain value, impair or even destroy the current acceptability of its own deposits.[20] It is therefore essential both to set limits of some sort on the IMF's holdings of any member's currency and to give the IMF effective tools or sanctions with which to enforce such limits. The following provisions are suggested, in summary outline.

6. *Limits on IMF Holdings of Member Currencies*

It is necessary to distinguish between convertible and inconvertible currencies. (*a*) In the first year or two after the inauguration of the new system, the IMF's *total* holdings of either group of currencies may be allowed to increase temporarily somewhat above the volume created initially (para. 3, above), if necessary to meet possible future pressures, but not ordinarily by more than say 10 per cent. This will permit a much greater expansion in absolute terms of convertible-currency holdings, of course, than of inconvertible. (*b*) The limits on temporary increases for any *one* currency should be substantially higher, again to meet possible future pressures: say 20 per cent instead of 10, provided that the total increase for the relevant group of currencies as a whole is still not exceeded. (*c*) The IMF should have power to exceed any of these limits temporarily by, say, another 10 per cent in severe emergencies. (*d*) If the total monetary reserves of a member A which holds IMF deposits exceed, say, 30 per cent of A's relevant demand liabilities, the IMF should have power to require A to repurchase with its IMF deposits any IMF holdings of A's currency, until the latter holdings are reduced to zero or the suggested reserve ratio is reached.

(*e*) Triffin has also proposed an automatic further increase in IMF

---

[20] For reasons given near the beginning of Section V, below, neither the solvency nor the liquidity of the reorganized IMF—in the sense of its ability to pay all its deposit liabilities in full and promptly—can ever be impaired in actual fact. General uneasiness about the value or the salability of a substantial part of the IMF's assets, however, might nevertheless make members hesitate to accept IMF deposits in payment—even though such hesitation would really be "irrational."

deposits, at, say, 3–5 per cent per year on the average. This would in general, of course, also increase IMF holdings of member currencies or securities. It has not been clearly established, however, that growth either in a member's real output or in the real or money volume of its international trade requires a corresponding increase in its international monetary reserves. Such reserves are required only to meet disequilibria in its balance of payments, not to carry the total volume of payments itself. With improved techniques for maintaining internal and external balance, and with a more powerful will to use them, the need for international reserves actually held may even decline. What is essential, rather, is to provide for the *availability* of additional reserves, on a temporary basis, to meet unusual pressures of those types for which the use of such reserves is appropriate. The provisions outlined above will ensure a substantial expansion of reserve availabilities, surely enough for some years, and until more evidence is at hand it would not be advisable to prescribe automatic increases in reserves actually held—which might prove merely inflationary.[21]

7. Sanctions

To enforce the limits just proposed the IMF should be given new powers, additional to those which it now has and will have over "direct" loans, to enable it to control "indirect" loans as well. Whenever the IMF feels that its holdings of a member's currency, from whatever source derived, are "excessive" in the sense of rapidly approaching or passing beyond limits such as those just outlined, it should have powers, which it should be free to use at discretion and in any order, to: (*a*) consult the member concerned, and recommend measures which the member itself should take; (*b*) suspend payment of interest on IMF deposits held by the member; (*c*) impose charges on *any* IMF holdings of the member's currency, as is now done with "direct" loans; (*d*) require the member to repurchase, either with gold or with another currency acceptable to the IMF, "excess" IMF holdings of the member's currency;[22] (*e*) declare an embargo on the mem-

---

[21] Also see the observations on the relations between international balance and liquidity, in somewhat the same vein, in the Radcliffe *Report*, especially paras. 679f.

[22] This step is, of course, much the same as Triffin's proposal for "extraordinary amortization" (*Gold and the Dollar Crisis*, p. 112 [see also p. 44 above]). But the settings and motivations are somewhat different in the two cases. In Triffin's system the IMF could itself be required to convert part of its deposit liabilities into gold, under specific conditions, and hence might be compelled to demand such "amortization" merely to protect its own gold reserves. Under my proposals these latter things would not be true. The IMF could hence concentrate solely on the best methods of dealing with the problems of the particular member or members whose currencies it held in "excessive" quantities.

ber's currency, and refuse to accept it for any purpose, until the situation has been corrected; (*f*) sell part or all of the IMF's holdings of the currency in the open market for what it will bring; and (*g*) expel the member from the IMF. Any one of the last three steps may also force a devaluation of the member's currency, but the devaluation will then occur in such circumstances that it is unlikely to spread in a chain reaction to other members —who can in any event be given help if adversely affected.

It may also be desirable to invoke sanctions such as (*a*) through (*d*) above against a member which has a seriously excessive international *creditor* position; and the IMF should have power, as proposed in para. 6 (*d*), above, to compel such a member to reduce its holdings of IMF deposits.

8. Investment of IMF Assets

The IMF should *not* make investments designed to promote the "development" of a particular country directly; the latter function belongs elsewhere. If its holdings of a member's currency are in excess of the IMF's own current requirements, however, the IMF should be free to invest the excess in the member's government or government-guaranteed obligations (with the member's consent). Such obligations should be short-term or not far from maturity, should be protected by the same guarantee against devaluation as the IMF's currency holdings, and should be included when the IMF determines the limits on its holdings of the member's currency (para. 6, above). The IMF should also have power to invest limited sums in the obligations of an approved intergovernmental agency, if the obligations are payable in a convertible currency and are subject to the provisos outlined in the preceding sentence—as if they were in fact obligations of the government issuing the currency in which they are payable.

9. Special Provisions for Primary-product Exporters

Many of the economically less-advanced countries that depend on exports of one or a few primary products face from time to time, as is familiar (see Section II, 1, above), severe balance-of-payments pressures that are substantially different both in their origins and often in their effects from those typically encountered by the more highly industrialized nations. So far as such pressures originate in overproduction, there is little in the strictly monetary field that other countries can or should try to do: measures of other sorts, perhaps including medium- and longer-term loans, would be more appropriate. When the pressures arise primarily from a decline in export proceeds which is itself due to a cyclical recession in the

industrialized importing countries, however, action by the international
monetary authorities is both possible and feasible.

Even in the latter situation it would be unwise for the IMF itself to
provide more than very limited and temporary assistance; otherwise an
unmanageably large proportion of its own total resources could quickly
become committed to illiquid situations. A solution can be found, however,
by utilizing a modification of a plan proposed by a United Nations Committee of Experts in 1949.[23] Under the conditions prescribed in the Committee plan, and at the request of the IMF, the principal importers A of
member B's primary exports to the group A would make interest-free loans
of their own currencies to the IMF (*not* to B), up to, say, perhaps 50 per
cent or more of any decline in B's average exports to them that was due
to recession within their own (A's) economies. The IMF would then create
an equivalent amount of its own deposit balances, and would lend them
(also interest-free) to B against the security of B's own currency.[24] Member B would then be able to maintain much of its own imports—thus also
helping to reduce and perhaps even reverse the recession in the industrial
countries that were the original lenders. The bigger the loans, the greater
the probable effect. Repayment of the IMF loans should, of course, be a
first charge on any subsequent increase in B's export proceeds above some
stated figure. The IMF should repay its own creditors A as it is itself repaid. The other necessary safeguards are largely self-evident, and need
not be spelled out.[25]

The interposition of the IMF in the loan operation, instead of having
the A group lend directly to B, seems desirable in order to provide unbiased

[23] *National and International Measures for Full Employment* (United Nations, 1949,
A Report by a Committee of Experts). The plan is commonly attributed to Mr. N. Kaldor,
who was a member of the Committee.

[24] Such increases in IMF holdings of A and B currencies should not, of course, be
counted in computing the limits proposed in Section IV, 6, above.

[25] This type of arrangement could be set up by a once-for-all agreement (with stated
maximum limits) between the IMF and the central banks of the larger relevant importing
members, and could be put into operation from time to time as required. Hence new legislative authority would not be required each time. The increases in the IMF holdings of
the currencies involved should not, of course, be counted in applying the limits on currency
holdings proposed in para. 6, above.

This arrangement also seems both more workable and more likely to be accepted than
the proposal for a "development insurance fund" recently made by another United Nations
group (International Financial News Survey, April 14, 1961). I have not yet seen the document in question, but the plan appears to contemplate the inclusion of the industrial countries as well, and to apply to *all* exports, not only primary products.

The arrangement proposed above obviously offers no solution, however, for the problems of underdeveloped countries that are *chronically* in need of much larger reserves.

determinations of times and amounts and an impartial agency for enforcing later repayment. Lending IMF deposits to B is preferable both because these deposits will be universally acceptable in payment for B's own subsequent imports, whereas some of the currencies of the importing group A might not be, and because the group A will in general be more willing to lend to the IMF than to B.

V. EFFECTS OF PROPOSED CHANGES

If the IMF is reorganized and is given the essential additional safeguards proposed above, and if the gold provisions are agreed to, the liquidity and general soundness of the IMF will be beyond question, even if no further increases are made in its subscriptions. Suppose, for example, that the reorganization had been effected on January 31, 1961, and that each member had been given a new IMF deposit balance equal to its total subscription at that date, minus any net claim of the IMF on it—as proposed above. The IMF itself would then have had deposit liabilities of roughly $14 billion. Its assets would have consisted of $2.4 billion of gold, $7.5 billion of convertible currencies (including gold-account investments of $800 million), $4.1 billion of inconvertible currencies and roughly $700 million of other assets—a total of $14.7 billion. The ratio of gold to deposits would have been 17 per cent; of gold plus convertible currencies to deposits, 71 per cent. The IMF would hence have been both highly liquid and on almost any definition "sound."[26]

If thus reorganized, and even without any further increases in subscriptions, the resources of the IMF should be more than sufficient for some years to come. It should be able to deal effectively with every probable future situation short of a general international collapse in which any substantial use of IMF funds at all is appropriate, provided only that the members involved on *both* sides of a payments-pressure situation also adopt appropriate internal policies. The IMF should even be able to combat "hot

[26] Any increase in subscriptions would now presumably increase the proportion of convertible currencies, and might also increase the quantity of gold held.

Triffin's proposals for inaugurating and expanding the IMF (*Gold and the Dollar Crisis*, pp. 107-10) [reproduced in part above, pp. 41-43] are not likely to be accepted in their present form because they would require large gold payments from some countries, especially the United States. Under the alternative proposals made above (Section IV, 2), the IMF would not ordinarily pay out gold at all, and hence would not need any additions to its stock. If subscriptions are later increased, I suggest that they be paid in as follows: (*a*) gold in excess of, say, 25 per cent of the relevant liabilities of the member's central bank; (*b*) convertible currencies up to, say, 50 per cent of the member's "official" holdings (but minus any payments in gold) ; and (*c*) the balance in the member's own currency.

money" flows successfully, except those due to political fear, since its intervention will in general reverse the speculative expectations which originally induced the flows themselves.[27]

Moreover, the IMF as thus reorganized can never become illiquid, in the sense of becoming unable to meet its deposit obligations promptly. A member wishing to withdraw its IMF deposits cannot convert them into gold (unless it were quitting the IMF entirely, when it would receive some *pro rata* share of IMF gold). The member can only convert its deposits into its own currency, if the IMF holds that currency; or, up to the amount that the IMF is able and willing to sell, into the currency of another member (see Section IV, 3, above; but of course the member can always offer its IMF deposits for sale to another member). Such conversions of deposits will reduce equally both the assets and the liabilities of the IMF, but will not impair its liquidity as just indirectly defined. Nor would a member ordinarily have any reason on balance-of-payments grounds to demand conversion into a second member's currency anyway: the latter currency would be needed only to make payments to the second or to another member, and all members will already be obligated to accept IMF deposits for such purposes (see Section IV, 4, above).[28]

Nor can the reorganized IMF ever become insolvent, in the sense of becoming unable to meet its deposits obligations in full, for essentially the same reasons. It is true that if a member became uneasy about the value of the IMF's assets it might refuse to accept IMF deposits—contrary to its agreement. But such a refusal would in actuality be irrational, for as just shown, the IMF will always be able to "convert" deposits in full. Only if the IMF were to be completely liquidated would a possible decline in the value of its assets below cost be a matter of legitimate concern.

---

[27] Here the procedure proposed by Dr. Bernstein (*International Effects of U.S. Economic Policy*), under which the IMF would issue its own debentures and use them as security to borrow gold or the debtor's currency from the member receiving the hot money, would also be most helpful. In a sense, this would temporarily reverse the flow. But the procedure is not powerful enough to be the chief reliance in times of major stress (in itself, it puts no pressure on the debtor; and some creditors might refuse to lend, as Professor Kenen has remarked in an unpublished manuscript which he kindly showed me), and it is rather clumsy. It is hence not an adequate alternative to the creation of a true international central bank.

[28] Had the IMF been reorganized on January 31, 1961, in the manner proposed above, and had all members then having convertible currencies withdrawn their deposits immediately after the reorganization, the IMF could still have paid them off in such currencies or in gold. Thereafter the IMF would have been protected from all dangers on this score by the provisions for reorganization themselves, as outlined above, and by the proposed measures relating to gold.

The real dangers to which the reorganized IMF will be exposed are different. First, there are various types of balance-of-payments pressures which, however severe they may be, the IMF cannot and should not try to deal with (see Section II, 1, above). If it nevertheless yields to temptation or the entreaties of its members, it will risk its own destruction. Second, it is also entirely possible that through bad judgment on the part of its managers the IMF's operations will become an engine of international inflation, despite the safeguards proposed at earlier points. This would be highly undesirable in itself, but would still not make the new IMF either insolvent or even illiquid. Moreover—though the thought may not be too comforting—the same risk of inflation attaches to the operation of *any* central bank or government, neither of which can ever be bankrupted involuntarily. One is always compelled to rely to some extent on the integrity, judgment, and will power of competent administrators.

VI. CONCLUSIONS

The preceding analysis has sought to establish three main points. First, an extensive and even drastic reorganization of our present international monetary arrangements is both imperative and urgent. Second, while the major objectives of Triffin's plan—the most comprehensive hitherto proposed—are the right ones as far as they go, the plan itself both contains serious internal defects and, with respect to gold, does not go to the real heart of the problem. Third, the adoption of the alternative proposals made above—especially those concerning gold, the specific limits and sanctions on IMF currency holdings, member reserves, primary-product exporters, the divorcement of IMF operations from development programs, and these and other arrangements permanently protecting the liquidity and the solvency of the IMF—will substantially cure these defects, and will permit the establishment of a really effective and adequate international monetary system.

Recognition of the validity of the first point is becoming increasingly widespread. On the other hand, the choice as between Triffin's plan for the reorganization itself, the alternative plan proposed above, and other present or possible future plans must obviously wait on further discussion and, eventually, on intergovernmental action.

Meanwhile, however, another and quite recent type of difficulty, which is as much political as economic, is threatening to block any action at all. This difficulty really has three aspects, though there is common ground among all three. First, the United Kingdom is understandably concerned about the effects of *any* general monetary reorganization on the interrelated financial, commercial, and political complexes of the Commonwealth and other sterling area countries. Second, in the leading European countries as a whole there is apparently an increasing disposition to urge that participation in any new international central bank be confined to the countries now possessing the major trading currencies—which is really a revival of Professor J. H. Williams' "key currency" idea—and thus to make the new IMF central bank a rich man's club alone. Finally, many countries all over the world are said to be increasingly uncomfortable over the dominating role which the United States would presumably play in the new institution. The United States subscription, and hence its vote if votes are proportional to subscriptions alone, would far exceed any other nation's.

These difficulties are not imaginary, and they could become serious or even fatal obstacles to any major reorganization. Although they cannot be examined here in detail, one or two comments may be suggested. First, there is obviously no *a priori* logical barrier to the incorporation into the proposed new IMF either of the sterling area or of more specifically localized regional arrangements, and without loss of that identity which is both so highly prized politically, and often so valuable in practical terms. Second, if there is enough good will on both sides the voting-power problem should be negotiable, and capable of a reasonable solution. Third, however, complete exclusion of the smaller countries from the new IMF would be both awkward with respect to the normal operations of the IMF and probably disastrous politically. It would be at once counter to the real spirit of the United Nations, and a wonderful weapon for the communist bloc.

But whatever the specific solutions that may be found for these very substantial problems, the one thing which is imperative is that serious work should begin promptly, at both governmental and intergovernmental levels, to develop and adopt an effective and adequate plan for the reorganization itself. Time may not wait much longer.

5

A Plan for Increasing Liquidity: A Critique

SIR ROY HARROD

This is a timely book. Professor Triffin, whose ideas were largely responsible for the shape of EPU, is a foremost authority on his subject. He writes with lucidity and persuasiveness. He has not only much practical experience of negotiations over a number of years, but also a rich knowledge of monetary history, such as is found in only a few contemporary writers. He is a fine theorist, and at the same time has a very good sense of how abstract doctrine should be resolved into practical proposals.

In his main theme he is, according to my view, on the side of the angels: he holds a sufficient provision of international liquidity to be of prime importance. And he has no difficulty in showing that the present provision is inadequate and, over the coming years, will grow more so.

In his wide-ranging discussions of monetary philosophy and in his historical retrospects, there is much that might call for comment. But it seems expedient in the space available to concentrate upon his constructive plan for increasing liquidity.

His proposal is to transform the International Monetary Fund into being in effect a world central bank; this is linked with a plan for terminating the use of the dollar and sterling as international currencies. Member countries would hold part of their reserves in the form of deposits with the IMF, drawable on by check, the deposits to be acquired in the first instance by the transfer of existing assets from the central banks to the IMF. These deposits would subsequently be increased by lending and open-market operations undertaken on a rising scale by the IMF and designed to increase world liquidity in the aggregate (i.e., including gold accessions) by 3 per cent (or 4 per cent or 5 per cent) a year.

A critique of *Gold and the Dollar Crisis*, by Robert Triffin (Yale University Press, 1960). Reprinted from the May 1961 issue of *Economica*, through the courtesy of the author and the publisher.

REDUCTION IN LIQUIDITY?

First, it is needful to deal with certain technical aspects of this plan. It is to be feared that it would not give so substantial an increase in liquidity as Professor Triffin appears to claim for it.

1. Initially there might be a rather large loss of liquidity. Central banks are to surrender certain liquid assets that they now have, mainly foreign exchange and gold, in return for deposits of equal amount with the reconstructed International Monetary Fund. Central banks are to be required to maintain 20 per cent of their gross reserves in the form of deposits with the IMF. These deposits can be used to discharge international indebtedness, but are to be maintained at 20 per cent of gross reserves. This requirement must be deemed to involve, like all percentage requirements, albeit in a modified form, the cab-rank fallacy.[1]

It must be remembered that the concept of liquidity cannot be completely divorced from a psychological element. An asset is liquid if its holder thinks of it as liquid. It may be useful, in order to bring the argument to a head, to consider specific numbers. Let a country have 100 units of gross reserve; let 80 units be the point at which it begins to get worried about the adequacy of its reserve and to consider taking measures to improve it; and let 50 units be the absolute bedrock, to prevent any fall below which it will adopt extreme measures. The Triffin plan requires that the country should transfer 20 units initially into deposit with the IMF. These 20 units can be drawn upon only in proportion to the fall in the rest of its reserves. If its gross reserves fall from 100 to 62.5, it will then have to have 12.5 on deposit with the IMF, so that it will have only 50 under its own fist. I submit that, as the basic bedrock reserve is thought of in terms of eventualities like war, the country will not think of letting the part under its own fist fall below 50. In that case it will not be able to allow its gross reserve to fall below 62.5. It would contemplate that, in the event of war, it could not be absolutely sure of drawing out the 12.5 from the IMF, if only because the IMF might be having difficulties about its own assets.

Thus, this provision reduces the excess of the initial 100 over the basic bedrock by 12.5 units, i.e., by 25 per cent. If the initial position was less favorable, the reserve being, say, 90, the reduction in the disposable re-

---

[1] [Professor Harrod appears to be referring to the story of the (no doubt mythical) town whose citizens were dissatisfied with the taxicab service in their community. They tried to remedy the situation by passing an ordinance requiring that one cab had to be at each cab station at all times.]

serve would be 31.25 per cent. Consequently, it appears to me that at the outset we have a very large initial loss of liquidity under this plan, which it would take a number of years of its working to offset.

PROBLEM OF INTERNAL FINANCING

2. Professor Triffin is incorrect in supposing that "the maintenance of a portion of a country's reserves in this form . . . would not raise the internal financing problems which some countries now find in financing their quota subscription to the Fund" (p. 106).[2] It is true that the initial subscription of 20 per cent of gross reserves would not entail an internal financing problem; nor would the further supplementary subscriptions by some countries, constituted by the handing over of the dollar or sterling balances remaining to them after the initial subscriptions had been paid (pp. 111–12);[3] but the initial subscriptions, and the supplementary subscriptions, by themselves, make no addition to international liquidity. The addition only occurs when the IMF starts lending or conducting open-market operations. The result of the lending or open-market operations is that aggregate deposits with it would rise above the level established by the initial and supplementary subscriptions. One of two things can then happen, or a mixture of both. Countries can withdraw in gold any deposits in excess of 20 per cent of their gross reserves. This is an essential feature of the scheme, designed to make it acceptable. If they withdraw all their excess deposits in this way, the power of the International Monetary Fund to lend or operate in the open market would be limited by the amount of the initial gold subscriptions (about $5 billion). If this happened, the whole scheme by which the IMF is to lend or invest enough to ensure a rise in total world liquid resources by 3 per cent a year or more would break down at the end of three or four years.

It is hoped, however, that countries would leave part, indeed the major part, of the extra deposits with the IMF; they would have the inducement of a sufficient rate of interest and the knowledge that excess deposits remained gold-convertible. Only to the extent that they did this in substantial degree could the scheme continue to work for more than three or four years. But precisely to the extent that they did this, the problem of internal financing would reappear. Let it be supposed that, in consequence of IMF lending to underdeveloped countries and thus giving those countries the power to increase their purchases, say from the U.S., American de-

---

[2] [Reproduced above, p. 41.]
[3] [Reproduced above, pp. 43–44.]

posits rose above their previous level. Underdeveloped countries could discharge their net indebtedness by paying in IMF "gold units," which the United States authorities would be obliged to accept. But the over-all external surplus of the U.S. is the net sum total of all individual dealings. American citizens, or their banks, who turned in these "gold units" to the Federal Reserve would expect to receive good American dollars in exchange. Where would these dollars come from? By internal financing on the part of the U.S. Government. The position would be exactly the same as it is in Britain when gold is paid into the Exchange Equalization Account. That Account can buy gold only to the extent that the British Government arranges internal financing.

Thus, although no internal financing would be required for the initial move, which in itself does nothing to increase world liquidity, but rather the other way round, all further increases of deposits with the IMF, which would be the consequence of lending or investment by the IMF, and would be equal in amount to that extra lending or investment minus gold withdrawals from the IMF, would require internal financing. Thus, apart from gold withdrawals, any net increase in world liquidity would have an equal counterpart in the form of internal financing by creditor countries.[4]

WHAT COVER FOR FUNDS?

3. Professor Triffin writes: "Countries would thus be required initially to hold in deposit with the Fund an amount of $11 billion. These would increase, year by year, by 20 per cent of the new additions of members' gross reserves and would be amply sufficient to cover prospective Fund lending for many years to come" (p. 107).[5] These words seem to suggest that lending to the extent of $11 billion plus 20 per cent of the new additions to members' gross reserves (due presumably, to new gold output) would be "covered." But in what sense "covered"? Some $6 billion out of the initial $11 billion would consist of dollar balances and sterling balances. These may be nominal cover, but are not really cover, since they would not be usable. Thus the lending power of the IMF seems to be exaggerated in this passage.

---

[4] To the extent that a country allowed the inflow of IMF "gold units" to increase the cash basis of commercial banks, there would be no problem. But in that regard there is no problem *now*. Professor Triffin's scheme would make no difference to the *present* position as regards internal financing in relation to any increase in the resources of the IMF.

[5] [Reproduced above, p. 41.]

DIFFICULTIES OF LIQUIDATING KEY-CURRENCY BALANCES

4. There is a proposal, however, that the dollar balances and sterling balances, not merely the $6 billion aforementioned, but also those turned in by the "supplementary" maneuver (see above), should be liquidated "at a maximum pace of, let us say, 5 per cent a year." It is intriguing to observe that Professor Triffin's plan involves that existing foreign holdings of dollar balances should be funded—a measure recommended for the British sterling balances after the war, but in very different circumstances.

This liquidation of all existing dollar and sterling balances would entail a great destruction of liquidity, albeit at a moderate pace, which must be offset against the creation of liquidity by IMF lending or open-market operations. It means that, in order to sustain an increase in world liquidity by the required amount, the IMF would have to do *more* lending or open-market operations each year than it would otherwise have to. (See below.)

THREAT TO LONDON'S FINANCIAL EMINENCE

5. It is an essential feature of Professor Triffin's scheme that the use of specific currencies, dollars and sterling, as international reserve currencies should be abolished. On the face of it such a destruction of liquidity seems gratuitous, when one is trying to increase liquidity. Professor Triffin argues, and frequently returns to the theme, that these specific currency holdings are precarious, and that, if something again goes wrong with one of these key currencies, world-wide disorders will ensue. He cites historic examples, from the collapse of sterling in 1931 and difficulties connected with sterling since World War II. It could be argued on the other side that both these unfortunate experiences were essentially due to war, the 1931 collapse of sterling being ascribable to the mistaken resumption of the pre-war parity in 1925, and that the British, at least, will in the future, with the guidance of past lessons, be more successful with sterling in normal times of peace.

This may be the suitable point to insert a plea on behalf of British interests. The external position of Britain was more heavily damaged than that of other countries in two wars, generally accounted to have been waged for freedom, and there might therefore be a case in equity for her not being asked to make another sacrifice which is not strictly necessary. To abandon the international use of sterling as a reserve currency would be the sacrifice of an existing asset, since the holding of sterling, invoicing in sterling, the use of British banks, British investment opportunities, and British export opportunities are all linked together. Such a further sacrifice Britain might be prepared to make, if it could be shown to be necessary, but not if it was required only to satisfy some academic criterion of general tidiness. There is no reason why sterling should not continue to be used as an international reserve and medium of settlement, alongside IMF deposits as established by some new system.

PROBLEMS OF ADMINISTRATION

6. According to Professor Triffin, in order to ease possible gold claims on the Fund, excess deposits arising out of the turning in of dollar balances should be regarded as gold-convertible, but those arising out of the turning in of sterling balances should not be, on the ground that dollar balances do, at present, but sterling balances do not, entitle their holders to gold. But now that Britain has moved out of transitional status (Article XIV), sterling is on a par with the dollar in being gold-convertible for the central banks of other member countries. Britain would certainly not agree that the inferiority of sterling that existed during the transitional period should be revived. And *de facto* the inferiority had already long since ceased to exist. Movement from the transitional status was merely the recognition of a *fait accompli*. Accordingly this proposal by Professor Triffin for reducing the gold claims on the Fund, by disallowing those resulting from the surrender to it of sterling, which would be of large amount, is unacceptable.

It remains to consider the lending and open-market operations of the IMF, on which the proposed increase of international liquidity would depend. The aggregate amount of lending and investment would have to rise year by year, but, as the lending would presumably be short-term, the amount of lending by fresh negotiations in any one year would be increased year by year. Although the extra liquidity consequent upon the lending would be a welcome contribution, it is to be noted that, insofar as the increase was due to lending and not open-market operations, it would be subject to perennial negotiations on a rising scale. Thus, this rising quantity of negotiations for loans is really an integral part of the proposed increase of liquidity. So far as the nations that are the beneficiaries of the lending are concerned, it is to be stressed that the opportunity of borrowing, however favorable—the psychological aspect of liquidity comes in again at this point—does not rank as a liquid asset in at all the same sense as gold or foreign currencies held in the coffers of one's bank. This is a mark to be set against Professor Triffin's plan for increasing liquidity.

Then as regards open-market operations, liquidity, once created, circulates. But if the actual creation of liquidity is to be by lending or investment, then the occasion of the creation of liquidity brings a balance-of-payments advantage to the country which secures the loan or investment. It would presumably be thought advantageous that these initial advantages should accrue to the underdeveloped countries. The investment would be by open-market operations. But the underdeveloped countries do not usually have open markets in which large-scale operations can be easily conducted. Thus, the benefit of the investments would probably have to accrue to the mature countries.

While the idea of a world central bank, able to create credit by lending and investment, is one to be greatly welcomed, it cannot be denied that the process of lending and investment would not be entirely smooth. This is another reason for deploring the plan for making the amount of lending and investment to be done by the IMF, in order to get a given increase in world liquidity, gratuitously larger, by providing for the absorption and liquidation of dollar and sterling balances. The proposal that loans should be made to the World Bank, for which acknowledgment is made to Mr. Maxwell Stamp (p. 118),[6] can be unequivocally welcomed.

Having dealt with these technical matters we may describe the contribution to liquidity that Professor Triffin proposes as follows. The principle of Keynes's Clearing Union was that liquidity should be increased by persistently creditor nations committing themselves to holding a rising quantity of bancor (originally called "grammor"), until such time as they were willing and able to use it for the purchase of goods and services abroad or for foreign investment. The maximum amount that might thus accumulate was to be equal to the sum of the quotas of the nations in over-all deficit. The creditors were not to be allowed to ask for gold in exchange for this bancor. Professor Triffin's scheme gives the right to nations to have any deposit in excess of the required 20 per cent minimum encashed for gold. But his scheme could work for more than three or four years only to the extent that the nations refrained from asking for their excess deposits to be thus encashed. Thus, Keynes says: "Make the potential creditor nations commit themselves to rising deposits (up to a certain top limit) without having a claim on gold." Professor Triffin says: "Let them have the right to claim gold, but hope that they will not exert it." The success of

---

[6] [See p. 49 above and Maxwell Stamp, "The Stamp Plan—1962 Version," reproduced as selection 3 in this volume.]

his scheme entirely depends on their not exerting it. That may be a tactful way to proceed; but it is precarious. It would also be slow working. The increase of liquidity would have, in the early years, to be set off against the loss of liquidity described in the paragraph numbered 1 above. Nonetheless it would be excellent if Professor Triffin's plan were accepted, subject to the reservations already stated.

There is one very grave matter with which Professor Triffin does not appear to deal at all. He provides for an annual increase of liquidity, but he provides nothing to relieve the existing shortage. Indeed, on its first inception, his scheme would increase the shortage. There have been arguments about how great the shortage now is. In my own judgment the shortage is already so great as to be the primary cause of the free world having shown inadequate growth rates in recent years. Relatively small oscillations in balances of payments have caused one nation after another to adopt restraining measures internally or import restrictions externally. If reserves were adequate, nations should be able to ride out temporary periods of deficit, which are bound to occur from time to time, since one nation's over-all surplus is another nation's over-all deficit, without resorting to deflationary or restrictive measures.

CHANGE IN PRICE OF GOLD

I would suggest that a scheme of the general kind proposed by Professor Triffin should be regarded as an essential *corollary* of a rise in the dollar price of gold. Once we had re-established liquidity by that method, we should need to think of further methods for maintaining a sufficient expansion, for ironing out the trade cycle, etc., etc. Nothing of the nature of Professor Triffin's plan could give us nearly a *large* enough initial increase in liquidity to meet the existing deficiency. Professor Triffin does indeed have a passage on the price of gold. He lists some arguments against it.

He says that the price increase would have to be very steep indeed, "to stimulate adequate annual supplies." What is "steep"? To get a realistic gold revision of the dollar, in line with its loss of its commodity value, the price should be at least doubled. This alone would double the annual supply and might well actually treble it, having regard to increased production and reduced seepage into hoards.

His second argument is that the price increase would have to be repeated. This does not appear to be so, if the annual supply were doubled or trebled. Any minor shortfall then accruing could be made good by a Triffin-type method.

The overnight revaluation might produce a temporary excess, but this would be soon absorbed by the increase of trade.

The initial benefits would, it is true, be distributed haphazardly. The record of recent grants and loans, however, does not show that they have gone to the most needy countries. Nor is it clear that the lendings and investments of the IMF would do so either. If lendings were insufficient, the investments would certainly be likely to go to the less needy countries, because they alone have broad capital markets. Now the great benefit to be derived from the gold price revaluation must not be thought of as the initial once-over present made to existing gold-holders, but as the lasting benefit due to the effect of greater liquidity in increasing world trade and production. The needier countries would benefit in the best possible way, namely, by the increased buying from them by the richer countries.

Professor Triffin makes the usual reference to the USSR and South Africa. It is very obscure why an operation, which gives the USSR a certain present but simultaneously gives the free world a much larger one, is said to benefit the USSR.

As for South Africa, the benefit would go, in the first instance, to the gold-mining companies. If it is desired to mitigate racial discrimination there, the more power that these companies, which on the whole have very enlightened leadership, have in South Africa the better. The benefit would go in the second instance to the Bantus, who work in mines; the gold companies are enlightened employers and would certainly pay more if they could afford to. There would be some transition to lower-grade ore-working, but their gross takings per man would be greatly increased. These Bantu mine workers save most of their earnings, and, when they return home with their savings, they take a more commercial view of agriculture, treating their cattle as economic assets rather than as mere ornaments available for dowries. Nothing could do so much to improve the racial relations in South Africa as rendering the unprivileged more economical viable and therefore better able to stand up for themselves.

6

Professor Triffin on International Liquidity and the Role of the Fund

OSCAR L. ALTMAN

In *Gold and the Dollar Crisis* Professor Robert Triffin of Yale University draws a bold picture of the dangerous state of, and prospects for, international liquidity. To cope with these problems he suggests expanding the role and changing the character of the International Monetary Fund. Triffin's proposals for a Fund with expanded functions and new responsibilities (called XIMF for convenience) appear to be designed to provide, at little or no cost, benefits for everybody. It will be useful to summarize these proposed benefits, as follows: (*a*) The world would benefit by obtaining, at long last, a currency both international and internationalized, described as being beyond question in quality, elastic in quantity, and responsive to the needs of trade. "Hot" money would be cooled off, and runs on currencies eliminated. (*b*) The United States would benefit because the possibility of converting official dollar balances into gold would be reduced, if not eliminated. The United States would be free to set interest rate policy without fearing repercussions via the outflow of official dollar balances and their conversion into gold or other currencies, and it would know that a payments deficit was no longer needed to increase international liquidity. (*c*) The United Kingdom would benefit because it would be freed from the specter of a flight from sterling into gold or dollars, and from the necessity of subordinating an interest rate policy appropriate to its domestic needs to the defense of the external position of sterling. (*d*) Holders of dollar, sterling, and other currency balances would be able to exchange their holdings for Fund deposits, which would

Reprinted from *IMF Staff Papers*, April 1961, through the courtesy of the International Monetary Fund and Mr. Altman. The original text included an accurate summary of Professor Triffin's proposals as they appeared at the time in his book *Gold and the Dollar Crisis* (New Haven: Yale University Press, 1960). This summary is not reproduced here. Two new introductory sentences have been substituted.

be of irreproachable quality because of an exchange guarantee, and which would probably earn interest into the bargain. (*e*) Less developed countries would benefit because the existence of the expanded Fund would make it unnecessary for them to transfer short-term capital to the United States or the United Kingdom in order to obtain exchange reserves. Instead, the flow could be reversed. A large part of the assets behind XIMF deposits could be invested directly, or through other agencies, to finance economic development, thus moving capital to the countries that need it most. (*f*) Even gold-mining countries and the gold-mining industry may be said to benefit in a backhanded way. Though gold as the basis for international reserves is held to be unnecessary, restrictive, and a waste of economic resources, it is nevertheless retained in the system, after its dangers have been neutralized, as a harmless example of cultural lag and as an inexpensive subsidy for the production of something that the world wants but does not need.

The following discussion attempts to determine whether Triffin's proposals are necessary or appropriate to realize all these benefits. It considers whether present and prospective dangers are as great as described. It inquires whether existing financial arrangements and institutions are as inadequate as alleged to cope with present conditions as well as those that are likely to develop. It examines the effect on the assets and liabilities of the Fund of the implementation of Triffin's proposals, both before and as a result of the expansion said to be needed during the next few years. Finally, it considers what fundamental policy changes are required for the proposed international financial mechanism, including further transfers of authority by countries to international agencies, additional responsibilities assumed by countries themselves, and new operating objectives of the expanded Fund.

TRIFFIN'S DIAGNOSIS EXAMINED

Is the Structure of International Reserves Unsatisfactory?

The first claim of the Triffin plan is that it will result in a more stable structure of reserves. It is proposed first to examine the present structure, in order to evaluate its advantages, disadvantages, dangers, and costs.

U.S. liquidity is very high in terms of the ratio of gold to *official* dollar balances. Even a large-scale conversion of official balances would have moderate effects, in view of the size of the balances and the need to maintain at least part of them for working purposes. The problem of liquidity really arises when account is taken of other present or potential liabilities. Banking and all other private dollar balances totaled $6 billion at the end of 1958; a change in leads and lags applied to foreign trade of $35 billion would amount to additional billions; repatriation of foreign funds invested in U.S. securities would amount to many more billions; and speculation against the dollar financed by funds borrowed by both nationals and foreigners would provide additional billions. All of these potentialities have increased since 1958, and banking and all other private balances alone reached $7.5 billion in June 1960.

At the end of 1958, short-term dollar liabilities totaled $14.6 billion, of which $8.7 billion was in official hands and $5.9 billion in the hands of banks and other private holders. On the same date, sterling liabilities[1] amounted to $9.4 billion, of which $6.7 billion was in official, and $2.7 billion in nonofficial, hands. Nonofficial holdings of dollars and sterling therefore totaled $8.7 billion, while official holdings totaled $15.4 billion.[2] Though Triffin's proposals refer to all official reserves, he recognizes that part of these will have to be held in liquid form. Countries

> have, in any case, to retain some working balances in a form other than gold in order to avoid repeated gold sales or purchases each time they wish to sell or buy [*sic*, O.A.] foreign currencies in the market to stabilize their own exchange rate. These working balances will have to be held either as excess deposits with the Fund or directly in the key currencies actively traded on the exchange markets. Either of these two alternatives would reduce substantially the danger of an excessive gold drain from the Fund. Working balances equal to only 5 per cent of annual imports, for instance, would absorb as much as $5 billion.[3]

Not all of the official holdings of exchange therefore involve the threat of conversion into gold.

Private holdings are, however, considerably more mobile than official ones. They are more responsive to interest rate differentials and speculative possibilities. Private dollar holdings cannot be converted into gold in the United States, but they can be used to buy gold abroad, or to buy any other key currencies at home or abroad. Either use could result in an outflow of gold. If nonofficial holders of dollars should switch to sterling

---

[1] At the end of 1956, approximately 40 per cent of sterling liabilities was held in the form of bank deposits and Treasury bills. The remainder (60 per cent) was held in the form of government securities, and of this, half had maturities longer than five years.

[2] Total exchange assets held officially are estimated at $19.2 billion as of the end of 1958 (*International Financial Statistics* [IMF], September 1960).

[3] *Gold and the Dollar Crisis*, pp. 113–14. It is not clear why the same consideration does not apply to official balances at the present time.

to take advantage of higher interest rates in the United Kingdom, the United States would have to support the dollar-sterling exchange rate by selling gold, unless the United Kingdom was willing to hold these dollars in the form of additional XIMF deposits or working balances. Similar considerations would apply for the United Kingdom and purchases of dollars with external sterling.

Under present arrangements, the United States could support the dollar with its gold reserves, and it could also draw other key currencies from the IMF, consistent with IMF policy. To draw these currencies the United States would pay dollars to the IMF; it would use these other currencies to buy dollars in the foreign exchange markets. The United States would thus relieve the pressure on the dollar, whether this stemmed from official or nonofficial sources.

The ownership of dollars would be transferred from their present holders to the IMF, and spot liabilities would be converted into term liabilities. The countries whose currencies were drawn from the Fund would automatically acquire credit balances, if it is assumed that the IMF initially held their currencies to the extent of only 75 per cent of their quotas, or lower debit balances, if it is assumed that the IMF held more than 75 per cent of their quotas. By using drawings to help counter pressure on the dollar, the United States would slow down the decrease in its gold holdings. Its *gross* reserve position would therefore be better than if it met all of the pressure on the dollar by selling gold. The effect upon its *net* reserve position would depend upon what liabilities were considered as contra items against gold reserves. Very short-term dollar liabilities—dollars being offered in the foreign exchange market—would be changed into dollars that had to be repurchased in three to five years (or, if there were no specific repurchase agreement, as gold reserves increased). The spot net position of the dollar would be improved immediately, while its five-year net position would remain unchanged.

The case for a full and open-end guarantee of dollar and sterling balances, given a realistic appraisal of present and prospective dangers to these currencies, and the resources that could be used to meet these dangers, must be considered as not proved. Perhaps some lesser kind of assurance may be useful, though even this is not clear. But if this is the case, only a few countries need be involved, since dollar and sterling balances, official and private, are highly concentrated.

In all probability, the risks of exchange instability have been overstated by Triffin, whose fears for the future of the dollar are colored by the large balance-of-payments deficits of the United States since 1958, deficits which must in any event be reduced or eliminated. On the other hand, the ability of the key currency countries to meet these risks has been understated. The resources of the Fund, supplemented by country credits and supported by appropriate domestic measures, were quite sufficient to halt heavy drains on sterling in 1956 and 1957. With much larger resources and with a larger assortment of convertible currencies, the Fund would be able to help even more in any future crisis. The United States has never drawn on the Fund, but there is no reason why it should not under conditions and for purposes consistent with Fund policy. The United States at the end of 1960 had a net creditor position in the Fund of $1.6 billion; after exhausting this, it could draw an additional $4.1 billion before Fund holdings of dollars would reach 200 per cent of quota. If the Fund needs more resources, it may obtain these by borrowing.[4] It is quite unlikely that sales of foreign currencies against dollars, up to as much as $6 billion, added to U.S. sales of its own gold, coupled with the determined attitude that such actions would proclaim, could fail to halt a run on the dollar.

Is the XIMF Needed to Expand International Liquidity?

The other leg of the dilemma described by Triffin is that the prospective growth of reserves will fall short of the requirements associated with the growth of trade. This shortfall over and above additions to gold reserves is calculated for the next decade and is declared to be far in excess of any safe expansion of dollar and other exchange reserve holdings. This conclusion rests principally upon Triffin's estimate of reserve requirements, since there is general agreement about prospective gold additions to monetary reserves.[5]

Triffin's view of the required growth of international reserves is essentially a mechanistic one based on a rough relationship of reserves to imports;[6] yet it is simply not true that the need for monetary reserves can be read off arithmetically from a table relating reserves to trade. The fact that this ratio—or more accurately, this family of ratios, since both trade and reserves can be thought of in many different ways—has been falling

---

[4] Under the present Articles of Agreement, the Fund can sell gold, or borrow, to replenish its currency holdings. It may be prudent, as E. M. Bernstein has suggested, to arrange for borrowing in advance of need by issuing to a small number of countries debentures which could be called for payment to meet large emergencies; see *International Effects of U.S. Economic Policy* (Joint Economic Committee, U.S. Congress, Study Paper No. 16 [Washington, 1960]), pp. 84–86.

[5] On this point, Triffin has generally approved the estimates in Oscar L. Altman, "A Note on Gold Production and Additions to International Gold Reserves," *IMF Staff Papers,* VI (1957–58), 258–88.

[6] *Gold and the Dollar Crisis,* p. 36 [reproduced on p. 19]. . . .

in the postwar period is no proof that reserves have been becoming less and less adequate or that they have reached some dangerous minimum. It is questionable that the level of reserves in 1957 or in 1958, the years used by Triffin as bases for reserve calculations, represented the minimum reserves required by the noncommunist world, and that in the future these reserves must grow as fast as world trade.

Equally, there is no reason to believe that in any period, and particularly in the next ten years, the demand for reserves will grow at the same rate as trade.

The demand for reserves is a result of the policy decisions by a relatively small number of countries. There was a great, but highly concentrated, demand during the 1950's. In this period, the major part of the increase in reserves was for the account of Germany, Austria, Italy, and Japan, countries which had been stripped of reserves by the war and had a problem of rebuilding them. If the demands for reserves for this particular purpose had not existed, dollar balances would in all probability not have grown as much as they did. If these countries (and a few others) had not been willing to add to their assets in the form of money (gold *or* dollars) rather than goods, the large and continuing deficits in the U.S. balance of payments in 1950–59 would not have occurred. The accumulation of reserves for this purpose must sooner or later come to an end, with important consequences for the future demand. Some of these countries have reserves which will be in excess of their needs for some years to come; thus they can be sources of reserves for other countries.

Many of the less developed countries, such as India, accumulated large reserves during World War II—only because they could not buy goods. These countries have already spent most or all of these reserves and show little sign of wishing to recapture reserve levels of ten and fifteen years ago. If appropriate reserves figures were available, some countries would show a negative *net* reserve position. The reserves of the less developed countries were remarkably stable during the decade of the 1950's, though this stability was the arithmetic result of a number of differing trends. The reserves of oil-producing countries (with the total largely influenced by Venezuela) increased until 1957 and declined sharply thereafter; those of the U.K. colonies increased steadily, doubling from 1950 to 1954 but increasing by only 10 per cent in the rest of the decade; and for all of the other less developed countries (with the total influenced largely by India), reserves decreased during the ten-year priod.

Gold reserves of the United States have decreased by $7 billion from their all-time peak of $24.6 billion at the end of 1949; but even so, they are at the level immediately preceding World War II. Reserves of the United Kingdom at the end of 1960 were $3.2 billion, or 6 per cent less than reserves at the end of 1950 and 20 per cent below those at mid-1951, the high for the decade.

The trend in gross reserves since World War II is the resultant of these and many other factors, and the future movement is not predictable on a statistical basis related to the growth of trade. Furthermore, the adequacy of the reserve position of any country is influenced not only by its gross reserves, but also by its debtor or creditor position in the Fund, the size of its unused Fund quota, the amount of its outstanding and overdue short-term commercial debt, official short-term borrowings, gold pledges, banks' holdings and other private holdings of exchange, and the like. Failure to take such factors into account, for example, leads Triffin to classify Argentina in 1953–55 in his group of high-reserve countries.[7] Countries that are in debt can, in the future, improve their real reserve positions by reducing their obligations rather than by increasing their gross reserves. This would not create any demand for reserves, and the world total of reserves would not need to grow, although it would become more adequate to meet demands. Finally, there is little reason to assume, as Triffin does, that the United Kingdom is actively pursuing policies compatible with the reserve target of $5 billion that has been talked about for a number of years.[8]

There are other difficulties in determining reserve requirements by applying a growth-of-trade factor to a base of present international reserves. For example, in his Wicksell Lecture (1958), Triffin said that "world trade and production are estimated to have increased in volume, over the last ten years, at a pace of 6 per cent a year. A parallel rate of increase in the world's monetary reserves ($62 billion at the end of last year) would require their expansion by about $3.7 billion annually."[9] This figure of $62 billion includes *all* the assets of the IMF (gold, convertible currencies, and inconvertible currencies), as well as country holdings of inconvertible currencies and balances under payments agreements. Would this imply that there is some requirement to expand reserves of inconvertible currencies, or to expand a total of which some components are much less useful than others? If a dollar's worth of inconvertible reserves becomes convertible, does it not become more efficient?

[7] *Gold and the Dollar Crisis*, p. 43 [reproduced on p. 23].

[8] *Ibid.*, p. 50. For purposes of calculating reserve requirements, Triffin assumes a figure of $4.6 billion as of the end of 1957 (*ibid.*, p. 50) [reproduced on pp. 27, 28]. . . .

[9] *The Future of the European Payments System* (Stockholm, 1958), p. 34.

A similar kind of question is posed by the treatment of claims on the European Payments Union (EPU). The $62 billion total of world reserves referred to in the Wicksell Lecture included claims on EPU totaling $1.3 billion. At a compound growth rate of 6 per cent a year, this inclusion created a demand for $1 billion of reserves over the next decade. But when claims on EPU were funded at the end of 1958, they vanished from the statistics on reserves. Triffin's calculations in 1959 of the required rate of growth of reserves for the next decade were reduced correspondingly. The reason for excluding these bilateral claims from reserves statistics was presumably that they represented longer-term assets; many of these funded claims had terms of a year or two, and a few had terms as long as seven or ten years. Germany was the largest net claimant on EPU and was interested in showing lower, rather than higher, reserves. Moreover, Germany's net bilateral claims of $1 billion in January 1959 had been reduced to $480 million by October 1960. The arbitrary nature of the classification of reserves is suggested by the subsequent rate of pay-off as well as by a comparison with overseas holdings of sterling. At the end of 1956, approximately one-third of sterling liabilities had maturities of more than five years; yet they were included in country reserves.

The currency holdings of the IMF present another problem in the calculation of requirements. Reserve requirements in 1958 were calculated by applying trade growth factors to a world total of reserves that included the currency holdings of the IMF. Since then, member quotas in the IMF have been increased by more than 50 per cent, and IMF holdings of currency enlarged by more than $4 billion. How, then, should requirements for 1960 be calculated? Should the procedure be the same as for 1958? Should the requirements for 1960–70 include an element for expanding this additional $4 billion at the assumed rate of growth of trade? At a 3 per cent rate, this involves a reserve requirement of almost $1.5 billion during the decade. Or should reserve requirements be calculated on the basis of 1960 figures that exclude this $4 billion, which in turn might be treated as a deduction from calculated requirements?

As these examples suggest, to calculate future reserve requirements by applying figures on the growth of trade to published figures on reserves may lead to results that vary considerably from one date to another. Arithmetic calculations of reserve requirements in relation to trade are simple—this would appear to be their outstanding virtue—but they are not necessarily convincing.

These comments should not be interpreted to mean that, because there is question about Triffin's rate of 3 per cent, or 5 per cent, or 6 per cent, some other rate is necessarily better. On the contrary, the search for any rate is vain. No mechanistic solution will serve. There are many roads to liquidity, many ways of increasing it, and many ways of judging when it is more or less adequate. The activities of the IMF, and the recent increase in its resources, affect the demand for reserves; also, the contracyclical activities of the industrial countries affect the demand.

An appropriate and expanding volume of world trade may be carried on with many different amounts of reserves, total reserves of many different compositions, and many different rates of growth of reserves. Any arbitrary determination that reserves should increase at some given rate may well lead to a lowering of credit standards and to inflation. In the end, stability of the reserve structure can be obtained only if the major countries really want it, and if they have access to credit to preserve it. Bagehot's doctrine that the Bank of England should be prepared always to be the lender of last resort has its counterpart in the international field. Access to IMF drawings and stand-bys has formalized and internationalized the granting of credit. This marks a great advance over the cooperation among central banks that characterized the period of the 1920's and has made it much more unlikely that a crack in the exchange structure can start, or, having started, that it can continue.

TRIFFIN'S REFORM PROPOSALS EXAMINED

Reserve Structure Proposed in the Triffin Plan

The foregoing discussion has shown that the existing structure of international liquidity is less vulnerable than Triffin's diagnosis suggests. Let us turn now to a consideration of his remedies for its weaknesses. He has claimed . . . that the Triffin plan will result in a more stable structure. This proposition is based upon the transformation of the IMF into a central bank to *hold*, in the form of deposits, part or all of the reserves of its members. This power is separable from the power to *create* deposits, a function also proposed for the IMF. The latter is based upon the assumption that the XIMF and the central banks of all member countries constitute a closed banking system, essentially similar to the central bank and commercial banks within any one country.

As a prelude to this discussion, it should be noted that adoption of Triffin's proposals would make no difference to the serious problem associated with the present balance-of-payments deficit of the United States and the recent increase in gold speculation and hoarding. On the surface, uneasiness about the dollar reflects the present state of reserves, liabilities, and rate of outflow of gold. But basically this uneasiness reflects trends. It reflects the series of large deficits which continue to reduce gold reserves and increase short-term dollar liabilities. Judgment about the adequacy of the reserve position of the United States and the strength of the dollar is highly colored—and correctly so—by fear that these trends will persist, by fear that the balance-of-payments deficit cannot or will not be eliminated.

Adoption of Triffin's plan will not eliminate this balance-of-payments deficit. It will not balance any country's external accounts. It should not relieve any country from keeping its balance of payments in order. Adoption of his proposal would probably reduce the proportion of the deficit currently settled in gold, but it would not affect the size of the deficit itself. To the extent that such a reduction of gold flows moderated present uncertainties and was considered as extending the time available for corrective measures, it might even result in a larger total deficit. Recent increases in gold speculation basically reflect the same set of problems. Speculation is not against the dollar in favor of other currencies; it is based on fear that the dollar—as well as other currencies—will be devalued. This is not a problem of a shortage of international liquidity. It is a problem arising out of the U.S. balance of payments.

To illustrate how the proposed arrangements would operate, let us apply the proposals to the data for the end of 1958, which were used by Triffin.[10] (The use of later data would not materially affect this analysis.) At the end of 1958, the United States had gross reserves of $22.5 billion, consisting of $20.6 billion of gold and $1.9 billion of net claims on IMF; its deposit requirement with the XIMF, at 20 per cent, would be $4.5 billion and would require an additional payment of $2.6 billion to the XIMF. Since the United States does not include exchange assets in its gross reserves, this deposit requirement would be met by paying gold. All other member countries would have deposit requirements of $6.7 billion. On the reasonable assumption used by Triffin "that all countries would initially prefer to hold onto their gold assets,"[11] the member countries would meet their deposit requirements with $600 million of present claims on the IMF, $800 million of gold, and $5.3 billion of exchange. The exchange payments probably would consist of approximately $1.9 billion of sterling

[10] These data were taken from *International Financial Statistics*, October 1959.
[11] *Gold and the Dollar Crisis*, p. 110 [reproduced on p. 41].

and $3.4 billion of dollars. Dollar balances held officially by all countries would be reduced from something over $9 billion (including bonds and notes) to $6 billion. As far as the United States is concerned, these payments of $3.4 billion of dollars would be rendered permanently inconvertible into gold unless the gross reserves of the rest of the world should fall below their total at the end of 1958, i.e., $33.7 billion. Such a development was very unlikely even in 1958, and it has become even more unlikely with the subsequent increase in reserves.

The effect so far upon the net reserve position of the United States would be the same as if the United States had redeemed $3.4 billion of dollar balances and paid out $2.6 billion of gold. But these transactions are only a first step. Under Triffin's proposals, all remaining official exchange balances would have to be deposited in the XIMF or converted into gold. Therefore, the $6 billion of dollar balances and more than $3 billion of sterling balances left after the required transfer to the XIMF of 20 per cent of gross reserves, which may be termed "excess" dollar balances, would have to be turned into gold or deposited at the XIMF. To the extent that countries chose this opportunity to buy gold which they might be unwilling to acquire under existing arrangements, they would create the pressure on the dollar and the outflow of gold that Triffin fears so much. In such circumstances, the help that could be provided by the XIMF to the United States to relieve the pressure would be no greater than the help that could be provided by the present IMF. Triffin is probably right, however, in thinking that XIMF deposits could be given such advantages over present exchange reserves in key currencies, notably an exchange guarantee and the prospect of earning interest, that the conversion would be made smoothly, with little additional demand for gold.

XIMF Deposits, Gold, and Exchange Guarantees

The XIMF would therefore begin operations, based on the data at the end of 1958, with $21 billion of deposits, of which $11 billion was required, in accordance with the 20 per cent deposit ratio, and the remaining $10 billion was "excess" in the sense that it was over and above the deposit requirement. The assets corresponding to these deposit liabilities would be $5 billion of gold and $16 billion of exchange; the latter would consist of more than $9 billion of dollars, more than $5 billion of sterling, and $1 billion of other exchange assets. (This ratio of gold to deposits subject to conversion is lower than the ratio of U.S. gold holdings, whether these are defined as total gold holdings or only those in excess of legal reserve requirements, to balances held officially by foreigners.)

Members could at any time use their "excess" deposit balances to buy gold or to convert them into gold through the XIMF. Thus, expanding the functions of the IMF would not necessarily rule out future switches into gold. If members should attempt to convert "excess" deposits into gold on a substantial scale, the XIMF would then have to make gold harder to get, call for more gold from its members, or both. It could raise the level of required deposits to 25 per cent or 30 per cent of reserves, or to even higher percentages. The higher deposit requirements would reduce the amount of "excess" deposits subject to conversion and simultaneously make the high-gold-reserve countries pay in more gold. For example, an increase of 5 per cent in the deposit requirement would call for $1 billion in gold from the United States. It would even be possible, as Triffin suggests, to make the gold-reserve countries finance the XIMF gold position to a larger extent by imposing "higher deposit requirements upon that portion of each member's reserves which exceeds the average ratio of world monetary gold to world imports."[12] Thus, a desire to convert "excess" dollars into gold rather than to deposit them in the XIMF would lead to a large gold drain from the United States, while an attempt at conversion of the same sums after they had once been deposited in the XIMF could be countered—to the extent that it was not financed by drawing gold from the United States—only by making a larger proportion of XIMF deposit balances inconvertible into gold.

Before pursuing the implications of these alternatives, we may follow through the development of XIMF over the next ten years, as contemplated in the Triffin plan. . . . He suggests that the Fund's net lending should be limited "over any twelve months' period, to a total amount which would, together with current increases in the world stock of monetary gold, increase total world reserves by, let us say, 3 to 5 per cent a year." If it is assumed that monetary gold stocks increase at the rate of $700 million or $800 million a year, the annual increase in XIMF deposits would be about $800 million based upon a 3 per cent rate, $1.4 billion at a 4 per cent rate, and $2 billion at a 5 per cent rate. Triffin comments that "these estimates would rise gradually, but slowly, with further increases in world reserves. They could decrease as well as increase, on the other hand, with future fluctuations in the current additions to the world monetary gold stock."[13]

How are annual net increases of such a size to be achieved by the expanded Fund?

12 *Ibid.*, p. 114 [reproduced on p. 46].
13 *Ibid.*, p. 104 [reproduced on p. 39].

It is unlikely that they could be significantly achieved by increasing short- and medium-term loans to member countries, for there is no suggestion that the lending policy of the IMF should be changed. Indeed, "the normal procedures for Fund advances need not differ substantially from those gradually developed by the Fund over its twelve years of existence."[14] The XIMF would continue to make short- and medium-term loans to debtor and creditor countries to meet temporary balance-of-payments difficulties. But it is highly doubtful that the net increase in deposits, calculated as being required, or as being obviously noninflationary, could be achieved by self-liquidating loans to meet temporary balance-of-payments difficulties. Unchanged lending procedures should not result in a larger net volume of lending after an expansion of the functions of the IMF.

The major part, if not all, of the net increase in deposits would necessarily depend upon investments by the XIMF, and these would have to be medium- and long-term investments. The criteria for these investments would have to include, as a major element, the desired increase in international liquidity. As a matter of policy, they could not be made to any substantial extent in creditor countries that were already exporters of capital. Sending capital to them would merely increase the size of their capital-exporting activities—carry coals to Newcastle. On the contrary, the investments would have to be made in countries that were net importers of capital, that is, less developed countries. This prospect would obviously have great political appeal for such countries.

It is assumed that monetary stocks of gold in the hands of countries would increase during the next decade by $7–8 billion; thus about the same amount of additional international liquidity in the form of XIMF deposits would have to be provided by the Fund. Accordingly, Fund deposits would increase by some $8 billion in the next decade, and in the process its total assets would increase to $29 billion. Of this total, perhaps $15 billion would represent required deposits, based upon a 20 per cent factor, while the remaining $14 billion would constitute "excess" deposits, with respect to which convertibility into gold might be requested. Under the assumptions already discussed, gold holdings of the XIMF would increase little, if at all, since exchange would be deposited to the maximum extent possible to satisfy deposit requirements. However, the quality of Fund deposits, and the liquidity of the Fund as measured by gold, could, of course, be increased by raising reserve requirements. This would result

---

[14] *Ibid.*, p. 115 [reproduced on p. 47].

in a substantial increase of the Fund's gold holdings; at the same time, the legal convertibility potentialities represented by Fund deposits would be reduced.

The $8 billion increase of Fund assets would consist of foreign exchange and securities: loans to members, direct investments in member countries, and investments in the securities of organizations such as the International Bank for Reconstruction and Development. These investments would be made on the initiative of the XIMF and would also be agreed by the monetary authorities of the country concerned. Such agreement would be necessary to secure for the investments a guarantee against exchange rate changes and inconvertibility risks.

The $8 billion of additional investments in the next decade would be in addition to the $16 billion of assets (almost wholly dollar and sterling balances) with which the XIMF began operations. The gradual change in the composition of XIMF assets during this period, and the probable structure of its assets at the end of the period, are matters of considerable interest.

The XIMF would have no immediate need to modify its initial investments, i.e., the dollars and sterling initially deposited with it, but "should be empowered to do so, in a smooth and progressive manner, insofar as useful for the conduct of its own operations. This purpose would be served by giving the Fund an option to liquidate such investments at a maximum pace of, let us say, 5 per cent a year."[15] This option would be noncumulative. This percentage applied to initial XIMF dollar and sterling holdings of $15 billion would correspond to an amortization requirement for the United States and the United Kingdom of $750 million a year. These countries could buy back the securities represented by this amortization requirement by paying gold to the XIMF or by transferring XIMF deposits, i.e., by reducing their reserves or by increasing their balance-of-payments surpluses. Amortization would not necessarily have to be undertaken at once, nor would it necessarily be required every year. On the contrary, if the United States or the United Kingdom should have balance-of-payments deficits in the early years of the XIMF, holdings of dollar and

---

[15] *Ibid.*, p. 110 [reproduced on p. 42]. The *Economist* (London) commented that "Professor Triffin proposes an orderly liquidation of such balances, say by 5 per cent a year . . ." (January 9, 1960, p. 134), and a number of other commentators drew the same unqualified inference. Triffin replied in a letter (*The Economist*, January 23, 1960, pp. 304–5) describing the proposal stated here. In his letter he also wrote, "I would indeed expect the Fund to *accumulate* instead additional sterling and dollar balances in the initial years." This expectation does not appear in *Gold and the Dollar Crisis*, or in earlier writings.

sterling assets might even increase. But the logic and the language of the Triffin proposals—the many animadversions on the policy of carrying coals to Newcastle—require a persistent, though orderly, liquidation of dollar and sterling balances.

> The resources derived from their progressive liquidation, however, would normally be re-employed in other markets whose need for international capital is greater than in the United States and the United Kingdom. A portion of such investments might even be channeled into relatively long-term investments for economic development through purchases of IBRD bonds or other securities of a similar character.[16]

If this policy were carried out at a rate of 5 per cent a year, the $15 billion of sterling and dollars initially turned over to the XIMF would be reduced to perhaps $8 billion at the end of a decade. Moreover, a policy of amortizing initial dollar and sterling assets would imply that new investments in such assets should be avoided. Instead, investments would be made in the securities of other countries. Investments in less developed countries would increase even more markedly than would otherwise be necessary. Some investments might be made through intermediaries (such as the International Bank for Reconstruction and Development) and some by encouraging the financial centers in Europe (Brussels, Frankfurt, etc.) to borrow on short term and lend on long term.[17] The change in the XIMF portfolio of assets may, in broad categories, be outlined as shown in Table 1. Thus, in a decade, gold holdings would be reduced from one-fourth to one-sixth of total assets. Obligations of less developed countries might equal more than half of the total assets of the XIMF. A substantial part of these obligations would necessarily be direct, and on medium and long term to the countries themselves; some would be obligations of international agencies.

The change in the character of the structure of international reserves to be accomplished by the XIMF is outlined by this numerical illustration. The present structure consists of gold and short-term obligations of net creditor countries. The proposed structure will consist of gold and XIMF deposits; and the deposits will increasingly rest upon the medium- and long-term obligations of the net debtor countries. (If the reserve situation

---

[16] *Gold and the Dollar Crisis*, pp. 117–18 [reproduced on p. 49]; *Employment, Growth, and Price Levels*, Hearings (October 1959), Joint Economic Committee, U.S. Congress (Washington, 1959), Part 9A, p. 2912.

[17] "Altman on Triffin: A Rebuttal," in *Banca Nazionale del Lavoro Quarterly Review*, No. 56, March 1961.

TABLE 1

ASSETS OF XIMF, 1958 AND 1968

(In billions of U.S. dollars)

	End of 1958	At End of 1968, on Assumption that Reserves Grow at Rate of 3 Per Cent a Year	
		Assumption: No Liquidation of Dollar and Sterling Balances	Assumption: Reduction of Dollar and Sterling Balances by 5 Per Cent a Year
Assets = deposits	21	29	29
Gold	5	5	5
Exchange and securities....	16	24	24
Dollars and sterling.....	*15*	*15*	*8*
Other	*1*	*9*	*16*

in 1960 had been taken as a starting point, XIMF assets and deposits would be larger than shown in the table, and the composition of assets would be somewhat different. Gold would be a smaller, and dollars a larger, proportion of total assets. The point of the calculation would, however, remain unchanged.)

If this transformation is not to impair member countries' confidence in the soundness of XIMF deposits, it would be essential to reinforce these deposits by appropriate guarantees. Such guarantees play a crucial role in Triffin's proposals. All XIMF deposits would carry an exchange guarantee, expressed in a gold unit of account. If the price of gold were raised, the amount of XIMF deposits standing to the credit of each member would be increased correspondingly. If any currency were devalued relative to gold—if the gold content of any currency were reduced while the world price of gold remained the same—an XIMF deposit would then buy more units of that currency. Such arrangements involve corresponding guarantees of XIMF assets and are the same as those applicable to IMF holdings of members' currencies under Article IV, Section 8, of the IMF Articles of Agreement. Under this provision, each member is required to maintain the gold value of the IMF holdings of its currency. If the par value of its currency declines, a member must pay to the IMF additional currency sufficient to restore the original gold value of the Fund's holdings. This provision is uniform for all members. It applies to members under Article XIV and whose currencies are not convertible within the meaning of the Articles of Agreement; it applies to members under Article VIII and whose currencies are considered to be convertible. It applies whether a member does, or does not, stand ready to buy and sell gold for official purposes at stated prices.

The significance of these guarantees would change, however, as the XIMF operations proceeded. With the passage of time, an increasing proportion of its assets would consist of direct obligations of less developed countries, and obligations of investing intermediaries, such as the International Bank for Reconstruction and Development (IBRD), "older financial centers" in Europe, and the like. Whereas XIMF's investments at the beginning would be in key currencies which are widely used and which are completely convertible on external account, investments later would be in national currencies having no international circulation and which may be subject to more or fewer exchange restrictions. Though all investments would be guaranteed against devaluation, additional quantities of various currencies paid in to compensate for devaluation would hardly have the same acceptability.

There are difficulties, also, in the concept of guarantees by the investment intermediaries. Bonds issued by the IBRD carry neither an exchange nor a gold guarantee. The bonds are issued in particular currencies and are repayable in those currencies on a legal tender basis, regardless of what their gold or exchange equivalent may be at the time of repayment. Members of the IBRD guarantee to maintain the value of their capital subscriptions in terms of a gold equivalent, but the IBRD itself does not issue bonds with a gold equivalent. Nor is it clear why, under these arrangements, the older financial centers would be prepared to lend long and borrow short. They have traditionally done this in the past, but they did not have to operate then with one-sided guarantees. It seems improbable that they would be content with the arrangements proposed by Triffin, under which their obligations to the XIMF would have to be guaranteed against exchange depreciation, whereas their foreign investments would be subject to all the risks of devaluation and restrictions on exchange and capital movements.[18]

But even if it is assumed that guarantees of the kind envisaged could be secured by the XIMF, an important question remains: Would not such a prospective change in the quality of its assets, first, encourage members to keep their excess reserves in gold rather than in XIMF deposits, and second, make it more difficult to secure agreement on an increase in reserve requirements? To the extent that it had these effects, it would limit XIMF

[18] Cf. *ibid.*

banking operations and reintroduce elements of instability resulting from sizable gold flows.

An alternative to these far-reaching proposals is that, if the United States and the United Kingdom wanted to, and could, avoid any threat to the dollar and the pound by a comprehensive guarantee, such a guarantee could be negotiated specifically to meet the degree of danger apprehended. It could apply to all countries or to only a few; it could apply to all official reserves or to only that part in excess of regular working balances; it could apply to existing balances or to additions. The Triffin proposals offer no such flexibility and are much more extensive. They formally apply only to official holdings of exchange. In the event of a run, however, nonofficial holdings are quickly converted into official holdings. Moreover, official holdings may come to include speculative flights from a currency financed by bank credit. The exchange guarantee under the Triffin proposals is thus likely to be more far-reaching than any exchange guarantee that might be negotiated by any individual country acting alone.

Even after the IMF was expanded to hold the exchange reserves of its members, private exchange holdings would remain outstanding and sensitive to profit opportunities. Interest rate policies that might be pursued by the United States, the United Kingdom, or any other key currency country would continue to affect short-term capital movements. To this extent, a differentially low interest rate adopted for domestic reasons might still be put under pressure by the outflow of short-term funds. To argue that such developments would in no instance result in the outflow of gold would be to assume that countries would be willing to accumulate XIMF deposits without limit and that they would abandon their views with respect to maintaining conventional proportions of their official reserves in gold.

There are, in fact, only two ways to eliminate the threat of a demand for gold. One is to maintain a 100 per cent gold reserve for deposits. The other, as Keynes recognized, is to establish one-way convertibility, so that gold can be used to buy "bancor," but "bancor" cannot be used to buy gold.[19] A fractional gold reserve system is always subject to disturbances, and both its proximate and its ultimate stability depend upon confidence. Confidence will, in turn, reflect the opinion that the system, whether it be a gold-exchange standard or the XIMF, will be able to honor its commitments.

---

[19] This was the arrangement suggested for the International Clearing Union; see *Proceedings and Documents of the United Nations Monetary and Financial Conference* (Washington, 1948), Vol. II, p. 1565, para. 29. [See also selection 2 in this volume, esp. p. 72.]

Furthermore, the acceptability of exchange assets (even with a country guarantee) depends upon maintaining balance-of-payments discipline, which limits the quantity of national currency paid out to foreigners. Gold flows may be disturbing, but they are a rude disciplinarian. Would the XIMF do as effective a disciplinary job? And could it do such a job without acting in much the same way as gold flows do? There may well be a conflict between the requirements for stability of the exchange structure in the short run and in the long run, and particularly if one *raison d'être* for an expanded IMF is to increase the growth of international liquidity.

There is no doubt that the calculated net increases in deposits could be obtained by a Fund whose objective would be to expand international liquidity (the money supply) even if it had to acquire large amounts of long-term obligations to do so. But three points should be noted. First, adherence to a lending policy based upon self-liquidating short-term borrowings will not necessarily expand the money supply at any predetermined rate, while adherence to a policy of expanding the money supply at a predetermined rate can hardly be based upon short-run borrowings. Second, the amount of additional investment required to achieve a given expansion of XIMF deposits is not necessarily in the ratio of 1:1. It may be less than this ratio if the key currency countries have balance-of-payments deficits. It may be more than this ratio if they are using balance-of-payments surpluses to reduce currency liabilities to foreigners—specifically, dollar and sterling assets held by the XIMF. This would be the situation whenever the XIMF exercised its option to have the United States, or the United Kingdom, amortize its liabilities to the XIMF at the rate of (say) 5 per cent a year. Finally, central banks have never been willing to adopt a policy of consistently and automatically expanding the domestic money supply in line with production or national income; they have invariably used a combination of criteria; and they have sometimes considered that increases in the money supply are not required for high levels of economic activity. An expanded IMF with responsibilities to attain the international liquidity that Triffin considers adequate would be put in the position of attempting to do internationally what no central bank has been willing to attempt nationally.

International Liquidity since 1956

To put Triffin's proposals in better perspective, and to see what they could imply for the international management of financial operations, a few comments may be in order on the course of international liquidity and on the use of IMF resources since 1956. It would not be unreasonable to

TABLE 2

INDICES OF VOLUME OF IMPORTS, 1955, 1956, AND 1959

(1953 = 100)

	1955	1956	1959	Annual Increase, 1957–59* (*in per cent*)
World	118	127	144	4.3
Developed areas	119	128	150	5.4
North America	104	116	136	5.4
Western Europe	125	134	158	5.5
Less developed areas........	117	124	129	1.3

Source: United Nations, *Monthly Bulletin of Statistics*, April 1961, Special Table A.

* Rates of increase are calculated on a compound basis.

expect, as a first hypothesis, that an inadequate rate of growth of international liquidity would be accompanied (with perhaps some lag) by one or more of the following: increased use of IMF resources, pressures upon world prices and trade, deflationary policies to gain reserves, and increased resort to impediments to trade. On the other hand, it would be difficult to conclude that, if most of these indications were not present, international liquidity was growing at an inadequate rate. The three-year period beginning with 1957 has been chosen for analysis partly because Triffin suggested a version of his present proposals in 1957, in his *Europe and the Money Muddle*, and partly because 1957 and 1959 appear to represent periods in the business cycle which are not too dissimilar; but there is no question that a longer period would have advantages. In commenting upon international liquidity and the effect of Fund operations, it may be noted that drawings on the IMF are statistically equivalent to increases in international liquidity, and that repayments are equivalent to decreases; however, liabilities (repurchase obligations) resulting from drawings are not deducted from statistics on country reserves.

In the three years 1957–59, the volume of world imports expanded at an average rate of 4.3 per cent a year. Imports of developed areas increased at a rate of 5.4 per cent a year, and those of less developed areas at the rate of 1.3 per cent.[20] The rates of increase are considerably greater

[20] As is evident from Table 2, in 1957–59 imports by North America and Western Europe increased at almost the same rate. Rates of increase based upon export data tell a very different story, since they were affected by the events at Suez. World exports in 1957–59 increased by 3.8 per cent a year. Exports by regions increased as follows: 3.4 per cent for developed areas including North America (−2.8 per cent) and Western Europe (7.0 per cent); 3.6 per cent for less developed areas.

if imports are measured through the second quarter of 1960, but the differences are probably attributable mainly to cyclical influences.

The increase of world imports at the rate of 4.3 per cent a year in 1957–59 was accompanied by some price reductions. World export prices fell by 3 per cent from 1956 to 1959; export prices of developed areas decreased by 2 per cent, and those of less developed areas by 8 per cent (Table 3).

TABLE 3

INDICES OF WORLD EXPORT PRICES, 1956–60

(1953 = 100)

	1956	1957	1958	1959	1960
By commodities					
All commodities	101	103	100	98	99*
Primary commodities	100	102	96	94	94
Manufactured goods	103	106	106	106	109
By area					
Developed areas	101	104	101	99	100
Less developed areas...........	101	101	97	93	94

Source: United Nations, *Monthly Bulletin of Statistics*, March 1961, Special Table A, and April 1961, Special Table A.

* Third quarter.

The total and the ownership of international reserves were affected by many events in the period 1957–59. Fund quotas were increased from $8.9 billion at the end of 1956 to $14.0 billion at the end of 1959, with one-quarter of this increase payable in gold. The major countries of Europe took far-reaching convertibility decisions at the end of 1958. At that time, more than $1 billion of reserves vanished from reserve statistics overnight, as short-term multilateral EPU credit balances were converted into longer-term bilateral balances. There was a substantial redistribution of reserves. Gold holdings of the United States fell sharply, and its short-term dollar liabilities increased substantially. Reserves of a number of other countries, notably India, Venezuela, and Egypt, decreased; although these decreases were much smaller than the decline in U.S. gold reserves, they were very significant for the countries concerned. Western Europe, including the United Kingdom, was the beneficiary of practically all of the gross increase in reserves and of the redistribution of reserves. Measuring the useful increase in reserves therefore presents some difficulties, while evaluating the increased effectiveness of reserves presents even greater ones. A number of separate indicators of changes in world reserves are given in Table 4.

TABLE 4

INTERNATIONAL RESERVES

(In billions of U.S. dollars; data pertain to end of year)

	1956	1959	Increase, 1957–59
All countries:			
Gold	36.1	37.9	1.8
Exchange	19.4	19.0	−0.4
Total	55.5	56.9	1.4
All countries excluding the United States:			
Gold	14.0	18.4	4.4
Exchange	19.4	19.0	−0.4
Total	33.4	37.4	4.0
International institutions:			
Gold	2.0	2.3	0.3
Exchange	6.4	11.4	4.9
Total	8.4	13.7	5.2
World:			
Gold	38.1	40.2	2.1
Exchange	25.8	30.4	4.6
Total	63.9	70.6	6.7

Source: *International Financial Statistics*, January 1961.

The stock of monetary gold held by countries and international institutions increased by 5.5 per cent during the three-year period, or at the rate of 1.8 per cent a year. Countries, because of payments to the IMF in connection with enlarged quotas, increased their gold reserves at a lower rate. Aggregate exchange reserves of all countries decreased by $400 million during the period and totaled $19.0 billion at the end of 1959; the amount of Fund drawings included in exchange reserves was $450 million larger at the end of 1959 than it had been three years earlier. According to one measure of over-all reserves, namely, world holdings of gold plus country holdings of foreign exchange, reserves increased from $57.5 billion at the end of 1956 to $59.2 billion at the end of 1959, or by less than 1 per cent a year.[21]

[21] As already noted, country holdings of exchange reserves were affected by the elimination of $1.3 billion of claims on EPU after the end of 1958. If adjustment is made for this nonrecurrent event, world gold plus country exchange reserves increased by $3 billion from 1956 to 1959, or by 1.7 per cent a year.

From 1956 to 1959 there was substantial easing in the international financial situation. Reserves of the countries in continental Western Europe increased to adequate, and in some cases admittedly high, levels. The major European currencies were made externally convertible at the end of 1958 and have been further liberalized since that date. Exchange restrictions in the world at large were reduced. A number of countries, including France, improved their reserve positions notably.

The Fund approved $3.4 billion of drawings from the beginning of operations through the end of 1959; $1.3 billion of this amount was outstanding at the end of the period (Table 5). In addition, it approved $2.0 billion of stand-by arrangements under which $208 million remained available at the end of 1959 for drawings. The years 1956 and 1957 were particularly active ones, accounting for one-half of all the drawings and three-fifths of all the stand-by arrangements agreed by the Fund from the beginning of operations to the end of 1959. In contrast, drawings and stand-bys in 1958 and 1959 were much less, while repurchases and expirations of stand-bys were substantial. Drawings outstanding at the end of 1959 were $450 million more than they had been three years earlier, but amounts available under stand-by arrangements were $900 million smaller. For the purpose of assessing the ease or the tightness of international liquidity, the most appropriate measurement of Fund assistance is probably drawings outstanding plus amounts still available under stand-by arrangements. By this measure, Fund assistance decreased from $1.9 billion at the end of 1956 to $1.5 billion at the end of 1959, and decreased further in 1960 to $1.25 billion. It should not be overlooked, however, that transactions with the United Kingdom are responsible for a substantial part of this trend.

TABLE 5

SUMMARY OF TRANSACTIONS OF THE INTERNATIONAL MONETARY FUND, 1955–60

(In millions of U.S. dollars)

	1955	1956	1957	1958	1959	1960
Activity during year:						
Drawings by members........	28	693	977	338	180	280
Repurchases by members.....	232	113	64	348	573	654
Stand-by arrangements agreed.	0	1,077	183	339	315	401
Position at end of year:						
Drawings outstanding	234	814	1,727	1,696	1,268	867
Available under stand-by arrangements	62	1,117	870	911	208	383

Source: *International Financial Statistics*, January 1961.

The immediately preceding discussion may be summarized as follows: In the three years 1957–59, the volume of imports increased 4.3 per cent a year, a rate of increase which was substantial, though somewhat lower than in earlier postwar years; export prices fell slightly, but were characterized by a stability which had been regarded only a few years before as most difficult to attain; the most important European currencies were made externally convertible; the over-all level of trade restrictions was reduced; and members' use of the Fund's resources decreased after 1957. The United Kingdom, Japan, and most of the industrial countries of Western Europe improved their reserve positions, in many cases markedly, without any of the severe deflationary measures usually associated with recovery from an inadequate level of international reserves. While all of these developments were taking place, international reserves increased at a slow rate, certainly less than 2 per cent a year. If the assumption is made that international reserves should increase as fast as trade, the events of 1957–59 would appear to be inconsistent with such a low rate of growth of international liquidity.

This three-year period nevertheless saw a number of disquieting developments. Perhaps the major one was the emergence in 1958 of the large balance-of-payments deficit of the United States, a deficit which has not yet been eliminated. But no one has ever suggested that this deficit was caused by an inadequate rate of expansion of international liquidity—nor that it can be cured by an increase in international liquidity. The balance-of-payments deficit of the United States did swell the reserves of the rest of the world, and to this extent may perhaps be considered as offsetting what would otherwise have been an inadequate rate of growth of reserves. But this is only to argue against the proposition that the *total* of world reserves is the only measure of adequacy and the only basis for financial policy. The distribution of reserves among countries has on many occasions been extremely important, and a number of other elements, particularly the quality of reserves and the substitutes for or supplements to reserves, also play important roles. In any event, the increase of reserves of all countries other than the United States during 1957–59 was somewhat smaller than the increase of imports, which was itself very highly concentrated in industrial countries.[22]

[22] In 1957–59, the volume of imports for the whole world increased by 4.3 per cent a year. Imports for the world excluding North America increased by 4 per cent. (The corresponding increases for exports were 3.8 per cent and 6 per cent, respectively.) Reserves of all countries other than the United States, including the contribution to reserves made by the balance-of-payments deficit of the United States, increased at the rate of 3.8 per cent a year.

The Fund at all times has had enough resources to operate on a substantial scale. Even the large operations in 1956 and 1957 did not rule out sizable additional operations, while the smaller operations in 1958 and 1959 clearly left room for additional drawings and stand-by arrangements.

This raises several questions: Why was it that the Fund was not more active? How could the Fund have engaged in additional operations if its policy had been directed toward pumping additional liquidity into the international system in order to increase the rate of expansion of reserves to 3 per cent a year, or even to higher rates closer to the actual rate of growth of trade? Was the lending policy of the Fund too "tough" and did it leave unsatisfied a large amount of appropriate demands for drawings and stand-by arrangements? Such a charge against Fund policy has not been made. There would certainly be no agreement that Fund policy was too "tough" if its objective was to make short- and medium-term (up to five years) advances. But if the policy objective was to increase further the rate of growth of international reserves, Fund policy undoubtedly was too "tough." The required increase of reserves for the three-year period 1957–59 at a rate of only 3 per cent a year was $5.2 billion, when the smallest reserve base, i.e., country reserves of gold and exchange, is used (Table 6). Reserves of all countries increased by only $1.4 billion. On this basis the Fund should have increased net drawings outstanding (plus undrawn stand-bys?) by an additional $1.3 billion a year. At a rate of 4.3 per cent a year, i.e., the rate of growth of imports during 1957–59, country reserves of gold and exchange should have increased by $7.5 billion instead of the actual $1.4 billion. This would have required an increase of $2.0 billion a year in international reserves.

A management of the IMF operating during 1957–59 on the proposition that international reserves should increase *pari passu* with imports, and that an annual rate of increase of 3 per cent was "definitely noninflationary," would have tried to increase reserves by at least an additional $1.3 billion a year. The IMF could have achieved this objective by making additional loans to nonindustrial countries, and it could also have engaged in investment operations. A large proportion of such funds would inevitably have been spent on imports from industrial countries, probably for economic development. Whether such an expansion in this period at this rate would have been desirable and noninflationary, and whether this procedure would have been the most appropriate for attaining the desired goal, are questions that would require extended consideration.

Alternatively, XIMF lending policy might be related to the growth of

TABLE 6

REQUIRED GROWTH OF RESERVES AT VARIOUS RATES, 1957–59

(In billions of U.S. dollars)

Reserve Base	Amount at End of 1956	Actual Increase, 1957–59	Required Increase, 1957–59, at Various Rates		
			3%	4%	5%
Country gold and exchange reserves.........	55.5	1.4	5.2	6.9	8.8
World gold reserves plus country exchange reserves	57.5	1.7	5.3	7.2	9.1
Country and international institution holdings of gold and exchange...........	63.9	6.7	5.9	8.0	10.1

reserves, and the determination of reserve adequacy, as measured for countries plus all international monetary organizations (IMF, EPU/EF, and BIS).

On this basis, reserves increased by $6.7 billion in 1957–59, of which the major part ($4 billion) represented currency payments (i.e., tendering of notes payable on demand in currency) by IMF members in connection with their quota increases of 1959. The increase of $6.7 billion was more than enough to meet requirements based upon a growth of imports of 3 per cent a year, but it fell short of meeting the actual rate of 4.3 per cent by almost $800 million.[23]

The large increase of reserves was achieved by enlarging Fund quotas. Why the delivery to the Fund of $4 billion of demand notes, which may not be cashed for many years, improves world liquidity immediately, may be puzzling. The explanation probably is that the usual meaning of the term "reserves" is too restricted, and that it would be useful to introduce such a term as quasi-reserves into the analysis of the statistics. Possibly published statistics on country reserves of Fund members would be more meaningful if their gold contributions to, their creditor positions in, and their drawing rights on, the IMF were considered along with their reserve holdings of gold and exchange.

International liquidity increases when the ability to borrow increases, whether from international, national, or private sources.[24] It also follows

[23] On the basis of world reserves (Table 4), the growth of reserves required to match world imports increasing at a compound rate of 4.3 per cent a year would have totaled $8 billion.

[24] When the United Kingdom made advance repayments to the Fund in 1960, Treasury officials are reported to have observed that these repayments did not in any way weaken the United Kingdom's reserve position. The repayments were considered to be merely a trans-

that, with a given amount of borrowable resources, liquidity is greater when countries are willing to borrow than when they are not. When countries can borrow, and are willing to borrow, it is unnecessary for an international organization to force-feed liquidity into the system and into the reserve statistics, in accordance with calculated requirements based upon the growth of trade. Nor is it meaningful after the fact to compare the actual growth of reserves with the actual growth of trade. It is sufficient to ensure that the amount of quasi-reserves is large—that the lender of last resort always has some resources to lend—and to let the reported total of reserves take care of itself. Countries will then rely on reserves and quasi-reserves in the proportion that seems to them most appropriate.

Some Political and International Implications

Triffin has remarked that "there is no doubt that these reforms could be viewed as a first step toward the setting up of a supranational monetary authority, to which central banks and governments are understandably reluctant to yield any parcel of their cherished national sovereignty and independence."[25] This is a consideration which is partly real and partly fictitious, but it is not one that can be put aside. It raises a number of complex issues, of which four are briefly discussed here: the role of the XIMF in national money markets; the role of the XIMF in international investment; some political aspects of exchange guarantees; and the present and future control of the Fund.

The XIMF would inevitably have to operate in many of the world's money markets, particularly those in the United States and the United Kingdom. The XIMF would begin operations with more than $9 billion of dollar assets and more than $5 billion of sterling assets, based on data as of the end of 1958.[26] These assets consist of demand and time deposits,

---

fer from front-line reserves to secondary reserves, since they enlarged U.K. drawing rights on the Fund (*The Wall Street Journal*, September 6, 1960). Governor Cobbold of the Bank of England stated in a speech in October 1960, "I hope that we shall all get more used to regarding the International Monetary Fund as a second line of reserves. Too little importance has been attached to the very large increase in their facilities which was arranged last year, and to the part they can play in offsetting these [short-term money, O.A.] movements. . . . I should like to see countries draw on these facilities as a matter of ordinary business when they need to reinforce reserves, and repay when reserves are rising."

25 "The Twilight of the Gold Exchange Standard and the World Dollar Crisis," in *Current Economic Situation and Short-Run Outlook*, Hearings (December 7 and 8, 1960) (Joint Economic Committee, U.S. Congress, Washington, 1961), p. 238.

26 It may be noted, by way of comparison, that the Federal Reserve System owns $27 billion of U.S. Government securities and all commercial member banks another $27 billion (data are for November 1960, from the *Federal Reserve Bulletin*, December 1960).

and short- and long-term government securities. Management of these portfolios would require many Fund decisions: to keep deposits in some banks rather than others, to hold assets in cash or to invest, and to vary the proportion of investments between short-term and long-term securities. Decisions of this sort could affect both the level and the structure of interest rates; they would be reinforced by exercise of the option to demand the annual liquidation of up to 5 per cent of XIMF holdings of dollars and sterling, equal to $500 million of dollars and $250 million of sterling.

The Triffin proposals would greatly increase the amount of internationalized investment. The decisions to invest, and the directions and the terms of investment, would be taken by the governing authorities of the XIMF. If the XIMF did not wish to make all of its investments directly in member countries, it could invest indirectly, through such other international agencies as the IBRD. The investments (apart from reinvestments) would be made with credit newly created by the XIMF; the real resources that would be bought with these funds would come from countries, very largely from developed countries. Injections of bank credit might be helpful if countries were in a recession, and inflationary if their resources were fully employed or if there were important bottlenecks in production. In either case, countries would have to readjust their ratios of domestic to overseas availabilities, and of savings to investment, in order to meet these additional export demands.

The political problems involved in negotiating an exchange guarantee of the scope proposed by Triffin are probably enormous in creditor countries with short-term foreign liabilities, particularly the United States and the United Kingdom. The long-term foreign investments of these countries are valued at billions of dollars. They are several times as large as foreign holdings of dollars and sterling. All of these investments in securities and business enterprises are exposed to risks: devaluation, changes in business policy and taxation, and, in some cases, the more than negligible possibilities of expropriation and "intervention." Countries with large foreign investments may well be unwilling that their own investments should not be guaranteed, but that external holdings of their currencies should be.

Finally, brief mention should be made of the membership of the Fund, now and in the future. The significance of stipulated voting majorities (one-half, two-thirds, three-fourths, etc.) depends very much upon the size of the XIMF, the number of its members, and voting rights once quotas are abolished. The membership of the Fund has increased substantially since 1946. It may well continue to increase. The Soviet Union attended the

Bretton Woods Conference, and its quota then agreed was slightly less than that of the United Kingdom and almost 15 per cent of the total. Czechoslovakia and Poland were original members of the Fund with combined quotas equal to almost 3 per cent of the total. These three countries could conceivably be admitted to membership in the XIMF under political conditions which cannot now be predicted. Other communist countries also could become members; and less developed countries that already have attained independent status, or that may do so in the future, may join the XIMF. These potential additions to membership should be carefully considered when it is proposed that the XIMF be given the power to create credit, to make international investments, and to exercise important powers in money markets.

The implications of Triffin's proposal are far-reaching. An international agency would be authorized to manage and systematically expand the international money supply. The character of the Fund's operations would be changed to facilitate expansion of international liquidity at what is conceived to be an adequate rate. The expanded Fund would have authority to create new money in the form of deposits, which would to an increasing extent rest on investments in underdeveloped net debtor countries. The process of creating deposits would involve drafts on the real resources of other members, largely the developed countries, and it could readily become inflationary. The character of the assets of the expanded IMF would increasingly be changed from currency holdings and three- to five-year loans, conceived to be self-liquidating and revolving, into medium- and long-term loans which would have a different character. These changes would rest on important exchange guarantees. They could involve intervention of the XIMF in the money markets of the United States, the United Kingdom, and perhaps other countries. They would involve changes in the sources of funds for, and in decisions over, long-term investment. The authority to require gradual liquidation of dollar and sterling balances would reduce either the gold reserves or the long-term capital exporting ability of the United States and the United Kingdom. The expanded IMF would inevitably be less liquid than the present one, and this might raise questions about its ability to create deposits as good as gold and to provide the key currencies that members may need, unless reserve deposit requirements are raised and the gold contributions of a few members increased far beyond the level initially proposed.

These far-reaching changes, and others which can be foreseen only dimly, are based upon findings of the dangerous state of, and prospects for, international liquidity. The proposals are based upon a simplified view of the statistics on reserves and trade that does not reflect such important factors as the distribution of reserves, the change in the quality of exchange assets, the state of balance of international trade and exchange rates, and the growing role of the IMF. At best, these findings of serious reserve deficiency are unproven; at worst, they are incorrect, at least for the next five or ten years. It may be argued that ten years is not a long time, and that the world should now anticipate developments over a much longer period. As to this, opinions differ. Since 1900 there have been many forecasts of reserve requirements based upon the rate of growth of trade. With practically no exceptions, these forecasts concluded that reserves would soon become inadequate, and that this inadequacy would cause deflation. There have been many forecasts since World War II of growing inadequacy. The remedies for this inadequacy have ranged from proposals to increase liquidity by raising the price of gold to Triffin's proposal to create a new kind of international deposit money. Yet for a large part of this period the problem was inflation, not deflation. Reasonable price stability, if it has indeed been achieved, is of recent date. Such threats as there are to this stability hardly stem from the side of deflation.

These comments in no way imply that international liquidity does not present many difficult problems. However, there is reason to believe that, in view of the recovery already made, the lines of development pursued in the postwar period offer the best chance for further progress. The international financial machinery has proved to be flexible and adaptable. Within its terms of reference, or with relatively small changes in them (compared with the large and controversial changes proposed by Triffin), this machinery is capable of further growth and adjustment. The IMF with its enlarged resources and its proven type of operation provides the guidance and monetary support that should facilitate further expansion and stability of the structure of international reserves.

7

International Monetary Reform and the New York Banking Community

DAVID ROCKEFELLER

I propose to address [this paper] primarily to the problem of international liquidity and to the changes in the international financial structure that may be necessary to deal with this problem. In doing so, I do not in any way wish to minimize the gravity of the balance-of-payments problem [the U.S.] faces, or the urgency of effective steps to achieve a viable balance in [the] international payments accounts. However, [it has been suggested that I discuss] the role of New York as an international reserve center. Thus, I [will] concentrate on the problem of what may need to be done to improve the world payments mechanism, since that ties in closely to the questions . . . posed.

DIAGNOSIS OF THE PROBLEM

At the outset, it seems to me important that we recognize that [the U.S.] faces two separate tasks in the international financial area. We must first deal with our balance-of-payments problem, for I do not believe there are any effective devices which could long withstand large continuing deficits on the part of the world's biggest trading nation and major reserve currency center.

However, success in bringing our basic payments position into balance will not solve the problem of international liquidity. That problem can be defined this way: We seek a world financial structure which will withstand short-term pressures against key currencies and meet the longer-term need for an adequate supply of assets acceptable in international payments.

This paper was prepared for the Joint Economic Committee's Subcommittee on International Exchange and Payments. It was published in the Committee's volume of Hearings on the topic *International Payments Imbalances and Need for Strengthening International Financial Arrangements*, U.S. Congress (Washington, 1961). This reprint has been made possible through the courtesy of Mr. Rockefeller.

The immediate problem is to improve the world payments mechanism to prevent short-term capital movements from becoming disruptive. In normal times, such movements perform a constructive function in financing international payments. However, short-term capital movements can place excessive pressure on any key currency where the country involved is experiencing temporary balance-of-payments deficits. Such capital movements are also highly sensitive to differentials in short-term interest rates. This fact restricts the ability of monetary authorities to ease money and credit in a recession since such action could drive down short-term interest rates and encourage an outflow of short-term capital. Consequently, we will face a problem of international liquidity even after our basic payments position has been righted.

This problem of short-term liquidity has arisen for two reasons. First, the spread of convertibility among industrial nations has made it possible to shift short-term funds from one market to another in response to interest-rate differentials, or in response to changes in the appraisals which holders of such funds make of prospects in various money markets. In many ways, this is a healthy development. Currency convertibility has been one of our foreign policy goals because of the benefits it brings in the form of more effective competition and enlarged trade. The greater mobility of short-term capital makes it possible to handle a much larger volume of trade and investments than was the case before the spread of convertibility. However, it does pose the problem I mentioned earlier of finding ways to keep such capital shifts within proper bounds.

A second reason for concern over the problem of short-term international liquidity lies in the change in the position of the United States. In the earlier postwar period, the dollar was universally regarded as invulnerable. The dollar was the leading reserve currency since dollar holdings could earn interest and were convertible into gold at a fixed price. Thus, foreign dollar holdings were built up from $8.6 billion to $21.4 billion between 1950 and the end of 1960.

This build-up in U.S. short-term liabilities, which has supplied a massive dose of needed international liquidity, now poses problems to the United States. The dollar is no longer invulnerable to any and all circumstances, as is shown clearly by developments of the past two years when the dollar has been under pressure.

In a sense, the position of our nation is somewhat like that of a commercial bank. The United States had demand liabilities at the end of last year amounting to $21.4 billion. Against these liabilities the nation held $17.8 billions of gold, of which nearly $12 billion was earmarked to back

Federal Reserve notes and deposits. U.S. long-term foreign investments are, of course, very substantial. But these long-term investments cannot be liquidated to cover short-term claims against the United States.

Thus, the United States has reached a point where it must be concerned about the pace and extent of the increase in its short-term foreign liabilities. The nation's reserves are large in relation to our trade and our short-term liabilities. Yet they are not so large in relation to the pressures that could be placed on them by short-term capital movements as to leave room for complacency. For that reason, the United States has a genuine interest in measures to improve the world financial mechanism to deal with the problem of short-term international liquidity.

If such a mechanism can be developed, the longer-term liquidity position of the world would appear to be satisfactory for at least the near-term future. Much has been made of the fact that official gold stocks have been growing at an average annual rate of 2 per cent while world trade has been expanding at a 5 per cent rate. However, there is no simple and mechanical relationship between the growth of trade and reserves. In large part because of the massive injections of dollars into foreign reserves in recent years, world liquidity is high in relation to world trade. As I shall say later, this may be a problem to watch in the years ahead. But it does not appear to be the problem to focus on at the moment.

REMEDIES ANALYZED

What, then, should be done about the short-term liquidity problem? Four approaches have been suggested to improve the world's financial mechanism: (1) increase the price of gold; (2) strengthen the present mechanism by internal measures and by increased cooperation among key-currency nations; (3) expand the scope of the IMF by increasing quotas and enlarging its power to borrow currencies in surplus; and (4) convert the IMF into a world central bank.

While an increase in the price of gold would appear to be a simple and direct solution, it actually has significant disadvantages. The gains from a mark-up in the price of gold would accrue chiefly to South Africa and the Soviet Union, the two largest gold producers, and to the Western industrial nations which hold gold. Lesser developed nations would receive minor benefits since they hold little gold. Nations holding their reserves in key currencies would find that these reserves would be worth less in terms of gold. Any hint of a possible gold price change would set off a widespread and disruptive speculative move. Consequently, the case against raising the price of gold is most persuasive.

A second approach would involve building on the present mechanism to bolster the ability of key currencies to withstand pressures. Since the dollar is a key currency, it is important to consider what might be done to strengthen the position of the United States as an international banker. There are a number of steps which could be taken unilaterally, and several others which would require international cooperation.

A first step which we could take would be to remove the requirement that gold be held against the note and deposit liabilities of the Federal Reserve banks. The Commission on Money and Credit discussed this problem at length, and I should like to quote the Commission's recommendation:

"The Commission believes that the threat of a confidence crisis would be greatly reduced if it were generally recognized, both here and abroad, that all of the U.S. gold is available to meet our international obligations. Any doubts about U.S. policy should be removed by elimination of the gold reserve requirement at the earliest convenient moment so that all of the U.S. gold stock is available for international settlements."

As a second measure I believe that continued efforts should be made to hold prices on the London gold market from rising unduly and thereby encouraging increased speculation. The speculation in the London market last fall, which drove the price of gold above $40 an ounce temporarily, was a factor that helped accelerate the outflow of short-term capital from this country. The U.S. Treasury (acting through the Federal Reserve) and perhaps other central banks as well, can cooperate with the Bank of England in efforts to prevent extreme moves in the gold price. The resulting cost may be low in comparison to the damage that can be done to confidence through wide speculative moves in the price.

U.S. domestic economic policies can also be adapted to reduce the pressure of short-term capital outflows in a period of recession. Such outflows are importantly influenced by differentials in short-term interest rates as between the United States and other industrial nations. The Federal Reserve can supply necessary reserves to the banking system by open-market purchases of intermediate-term securities, thus reducing short-term rates less than would be the case if short-term securities were purchased. The Federal Reserve has been following this policy in recent months and I believe the record shows that it has been generally successful.

At the same time, greater reliance on fiscal measures could reduce the amount of monetary ease needed to facilitate business recovery. The re-

sulting deficits could be financed with short-term securities, which would
help keep short-term interest rates from declining to unusually low levels.
The use of short-term financing by the Treasury is an appropriate procedure
in a recession.

Regulation Q, under which the Federal Reserve sets ceilings on interest
rates which commercial banks can pay on time deposits, should be revised
to enable commercial banks to compete more effectively with interest rates
abroad, and thus be better able to retain holdings of foreign dollars in the
United States. This is particularly important in the case of large dollar
holdings of foreign central banks and official institutions, some of which
might otherwise be converted into gold.

Steps can also be taken to reduce the profitability and hence the volume
of short-term capital flows. To avoid the foreign exchange risk, those who
shift short-term funds abroad frequently cover themselves through purchases of dollars in the forward market. By operating in this market, U.S.
authorities could increase the cost of purchasing forward dollars, perhaps
to the point where shifting funds would not be worth while. This would
increase the risks of temporary movements of funds and reduce the volume.
U.S. authorities could cover their short position by borrowing from the
IMF or from foreign central banks. Such operations have been carried on
recently in German marks.

Several other steps could be taken by agreement among the six or eight
countries which are the main holders of foreign currencies. Central banks
could agree to hold other currencies for limited periods rather than convert them into gold. This would reduce the possibility of an exchange crisis
arising from large shifts of short-term funds. Such cooperative arrangements among central banks have been used in part to cover the shifts in
funds following the German revaluation.

It seems to me that the key-currency approach is a constructive one.
The experience now being accumulated through cooperative efforts could
pave the way for further steps to improve the world financial structure.

However, I believe we must soon take such further steps to develop a
structure that will withstand the massive movements of short-term funds
which are now possible as well as to meet eventual needs for a growing
volume of international reserves. I believe the most effective approach lies
through strengthening the International Monetary Fund along the general
lines proposed by Mr. Bernstein. . . .

It seems to me that these proposals would, if they could be adopted
on the proper scale, deal with the problems we confront in the foreseeable
future. It would be possible for key currency countries to rely on drawings

from the Fund to finance temporary exchange deficits, since the Fund would be in a position to extend credits in the currencies required. Thus, such nations would have an incentive to integrate their Fund quotas with their reserves. The use of Fund drawings to finance shifts of short-term funds would greatly reduce the possibility of an exchange crisis. Such an arrangement would also provide an incentive to surplus countries to adopt policies to reduce their surpluses. They would have an incentive to increase their imports of goods and services, or engage directly in international aid or investment, rather than to provide funds to the IMF for the use of other countries. The fact of borrowing from the Fund, plus the cost, would give deficit countries an incentive to take steps to eliminate the deficit.

For some years ahead, increased reliance on the Fund, plus new gold production, could cover the needs for increasing liquidity. If necessary, it would be possible to increase country quotas, as was done in 1959. As I said earlier, I do not believe that there is any immediate problem of a shortage of over-all liquidity in the sense that world reserves of gold and foreign exchange will be inadequate to finance the potential expansion in trade.

At the same time we must not lose sight of this as a long-run problem. Forecasts in this field are notoriously hazardous and unreliable, so I would hesitate to make the judgment that increased reliance on the Fund can solve for all time the problem of liquidity. But I do feel that it can be sufficient in the years immediately ahead. I would caution only that this is a problem that must be kept under surveillance.

It is implicit in what I have said that I do not believe we need go to the extreme of a world central bank, as proposed by Professor Triffin, to deal with the problem of liquidity in the years immediately ahead. Looking into the distant future, it may well be that we should work toward the eventual development of a world central bank. Virtually all national banking systems have evolved toward a central banking system as the most effective and efficient way to operate a financial mechanism. However, I doubt that the world has reached a point where the member nations of a central bank could be counted on to maintain the discipline in their financial policies needed to make such a bank successful.

Moreover, I believe the Triffin proposal has a number of serious disadvantages. I am sure you have heard the general arguments against the Triffin plan so I will mention some of them only briefly, and then turn to its effects on the New York money market.

To my mind, the most telling general arguments against the Triffin proposal can be summed up in the following manner:

First, the cost to the United States would be high in terms of reducing our freedom of action in financing any balance-of-payments deficits. If the Triffin plan had been in effect, the United States would have been under great pressure to reduce its payments deficits in recent years. Yet the fact that foreign recipients of dollars have been willing to hold a good part of them has enabled this country to carry on programs of foreign aid, investment, and military assistance that have been in the national interest. In the future, the Triffin plan would mean that the United States would give up the possibility of financing at least a part of a temporary balance-of-payments deficit through the further build-up of dollar holdings by other countries.

Second, the gold guarantee of deposits in the Fund Bank and of its investments imposes a high price on the United States. Circumstances could arise under which it would severely constrict our freedom of action because of our large liabilities to foreign holders of dollars. The fact of this huge commitment might push us into restrictive domestic policies well before such policies would be genuinely needed.

A third general objection is that the political and technical problems involved are formidable. It is far from clear that the technical knowledge exists to operate a world central bank without complicating unduly the problems of maintaining prosperity and growth without inflation throughout the free world. I doubt whether most countries, including the United States, would be willing at this time to delegate to an international agency the powers necessary to operate a world central bank.

Over time, many of these problems might be overcome, given the continued cooperation among members of the world financial community. To a large extent the problems are political as well as technical. Certainly nothing like a world central bank would be feasible unless or until a closer economic alliance had been achieved, at least within the Atlantic Community. At the same time I feel that there are many technical and operational problems that would have to be solved before a world central bank could operate properly. Thus, I believe the proper approach is one of evolution through increased international cooperation along the lines I suggested earlier.

THE TRIFFIN PLAN'S IMPACT ON NEW YORK BANKS

Some of the technical problems involved can be highlighted by considering the impact of the Triffin plan on the New York money market. As a practical matter the first problem would arise during the extended period of delicate negotiation which would be involved in trying to work through an agreement to establish a world central bank. This would be a period of great uncertainty, in which an upsetting move out of key currencies into gold might develop. The New York banks would face the possibility that their foreign deposits—as much as 15 per cent of their total deposits— might be withdrawn on short notice. Even if the Federal Reserve should move to counter such a withdrawal if it occurred, such action would affect the banking system as a whole and New York banks could face a painful readjustment.

Assuming that the Triffin plan were put into operation with no such anticipatory moves, foreign central banks would transfer to the new Fund Bank almost $2 billion of foreign official deposits now held in New York by commercial banks, plus a substantial amount of short-term investments (treasury bills, acceptances, etc.) held by these banks for their foreign correspondents. From that point on, additional dollars secured by foreign central banks would be deposited with the Fund Bank.

Thus, the New York banks would be in a position of dealing with the Fund Bank rather than with central banks around the world. Each commercial bank's share of international deposits would depend, not on its competitive ability and the quality of the service it rendered, but on the decision of the Fund Bank acting in agreement with U.S. authorities. Long-established relationships based on mutual confidence and services rendered over many years would be disrupted. In all probability, the Fund Bank's deposits in the United States would be allocated on some quota basis which would act to penalize banks that had performed the larger share of the services involved in international banking.

One such service is the loans New York City banks have made to both government institutions and private organizations abroad. In many cases these credits filled pressing needs which could not have been met from any other source. It was possible for New York City banks to extend them because of long-standing relationships abroad and because of the large deposits which foreign central banks and official institutions have maintained in New York. If the banks held such deposits for the account of the Fund, rather than for foreign banks directly, it is very doubtful that New York City banks could continue to assist foreign countries with necessary credits to the degree they have in the past.

Another source of uncertainty would relate to what the Fund Bank might do with its deposits and how its operations might affect nonofficial foreign dollar holdings. The Fund Bank's right to liquidate its dollar holdings, even if it were used sparingly or not at all, would introduce a new dimension of uncertainty into the New York money market. While it would undoubtedly be possible to adjust over time to such changes, the adjustment would certainly not be easy, and it could interfere with the ability of the New York banks to provide their traditional services to domestic and oversea customers.

[This analysis leads to another question:] Is the role of New York as an international financial center a source of strength or weakness to the United States? I would say that it is an important source of strength. I believe the United States must exercise a role of leadership in international financial matters. This is a part—an important part—of our role in con-tributing to the defense and development of the free world.

I believe that the New York commercial banks and the New York money market institutions are now making a considerable contribution to these broad national objectives. A major part of the financing of our exports and imports of goods and services—a total of some $50 billion a year—is handled in New York. This involves a tremendous amount of detailed work and expert knowledge. Financing foreign trade is a business for specialists who possess the knowledge, ability, and experience to handle transactions throughout the world. These skills have played an important part in making the United States the world's largest trader. And it should be remembered that our foreign trade is many times the size of our foreign aid, so our impact on the rest of the world through our trade and its financ-ing is a most significant part of our over-all foreign relations.

In addition, New York commercial banks and investment houses have provided the means through which many foreign governments and foreign businesses have obtained funds essential to their financial and economic progress. At the end of 1960 private loans and portfolio investments from the United States to other countries amounted to no less than $15 billion, and the great bulk of this financing was organized through the financial community in New York.

New and flexible means are constantly being sought to increase the effectiveness of international financing. One such development has been the formation of venture capital investment companies. These companies perform a unique role in setting up joint ventures to develop private busi-ness abroad. Typically, such a venture might include participation by a U.S. manufacturing corporation to provide technical knowledge as well as part of the capital, the venture capital company, and investors from the host country. The Chase Manhattan Bank has had such a facility operating in the past few years in the form of an Edge Act subsidiary, the Chase International Investment Corporation. There are also a number of similar ventures. Another example is provided by the efforts now under way by commercial banks and insurance companies to work out procedures to provide export credit insurance and medium-term export credits in cooperation with the Export-Import Bank.

Finally, New York City provides the institutional mechanism necessary to make the United States the great reserve currency center of the world. It is not only the banks which are involved, but the money market as a whole—the Government securities market and the dealers who are an integral part of it, the market for commercial paper, acceptance and other short-term paper. This complex mechanism provides safe, liquid investments which attract and retain foreign exchange reserves from foreign commercial and central banks from all over the world. The dollar in consequence of this, and because of the basic strength of the United States, is used as a currency to finance trade, investments, and other transactions in many areas of the world.

All of these matters not only have important economic implications for the United States but also add to the political strength and position of leadership of the United States in world affairs. Today New York City in many ways is the financial center of the world. That is an inevitable accompaniment of the nation's position in political and military affairs. We cannot have the one without the other.

8

The Triffin Plan:
Diagnosis, Remedy, and Alternatives

LELAND B. YEAGER

DIAGNOSIS

Professor Robert Triffin's diagnosis of and prescription for international monetary ills have been commanding widespread attention, including that of the Kennedy administration. The next few years are likely to see far-reaching decisions made on international monetary organization. The Triffin plan and its alternatives warrant the careful consideration that its author himself has called for.[1]

As world income and trade continue to grow, Triffin argues, countries will need more and more international liquidity (gold and foreign exchange) to finance temporary deficits in their balances of payments. Experience punctures any hope that gold production alone can fully meet this need.[2] For decades, many countries have been "economizing" on gold by also holding key currencies, particularly sterling and dollars, in their international reserves. In the last decade, gold production has provided hardly more than one-third of the growth of international liquidity held

Reprinted from *Kyklos*, XIV (1961), Fasc. 3, through the courtesy of the publisher and author.

[1] See his testimony before the Joint Economic Committee, October 1959, in *Employment, Growth, and Price Levels*, Hearings, U.S. Congress (Washington, 1959), Part 9A; his *Gold and the Dollar Crisis* (New Haven: Yale University Press, 1960), which permits part of the 1959 testimony; and his testimony and related material in Hearings before the Joint Economic Committee, U.S. Congress, December 1960, entitled *Current Economic Situation and Short-Run Outlook* (Washington, 1961), pp. 170–260. Without implicating them, the present author thanks Professors Alexandre Kafka and Daniel Edwards for reading an earlier draft of this paper and making valuable comments.

[2] Assuming, of course, the continued growth of world trade and the avoidance both of price-level deflation and of increases in the price of gold. For some of the many persuasive arguments against a gold price increase—which this paper will not consider further as an alternative to the Triffin plan—see *Gold and the Dollar Crisis*, pp. 81–82.

by countries outside the United States; the great bulk of this growth has come from American gold losses and, in particular, from increased foreign holdings of American liquid liabilities.[3] This system requires a paradoxical flow of capital. While the United States is providing private foreign investment and government loans and grants to other countries, these other countries—many of them quite poor in comparison—are at the same time providing free or cheap loans *to* the United States by acquiring accounts in American banks, U.S. Government securities, and similar liquid claims.

A still more patent "absurdity"[4] of existing arrangements has been dramatized by the balance-of-payments troubles of the United States from 1958 on. Over the long run, the key-currency countries must have deficits to expand the reserves of other countries. Yet the key-currency countries thereby incur ever larger liquid liabilities to foreigners; as a percentage of these liabilities, and perhaps in absolute amount also, their gold reserves become smaller and smaller. While there simply is not enough gold for all countries to hold their international reserves in gold alone, the monetary authority of any individual country, acting by itself, is free to hold as much of its reserve in gold as it wishes. The only real incentive (apart from international cooperation and the like) for holding some or most of the reserve in key currency instead is its convenience and interest yield. Precisely because of its reasons for holding any international reserves in the first place and because of its own sophistication, a national monetary authority will actively consider getting rid of a key currency whose gold parity seems shaky. If more key currencies than one serve as international reserves, the rush may be from the weaker to the stronger. If the threatened key currency has no rivals, the rush will be into gold. The 1931 monetary collapse shows how history might some day repeat itself.

To maintain confidence in its currency and avoid a flight from it, a key-currency country must watch its balance-of-payments position closely, as the United States is doing today, and must perhaps take action to cure deficits. But in doing so, it restricts the growth of international liquidity in the form of foreign holdings of its currency.

In summary, Triffin finds that under existing arrangements, long-run balance-of-payments deficits of key-currency countries are both necessary yet alarming. This haphazard system is fated to become more and more precarious as time goes on.

[3] *Gold and the Dollar Crisis*, pp. 54–55; *Current Economic Situation*, pp. 209–10. [See pp. 29, 30 of this volume.]
[4] *Gold and the Dollar Crisis*, p. 67.

TRIFFIN'S PROPOSAL

The remedy Triffin prescribes is worth considering not only for its own sake but also for the deeper insight it provides into his diagnosis. Countries belonging to the International Monetary Fund would initially be encouraged to transfer parts of their foreign exchange holdings to the Fund in return for deposits with it. We need not describe the suggested details of negotiating and carrying out a piecemeal and gradual transition; we can best appraise the new system by considering its logical extension to its final form. Ultimately, countries would hold substantially all of their official international reserves—beyond some maximum allowable gold percentage—in the form of deposits with an expanded International Monetary Fund (hereafter called XIMF[5]). The XIMF could pay its members interest on their deposits because it would be earning interest on the foreign exchange assets initially transferred to it and on the other loans and investments that it would subsequently acquire. International settlements nowadays made by official transfers of gold and key currencies would be made, under the new system, by transfers of deposits at the XIMF. Central banks could draw on their XIMF deposits to obtain currencies actually needed for their stabilizing interventions in the foreign exchange markets.

Deposits at the XIMF would constitute a new international money, perhaps known as "bancor" (the name suggested by Keynes in his plan of 1943 for an international clearing union). [See selection 2 of this volume.] Bancor, gold, and national currencies would all have fixed parities in terms of one another, though individual countries might presumably change their own parities, as under existing IMF rules, in infrequent cases of "fundamental disequilibrium." The XIMF would be a central bank for central banks, adjusting the total supply of bancor to the liquidity needs of the world economy. It could expand the bancor supply gradually over time by making loans and acquiring securities, just as a national central bank can expand the national stock of currency and commercial bank reserve funds. Under the new system, the total supply of bancor, and therefore of bancor plus gold, could be subjected to a rational management impossible for gold alone or for gold and foreign exchange.

The Triffin plan stems from a perceptive diagnosis of existing ills.[6] Its

---

[5] Following the example of Oscar Altman in his penetrating critique of the plan reprinted in *Current Economic Situation*, pp. 175–207. [See also selection 6 of this volume.]

[6] One reservation about the diagnosis, however, must be developed later on. The essen-

adoption probably would represent a genuine improvement. It would convert a dilemma into a mere problem: the United States could strive to remedy its balance-of-payments deficit without threatening to strangle the growth of international liquidity. Still, there is ample reason for accepting Triffin's invitation to discuss his plan in the light of possible improvements or alternatives. The plan would expand governmental institutions and discretionary authority and thus depart still further from the ideal of simplicity and automaticity in social and economic arrangements. Its adoption would be difficult to reverse. We may quickly pass over the obvious points connected with expansion of the staff of the International Monetary Fund and the self-perpetuating character of governmental and international organizations—tendencies described by Parkinson's Law. What requires emphasis is that when the XIMF had come to have a large volume of deposit liabilities, backed only fractionally by gold and with much of the other assets being long-term loans and securities, liquidating it and repaying the depositors would be awkward. This is especially true because the scheme would ultimately have become dependent on *requiring* member countries to hold no more than a specified percentage of their total reserves in gold. If one or more economically important members wanted to withdraw from the scheme, the XIMF would find itself in difficulties, especially in view of the guarantee of the gold value of their deposits extended to all members. To safeguard the scheme and protect all other members, it might be essential to forbid any country to withdraw, ever. Countries would probably be unwilling to commit themselves so irrevocably; but even if they did make the commitment, some future government of some important country might still possibly repudiate it. The Triffin plan is no stopgap to be tried pending invention of something better. As a practical matter, its adoption would block any fundamentally different solution to the world liquidity problem. It is much more fully true of the Triffin plan than of economic reform proposals generally that we cannot afford to experiment, hoping to guide ourselves by how the plan works out in practice. It is necessary to reason out, in advance, how the plan is likely to work.

---

tial trouble nowadays is not the use of national currencies as international liquidity, but the use as international liquidity of national currencies *precariously tied to gold on a fractional-reserve basis.* Triffin does not make this distinction because he takes for granted the continued pegging of currencies to gold. Some criticisms (e.g., "World Shortage of Money?" First National City Bank of New York, *Monthly Letter*, March 1961, pp. 31–35) dispute whether there actually is any liquidity problem. Perhaps Triffin's diagnosis is a bit premature, but it is hardly fanciful.

GOLD UNDER THE TRIFFIN PLAN

The plan would allot a peculiar role to gold. National currencies would be pegged to bancor (XIMF deposits), which would in turn be pegged to gold. The needed long-run growth of international liquidity would make gold become an ever smaller fraction of bancor deposits. In the Joint Economic Committee Hearings of December 1960, Representative Coffin in fact asked Professor Triffin: "In view of your analysis of the failure of gold supply to keep up with the business of the world, would you not run into a problem; maybe we would be delaying the problem by decades, but to the extent that we may be building on a gold exchange guarantee we are basically coming back to the Achilles' heel of the system as you see it?"[7]

The answer has two interlocking parts: (1) the so-called gold or exchange guarantee will prevent any loss of confidence that might touch off a run from bancor into gold, and (2) anyway, the XIMF will narrowly limit the convertibility of bancor into gold for purposes of hoarding. XIMF deposits would be expressed in a gold unit and thus escape foreign exchange risk. The depositor "is guaranteed against devaluation . . . and will always get the same amount measured in terms of gold; in case, for instance, of a devaluation his currency deposit would be increased to make up for the devaluation."[8] The XIMF would be able to guarantee the gold value of its deposit liabilities because, for one thing, the gold values of its assets would also be guaranteed: countries that had borrowed from the Fund would (as is also true under existing rules) owe a debt fixed in gold and unchanged by any devaluation of national currency, and countries in which the Fund made investments would also guarantee the Fund against loss through devaluation of their currencies.[9]

It is unlikely that debtor countries would ever default on their guarantee of any sizable fraction of the Fund's assets. But if such a thing *should* happen, would it not weaken the Fund's ability to protect its own depositors? A more fundamental question is this: What could conceivably happen that could force the XIMF to devalue bancor in terms of gold and yet leave it able to honor its gold guarantee of deposits? If a lack of gold in the Fund should ever force a devaluation, how could the Fund nevertheless stand ready to give its members just as much gold per unit of bancor

---

[7] *Current Economic Situation*, p. 246. Compare the similar worry expressed by Oscar Altman on page 187 of the same Hearings.

[8] Triffin, *ibid.*, p. 246; cf. *Gold and the Dollar Crisis*, p. 105 [reproduced on p. 40].

[9] Triffin in *Current Economic Situation*, p. 212; Altman, *ibid.*, pp. 190, 200.

as before? And guarantee or no guarantee, how could the Fund overcome the fact that there ultimately just would not be enough gold in existence to redeem any sizable fraction of its members' deposits?

The XIMF will *not* stand ready, after all, to redeem its deposits in gold, except subject to very narrow limitations. As Triffin has himself said of the gold guarantee, "It does not necessarily mean that a depositor would be entitled to take gold out of the Fund in exchange for his deposit." "Provision would have to be made to safeguard the Fund's liquidity both against unforeseen conversions of excess deposits into gold and, in the long run, against the increasing gap between the probable level of world gold stocks and the desirable expansion of over-all monetary reserves."[10] Specifically, members would be required to hold ever larger fractions of their total international reserves in bancor and would be permitted to hold ever smaller fractions in gold.[11] The Fund's ability to satisfy all legitimate demands for conversion of bancor into gold would be safeguarded by defining "legitimate" demands very narrowly and ultimately even by requiring national monetary authorities to turn over to the Fund most of any new gold they might acquire.

Increasingly tight restrictions on gold ownership by national monetary authorities would almost certainly require an accompanying ban on private gold ownership in all member countries. Otherwise, governments might sometimes have an incentive to exercise whatever limited right they still retained to redeem bancor in gold in order to resell the gold to their own citizens. In so doing, they could mop up domestic liquidity when they considered it excessive and could at the same time keep the gold outside their official reserves in calculating the volume of XIMF deposits that they were required to hold.

The need to ban private as well as limit official gold ownership emphasizes how little the fixed gold content of money units would still mean operationally. What is the difference, really, between saying that a dollar is worth 1/35 of an ounce of gold but that no one can have the gold and saying that a dollar is worth 1/50 of an ounce of gold but that no one can have the gold? The only real difference is in the degree of subsidy to gold mining. As rights to redeem XIMF deposits in gold became ever more narrow, the gold guarantee of the bancor unit would likewise become ever more completely a matter of empty words.

---

[10] Triffin, *ibid.*, p. 246; *Gold and the Dollar Crisis*, p. 114 [reproduced on p. 45].

[11] It is unnecessary to consider here the details of the form in which these requirements would be expressed, or the rules for voting or otherwise deciding on each successive tightening. On these matters, see *Gold and the Dollar Crisis*, pp. 114–15.

The original logic of a gold standard was to safeguard the value of money by linking the amount of money to something that could not be simply printed but had to be laboriously produced. The linkage was to be kept fairly definite by using gold coins in actual circulation and keeping all kinds of money redeemable in them. Redeemability and a concern for their reserves would keep the authorities cautious in creating money and in permitting its creation by the banks. Almost all of the countries returning to what they supposed to be a gold standard after World War I weakened this linkage and increased the pyramiding of money on a narrow gold base by withdrawing gold coins from circulation and making money redeemable only in expensive gold bars. The gold exchange standard, widely recommended and adopted in the 1920's, went further by basing domestic money on a fractional reserve of foreign exchange, in turn only fractionally based on gold. A still further step, widely taken during the 1930's, was actually to forbid private gold ownership. The "modern" gold standard became an effort both to preserve and to escape from the linkage of money to gold, an attempt to preserve an appearance while destroying its meaning. The Triffin plan carries this development practically to its ultimate.

Insofar as any meaning at all remains, it is the practice of subsidizing production of the very commodity whose real monetary significance has been destroyed. Curiously enough, it is Triffin himself who has made the appropriate comment: "Nobody could ever have conceived of a more absurd waste of human resources than to dig gold in distant corners of the earth for the sole purpose of transporting it and reburying it immediately afterward in other deep holes, especially excavated to receive it and heavily guarded to protect it."[12]

Under the Triffin plan, bancor, not gold, becomes the ultimate international currency.[13] Gold becomes a mere appendage, apparently serving as nothing more than a public relations device. It is an unnecessary complication to have rules about defining and guaranteeing money units in terms of it, about restricting national and private ownership of it, and about tightening these restrictions from time to time. More disturbingly, the fact that even an economist of outstanding competence and known love of innovation advocates an apparently key role for gold (and a continued subsidy to its production) tends to retard public understanding of monetary fundamentals. The task of spreading enlightenment becomes all the more difficult

---

[12] *Ibid.*, p. 89.

[13] Triffin of course understands this. See his reply to Senator Butler's question whether the plan would spell the end of the international gold standard; *Current Economic Situation*, p. 247.

for economists who are willing to keep their analyses and recommendations consistent with their understanding of how unnecessary, irrelevant, and troublesome gold really is in modern monetary systems. Perhaps it is true that a gold basis might as well be retained "as a harmless example of cultural lag and as an inexpensive subsidy for something that the world wants but does not need."[14] But if people do want gold, the reason is that they think they need it. And in the long run, what people think about economic issues depends largely on what beliefs economists either actively promote or passively allow to pass unchallenged. The true mission of expert advisers is the very opposite of adjusting to popular prejudice and misunderstanding.[15] To the extent that some advisers do so adjust, incidentally enhancing their own reputations for the supposititious merit of practicality and political realism, they cast undeserved discredit, however unintentionally, on other advisers who take a different view of their professional responsibilities.

INTERNATIONAL MONETARY LINKAGE

The gold link might perhaps be defended as a device for pegging currencies to bancor and to each other. A reply, beyond repeating that this is an unnecessary complication, might question the very idea of international monetary linkage.

In perpetuating this linkage, the Triffin plan fails to restore any "automatic" mechanism for balancing international transactions. Triffin himself recognizes that his plan deals only with liquidity problems and not with balance-of-payments problems.[16] It provides more adequate financing of the present-day practice of "riding out" deficits while waiting for them to reverse themselves somehow. Deficits can be allowed to grow larger and

---

[14] The interpretation and words are Oscar Altman's, *ibid.*, p. 184.

[15] Cf. Clarence E. Philbrook, " 'Realism' in Policy Espousal," *American Economic Review*, XLIII (December 1953), 846–59.

[16] Regarding the American balance of payments, for example, he has admitted having "no really original advice to offer regarding the policies which we should follow to plug these persistent and growing deficits" (*Gold and the Dollar Crisis*, p. 7). The *Current Economic Situation*, pp. 249ff, contains passages in which Triffin and other participants emphatically draw the distinction between the two sets of problems.

One feels apologetic in belaboring so obvious a point as that needs for liquidity are related to imbalances of payments, which in turn are related to destruction of any "automatic" international adjustments working through either exchange rates or gold standard processes. The excuse is that this obvious yet crucial point is curiously neglected in the great bulk of contemporary discussion. Perhaps, indeed, most participants in the discussion distrust or dislike automaticity; perhaps they positively like having national and international authorities deal with balance-of-payments troubles on an *ad hoc* basis. Value judgments certainly enter into the matter.

last longer than otherwise; but avoiding ultimate crises still requires conscious governmental attention to each country's balance of payments. No excessively rigid version of the purchasing-power-parity doctrine is necessary to show that price levels in various countries will have to move roughly in parallel if their currencies are to stay linked together meaningfully—in substantially free markets and without a panoply of controls. A country that inflates too fast will incur balance-of-payments deficits; a country that lags behind in a general inflationary procession will find the danger of imported inflation thrust upon it. Somehow, actively or passively, monetary conditions within the various countries will have to be more or less coordinated.

Coordinating national monetary managements among themselves and with the international management of bancor will be a delicate task. The quantity of bancor in existence at any given time and the quantities and purchasing powers of national currencies must be connected. One reason is that the volume of bancor "needed" to lubricate the flow of trade depends largely on the price level of internationally traded goods. National inflations can thus increase the quantity of bancor needed and the quantity presumably provided by the XIMF. Causation runs the other way, too: by allowing some countries to have larger or more persistent deficits than they could otherwise have afforded, creation of bancor will strengthen demand and raise prices in the world markets for their imports and exports.

International liquidity management cannot follow some simple criterion of stabilization, for the purchasing power of bancor consists of the purchasing powers of the national currencies tied to it; and national price levels are subject to domestic policies. The difficulty is that under the Triffin plan, money-supply management would be taking place on two levels—the international and the national. This problem of two levels would be absent only if countries forwent national monetary independence and behaved according to the rules supposedly governing the international gold standard before World War I. In such a world, countries would orient their domestic monetary conditions above all toward keeping their international transactions balanced. A country's money supply, price level, and state of business activity would be related to its holdings of gold or the equivalent. A world gold shortage would then be unambiguously deflationary. But when, as nowadays, countries orient their policies toward maintaining full employment (or even toward financing government budget deficits) and refuse to accept deflation to keep in step internationally, liquidity need not always be deficient or excessive on the national and international levels both at the same time. In particular, a shortage of international liquidity need not mean a deflationary shortage of domestic liquidity. An international liquidity shortage will breed restrictions on international trade, to be sure, but ordinarily not deflation.[17] As the early years after World War II amply illustrate, inflationary abundance of domestic liquidity can coexist with impediments to international trade that might somewhat plausibly be blamed on a shortage of international liquidity available for riding out deficits (although the deficits themselves were partly attributable to divergent degrees of inflation within countries).

In such situations, remedying an international liquidity shortage would mean creating more bancor even when it was not needed to avoid any price-level deflation. This important point will bear repetition to avoid any misunderstanding: the argument is not that liquidity is inherently "bad" or "inflationary," but simply that creating additional liquidity even when there would otherwise be no deflationary deficiency does tend toward inflation. Triffin counters the fear of inflation by suggesting some conservative limit to the annual increase in the supply of bancor.[18] But then, as just shown, the supply of bancor might sometimes fall short of the needs of international trade.

Is the opposite sort of conflict also possible—too much liquidity to lubricate international trade but not enough to prevent deflation within countries? This is unlikely. An excess of international liquidity hardly has any meaning, apart from its effect on price levels; and domestic policy can avoid domestic deflation. The conflict is asymmetrical: the needs of international trade may sometimes promote but never restrict the creation of liquidity when an opposite policy is advisable on domestic grounds. The inconsistencies of trying to manage liquidity on two levels at the same time shake the hope that international liquidity would never be created in inflationary excess, but always created only to stave off a deflationary deficiency.

Let us consider this inflationary bias further. New international liquidity would seldom be created to prevent deflation of prices and business activity; domestic policies would be taking care of that, anyway. Controls or currency devaluation, not deflation, are the ultimate response to bal-

---

[17] A *Business Week* article of September 26, 1959, reporting on a meeting of the International Economic Association, misinterpreted Triffin as warning that an impending international liquidity shortage made deflation rather than inflation the real threat to the world economy. As Triffin later explained, he considers "a new spiral of devaluations and of trade and exchange restrictions" far more likely "than a wave of deflationary adaptations" (*Gold and the Dollar Crisis*, p. 151).

[18] *Gold and the Dollar Crisis*, pp. 103–4 [reproduced on pp. 38–39].

ance-of-payments crises. Domestic policies err more generally and substantially on the inflationary than on the deflationary side. The supply of bancor does not significantly *restrict* domestic money supplies; yet this in no way means that creating additional bancor will not expand them. New bancor adds new spending power even to not-otherwise-deflationary situations. Its purpose is to let deficit countries avoid or postpone or mitigate the controls or devaluations otherwise necessary, financing larger or longer-lasting deficits than if new bancor had not been created. The hope that payments surpluses will alternate with deficits provides little reassurance, for the alternation will take place at generally higher levels of spending.

When some countries are financing larger or longer-lasting deficits than would have been possible without the new bancor, other countries will be experiencing the corresponding surpluses and facing inflationary influences with three interrelated aspects: (1) net exports and thus withdrawal of real goods and services from the home economy; (2) expansionary operation of the "foreign-trade multiplier"; and (3) creation of new domestic money as the authorities absorb the local residents' surplus earnings of foreign exchange to keep exchange rates pegged. Under a fractional-reserve banking system, official purchases of foreign exchange or gold, as of securities or anything else, expand the volume of bank reserves and set the stage for a multiple expansion of ordinary money. Deliberate monetary or fiscal measures can in principle counteract or neutralize these spontaneous inflationary pressures, but successful neutralization tends to frustrate any spontaneous balance-of-payments adjustment, perpetuating the troublesome surplus and the need for domestic measures to resist its inflationary impact. Furthermore, the policy involves the cost of imposing higher taxes or tighter credit[19] on the home economy for the sake of being able, without inflation, to make the involuntary loans to foreigners that the foreign exchange accumulations represent. Domestic policies for monetary stability cannot proceed with as much consistency, vigor, and relative painlessness as would be possible if some mechanism were continuously correcting balance-of-payments disequilibria.

A surplus, with its inflationary impact, may indeed reverse itself in time. But the deflationary impact of a subsequent balance-of-payments deficit is hardly a full and satisfactory remedy for what may have hap-

[19] The dilemma is compounded if relatively high interest rates attract funds from abroad, increasing the amount of foreign exchange that the central bank must buy to maintain exchange-rate stability. These official purchases themselves tend to expand the domestic money supply, and the country presumably pays higher interest rates on the inflowing foreign funds than it earns on its involuntary foreign exchange holdings.

pened earlier. Trying belatedly to undo an accomplished inflation in the face of well-known rigidities is to court unemployment and recession. A country will resist deflationary pressures from abroad even when they come against a background of inflation imported earlier. A "ratchet" is at work.

A related aspect of this "ratchet" can be illuminated by an admittedly oversimplified example concerning either several industries within a single country or several countries in a world of linked currencies. Suppose that something (perhaps changes in consumer preferences) shifts demand away from the products of industry or country A onto the products of industry or country B. Prices and wages are bid up in B but exhibit downward rigidities in A. Demand next shifts from B to industry or country C, again raising some prices and wages without correspondingly reducing others. Now demand may shift back toward A, perhaps still depressed from the first shift. Wages and prices may or may not go up there; but anyway, they have gone up and stayed up in B and C. Mere shifts—perhaps only temporary shifts—in the pattern of demand may thus raise the *average* level of wages and prices.[20] Under policies of stabilizing money supplies or total spending, these wage-and-price increases would entail unemployment; acquiescent monetary expansion, on the other hand, would consolidate them. Within a country, this dilemma stems from inadequate two-way flexibility of wages and prices; internationally, it stems from lack of continuous balance-of-payments adjustment either through domestic price-and-wage flexibility or through the less painful substitute of exchange-rate flexibility.

Inflationary biases could even make the Triffin plan partially self-defeating. Increased price levels would increase the amount of international liquidity needed to lubricate any given real flow of international trade. If the XIMF expanded the volume of bancor to meet these needs, the process could proceed for another round. If, on the other hand, the XIMF was determined to avoid contributing to price-level inflation—if it operated according to liquidity requirements on the *national* level—only happy but improbable coincidence could assure adequate liquidity on the international level as well. A further complication is that liquidity requirements even on the national level would diverge among countries. It would be beyond the power of the XIMF to guarantee adequate but not excessive liquidity for all countries at the same time.

---

[20] Charles L. Schultze has detected some such ratchet mechanism at work domestically. See his *Recent Inflation in the United States* (Joint Economic Committee, U.S. Congress, Study Paper No. 1, Washington, 1959).

INTERNATIONAL TRANSFERS OF RESOURCES

The XIMF, when reaping what might be called "seigniorage" by transforming the cheap paper and ink of account books into valuable bancor, is not obtaining real resources out of some fourth dimension. The losers are the countries that wind up having parted with real goods and services and holding bancor in excess of their actual desires, while who gains the seigniorage is a question of some interest.[21] Some of it is presumably absorbed in covering the Fund's operating expenses. Much presumably goes to the countries that first receive newly created bancor, that is, the countries to which the XIMF makes loans and in which it makes investments. Of course, the bancor does not come as an outright gift; countries must sooner or later repay their loans (or keep getting them renewed—the secular growth of XIMF deposits does imply a corresponding long-run growth of outstanding loans). The fact that new bancor comes into existence through loans and investments suggests that the borrowing countries reap seigniorage in the form of slightly lower interest rates than would otherwise prevail. The way in which this part of the seigniorage is distributed apparently rewards balance-of-payments deficits; for precisely the countries to which the XIMF lends are ones running deficits, and those in which it invests are presumably those expected to put most of the increments to their bancor reserves into international circulation by using them to finance deficits. (To buy securities in some country on its own initiative,

---

[21] Strictly speaking, seigniorage is the value of coins in excess of the value of their metallic content; but the word may be extended to mean the value of any kind of money in excess of its cost of production. Within a country whose domestic money supply is gradually expanding only enough to satisfy a demand for real cash balances growing along with population and production, seigniorage need not arise at anyone's expense. The particular way that the new money gets into circulation simply determines who gets the seigniorage. Even if the nominal money supply were held constant and the real money supply allowed to grow through price-level deflation, seigniorage would still emerge, accruing, in the form of increased real purchasing power, to persons and firms already holding cash balances.

Internationally, the seigniorage on the creation of bancor is less likely to be at no one's expense. Bancor is held only by official agencies and not by private persons or firms operating according to the same kinds of ordinary motives as govern the demand for domestic cash balances. Bancor cannot, in the same sense as domestic money can, be created solely to satisfy the growth in demand for real balances of it. While domestic money can be created without being forced on anyone, new bancor can gravitate, unwanted, into the possession of countries incurring unwanted balance-of-payments surpluses. As Edward M. Bernstein has said, "It is not desirable to give an international institution the power to create reserves through credit operations, with the obligation on the part of member countries to provide the real resources equivalent to the Fund deposits they acquire" (*International Effects of U.S. Economic Policy*, Joint Economic Committee, U.S. Congress, Study Paper No. 16 [Washington, 1960], p. 85).

the XIMF would presumably buy the necessary local currency from the country's central bank, paying by crediting it with an addition to its bancor deposit.) The XIMF will presumably lend and invest more on the basis of supposed "need" and less on the basis of prospective productivity than do ordinary commercial banks. This conjecture is supported by the suggestion that XIMF investments be made largely in underdeveloped countries.[22]

The XIMF is not the ultimate saver that furnishes these loans; it is just a financial intermediary. In effect, it enables deficit countries to borrow from the surplus countries that eventually absorb the additional bancor. It is true that the surplus countries will earn interest (at a low rate) on their bancor, but this is no proof either that they are sharing in the seigniorage or that their loans of real goods and services, corresponding to their accumulations of bancor, are wholly voluntary. If they were, one might ask, then why wouldn't the surplus countries do just as much lending or investing in the deficit countries even without the intermediation of the Fund? The obvious, though not decisive, answer is that indirect lending and investing have advantages—the safety of bancor and its liquidity as the ultimate international means of settlement—that more than compensate for the lowness of interest rates caused by the dumping of newly created funds onto the money and capital markets. One reason why this answer is unsatisfactory is that central banks sometimes accumulate bancor involuntarily in stabilizing exchange rates, rather than solely according to the ordinary motives that guide ordinary individuals and business firms in the management of their domestic cash balances.

ALTERNATIVES TO THE TRIFFIN PLAN: INCREASED RESOURCES FOR THE EXISTING IMF

The most questionable features of the Triffin plan, to recapitulate, are: the great difficulty of dismantling it should it prove unsatisfactory, the paradoxical and even deceptive role it gives to gold, the continued need for *ad hoc* expedients to deal with balance-of-payments disequilibria because no adjustment mechanism is allowed to operate continuously, the linking together of national currencies under arrangements biased toward inflation (especially because of the dilemmas involved in trying to manage liquidity on two levels), and international transfers of resources that are

---

[22] The XIMF might invest in underdeveloped countries either directly or by buying World Bank bonds. See Triffin, *Gold and the Dollar Crisis*, pp. 117–18 [reproduced on pp. 48–49], and Altman in *Current Economic Situation*, pp. 197–98, 207.

incidental to the creation of liquidity rather than consciously chosen on their own merits. Whether the Triffin plan should be rejected on these grounds, however, depends on the alternatives to it.

Probably the most popular alternative is to keep the International Monetary Fund and its operations much as they are today, but with increases in the Fund's lending power and in members' drawing rights. Members' quotas could be increased periodically, as was done in 1959. The contingent reserve system suggested by E. M. Bernstein might also be adopted.[23] The major trading countries would agree to buy up to specified amounts of medium-term debentures issued by the Fund under certain conditions when the Fund needed additional amounts of their currencies in order to provide emergency assistance to other members. No country undertaking to buy these debentures would endanger its own payments and reserve position, since it would not be called on to take up its subscription unless it had a balance-of-payments surplus and was increasing its reserves and since it could always use the debentures even before maturity to buy any currency in the Fund that it might need to meet a subsequent deficit of its own. The slower growth of gold and foreign exchange reserves than of world trade would matter little, since the member countries would have a growing "second line of reserves" in the form of their drawing rights at the Fund. The Fund would continue to serve as an intermediary for loans from surplus to deficit countries but, unlike Triffin's XIMF, would issue no monetary liabilities of its own to serve as actual liquidity. Expansion of the Fund's resources would provide an adequate substitute for international liquidity while not steering the world irreversibly onto some unfamiliar path.

Like the Triffin plan, however, this is an expedient for perpetuating the existing lack of any "automatic" balancing mechanism in international transactions. A different disadvantage is that loans which a central bank hopes to obtain in case of need are hardly the same as gold and foreign exchange that it actually owns. Authorities will presumably resort more

[23] Cf. *International Effects of U.S. Economic Policy*, p. 86, and a privately circulated paper by Bernstein as summarized and quoted in Brian Tew, *The International Monetary Fund: Its Present Role and Future Prospects* (Essays in International Finance, No. 36; Princeton: Princeton University, 1961), pp. 25–26. Tew, incidentally, expects "a considerable proliferation of reserve media": the German mark and several other currencies are likely to supplement the pound and the dollar, enabling the total amount of national currencies in international use to grow as rapidly in the 1960's as in the 1950's. The support of the International Monetary Fund would help lessen the aggravated danger of flights from one reserve medium to another. Nevertheless, Tew finds the case for the Triffin plan "convincing" (pp. 9–10, 24).

quickly to trade and exchange controls to safeguard the balance of payments when they have to eke out skimpy reserves with drawing rights at the IMF than when they own adequate reserves outright. With owned reserves failing to grow in step with trade, countries wanting to ride out deficits without trade and exchange controls would have to resort to the Fund more frequently and on a larger scale as time went on. Attitudes might change, of course, but resort to the Fund is still generally regarded as a sign of crisis.

A more fundamental objection is that IMF expansion deals only indirectly, at best, with Triffin's worry about key currencies serving as international reserves but becoming ever more shakily backed by gold. The growth of drawing rights at the Fund does reduce the *need* for countries to accumulate key currencies (and so reduces the need for deficits of key-currency countries), but, unlike the Triffin plan, it does nothing directly to restrict attempted accumulation of key currencies. Nor does it do anything directly to cope with the failure of gold stocks to grow in step with world trade, with foreign holdings of key currencies, and with total money supplies. It does not demonetize gold or even palliate the problem by restricting official as well as private acquisition and holding of gold. The IMF-expansion approach, in short, means muddling through while waiting to see how things work out.

A SECOND ALTERNATIVE:
A NONGOLD KEY CURRENCY

The United States might simply cut any link between the dollar and gold, relegate gold to the status of an ordinary commodity, and stop buying it while remaining alert to opportunities to unload the stock already on hand. Foreign authorities might then stop pegging their currencies to the dollar and holding dollars as reserves. But the continued use of the dollar as a key currency is quite conceivable. As mentioned in footnote 6 above, the crucial flaw in existing arrangements is not really the use of key-currency reserves, as such, but the use as international liquidity of key currencies *precariously pegged to gold on a fractional-reserve basis.* With no official gold reserve whose shrinkage could sap confidence and with no possibility of one-way-option speculation on a possible devaluation of the dollar against gold, the precariousness of today's system would be gone. (If more key currencies than one were used as international liquidity, however, and if they were pegged together at fixed rates, the possibility would remain of flights from relatively distrusted to relatively trusted key currencies. The nongold key-currency system works best when there is only a single key currency.)

Any run from the dollar would have to be a run into American goods and services (if some foreigners unloaded their dollars onto other foreigners, this would not be a run from the American point of view). Unlike a run from a gold standard dollar, this could cause no crisis for the American monetary authorities; the capital outflow would finance itself by and coincide with an American export surplus on current account. Even this development would be limited to the extent that the dollars were held by foreign monetary authorities and banks rather than by business firms, for it is hardly conceivable that central and commercial banks would fly on any large scale from dollars into commodities. To persuade residents of their own countries to take dollars off their hands and use them for purchases in the United States, the foreign authorities might relax import and exchange restrictions previously in effect or sell the dollars at a reduced price (that is, revalue the local currency upward against the dollar). The only devaluation of the dollar relative to foreign currencies to worry about would have to come at the initiative of foreign authorities, since the United States would not have been pegging the dollar in the first place.

Fears of continuing American inflation might conceivably motivate a flight from foreign-held dollars into American goods and services. This would differ little from a flight out of domestically held dollars. Foreign and domestic flight would occur together, if at all, developing gradually as a continuing inflationary drift in American monetary policy undermined confidence in the purchasing power of the dollar. In a key-currency country as in a non-key-currency country, the monetary authorities might either succeed or fail in recognizing and preventing such an inflationary drift. Failure would motivate a rise in velocity and further inflationary pressure. The essential point is that with the key currency unpegged from gold, there could be no clash between the domestic and external criteria of monetary policy. With its task simplified—its objectives made fewer—monetary management in the key-currency country would have a better chance of success.

The nongold key-currency system does not imply fluctuating exchange rates. Foreign authorities might peg their own currencies among themselves and with the dollar and even to gold as well, thereby indirectly linking the dollar and gold. Any distrust of this link—any fear that the dollar might lose value relative to gold—would imply expectations of either an upvaluation of foreign currencies against the dollar while leaving the foreign currency price of gold unchanged or an increase in the foreign currency price of gold while leaving exchange pegging against the dollar unchanged. If private parties were acting on expectations of the first alternative, foreign authorities would have to absorb dollars to keep exchange rates fixed until, if ever, they made the expected decision to change the level of pegging. For reasons already mentioned, an official flight from dollars is unlikely. Expectations of the second alternative would motivate a flight into gold from dollars and foreign money alike. In neither case would the American authorities face any crisis, since it is not they who would have been doing any pegging and worrying about drains on reserves in the first place. The foreign authorities would meet difficulties (akin to those of bimetallism) in trying to peg their currencies to each other, the dollar, and gold all at the same time; but the difficulties would be theirs, not American. The nongold key-currency system is most coherent, of course, when gold is demonetized everywhere.

Even under this system, individual foreign countries would occasionally face deficits, reserve losses, and one-way-option speculation on devaluation, or surpluses and unwanted large accumulations of dollar reserves. These are difficulties of exchange-rate pegging as such rather than of the choice of a particular international reserve medium. For the United States, balance-of-payments problems would be less serious, though a conceivable run out of dollars into goods and services, meaning an export surplus, would presumably be more nearly troublesome than a deficit. Even such a surplus would be nothing worse than repayment of real resources previously lent especially cheaply by foreigners.

Over the long run, a *deficit* would be more likely as foreigners accumulated dollar reserves. Far from being troublesome for the United States, this would mean receipt of cheap loans. From the foreign point of view, this is a defect of the nongold key-currency system, but no worse than the present system of in effect exporting capital by accumulating not only gold-pegged dollars but also gold itself.

The "coals-to-Newcastle" capital flow into the key-currency country aggravates what Triffin considers to be a defect of the present gold key currency system (and all the more so, one might add, of the nongold key-currency system), namely, that it weakens "the discipline of the gold flows" by distorting their timing. Foreign accumulation of key-currency reserves postpones gold settlements and permits the key-currency country to continue its deficits, though at the cost of danger of a run later on. The

United States would hardly have been able to accumulate a deficit of more than $15 billion over the decade 1950–59 if foreigners had not relaxed the "discipline of gold outflows" by accepting more than $11 billion of the settlement in dollar balances.[24] Under the Triffin plan, by contrast, the use of bancor instead of dollars as international reserves would prevent this discipline-relaxing flow of capital. The loss of bancor reserves would force even a former key-currency country to take corrective measures (such as internal disinflation) *at the time* it was running a deficit. The Triffin plan has this advantage, if it is one, over the gold and nongold key-currency systems alike: a key-currency system without gold is qualitatively little different in this respect from one based on gold, and the absence of gold avoids the precariousness of the latter system.

A THIRD ALTERNATIVE: NO OFFICIAL RESERVES

Most of the problems so far discussed would vanish if national and international authorities ceased to concern themselves with international liquidity, external reserves, or operations in the foreign exchange market. Foreign balances would be held only by individuals, commercial banks, and other business firms and private organizations (as well as by government agencies solely in connection with their regular international transactions rather than to influence the exchange market). Holders would determine and manage their foreign bank balances according to the same sorts of motives that govern their domestic bank balances and their inventories of ordinary commodities. (For private businesses, foreign exchange is indeed a kind of intermediate good, like fertilizer, office supplies, pig iron, or cloth; it is an "ingredient" in the process of "producing" imported goods and services and is itself "produced" by domestic labor and resources in the export industries.)

Even under the Triffin plan, which seeks to rationalize official reserves only, private holdings of foreign exchange would presumably remain substantial. As of late 1960, some one-third of U.S. liquid dollar liabilities— and some two-fifths of liquid dollar liabilities owed other than to international organizations—was held by foreign commercial banks and business firms rather than by official agencies. Even with the Triffin plan forbidding official ownership of other countries' currencies, private holdings of foreign exchange could become subject to one-way-option speculation from time to time; for the XIMF could hardly guarantee all national currencies,

---

24 Triffin in *Current Economic Situation*, p. 211.

as well as bancor, against devaluation. A private flight from dollars into sterling, for example, could force the Bank of England to accumulate dollars in its exchange-stabilization operations. Since the Bank would be forbidden to continue holding these dollars, it would require the United States to redeem them in bancor. The drain on the bancor reserves of the United States could be quite as serious as a gold drain nowadays. The United States might borrow from the XIMF, but this would not so much prevent as palliate the dangers of one-way speculation.

Avoiding official reserves and intervention and relying exclusively on privately owned foreign exchange reserves, by contrast, would enlist the law of large numbers on behalf of a resilient national and international monetary structure. But nowadays, the law of large numbers is inapplicable in two ways: one or two currencies alone make up the great bulk of foreign exchange reserves, and a small number of national authorities hold the bulk of the total.[25] When just one leading currency comes under suspicion, a large fraction of all international reserves is by that token under suspicion and particularly dependent for its fate on the decisions of a relatively few authorities. But if all foreign exchange holdings were private, there would be no dominant holders of sizable percentages of particular currencies. Each international reserve currency would be held by thousands of merchants and banks, no one of which held more than a very few per cent of its total amount. Furthermore, no one currency would fully retain its present-day dominance as an international reserve medium. Each merchant would probably hold bank accounts in the currencies in which he ordinarily made and received payments. Each bank, similarly, would hold foreign balances in many currencies in rough proportion to the volume of its customers' transactions in each. Speculative opinion would be diffused over a large number of currencies and among many holders, none of whom would be of dominant size. In contrast with the present system, only a widespread realignment of opinion could seriously strain international monetary relations.

[25] As of November 1960, of the total of short-term liabilities to foreigners (not including international institutions) reported by banks in the United States, over one-third was owed to only two countries and over half to only four countries (computed from *Federal Reserve Bulletin*, January 1961, pp. 110–11). These figures refer to official plus private holdings of liquid claims on the United States but presumably give a clue to the degree of concentration of official holdings. Another clue is the distribution of ownership in mid-1960 of all foreign exchange held by official holders except international institutions and countries in the Outer Sterling Area. Of this amount, nearly one-third was held by only two countries and fully one-half by only six countries (computed from *International Financial Statistics*, February 1961, p. 23).

This distinction needs some qualification. As is illustrated by bank runs even in a country with many separate banks and depositors, distrust may spread and destroy the independence of decisions necessary for the law of large numbers to be applicable. A similar linkage of opinion might similarly affect private holdings of international reserves, though presumably less than when attention had been concentrated all along on one or two key currencies largely held by a few dominant holders. A more important consideration derives from the absence of exchange-rate pegging. Incipient distrust of a currency can express itself by a slight weakening of its exchange quotation, producing a new alignment of speculative opinion. An exchange rate determined by truly free private supply and demand almost by definition cannot be lopsidedly expected to move in one particular direction rather than the other. There is no one-way option.[26]

With the pricing of currencies as free from official intervention as the pricing of ordinary commodities, the profit motive could usually be trusted to keep inventories of foreign exchange, as of any ordinary commodity, tending toward a level appropriate to the needs of its holders and to the cost of tying up resources in that form. Foreign exchange even contrasts favorably with flour, paint, salt, and other ordinary commodities in that large amounts of it could, at a price, be "produced" quickly if necessary. Banks could borrow abroad; balances in one money can turn instantly into foreign exchange by mere change of ownership. Severe inflations or deflations may conceivably distort holdings of foreign exchange away from a socially optimum level, defined in any plausible way. But these distortions, stemming from price-level instability and the resulting expectations, would be similar for inventories of foreign exchange and ordinary commodities alike. This consideration strengthens the argument for aiming at domestic monetary stabilization.

Under the system outlined here, there could be no such thing as a shortage of international liquidity *apart from* deflationary shortages of the domestic currencies of particular countries. Anyone who wanted to obtain more than he already held of some particular foreign currency could always do so at some price, a price at which its total quantities supplied and demanded were equal. Of course, the addition of an intensified foreign demand onto the domestic demand for cash balances of a particular country's currency would exert a deflationary tendency on that country. (The deflation can be understood either in terms of the demand for and supply of

---

[26] Pursuing these points further would lead into the general theory of exchange speculation, which is beyond the scope of this paper.

cash balances or in terms of appreciation of the affected currency on the exchange market and a resulting import balance of goods and services, with the foreign trade multiplier operating to contract domestic income.) Far from being burdensome, the opportunity to create additional domestic money to meet the intensified foreign demand for balances of it would allow the country to acquire real goods and services on indefinite loan at zero or low interest from the foreign holders of its money or near-moneys. In any country, stable economic growth requires satisfaction, somehow, of the growing demand for real cash balances that accompanies long-run growth of population and production; and the fact that foreigners account for part of the growth in demand for cash balances need cause no particular complications. Changing demands for cash balances (changing velocity) may admittedly pose problems for the ideal management of a country's money supply; but the changes are of many kinds, and the state of foreign demand for the currency is by no means the most troublesome. The exclusively private holding of foreign exchange at least avoids the especially troublesome conflict between domestic and international considerations caused by the existence and management of a separate international money in addition to the various national currencies. Monetary stabilization has a better chance of success when it can be pursued in accordance with fairly simple criteria on the national level and for national objectives alone than when the task is complicated by liquidity management for international objectives as well.

Triffin recognizes that general reliance on fluctuating exchange rates is an alternative to his own plan. It is to his credit that he does not emphasize the familiar but dubious objections concerning speculation, "perverse elasticities," and the like. But he does find one objection rather persuasive.[27] With fluctuating exchanges keeping balances of payments continuously in equilibrium (except as speculators voluntarily financed imbalances that they expected to be temporary) and with downward inflexibility of wages and prices making a ratchet, accidental domestic inflationary impulses that might otherwise prove temporary and remediable threaten to become consolidated in wage and price structures. The deficit tendency in the balance of payments is checked by exchange depreciation, which promotes a rise in import and export prices and, together with the monetary expansion that may have been the initial disturbance, promotes

[27] *Gold and the Dollar Crisis*, pp. 82–86. The present discussion obviously makes no pretense at a full appraisal of fluctuating exchanges; it is limited to points raised by Triffin and to closely related matters.

a general rise in prices. Fluctuating exchanges thus create an inflationary bias. But exchange-rate pegging enables the country, while taking domestic measures against the initial inflationary disturbance, to enjoy the three-fold anti-inflationary assistance of an actual deficit: the real goods and services being in effect borrowed from abroad cushion the impact of increased spending on prices, the foreign trade multiplier works in a downward direction, and the sale of foreign exchange drawn from official reserves or borrowed abroad mops up domestic liquidity. In broader terms, the gearing of the home economy into a not-yet-inflated world environment provides a breathing spell for dealing with inflationary tendencies before they become irreversibly consolidated in wages and prices.[28]

Though perhaps the strongest of all arguments in favor of fixed exchanges, Triffin's is just one of many considerations on both sides that must be weighed in a final appraisal. One minor answer is that if inflationary tendencies in a country really were likely to be stopped by quick and successful countermeasures, then speculators would accumulate that country's currency when it first weakened slightly. They would thereby enable the country to have a temporary current-account deficit, providing the benefits that Triffin expects from an officially financed deficit. If the prospects for quick and successful action against inflation were too poor to convince private speculators, who, unlike government officials, have a profit incentive to get the facts straight and to weigh the probabilities dispassionately, then the prospects might really be poor after all.

Especially in the latter case, the reminder is relevant that a country is not so much preventing its inflation by running a balance-of-payments deficit as, rather, obscuring its effects by diluting them onto the outside world. The more the creation of international liquidity allows such countries to enjoy larger or longer-lasting deficits than they could otherwise finance, the more other countries risk importing their inflation. One might say that the inflationary impulses diluted onto these other countries are too

---

[28] Triffin might have used but did not explicitly use an argument offered by Lionel Robbins (for example, in *The Balance of Payments*, Stamp Memorial Lecture [London: The Athlone Press, 1951], pp. 31–32). If a fixed exchange rate is considered almost sacred, the discipline of the balance of payments restrains inflationary decisions in domestic policy. On the other hand, this discipline is unwelcome when it imposes the contagion of foreign deflation rather than mere resistance to domestic inflation, just as when, in the opposite direction, it imposes the contagion of inflation originating abroad. Furthermore, a free exchange rate may be a useful alarm signal, indicating domestic inflationary tendencies more conspicuously than an external deficit would and rallying public protest more promptly. But none of these points is decisive. On the question of what exchange system best promotes resistance to inflation of domestic origin, much can be said on each side.

widely dispersed to be serious, but this is a denial less of the existence than of the conspicuousness of the international contagion. Even when only one single country shoves part of its own problem onto others in many small inconspicuous bits, it is not clear that the aggregate harm falls short of the benefit.

This reminder of inflationary biases from monetary linkage (including ratchet effects and the fact that the need for international liquidity to lubricate trade may sometimes promote but hardly ever restrict the creation of domestic liquidity) counters Triffin's argument. Fixed exchanges subject to occasional adjustment present still another bias: since balance-of-payments deficits and reserve losses are more *critical* problems than surpluses and reserve gains, countries are far more likely to devalue to adjust to international inflation or to escape external deflationary pressures than they are to revalue upward to escape external inflationary pressures.[29] Furthermore, devaluations tend to err on the large side, possibly because the authorities typically want to avoid risking the need for a confidence-shaking second devaluation soon afterward and want to rebuild their depleted reserves; and excessive devaluation sets the stage for inflationary influences working through the balance of payments. Over the long run, the devaluation bias means that even a fixed world stock of gold or bancor would grow in value expressed in national currencies; and, as already argued, an abundance of international liquidity is far more likely to promote than a scarcity is to restrain the inflation of national currencies. Free exchange rates work in both directions and escape this bias: surplus-country currencies can appreciate just as well as deficit-country currencies can depreciate (both in relation to the currencies of countries in approximate equilibrium, since there would be no particular international reserve medium to serve as a point of reference).

Although a country may follow Triffin's advice, using its monetary linkage with other countries to gain time while correcting domestic inflationary pressures, it may just as well not do so. Inflation, especially wage-push inflation, has aptly been characterized as an attempt by different economic interests to divide up among themselves more than the total national output. Under fixed exchange rates these excessive claims against national output can partly be met—for a while—by dipping into reserves or borrowing abroad. It is not unprecedented for countries to enjoy the tempo-

---

[29] For historical documentation of the devaluation bias of fixed exchanges, see Henrik Akerlund, *Guldparistandarden* (Stockholm: Grafiska Konstanstalten Tryckeri, 1959), pp. 85–88. Upward revaluations—when such rarities occur—are likely to err on the small side.

rary delights of living beyond their means while passively hoping that the longer-run necessary adjustment will somehow easily take care of itself. It is not unknown for the authorities in power to continue dissipating the country's international resources, leaving it to successor regimes to impose "austerity." The large measure of monetary insulation offered by fluctuating exchanges, on the other hand, leaves each country more immediately exposed than it would otherwise be to the wanted or unwanted consequences of its own domestic policies. One particular aspect of this feature in fact constitutes Triffin's argument against independent national monetary systems. It is largely a question of value judgments whether this independence is good or bad, all aspects considered, and whether, on the contrary, other countries *ought* to help carry the burden of some countries' inflationary blunders.

Triffin has aptly exposed the "absurdity" of economizing on gold by the growing use, as international liquidity, of national currencies precariously pegged to gold on a fractional reserve basis. Turning the International Monetary Fund into a world central bank to manage liquidity on the international level would probably be an improvement over present-day arrangements. However, the Triffin plan still does not provide the world with any payments-balancing mechanism. Furthermore, the complexities of managing liquidity on two levels, and the creation of additional liquidity even when not required to ward off actual deflation, threaten inflationary pressure on countries whose balance-of-payments surpluses correspond to the more amply financed deficits of others. A full appraisal of the plan requires considering the alternatives. One is periodic expansion of the International Monetary Fund much as it exists today. Another is the use for international liquidity of a single national currency not tied to gold. Still another is to leave the holding of foreign exchange entirely to decentralized private decisions, with national monetary authorities free to guide themselves consistently by domestic objectives alone. This last approach would spare the monetarily most prudent countries, at least, some of the inflationary biases inherent in the rival systems.

Part II

IMPROVEMENT OF THE GOLD EXCHANGE STANDARD SYSTEM

9

Proposed Reforms in the International Monetary System

EDWARD M. BERNSTEIN

DEFICITS AND RESERVES

The balance of payments of the United States has shown a large deficit for a number of years. This deficit has been met by sales of gold by the U.S. Treasury and the accumulation of dollar claims by other countries. The gold reserves of the United States have declined by $6.9 billion since 1958. In this period, the short-term and liquid dollar claims of foreign official institutions and banks have increased by $5.9 billion. To some extent, this transfer of reserves from the United States has been extremely helpful in restoring the liquidity of the other large industrial countries and in enabling them to undertake the convertibility of their currencies. The continuation of the deficit has, however, caused a greater depletion of U.S. gold reserves than is desirable. Furthermore, the large foreign holdings of short-term and liquid dollar assets expose the United States to the danger of massive conversion of dollars into gold in the future.

There is no way in which U.S. gold reserves can be protected except through the elimination of the balance-of-payments deficit. That is and must be a major objective of our economic policy. There are, indeed, problems regarding reserves whose importance has been accentuated by U.S. payments difficulties. The solution of these problems is essential to the functioning of the world economy under a system of fixed exchange rates with convertible currencies. A better system of reserves will make it possible for countries to deal with their balance-of-payments problems without relying on exchange control or quantitative restrictions on imports and without the necessity of imposing harsh deflationary measures on the

Reprinted from *Outlook for United States Balance of Payments*, Hearings (December 14, 1962), Joint Economic Committee, Subcommittee on International Exchange and Payments (Washington, 1963), with permission from the author.

domestic economy in order to force an immediate adjustment in the balance of payments. For the United States, a better reserve system would minimize the risks inherent in its unique position as a reserve center with large short-term obligations to the rest of the world. Nevertheless, it should be emphasized that no system of reserves can obviate the need for maintaining a balancd international payments position over the course of a reasonable period of time—say, the length of a business cycle.

LEVEL AND DISTRIBUTION OF MONETARY RESERVES

At the end of September 1962, the gross official gold and foreign exchange reserves of all countries outside the Soviet bloc amounted to $60.9 billion. Of these reserves, $38.9 billion consisted of gold. The other $22 billion of reserves was in the form of official holdings of dollars, sterling, and various other currencies, including deposits with the Bank for International Settlements. In the five years ending in 1956, the increase in official gold and foreign exchange reserves amounted to $6.8 billion—an average annual increase of slightly more than 2.6 per cent. In the five years ending in 1961, the increase in official gold and foreign exchange reserves amounted to $5.3 billion—an average annual increase of just over 1.8 per cent. There was no increase at all in gross official gold and foreign exchange reserves in the first three quarters of 1962.

Of the increase of $6.8 billion in gross reserves of all countries in the five years ending in 1956, only $2.2 billion was in gold; and of the increase of $5.3 billion in reserves in the five years ending in 1961, about $2.8 billion was in gold. The remainder of the increase in the reserves of all countries is accounted for by larger holdings of foreign exchange, primarily dollars. As it is impossible for the United States to continue indefinitely a balance-of-payments deficit of the magnitude of recent years, this source of reserves for the rest of the world may be expected to disappear in the course of the next few years. Foreign holdings of sterling, the other reserve currency, have not increased during the past ten years. The steady and moderate growth of reserves that is essential for an expanding world economy must be provided in some other way.

The holdings of gold and foreign exchange reserves are very heavily concentrated in the industrial countries. Total reserves of the United States, the United Kingdom, continental Europe, Canada, and Japan at the end of September 1962 amounted to $47.9 billion and constituted nearly 80 per cent of the world total. All of Latin America, all of the

GROSS OFFICIAL GOLD AND FOREIGN EXCHANGE RESERVES*
(Billion U.S. dollars)

	1951	1956	1961	Sept. 1962	Sept. 1962 Gold	Exchange
United States	22.87	22.06	17.06	16.53	16.08	.45
United Kingdom	2.37	2.28	3.32	2.80	2.60e	.20e
Canada	1.83	1.95	2.06	2.45	.69	1.76
Japan	.....	.94	1.49	1.72	.29e	1.43e
Belgium	1.05	1.16	1.66	1.63	1.34	.29
France	.62	1.18	2.94	3.53	2.48	1.05
Germany	.52	4.12	6.54	6.47	3.67	2.80
Italy	.77	1.24	3.42	3.25	2.24	1.01
Netherlands	.55	1.04	1.72	1.78	1.58	.20
Sweden	.....	.51	.67	.76	.18	.57
Switzerland	1.64	1.88	2.76	2.63	2.45	.18
Total, 11 countries.....	32.22	38.36	43.64	43.55	33.60	9.94
Other Europe	2.29	2.44	3.90	4.35	1.81e	2.54e
Latin America	2.98	3.68	2.78	2.28	1.28e	1.00e
Other sterling area......	7.44	7.54	7.12	7.08e	1.03	6.05e
All other countries......	4.11	3.88	3.69	3.66e	1.19e	2.47e
Total, all countries†....	49.05	55.89	61.20	60.92e	38.91e	22.01e

Source: *International Financial Statistics* (IMF), December 1962, p. 17.
  * Data are for end of period shown ["e" after figures indicates estimate].
  † All countries outside the Soviet bloc.

sterling area outside the United Kingdom, and all of the rest of the world except Japan held $13 billion of reserves. Even more striking is the fact that while the gross reserves of all countries increased by $12 billion in the ten years ending in 1961, the reserves of the countries outside Europe, North America, and Japan actually decreased by $1 billion in this same period. These countries held nearly 30 per cent of the total reserves at the end of 1951; they now hold just over 20 per cent. The fact is that the raw materials–producing countries do not, and perhaps cannot, hold reserves on the scale necessary for their trade and payments.

The concentration of gold reserves, as distinguished from total reserves, is even greater. Eleven major industrial countries hold their reserves predominantly in this form. The gold reserves of these countries— the United States, the United Kingdom, the Common Market, Switzerland, Sweden, Canada, and Japan—constitute about 87 per cent of the total held by all countries. In the past ten years, these eleven countries have absorbed all of the newly mined gold and the gold sales of the Soviet Union that did not go into private hoards or into international financial institutions. In fact, they acquired, in addition, about $1.5 billion of the gold reserves of the rest of the world. Over 80 per cent of the gross sales of gold by the U.S. Treasury to foreign countries in the past five years has been to the other ten major industrial countries. They are the only countries that can put serious pressure on the United States through the conversion of their dollar holdings into gold. The strength and stability of the present reserve system, based on the equivalence of gold and dollars, depend on the willingness of the eleven major industrial countries to hold a reasonable part of their reserves in foreign exchange.

These three practical problems regarding monetary reserves can be summarized as follows:

1. How to protect the financial centers from the disruption of massive capital movements and large-scale conversions of currencies into gold.
2. How to meet the reserve needs of the low-income countries that hold, and prefer to hold, very small monetary reserves.
3. How to provide for the orderly growth of monetary reserves in the future so that world trade and payments can continue to expand.

The reserve problems are specific problems calling for specific solutions. They do not require radical changes in the structure of the present reserve system; but they do require the adaptation of the present reserve system to the requirements of the modern world. The view that the payments difficulties of the United States or of other countries are due to the inadequacy of the present level of monetary reserves or that they can be solved by merely changing the reserve system is entirely mistaken. These reserve problems will grow more acute after the deficit in the U.S. balance of payments has been eliminated.

GOLD AND THE FINANCIAL CENTERS

Because the dollar is a reserve currency, the gold reserves of the United States are affected not only by its own balance of payments, but also by the payments of other dollar countries with the rest of the world and the attitude of other financial centers toward the holding of dollars as a part of their reserves. It is likely that even after the balance of payments of the United States is no longer in deficit, there will be a gold outflow for a time. This is because the dollar component of the reserves of other financial centers is at present larger than they customarily hold. Once the U.S. payments position is strengthened, their reluctance to convert dollars into gold may be very much diminished. To halt a gold outflow in the future, the United States may have to have a sizable surplus in its balance of payments for many years in order to reduce the dollar holdings of other countries. Such a reduction in dollar assets would deflate the gross reserves of the world.

The difficulty in providing more of the world's reserves through dollars and other currencies arises from the fact that some of the large financial centers hold a very large proportion of their reserves in the form of gold. There are various reasons for the preference of these countries for gold as reserves. Prestige, tradition, security, liquidity—all affect the decisions of the financial centers in determining whether to hold gold or foreign exchange as reserves. As a practical matter, it will not be possible for the leading financial centers to continue to concentrate their reserves in gold. The increase in the monetary gold stock outside the Soviet bloc amounted to $550 million a year in the ten years ending in 1962. This is an average annual increase of about 1.3 per cent. If all of this gold were added to the monetary reserves of the eleven major industrial countries, the gold component of their reserves would increase by about 1.6 per cent a year. This is not sufficient even for a moderate growth in the reserves of the financial centers. The practice of many of the gold-holding countries, including the United States and the United Kingdom, of keeping their reserves almost exclusively in gold can only lead to a serious deficiency in the reserves of the financial centers. These countries, and particularly the United States and the United Kingdom, must increase their holdings of foreign exchange as reserves. Secretary Dillon has already stated that this will be the policy of the United States.

There is another difficulty that confronts the large industrial countries. As financial centers, they are exposed to the risk of large and sudden movements of liquid funds either for interest arbitrage, to take advantage of interest rate differentials, or for speculation, in anticipation of changes in exchange rates or exchange controls. The United States has had to meet an outflow of $2.8 billion of U.S. private short-term funds in 1960 and 1961 and additional net payments of $1.2 billion on unrecorded transactions, some of which were undoubtedly capital movements. Such a large outflow of liquid funds can occur in other countries, as happened in fact in the periods 1937–41 and 1947–49. In the former period, unrecorded transactions and short-term capital movements required payments of $3.7 billion to the United States. In the latter period, unrecorded transactions and short-term capital movements required payments of $2.8 billion to the United States. The outflow of gold from other financial centers to the United States was enormous in both periods.

With all of the major currencies freely convertible, occasional large movements of liquid funds from one financial center to another are inevitable. Differences in monetary policy to deal with the domestic economy or the balance of payments will encourage an outflow of funds from countries with easy credit to countries with tight credit. Furthermore, a serious recession or a political crisis in any part of the world may induce large movements of liquid funds in search of security. These are contingencies for which the financial centers must be prepared. It would be a backward step to depend on exchange controls to avoid such capital movements. A more practical way to deal with the problem is to have a greater degree of international cooperation on monetary policy to minimize the outflow of short-term funds and to provide reciprocal credits to finance such capital movements as do occur.

The financial centers have already taken major steps to deal with the problem of short-term capital movements. They have frequent consultations on monetary problems and monetary policies. In the course of 1962, differentials between short-term interest rates in the United States and Europe have been very much narrowed. In Switzerland, Netherlands, Germany, and Belgium the yield on money market funds is lower than the yield on three-month Treasury bills in the United States. Just a year ago, the financial centers (except Switzerland) subscribed to the Paris Agreement under which they undertake to provide $6 billion of special resources to the International Monetary Fund principally for the purpose of financing short-term capital movements from one country to another. The Managing Director of the Fund has been consulting with Switzerland, which is not a member of the Fund, for association in some form with these borrowing arrangements. Clearly, a great deal has been done to enable the reserve centers to meet the special problems that may arise from massive capital movements.

The financial centers must now take further steps to decrease their excessive reliance on gold for their monetary reserves. A very ingenious plan for this purpose has been proposed by Professor Posthuma, a director of the Netherlands Bank. If the countries that have subscribed to the Paris

Agreement and Switzerland were to enter into an arrangement for holding a minimum proportion of their reserves in foreign exchange, they could bring about the most important advance in the reserve system since the establishment of the International Monetary Fund. The demand for monetary gold comes almost entirely from these eleven countries. No other countries can support the balance-of-payments surplus or the investment in monetary reserves that would enable them to acquire very large amounts of gold. If these eleven countries were to undertake to hold 40 per cent of their gross reserves in foreign exchange, their reserves in this form (on the basis of present gold holdings) could be increased by about $11 billion. Some provision would have to be made in the Posthuma plan for an appropriate and predetermined allocation of the various currencies to be held as reserves. This is particularly important for the United States, as an increase in the holding of dollars as reserves by the financial centers is desirable in order to relieve the pressure on U.S. gold reserves.

RESERVE PROBLEM OF THE UNDERDEVELOPED COUNTRIES

With very few exceptions, the underdeveloped countries do not hold sufficient monetary reserves to meet the recurrent fluctuations in their international payments. With the decline in the prices of basic products over the past ten years, these countries have reduced their reserves until they are now at the bare minimum necessary for financing their international payments. As a consequence, when their exports fall because of a deterioration in world markets, the underdeveloped countries are compelled to reduce their imports sharply and immediately. In their own interest, it would be desirable for these countries to hold somewhat larger reserves in order to avoid such severe fluctuations in their imports. Nevertheless, because of their great need for capital, these countries feel that they cannot afford to invest real resources in holding larger reserves.

During the past ten years a number of proposals have been made to deal with the difficulties arising from fluctuations in the prices of basic products and the recurrent payments problems of the countries dependent on such exports. The United Nations has issued a number of reports recommending measures to compensate countries exporting basic products for a decline in the prices of such commodities. The Organization of American States has studied the commodity problems of Latin America and has recommended the establishment of a fund for the stabilization of the export receipts of low-income countries dependent on exports of basic products. A resolution was adopted by the Alliance for Progress at its meeting in Punte del Este in 1961 supporting this proposal. A tentative plan has been drawn up and it is now under study by the United Nations.

Under this plan, an Export Receipts Stabilization Fund would be established, either as a subsidiary of the International Monetary Fund or as an independent institution. The Export Receipts Stabilization Fund would have resources provided by both the high-income and the low-income countries. However, only the low-income countries would be eligible to make use of the resources of the institution. It is not feasible, whatever its merits, to provide aid to the United States, Canada, Australia, and other high-income countries when their exports of primary products decline. On the other hand, it is feasible to secure sufficient resources to provide aid for the low-income countries when their exports of primary products fall.

The principal provisions of the plan for an Export Receipts Stabilization Fund can be summarized briefly as follows: Whenever the export receipts of a low-income country fall below the average of the three preceding years, it would be entitled to secure credits from the institution, on a virtually automatic basis, to the extent of two-thirds of the shortfall in its exports. When the export receipts of a country indebted to the institution rise above the average of the three preceding years, two-thirds of the excess would be used to repay the export receipts stabilization credits it previously received. When any credit has been outstanding three years, one-half of the balance would have to be repaid in the fourth year and the remainder in the fifth year, even if a country's exports have not increased.

There are a number of other provisions that are intended to assure the equitable use of the resources of the institution. No country could secure export receipts stabilization credits in excess of 20 per cent of the average of its exports in the three preceding years. If a country should use the resources of the institution in a manner not consistent with its purposes, the country could be declared ineligible to receive export receipts stabilization credits. Furthermore, if the institution were to find that its resources would not be sufficient to meet all requests for export receipts stabilization credits, it could ration the amount of credits it extends. Notwithstanding these limitations, a country could apply for additional special credits if it finds that the amount of export receipts stabilization credits to which it is entitled does not properly reflect the impact on its economy of the decline in its exports.

This is essentially a plan to deal with the reserve problem of the underdeveloped countries. Needless to say, it would not achieve its purposes if it merely resulted in a further reduction of the independent reserves held by the low-income countries or if export receipts stabilization credits were to induce a corresponding reduction of the drawings of low-income countries on the International Monetary Fund. The plan is no solution to the basic commodity problems of the raw materials–exporting countries. On the other hand, there is no reason why it should hamper international commodity agreements in any field in which such cooperation is possible. Within its limited scope, the Export Receipts Stabilization Fund could be of great practical help to the low-income countries in minimizing the adverse effects of large fluctuations in their export receipts.

THE IMF AND RESERVES

Any program for dealing with monetary reserves must start with the basic fact that the International Monetary Fund has responsibilities in this field that it has been meeting for more than fifteen years. The Fund holds resources of $14.6 billion in currencies and gold, and it has borrowing arrangements with ten major industrial countries aggregating an additional $6 billion. From 1947 to the end of October 1962, the Fund's sales of currencies amounted to $6.7 billion, of which $5.1 billion has been repaid. The cumulative total of its stand-by agreements with members is $5.5 billion, of which $1.6 billion is still available for drawing. An institution with such vast resources and with extensive experience in dealing with the payments problems of its members is uniquely suited to provide for the orderly growth of reserves. In order to meet the reserve needs of the future, the resources of the Fund must be integrated with the working reserves of its members.

The first step in this gradual process would be to regard the Fund quota as part of a country's reserves. A number of countries already include the net creditor position in the Fund (what the Fund calls the gold tranche) in their reserves. What is proposed now is to include a country's quota (the credit tranches) as part of its gross reserves. The Fund recognizes that the right of members to draw on its resources is in some sense equivalent to reserves. In *International Financial Statistics*, the Fund includes a member's position in the Fund under the general heading "Gold, Foreign Exchange, and IMF." There would be nothing misleading in regarding the gold and credit tranches of a country as part of its gross reserves. Of course, it would be necessary to show among the reserve liabilities the contingent obligation to provide additional currency when a country draws on the Fund.

The second step in integrating the resources of the Fund with the working reserves of members would be to permit countries to draw freely on their quotas, without prior approval, to the limits prescribed in the Fund Agreement. After the Fund's holdings of a member currency have reached 75 per cent of the quota, a member may draw only 25 per cent of its quota in a twelve-month period until the Fund's holdings of its currency have reached 200 per cent of the quota—that is, net credit equal to its quota. At present, the policy of the Fund is to give members a virtually unconditional right to draw an amount equal to their net creditor position—the gold tranche. Thereafter, drawings, even within the quota limits, require justification and the justification becomes more stringent as a member draws successive credit tranches of its quota.

A further liberalization of this policy is now called for. Members of the Fund should have the right to draw the gold tranche plus the first credit tranche of 25 per cent in a twelve-month period. This could be done by a general waiver applying the 25 per cent limitation only after the gold tranche. Beyond that, a member of the Fund should be permitted to draw 25 per cent of its quota each year, when necessary, until the Fund's holdings of its currency have reached 200 per cent of the quota. Drawings within these limits should be freely permitted to any member that has not been declared ineligible to use the resources of the Fund. Larger drawings than 25 per cent of the quota in a twelve-month period or drawings in excess of 200 per cent of the quota would, as now, require a waiver and such drawings would be permitted only on terms and conditions agreed with the Fund.

There is no reason to fear that such a policy would be abused. Members are aware that drawings on the Fund are transactions in reserves, and that their position in the Fund must be restored as soon as possible—in any case, within three years with an outside limit of five years. No country has failed in its financial obligations to the Fund. There might be some members that would be tempted to use the resources of the Fund as a source of credit rather than as monetary reserves. These countries are few in number and their aggregate quotas are small. As a practical matter this happens now. To prevent this, the Fund could call the attention of a member to the importance of avoiding improper use of its resources and, in an extreme case, it could suspend a member's right to draw on the Fund.

The influence of the Fund in advising members on exchange, payments, monetary and fiscal policies would not be diminished by providing assured access to its resources. The best way for the Fund to influence the policies of its members is not on the few occasions when they come for large drawings under waivers. By that time, the disruption in the balance of payments may already have gone very far. Instead, the Fund must work with its members as their problems emerge. This is the method the Fund now uses in its annual consultations. As countries come more and more to count on the Fund's resources as part of their working reserves, the influence of the Fund with its members should become even greater than it is now.

The third step in integrating the resources of the Fund with the working reserves of members would be for them to draw on the Fund as a matter of course whenever they use their own reserves. Forty-seven countries have drawn on the Fund. Many of them have come to the Fund for very large drawings to help them meet a payments crisis. The Fund has shown a great capacity to cope with such needs while creating an atmosphere of confidence. Nevertheless, it is not wise for countries to limit their use of the Fund's resources to rare occasions and for very large sums. Such a practice gives substance to the impression that a drawing on the Fund is a sign of weakness rather than a normal use of reserves. The major industrial countries should draw on the Fund for relatively small sums at frequent intervals, in the expectation that their position would be restored when their currencies are drawn by other members.

The present system of charges could be modified to encourage use of the Fund in conjunction with a member's own reserves. The Fund Agreement provides for a service charge of not less than one-half per cent on all exchange transactions. This charge is levied at the time a member draws on the Fund and is applied to the gross amount of the drawing. If possible, the transactions charge should be levied at the close of the Fund's financial year and should apply to the net currency transactions of a member. Thus, the exchange purchases of a member would be offset by the Fund's sales of its currency to determine its net currency transactions. A service charge based on net purchases would permit a member to draw on the Fund in the expectation that such drawings would be largely offset by Fund sales of its currency.

The Fund Agreement provides for a quinquennial review and a general revision of quotas when this becomes necessary. During 1959, the quotas of nearly all members of the Fund were increased by 30 per cent or more. In the future, it should be possible to have a continuous review of quotas and moderate increases from time to time. This would assure a gradual growth in the resources of the Fund to meet the greater reserve needs of an expanding world economy.

With the present quotas, which are generously large, the world would be well provided with reserves if the resources of the Fund were gradually integrated with the working reserves of members. The evolution of the Fund's policy on the use of its resources has been going on for some years. It is necessary to proceed with the further development of this policy. If this were done, there would be no danger that aggregate monetary reserves would be inadequate for financing deficits in world payments.

The striking fact about the reserve problems is not that they have become more acute. Gross reserves for the world as a whole are more adequate now than at any time in the postwar period if account is taken of the availability of the resources of the Fund. What has been happening in recent years is a wider recognition of the reserve problems inherent in the present reserve system. Fortunately, the major industrial countries and the Fund are aware of the necessity of dealing with these problems. I am confident that the measures now being considered will bring about a gradual modification of the present reserve system to enable it to meet the reserve needs of an expanding and prosperous world economy.

. . .

A NOTE ON THE TRIFFIN PLAN*

The difficulty of providing for future reserve needs through increased holdings of dollars, sterling, and other foreign exchange, and the danger that the reserve currencies could be exposed to serious pressure from the conversion of present holdings into gold have led Professor Robert Triffin to conclude that a completely new system of supplying monetary reserves is necessary. He had proposed that this be done by transforming the International Monetary Fund into a world central bank with the power to accept deposits and to create credit denominated in a new international currency unit. These deposits would be transferable among central banks and would act as monetary reserves.

The first step in Professor Triffin's plan would be to abandon the present quotas and to terminate the present drawing arrangements under the Fund Agreement. Countries with a net creditor position in the Fund would be given deposits to their accounts in settlement of their claims. Countries with a net debtor position in the Fund would have these debts converted into loans repayable over a period of three to five years. All countries

* Addendum, reprinted from *Outlook for United States Balance of Payments.*

adhering to the world central bank would be required to deposit a pre-scribed fraction of their gross monetary reserves, say one-fourth, in the new institution. Countries holding dollars, sterling, and other foreign ex-change reserves could fulfill this requirement by depositing balances of these currencies. The United States, the United Kingdom, and other gold-holding countries would have to make their required deposits largely or entirely in gold. The dollar, sterling, and other foreign exchange acquired by the world central bank through such initial deposits would be funded into debts repayable over a reasonably long period.

For all practical purposes, the dollar and sterling would cease to be reserve currencies, although most countries would continue to hold modest balances of such currencies for their ordinary payments needs. Instead of supplying the world with additional reserves through the increase in foreign holdings of dollars and sterling, the United States and the United Kingdom would be compelled to deplete the reserves of other countries by maintain-ing an over-all balance-of-payments surplus in order to repay their debts to the world central bank. With the change in their status under such a system, the capacity of the reserve centers to act as exporters of long-term capital or as the source of additional short-term international credit would be very reduced. The world central bank would, of course, attempt to pro-vide the additional reserves that would no longer be supplied through increased holdings of dollars and sterling. It would be more difficult to replace the function of the reserve centers as suppliers of capital for the world economy.

The basic technique for assuring an adequate growth of monetary re-serves under the Triffin plan would be the extension of credit by the world central bank. To provide the necessary supplement of reserves, the world central bank would have to create reserve deposits (that is, excluding de-posits of gold) at an average rate of $1 billion net a year. To achieve this, the new institution would have to undertake a vast lending program. If the loans of the world central bank were repayable in about three years, the period now regarded as normal by the Fund, the turnover of loans to assure an average growth of $1 billion a year net in reserve credit deposits would soon reach enormous proportions—say, about $4 billion a year or more in about ten years. In fact, as many loans would be repaid before three years, the turnover of loans would have to reach a much higher level much sooner.

It would be impractical to count on such a steady increase in loans to central banks of member countries to provide for the growth of monetary reserves. The large industrial countries would have no reason to incur indebtedness merely to facilitate the growth of the world total of monetary reserves. Other countries could not be expected to qualify for the enormous increase in loans that would be necessary for the growth of the world total of monetary reserves. The experience of the Federal Reserve System is pertinent on this point. Among the factors supplying reserve funds to the member banks of the Federal Reserve System, discounts and advances (loan) are of negligible importance. In the week ended December 12, 1962, member bank borrowings accounted for $107 million out of a total of $2,629 million of Federal Reserve Bank credit outstanding. At present, about 94 per cent of Federal Reserve Bank credit is provided through holding U.S. Government securities.

Professor Triffin is aware that it might be impossible to make loans to countries on the scale required for an adequate growth of monetary reserves. He would, therefore, empower the world central bank to enter into open-market operations through the purchase of government securities in the leading financial centers. This would, of course, have to be done with the approval and through the agency of the monetary authorities. Countries acquiring reserves through the open-market operations of the world central bank would be expected to use the reserves to increase their foreign investment so that the reserves would be spread throughout the world economy. It is difficult to believe that any large country would consent to such an arrangement. It would impose on the reserve centers a greater obligation for supplying capital and reserves to the rest of the world than they now have.

To avoid this difficulty, it has been proposed by The Honorable A. Maxwell Stamp that the creation of reserves by a world central bank should be linked to development loans. This could be done by having the world central bank buy the securities of the International Bank for Reconstruction and Development and the Inter-American Development Bank, leaving to these institutions the responsibility of deciding in which countries to make development loans. If the development loans, which would be the basic securities behind the reserve deposits with the world central bank, had to meet reasonable standards of creditworthiness, it would not be possible to find eligible borrowers for the amount needed to increase monetary reserves at a moderate but steady rate. It is difficult to believe that countries reluctant to absorb additional reserves in the form of dollar and sterling claims would be receptive to holding reserves in the form of international currency units created by a world central bank through credit operations under such a plan.

There is a widespread fear among central banks that the Triffin plan would inevitably involve an excessive creation of monetary reserves and generate inflation in the world economy. There is this possibility, although it is unlikely. Professor Triffin recognizes the desirability of limiting the capacity of a world central bank to create reserve credit by providing for a fractional gold reserve and for the conversion of excess deposits of currency units into gold. Other reasonable safeguards could be imposed on the operations of a world central bank, such as a limitation on the annual increase of reserve credit, or a limitation on the amount of deposits with a world central bank that any country could be required to hold. These are feasible devices for preventing the excessive creation of reserve credit by a world central bank. They would be adequate to restrain any tendency toward a rapid expansion of reserve credit under the Triffin plan.

In my opinion, the Triffin plan is much more likely to be deflationary. As already noted, a world central bank would have great difficulty in finding acceptable borrowers to whom to extend loans on the scale necessary for the growth of monetary reserves. A prospective borrower would have to satisfy a world central bank that it is creditworthy and that it is following responsible financial policies. Even this would not assure a country that it could secure credit when its balance of payments is under pressure. It must be presumed that in determining whether to create reserve credit, a world central bank would have to take account of the state of the world economy. It is quite conceivable that a country with a balance-of-payments deficit, not attributable to its own inflation, would be denied credit on the grounds that the world economy has adequate reserves and is suffering from excessive demand.

The point that must be emphasized is that the grant of such a far-reaching power as the creation of monetary reserves would impose on a world central bank a corresponding responsibility to use such power with great caution and in the general interest. Inevitably, the policy of a world central bank in creating monetary reserves would be determined by the general state of the world economy. Although the interdependence of countries in the world economy is far greater than it has been in the past, the economic situation differs radically from country to country. It would be unfortunate if the provision of reserve credit for any country had to be dependent on the capacity of other countries to absorb more reserves with-

Edward M. Bernstein

out putting pressure on their domestic economy. At this stage, it would seem far wiser to give countries access to predetermined, but limited, reserve credit when their own balance-of-payments position makes this necessary. This is done through the quotas of the International Monetary Fund. The improvement of the reserve system does not require the elimination of quotas, but a more effective means of integrating them with the working reserves of members of the Fund.

10

Liquidity

SIR ROY HARROD

DIAGNOSIS

Internal Liquidity

The concept of liquidity was brought into prominence by the late Lord Keynes. The desire for liquidity has a key role, according to his theory, in the determination of the general macro-economic equilibrium. The marginal disinclination to part with liquidity is measured by the rate of interest. How high or low this rate is depends on where the margin is. If there is plenty of liquidity in relation to the desire for it, the rate of interest will be low; and conversely.

The rate of interest has also an influence on the amount of investment undertaken. Keynes represented the matter schematically by positing that an investor (in real capital) would compare the market rate of interest at which funds could be borrowed with the expected yield over cost of projected capital installations. In some recent writing there has been a disposition to doubt the potency of the interest rate in having any large effect on the volume of investment; it has been questioned whether those contemplating capital outlay often in fact make so precise a calculation as that set forth by Keynes. But this doubt may spring from too narrow an interpretation of Keynes's theory; it was expedient for him to present it in abstract terms, since he wished it to displace older established theories of equally abstract formulation. Looking at the matter more broadly, one may think of the ruling rate of interest, as registered in certain organized markets, as being a symptom of the current ease or difficulty in borrowing. Many firms, perhaps most firms, when contemplating capital outlay will not

This article is made up of excerpts from two papers, "Liquidity" and "Growth and Liquidity," which were published in 1961 and 1962 in *Rivista di Politica Economica*. The fifteen paragraphs beginning "The U.S. and the Price of Gold" are from the later article, the rest from the earlier one. This reprint has been made possible through the courtesy of the author.

make the precise calculation defined above, but will be influenced in favor or against an investment project by whether it is easy or difficult to find finance. The high rate of interest may be regarded as a barometric reading indicating that the capital market is tight.

Thus in the Keynes scheme a shortage of liquidity, which would be reflected in a high rate of interest, would be an obstacle to investment. Such an obstacle might, in certain circumstances, be salutary, as on occasions of an investment boom giving rise to inflationary pressure. At the time when Keynes was evolving his theories, the general trend throughout the world was in the opposite direction, namely, toward underinvestment and industrial depression.

His remedy for this state of affairs was to stimulate investment by bringing down the rate of interest and to bring down the rate of interest by increasing liquidity. For him the quantity of liquidity was regarded, by way of rough approximation, as simply the quantity of money (bank deposits and notes). Thus to increase liquidity, one increased the quantity of money. He did not consider that this would have an inflationary effect of any significance except when economies were nearing the point of full employment. He considered that there was a shortage of liquidity in the 1930's *both* internal and international.

In a broad way his theory of the dependence of the rate of interest on the quantity of liquidity may be thought to have been verified in Britain since the war. The primary determinant of the *demand* for liquidity may be taken to be the money value of the national income. The first column of the following table shows the value of the national income in each year divided by the quantity of bank deposits outstanding (average) each year. This figure may be designated the "income velocity of circulation" of money. It has no direct relation to the velocity of circulation in the ordi-

Year	Measure of Scarcity of Liquidity*	Yield of Consols	Year	Measure of Scarcity of Liquidity*	Yield of Consols
1938	2.557	3.38	1954	2.746	3.75
1947	1.978	2.76	1955	2.973	4.17
1948	2.014	3.21	1956	3.268	4.73
1949	2.097	3.30	1957	3.361	4.98
1950	2.157	3.54	1958	3.380	4.98
1951	2.442	3.78	1959	3.384	4.82
1952	2.586	4.23	1960	4.524	5.42
1953	2.695	4.08			

* National income divided by quantity of bank deposits. Higher figures denote greater scarcity.

nary sense, since the goods that go to compose the national income change hands a number of times in the course of processing and distribution. The figure simply shows the average number of times that each unit of money would have to be used during the year, if it was used only to purchase the final product, consisting of goods and services. For this purpose, what is called the "total domestic expenditure at market prices" in the British national income year book has been chosen.

The income velocity of circulation is the precise reciprocal of the abundance or shortage of liquidity. If the velocity is high, this means that money balances in hand are low in relation to the work that they have to do. Thus the column is headed "measure of scarcity of liquidity."

There is no exact annual correlation between the scarcity of liquidity and the rate of interest. Special factors affecting the capital market, including expectations, doubtless played their part. The most notable deviation was in 1952, which followed a great funding operation for converting treasury bills into longer-term debt. But the broad pattern is fairly clear. The period of ultra-ease in monetary policy, 1947, when Lord Dalton was Chancellor of the Exchequer, stands out. The rate of interest was then below its prewar level. After that there was a progressive reduction of liquidity, finally going far beyond the level ruling before the war, and the rate of interest rose accordingly. The stiff decrease of liquidity during the credit squeeze period (1954–57) is to be noted and the sharp rise in the rate of interest in that period. In the following two years (in 1958 and 1959) the scarcity of liquidity remained roughly constant, and the rate of interest also; the authorities allowed a moderate increase in the quantity of money in line with the rising value of the national income. In 1960 there was a renewed pressure on liquidity, and the rate of interest rose.

The pattern of events was doubtless affected by the important change that took place in this period in the attitude of investors to gilt-edged stock, as compared with "equities." This might be expected to produce, on its own account, some rise in the yield of gilt-edged securities. (Note that the yield of the undated consols has been taken, since it is difficult to get a consistent index of the yield of dated stocks, the remaining lengths of life of which before maturity were varying during the period.) While some of the rise in gilt-edged yields must be attributed to this cause, it may well be thought that the main part of the rise was due to the progressive decline in liquidity; indeed one may regard this as a very striking posthumous vindication of Keynes's theory.

The pre-Keynesian school might hold that the rise in interest rates was due to the high level of investment and its pressure on available savings. This might be an arguable view up to 1955, but since 1955 there has been no pressure on productive resources, such as would be expected if investment was running ahead of the saving potential of the community. In all that period, except perhaps for a few months at the beginning of 1960, the economy has been notably slack. If the high interest rate has been deemed to be fulfilling its classical function of holding down investment, it is rather curious for the authorities to have in operation a subsidy to investment, in the form of what is known as an "investment allowance." It would be simpler to have a lower rate of interest, in order to stimulate investment, and to hold the possibility of a subsidy in reserve for use in the event of its being found that a lower interest rate did not stimulate investment as much as might be thought desirable. Alternatively the older school might argue that the higher interest rate was performing the function of stimulating saving. It seems extremely unlikely that saving would be appreciably lower, if the interest rate was lower. Indeed saving might well be higher, if the economy was growing in accordance with its full potential and households and firms had higher (real) incomes out of which to set savings aside. Much the greater part of personal saving is done through insurance policies and pension funds. To this must be added that due to home ownership. These principal forms of saving would not be likely to be diminished by a lower interest rate.

International Liquidity

Keynes was very strongly convinced that before the war the world was suffering from a shortage of international liquidity also. At the time of the World Economic Conference in London (1933), which was convened to deal with the great depression, he put forward a scheme for the issue of international "gold notes." Later his primary purpose in devising his plan for a "clearing union"[1] was to secure such increase of liquidity after the war as would facilitate a return to more liberal multilateral commercial policies. In the event the International Monetary Fund, which was conceived on a less generous scale than his clearing union, has not achieved any *net* increase in world liquidity, but only offset, in a small degree, the decline in international liquidity, which has been caused by the reduced commodity value of an ounce of gold.

---

[1] "Proposals for an International Clearing Union," British Government Publication, Cmd. 6437 (London: H.M. Stationery Office, 1943) [reproduced above, pp. 55–79].

Internally the amount of liquidity may be regarded as represented roughly by the amount of bank deposits outstanding. For international purposes, liquidity consists of gold reserves and foreign exchange holdings, and, to a lesser degree, of drawing rights on the International Monetary Fund. Internally the adjustment to a shortage of liquidity is made by the millions of individuals (households or firms) affected by it. They have a tendency to restore their position by selling assets, thereby lowering the values of the assets and raising their yields (interest rates). By contrast, the shortage of reserves for international settlement acts upon the economic policy makers in each country. The authorities may have the choice, when their reserves run too low, between adopting a policy of import restriction or internal deflation; they may adopt both.

Some countries in continental Europe may be rejoicing at, or may even be embarrassed by, their recent increases in liquid reserves. But it is to be observed that in 1961 *both* the United States and Britain are very short of reserves. The fundamental balance of payments of the United States improved considerably in 1960, but that country has not yet reached the end of her difficulties. The difficulties of Britain are likely to become manifest presently. Outside Europe there are many other countries also experiencing reserve shortage. If it is felt that reserves, say in Germany and Italy, are somewhat in excess, it must be rememberd that the redistribution of what those countries might regard as surplus to their requirements would have a very small effect on the shortages felt elsewhere. If a turn of events occurred that swept away the continental surpluses, the rest of the countries would not feel their own improvement to be appreciable.

In a comparison with the prewar period it may be better to take 1937 than 1938, since the latter was a year of depression and diminished value of international trade. In 1937 gold and foreign exchange held by central banks or financial authorities ($27.575 million) was slightly in excess of the value of world imports ($27.275 million). It might at first be thought that this, representing as it does a lower velocity of international than internal circulation, indicated a needless abundance of liquidity; but the requirements for international settlement are really quite different from those for internal settlement. In the latter case the individual can react promptly in adjusting his own position. By contrast the national authorities, who are responsible for the solvency of their respective countries, have to rely on general policy measures, which may be slow working. Furthermore the individual may in certain cases let his cash run down to zero (and even become "overdrawn" at his bank). The national authorities could not contemplate this; and they probably have in mind a certain "bedrock" level of reserve, to be kept available for use in extreme emergencies—war, etc. A further point is that the figure for world trade given above represents visible trade only; the monetary authorities have to think also of "invisible" items due out and also capital outflow in the form of repayments due and overseas investments for which there have already been commitments. By 1948 the ratio of world trade to reserves had risen by 30 per cent. By 1951 it had risen by about 70 per cent. Thereafter there was a certain slackening until 1955. Between then and 1960 there was a further rise, and in the latter year it was double its prewar level.

The level of international liquidity, as distinct from internal liquidity, may be thought of as having its direct effect on short-term interest rates. For rough guidance, I have taken the arithmetic unweighted average of the official bank rates in the United States, Canada, Belgium, Britain, Denmark, France, Germany, Holland, Italy, Norway, Sweden, and Switzerland. In 1937 we get an arithmetic average of 2.7 per cent. In 1948 we find an average of 2.8 per cent only. In 1951 it had risen to 3.25 per cent. It will be recalled that in this period most currencies were inconvertible, except for the U.S. dollar, where there was at that time still an ample reserve margin; and that the foreign trade of most countries was still subject to severe controls. By 1957, when the ratio of world trade to reserves had almost reached its 1960 peak, the average of bank rates had come up to 4.4 per cent. In 1960 it stood at 3.9 per cent. There is doubtless interaction between the long-term interest rate, which is related mainly to the condition of the internal economy, and the short-term rate which has more relevance to the need to protect reserves in relation to balance-of-payments problems. The Americans have recently recognized this distinction in a notable way by adopting a federal reserve policy for bringing down the rate of interest on U.S. bonds, as required by the internal situation, while maintaining (or even raising?) the rate on bills.

One may think of the short-term rates in the various countries being levered upward, largely by mutual competition, through the need of the countries to protect their inadequate reserves. If there had been an over-all sufficiency of reserves, some countries would doubtless have been short from time to time and have had to raise their own rates; but there would have been no cause making for a general increase. Individuals inside a country may adjust their own positions by selling securities, but this will not have a general effect on the yields of securities unless there is an over-all internal shortage.

The high short-term rates, thus levered upward, have their effect on the

long-term rate (and the long-term rate also has some significance in relation to the international flow of capital). If countries which are forced to
maintain relatively high short-term rates had all-out drives for decreasing
their long-term rates, this might jeopardize the high short-term rate policy.
Will the Americans now disprove this by the policy aforementioned? To
maintain the long-term rates in reasonable relation to the short-term rates,
internal liquidity has to be kept in restraint.

Some countries in continental Europe have recently maintained satisfactory growth rates, but not all. The growth rates both in the United States
and Britain have been profoundly unsatisfactory. A turn of events could
easily put the European countries into similar difficulties as regards reserves, and indeed almost all of them have been hampered in some period
or other since the war in their growth policies by the external position.

Quite apart from the problem of internal growth, high interest rates in
the mature industrial countries are very unhelpful in this phase of world
history. It is to be hoped that these countries, with their high rates of
saving, will be able to increase their rate of investment in the developing
countries of the world. It is desirable that these developing countries
should make the utmost effort to finance their internal investments by their
own savings. But it is not likely that they will be able to do all that is
required by this method; and from the point of view of their own balances
of payments it may be needful to get external assistance, if their development requires the importation of capital goods on a big scale. Borrowing
abroad is for these countries a *pis aller*. They do not want to encumber
themselves with service charges, unless they have the prospect of improving
external balances of payments. But some borrowing in moderation may
be quite essential for them. Precisely because of the difficulty of meeting
resultant service charges, they need to borrow at the lowest possible interest
rates. The World Bank itself may be hampered in its efforts to assist them,
if the cost of raising capital in the mature countries is too high. Thus, even
if it is contended that the gimmick of a high interest rate is not seriously
impeding growth in the mature countries, it can do grievous harm if it
substantially reduces the feasible outflow of capital to help the developing
countries.

PRESCRIPTIONS

Change in Price of Gold

The figures cited above, showing a rising ratio of world trade to liquid
reserves, amounting now to double the prewar level, give a *prima facie*
case for taking steps to increase world liquidity. This is likely to become

a subject for international consideration. Indeed Anglo-American discussions have already begun.

The simplest method for obtaining the desired result would be to realign the dollar price of gold in proportion to the loss in the goods value of the dollar, which, by any mode of reckoning, has fallen to less than half its prewar value. This would not necessarily be a final solution, since there is doubt about how much the annual accessions of newly mined gold will be. Doubling the price of gold would at least double the value of those accessions; and there are good grounds for hoping that physical production might also become larger and the abnormally high postwar diversion of gold into private hoards might be reduced. Even if gold accessions did prove sufficient, it might be desirable to introduce greater flexibility into the International Monetary Fund, with a view to its carrying out an anticyclical policy.

The idea of raising the currency price of gold, so as to restore the prewar position of liquidity, is such a simple one that it is strange that it has not long since been brought into the forum of international discussion, and adopted. It is important to notice at this point, however, that the incidence of international liquidity shortage would have been much more severe, had it not been alleviated by the large increase in foreign exchange holdings, namely, sterling balances and dollar balances. It is evident that the increases in the holdings of these two currencies cannot be continued at the rate of the last twenty years, so that the problem of international liquidity shortage is bound to become more acute.

The reason why this simple recipe has not been more canvassed has apparently been a gust of fashion. For many years before the war Keynes inveighed against the rigidities of the gold standard, and, although his words were not much heeded at the time—countries abandoning the gold standard did so under *force majeure* and not because they were Keynesians—they have sunk in since. In the minds of many gold has come to be thought of as something outmoded and belonging to a bad old world; but Keynes himself did not take this view. In 1933 he wrote: "At all stages of postwar development the concrete proposals which I have brought forward from time to time have been based on the use of gold as an international standard, while discarding it as a rigid national standard." In the pages of his plan for a clearing union he wrote: "Gold still possesses great psychological value which is not being diminished by current events . . . gold also has the merit of providing in point of form (whatever the underlying realities may be) an uncontroversial standard of value for international

purposes for which it would not yet be easy to find a serviceable substitute."
He proceeds to explain how gold would continue to play a part of substantial importance in his clearing union plan.

It is a paradox that in a world which has come to lay greater stress on multilateral trade and the value of automatic mechanisms of adjustment—a trend which would have surprised people in the 1930's—so little attention has been paid to the substance that has throughout historic times been the prime lubricant for facilitating the flow of trade. If liquidity were reduced to zero, trade would have to follow the channels of strict barter.

Perhaps this neglect has been due to the idea that a substitute has been found through the institution of the International Monetary Fund, or could be found through its further modification. But, as Keynes said, "it would not be easy to find a serviceable substitute."

Unless a severe dollar crisis arises fairly soon and causes a rise in the dollar price of gold, there is likely to be a prolonged process of discussion on precisely this question of a substitute for gold; but it is by no means certain, or a pessimist might say, by no means likely, that an effective substitute will be found. In that case renewed crises of liquidity are likely to occur and give rise in the end to that revision in the price of gold that it would be so easy to undertake at once.

The U.S. and the Price of Gold

Before proceeding to considerations about the wider international liquidity position, it may be well to analyze how an increase in the price of gold would help the United States economy and render a more expansionist policy there possible.

1. Too many commentators think of what they call the "devaluation" of the dollar as something which would give American exporters a competitive advantage. To this it is objected that other countries would also devalue at the same time, so that no such competition advantage would accrue. The British would certainly not be willing to agree to a devaluation of the dollar against sterling, since they have their own balance-of-payments difficulties. If sterling was kept level with the dollar at its new valuation, that would cover the whole of the sterling area. There would be very few developing countries who would be prepared to have their currencies upvalued relative to the dollar. There may be one or two countries in continental Europe which would be willing to see some moderate upward revision. Thus, if the Americans raise the dollar price of gold by 100 per cent, they might be content to raise it by, say, 90 per cent. Therefore in

relation to these countries one ought to think of them deciding to up-value against the dollar, for special reasons, rather than to think of the dollar being devalued in relation to other currencies in general. It is doubtful if France is one of the countries for which an upward valuation should be desired. For the French still have the continuing problem of internal inflation. It is often said that this has been checked through the influence of the President or of the famous report made by M. Rueff. The statistics to which one would naturally have first resort to illustrate this opinion do not seem to verify it. One may take "the cost of living" and "wages" as supplied by *International Financial Statistics*. Whereas in the five years up to 1958 the cost of living rose at the average rate of 3.9 per cent a year, it has since risen to date at the average rate of 4.6 per cent a year. Wages rose in the earlier period at 8.6 per cent a year (average) and in the later period at 8.3 per cent. These figures do not suggest any abatement of the inflationary tendency inside France; rather the contrary.

The course of U.S. exports and imports does not suggest that the United States is being progressively priced out of world markets. No doubt the question of dollar valuation relative to other currencies is a matter for legitimate argument. A rise in the dollar price of gold should be considered quite apart from such argument, and it ought to be strongly laid down that the recommendation of it should not be taken to imply that the dollar is overvalued relatively to other currencies.

2. An increase in the dollar price of gold would add substantially to the dollar value of the U.S. gold reserves; also to their value in terms of all other currencies and in terms of goods. This is an important point, but not the main point in relation to a rise in the dollar price. It is important because it would further postpone any need for unneighborly action by the United States. Its authorities have done their best, very gallantly, to avoid taking unneighborly action so far. But if pressure on the dollar continues, such action might eventually become unavoidable. It might consist in a raising of tariffs or other barriers to imports, or in a reduction in aid given to the developing countries, or in a reduction in military expenditure overseas which are so important for the defense and morale of the free world. Given a sufficient passage of time, we should be able to rely on natural forces, as envisaged not only by Adam Smith but also by Keynes, gradually to bring the U.S. external account into balance. The increased goods value of the reserves would also have a very valuable effect, both from the world and the American point of view in enabling the present Administration to adopt a bolder policy of internal expansion.

Doubtless the question will arise as to whether there would have to be gold compensation in relation to any of the external dollar balances now held. It is understood that there has in no case been any gold guarantee of the dollar in relation to a possible devaluation in terms of gold. That is evidently satisfactory, if correct. None the less there might be some question as regards a moral claim in certain cases. When the dollar came under pressure a few years ago, certain central banks allowed their dollar balances to rise, so as not to embarrass United States authorities. It has been said that this occurred in consequence of a "gentlemen's agreement." The existence of any such agreement has been denied by the United States authorities. But what is a gentlemen's agreement? It may be something "as light as air, but strong as links of iron." It may be something, not written down, not even orally formulated, but yet mutually understood. When sterling came under pressure in 1961, there occurred what was known as the Basel Agreement. This has been openly referred to and the precise amount of sterling held in consequence of it by other central banks has been stated. Perhaps it may be taken to be a tribute to the higher authority and greater power in the world of the United States that an agreement with it, if so it ought to be called, may be something unnamed, unquoted, and unmentionable by discreet people. That something of this sort has existed, agreement or no agreement, can hardly be denied since dollar balances in central banks have been allowed to rise beyond the point of normal convenience; and why should this have happened, save as a contribution to easing American difficulties.

It might be held that the central banks which from some undated day allowed their dollar balances to rise up beyond the normal level, are morally entitled to a gold reimbursement in the event of a rise in the dollar price of gold. Such matters will anyhow have to be considered.

Reimbursements could be strictly confined to central banks, and to those balances held by them in excess of what might be computed as normal. Even when allowance has been made for such reimbursements, if any, the net increase in the goods and currency value of the U.S. gold holdings would be very large. It is to be noted that no consequence of the revaluation would be such as to lead to any increase in the basic U.S. external deficit, expressed in dollars. Therefore the rise in the dollar value of the remaining gold reserve would give the U.S. authorities greater freedom of action in the years immediately ahead.

3. We now come to the more important forms of assistance which a rise in the dollar value of gold would give to the United States. It would

indeed, as stated in the last paragraph, help the U.S. authorities to tide over a longer period of basic deficit without taking unneighborly action. The much more important point is that it would tend to *cure* their basic deficit. It would tend to cause interest rates to fall throughout the world. Figures were given in my article of July 1961 showing that short-term interest rates, taking an average of all the more important countries, in 1960 were 44 per cent above their 1938 level. There need be no doubt that this was the direct consequence of the liquidity shortage; each separate country has had, from time to time, to maintain its bank rate at a higher level than would otherwise be desirable, in order to protect its reserve. The same cause that has resulted in a levering up of short-term interest rates in the various countries would, in reverse, result in their easing off. In the more recent period the United States has been plagued by an outflow of capital, both short-term and portfolio, in quest of higher interest rates elsewhere; thus a lowering of foreign interest rates would bring an immediate advantage to the U.S. balance of payments on this account.

The United States, a mature country of high saving propensity and an already existing capital equipment of unsurpassed magnitude, must have low interest rates internally, if growth is to be maintained. Therefore it would be a great advantage to the United States to have interest rates coming down somewhat in other countries, thereby reducing the outflow of capital in quest of higher yields elsewhere.

The late Lord Keynes, when he argued for very low interest rates in Britain to care for the unemployment problem between the two world wars, held that the British ought to be prepared to control the outflow of capital. He feared that other countries would not be so adventurous in a policy of low interest rates, or that even, in many cases, such a policy might be undesirable for them, from the point of view of their own internal economics. Accordingly he held that the British should safeguard themselves against an unduly large outflow of capital in quest of the higher yields elsewhere by some direct control. It was partly through his influence that the idea of countries controlling the outflow of capital was made respectable by incorporation in the Articles of Agreement of the International Monetary Fund. The British have kept in being the machinery for controlling the outflow of capital beyond the sterling area since World War II.

The Americans never had such controls. It might be very difficult to get the necessary legislation through Congress, since it would seem to many to be an intolerable limitation on the freedom of American citizens to do what they liked with their own, e.g., by making portfolio or direct investments in other countries. It may be noted at this point that it might be helpful to the Americans if the countries of Europe obtained the same result by limiting the inflow, by direct control, of capital from the United States. This would not be so difficult for them from administrative, political, or constitutional points of view. It would be to the long-run advantage of the European countries, since their balances of payments are likely to be burdened in future years by the profits or service charges that will have to be remitted in respect of the American capital investment now proceeding into Europe. The rise in the dollar price of gold would help to check this overspill of American capital into Europe, which is unhealthy from a European point of view and is causing the most serious balance-of-payments embarrassment to the United States.

4. A rise in the dollar price of gold would have an immediately favorable effect on United States exports. It is true that the countries of continental Europe have had favorable growth rates in recent years. An enlargement of its reserves would undoubtedly render possible a more expansionist policy in the United Kingdom and there are probably some other countries which would be influenced in the same direction. This would have a stimulating effect on primary product prices and on the incomes of their producers. Thus there would be an enlargement of purchases throughout a considerable part of the world and the United States would get its fair share in the resulting increase of exports.

A diminished outward movement of capital and an increased outward movement of merchandise exports should bring the United States balance of payments to rights, and at the same time facilitate an easier monetary policy at home. This in turn should promote expansion by giving a lift to prices in Wall Street and to the expenditures on consumer investment account of those influenced by the prices there, and at the same time in itself stimulate investment, by the normal causation of easier finance making many firms able to finance outlays on modernization, etc. . . .

A change in the price of gold ought not to be thought of as an *ad hoc* expedient or as a last desperate measure that has to be adopted, failing other ways out of difficulties. Rather it should be thought of as something right and good, something that it would be desirable to adopt on its own merits, even if there were no difficulties. For centuries of economic thinking the question of the abundance or scarcity of the precious metals has been thought to be one of primary importance. In the old days the goods value of the metals used for money was adapted to requirements, through a rise in general prices when the metals were becoming more abundant, and conversely. But since the days of monetary management the valuation of currencies has been determined in other ways; the resistance of wage demands to downward revision, which has its own merits, has been a factor here. All this may not work too badly, if a rough stability in the price level can be maintained. But something like World War II is too powerful for its effects on currency values to be nicely arranged by the monetary authorities. Since 1939 the goods value of currencies has not been determined by the abundance or scarcity of gold; rather the goods value of gold has been determined by the changed goods values of the currencies. In existing circumstances of shortage of international reserves, violent forces would, under the old dispensation, come into operation to depress wages and prices, and therewith gold; the liquidity shortage would have come to an end and the growth of economies rendered possible once more. No such way out of the difficulties is available today. For other reasons we may think that that is a good thing. But it does carry the corollary that we must relieve the pressure in the way that is open to us, namely, by altering the gold value of the currencies.

Unfortunately this has become entangled with a prestige point on the side of the Americans, which, however, is ill conceived. The real devaluation of the dollar took place long ago, during World War II and after it. The Americans appear to have a certain temperamental unwillingness, which appears in the political field also, to recognize existing facts. If there was any loss of prestige, it was when the dollar became devalued in terms of goods. Rightly considered, its devaluation now in terms of gold should not be thought to diminish American prestige, but merely to indicate that they are capable of dealing with realities in a businesslike way.

Historically the medium for international liquidity has been gold, or silver. It is important to observe that these were acquired from producers in exchange for goods which had had a cost of production. Both the precious metals and the goods for which they were exchanged had costs of production. Thus media for international liquidity could only be earned at a price. Since they carried an advantage, and were subsequently to be exchanged for other valuable goods, nations were prepared to buy them at a price. The other important, and by now time-honored, medium of liquidity, foreign exchange, could also be obtained only at a price. It is true that this could be manufactured by the nation providing this asset by a mere stroke of the pen; but this arrangement was acceptable, since the providing nation was under a potential obligation, sooner or later, to honor this liability, and to liquidate the claim upon it by the discharge of an excess of exports. Thus, under this arrangement, no one was getting anything for nothing. The producers of the precious metals were entitled to their *quid pro quo* because the precious metals had required labor for their production.

This arrangement began many centuries ago and our modes of thought have become accustomed to it. It accordingly seems unnatural that an asset, carrying the advantage of liquidity and the purchasing power implied, should be obtainable otherwise than by exchange for goods having their own cost of production. If media for international liquidity can be manufactured by a mere stroke of the pen, why should their producer be paid anything for them? Why should not such media be obtainable from time to time, by some equitable system of distribution among the nations as gifts? If they are to be purchased only by exchange for goods, who is to receive the goods? Why should the issuing authority be entitled to receive goods, since it sustains no cost in producing paper in question?

If the idea of gifts is unacceptable, it would seem that, if it was desired to supplement the medium of liquidity furnished by gold, one should think of some other medium of liquidity, which also had its own cost of production. It is easy enough to think of another. One could think of silver; but to do so seems absurdly archaic. There would be much to be said for supplementing gold, in this era of shortage of liquidity, by silver. The true objection to this way out of the difficulty is that the value of the total supply of silver, supplementary to its requirement for industrial use, would be insufficient to make a large difference. One might indeed think of the use of other commodities also as a reserve and medium for international settlement. This might one day be the solution (see below), but probably involves going forward too much in time in relation to what the human mind is at present prepared to accept.

There is an instinctive feeling that there must be some alternative method for providing additional liquidity, *other* than basing it on central reserves of gold or commodities. If an attempt is made to translate this feeling into intellectual terms, it appears difficult to give it precise articulation. It is vague and amorphous; and this is precisely where the difficulty that will confront international negotiators lies. There is a "feeling in the air." But when it comes down to "brass tacks," they will find themselves faced with something elusive, that they cannot translate into concrete terms. One has only to suggest the idea that all the nations of the world should be provided with media of payment as *gifts*, in proportion to the value of

their foreign trade or national income, for this to jar violently with preconceived concepts. Why, indeed, should the nations not receive these
media as gifts since they cost nothing to manufacture? But, against this,
it will be asked why nations should be entitled to receive anything as gifts.
This is the central problem.

Internal liquidity is created by a mere stroke of the pen by central
banks. The process by which this is done accords with historic modes of
thought. Households and firms in the nations do not receive their media
of liquidity by way of gift; they receive them in exchange for securities
surrendered to the Central Bank. Some part of the media of internal liquidity comes into the hands of its holders in exchange for gold or foreign
exchange acquired in international trade. But the greater part comes into
their hands through the "open market operations" of the central banks;
the individuals receive them in exchange for securities. This again, by
traditional modes of thinking, is fair enough. The individual surrenders a
security, which he had originally acquired for services rendered or goods
produced by him, in exchange for a bank balance. He thus pays for the
advantage that he gets, which currently takes the form of liquidity and
later his own power to acquire value in exchange for his bank balance.

The Triffin Plan

In principle it would be perfectly proper for a world central bank to
create international liquidity by open-market operations. This indeed is
part of the plan put forward by Professor Triffin, which has received much
attention. The creation of international liquidity by open-market operations by a world central bank might seem to be a happy solution of the
problem of securing an increase in world liquidity by a painless method,
viz., otherwise than by the laborious process of digging more gold out of
the ground, or platinum, or uranium, or whatever it might be.

The difficulties of securing general agreement to such an arrangement
are practical. First and foremost there is a feeling which is, perhaps, a
mixture of jealousy and anxiety, about donating such terrific power to an
international committee, which would cause a strong psychological resistance in the minds of the Americans and all others concerned. People
are unwilling to create a new body to which great power is to be donated.
This is partly unreasoning prejudice; but it is always founded on the reasoning that such a committee might act injudiciously. Perhaps this is a
little too cynical; but so far international committees have not always

given evidence that such cynicism would be misplaced. There are other practical difficulties.

While it must be emphasized that the benefit of additional liquidity does not accrue solely or mainly to its initial recipient, but arises from the growth of production and international trade which is the consequence of this additional liquidity circulating around in the world, the fact remains that someone does receive an initial benefit. By definition open-market operations must be carried out in an open market; and it is also implied that what is purchased by the operation is a marketable security. Only a small number of the nations of the world have sufficiently wide-open markets to sustain open-market operations in terms of hundreds of millions of dollars' worth of purchases per annum at the outset, mounting up to billions of dollars' worth later. Furthermore only a relatively small number of nations issue securities of a kind that would be eligible for this purpose. These are the rich nations. Accordingly if the initial generation of additional liquidity were to be by open-market operations of a world central bank, the benefits would flow in the first instance to rich nations. This would be considered inequitable. Even as between the wealthy nations such operations might indeed be inequitable. How would the world central bank decide how many U.S. bonds to purchase, how many British, French, German, Italian bonds, etc.? It would look as though there would have to be something rather arbitrary in this. The bank might proceed in relation to the existing balances of payments, so as to help those nations in temporary adverse external balance; but even about this there might be some disagreement. How draw the line between those nations the securities of which might be regarded as eligible from a banking point of view and those not so?

Putting the matter in this way suggests the idea that, instead of purchasing securities already in circulation in open markets, the world central bank had just as well given checks to the various member nations, on some equitable principle, viz., in proportion to the value of their foreign trade, etc., in return for I.O.U.s by the governments concerned. As it would be expected that the amount of liquidity required would increase year by year, these I.O.U.s would never have to be redeemed. This would in fact be tantamount to the distribution of gifts. And it is precisely against this idea that ordinary thinking, habituated to the process by which liquidity can only be acquired in exchange for the products of sweat and toil, revolts. It will take a vast change of thought to get acceptance for the

proposal that a supplementary medium for international liquidity should
be provided through a world-wide distribution of drawing rights on a world
central bank in exchange for I.O.U.s of member nations which would never
be called upon for redemption.

There is a further objection. "Open-market operations" imply intervention by purchase and sale in open markets. On the whole, as we have
seen, this would be a one-way intervention; sales would not normally be
required. If the idea of sales was ruled out *in principle*, then we should be
back to the notion of pure gifts. National authorities would not welcome
the idea of intervention by so powerful a body as the world central bank
in their own markets in the way of purchases and sales of their own securities on a great scale. They would regard this as carrying the possibility of
uncomfortable disturbance to their own policies of debt management. This
very point came up in an acute form in the negotiations between the United
States and Britain prior to the Bretton Woods meeting. Rightly or wrongly,
the British laid great stress on the principle of "passivity" in regard to
International Monetary Fund operations. The British wanted it made absolutely clear that the International Monetary Fund would not be able to
barge into foreign exchange markets with purchases and sales according
to its own discretion. This principle was established. This clearly has relevance to what nations would be prepared to allow in relation to open-
market operations in national security markets.

The other way by which a central bank creates liquidity within its do-
main is by lending, e.g., by the discount of bills. In a well-seasoned country
like Britain, the liquidity thus created is only a minute fraction of total
liquidity. In the British market there is the expectation of very prompt
repayment of such borrowing, reinforced by the fact that Bank of England
lending is at a penal rate. In the United States there is greater laxity, the
borrowing by "member" banks being allowed to run on for longer periods.
But even there the duty of repayment hangs over the heads of the member
banks that are in debt to Federal Reserve banks. While they are in debt,
they feel that this is a *reduction* of their own liquidity, and they are more
reluctant to extend advances until such time as the indebtedness is paid off.
Thus "lending" is only a partial answer to the problem of how to create
additional liquidity even internally. The matter is more difficult when we
come to the question of a world central bank. Inside the nations there are
established rules, legal or conventional, for the eligibility of paper put up
for rediscount, and there is a sort of implied obligation on the part of the
central bank to rediscount eligible paper. The Bundesbank has a certain

quota for the amount of discount. These arrangements and limitations are facilitated by the fact that there is a certain homogeneity of paper within the national unit. It would be more difficult to arrange for standardized rules of eligibility applying to discount paper as manufactured by all the different nations. If rediscount facilities were allowed by the world bank, there might be a mushroom growth of all sorts of discountable paper manufactured in unlikely quarters.

The question of the repayment of such lending is of paramount importance. Firms acquiring cash by rediscount with the national central bank normally expect to repay. Indeed the very form of this mode of borrowing implies a repayment date, since the paper has a certain maturity. This does not matter very much from the point of view of internal liquidity, since it is understood that the central bank will maintain a certain global supply of liquidity through its open-market operations. It is these open-market operations that are the centerpiece of the whole system. Lending by rediscount is subsidiary. And so it would probably have to be with the world central bank.

The question of repayment presents itself differently on the international scale from that within a national orbit. In the latter case the individual borrower, whether bank or discount house, expects as a matter of course to repay. For him the borrowing right is not considered a part of his own liquidity, but rather the contrary. He is illiquid until he repays. But in the international field the objective is to increase total liquidity. If the borrowing nation regards its debt to the world central bank as subject to the obligation of repayment, whether at a named date or otherwise, it would regard this obligation as a subtraction from its total of liquid assets. This is why the drawing rights established at the International Monetary Fund cannot be regarded as an increase in international liquidity in the full sense. If a nation lets its gold reserve run down to meet an external deficit, it feels at perfect liberty in regard to rebuilding its gold reserve again, whether within a given date or ever. But that is not so if it has borrowed from the International Monetary Fund; there is an implicit obligation to repay before too long. To that extent the drawing rights are not a real addition to international liquidity in the full sense.

There is a further point. Within the nation a check upon the central bank is regarded as a full and final discharge of debt. Thus a balance at the central bank is a perfect form of liquidity. Are nations prepared to accept checks on the International Monetary Fund as a full and final discharge of international indebtedness? Keynes thought that they should, and it was an integral part of his original scheme that checks on the clearing union, expressed in bancor, in his lingo, were *not* redeemable in gold. Bancor checks were to be co-equal with gold as a medium for the final discharge of international debt. But in the negotiations the Americans refused to accept this. They were only prepared to allow this form of settlement up to the limit of their quota.

It was this conflict between Keynes's view and the American unwillingness to accept it that gave rise to the "scarce currency" clause in the Articles of Agreement. If nations, having certain drawing rights on the International Monetary Fund, required them to be encashed in dollars, and if the American quota had run out, this requirement could not be met; in these circumstances the dollar was to be declared a "scarce currency," and, when that happened, discrimination against the United States was to be allowed. The proposal for a "scarce currency" clause resolved an impasse at the time, and was therefore to be regarded as a favorable concession by the Americans. But it has its awkwardnesses and has never been put into operation. The fact that the drawing rights, although established, would not be in fact usable if one particular nation happened to be in a strong creditor position vis-à-vis the rest of the world was a serious detraction from the amount of liquidity that the International Monetary Fund was supposed to create.

Keynes held that his bancor should not be convertible into gold; but the Americans would not consent to the acceptance of bancor (or its currency equivalent) as a final discharge of debt, except up to the limit of their quota. A compromise is to be found in Professor Triffin's plan. Balances at a reconstructed International Monetary Fund are, under it, to be convertible into gold; but he hopes that nations would not in effect want to convert these balances. International liquidity would be increased only to the extent that they did not insist on doing so. It might be thought that this was the path of wisdom. Make the balances in principle convertible and hope that no one will wish to convert them. It might be worth while to experiment with such a plan, which might be designated as a "ruse," if nothing better could be accepted. But the Triffin plan is also subject to the difficulties, as already set out, that surround the creation of an additional amount of liquidity by open-market operations or lending.

It may be well at this point to make a digression on the Triffin plan. While, subject to the objections mentioned, it has attractions, it has also grave disadvantages. It may well be deemed likely not to create, but to destroy, international liquidity, anyhow for a number of years after its first inception. In the first place, all nations are required to hold deposits up to 20 per cent of their gross liquid assets, these deposits to be acquired by the surrender of existing liquid assets. These minimum deposits (20 per cent of gross reserve) could not be drawn down, and would not therefore be usable for the discharge of international debt. This is a grave drawback in the Triffin plan compared with Keynes's plan. Since nations will wish in any case to retain a certain "bedrock" reserve, as explained above, their "available" liquidity can only be regarded as what they have in addition to the bedrock reserve. Professor Triffin's 20 per cent requirement increases the bedrock reserve by 20 per cent and thus reduces the "available" liquidity that nations at present have in excess of what they regard as their bedrock reserve.

Second, Professor Triffin proposes to destroy a large quantity of existing liquidity, namely, outstanding dollar and sterling balances. These are to be liquidated (in gold) over a term of years. The Triffin plan is presented as furnishing a medium of liquidity to take the place of existing dollar and sterling holdings; thus it is suggested that there would be no loss in the abolition of those holdings. But his liquidity can only be created by a rising quantity of lending and open-market operations by the reconstructed International Monetary Fund. He sets this Fund the task, not only of providing such extra liquidity as may be required by the nations year by year—all to be done by lending and open-market operations—but also of providing liquidity in lieu of the existing dollar and sterling balances. This is a wanton addition to its anyhow very difficult task. It is in virtue of these two features, namely, the 20 per cent requirement and the liquidation of existing dollar and sterling balances, that I deem that the Triffin plan would involve a net loss of international liquidity, anyhow for a good many years ahead. Indeed before it actually began to add to liquidity, the difficulty of further expanding its lending and open-market operations might prove insuperable.

In Keynes's plan for a clearing union, it was laid down that drawing rights should increase year by year. "The quotas should be revised annually in accordance with the running average of each country's actual volume of trade in the three preceding years, rising to a five-year average when figures for five postwar years are available."[2] Such a provision for increase is absolutely essential, if the problem of international liquidity is to be solved. There is no such provision in the IMF Articles of Agree-

---

[2] *Ibid.*, II. 6 (5). [Reproduced above, p. 60.]

ment. There will be great difficulties in getting acceptance for such an automatic increase.

It is by no means certain that the procedures for increasing international liquidity by lending or by open-market operations can meet the case. If reliance were placed mainly on lending, which would presumably be of short term, the volume of loans to be negotiated with the International Monetary Fund would rise progressively year by year, and would amount before long to many billions of dollars each year. It is most doubtful if nations will be prepared to renegotiate loans on such a scale. If these methods of extending liquidity are impracticable, then one would have to fall back on establishing automatic drawing rights, in return, say, for irredeemable I.O.U.s by the different national governments, which would in effect amount to gifts. And it is on this point that the implacable mental prejudices would be likely to be a fatal obstacle to the acceptance of the scheme. We have been in the habit of "earning" our liquidity, and the human mind, let alone the minds of persons concerned with international banking, is unlikely to accept an idea which is so novel. Totally new procedures from time to time gain a footing in human affairs; but this is usually by imperceptible processes, in which, in the early stages, people do not realize the novelty of what is happening. It is very difficult to get acceptance for a plan of action based on a totally new idea, just because it is argued that the idea is good.

But not only has the principle of gifts, rising periodically with the growth of world trade, to be accepted, but also nations have got to accept checks upon the reconstructed International Monetary Fund as full and final discharge of indebtedness—just as checks on a country's central bank are so accepted by its citizens. In the majority of countries these citizens have not even a nominal right to convert their balances into gold for internal monetary use; and in practice this is nowhere done, save in exceptional cases. The Americans showed not the slightest inclination to agree to accept checks on the IMF as a final discharge of international debt in the period prior to Bretton Woods; it is doubtful if they have yet changed their minds, and there are some other nations that might not be willing to accept the principle either.

Alternative Measures

Thus, when we proceed into the "discussions" about increasing international liquidity, which appear likely to take place, it may well prove that no radical solution is acceptable. Thus we may have to be content with a few makeshift arrangements that would ease the position a little for a year or two ahead. But the major problem will come up again.

There is one way of getting out of the difficulty without accepting the principle of gifts. That is that the reconstructed International Monetary Fund should, on its own account or through an agency, finance a world buffer stock, to hold stocks of the various primary products that are amenable to storage. It is well known that there are many arguments in favor of the establishment of such a buffer stock for its own sake, to iron out undue oscillations in primary production prices, and thus help development in the countries mainly reliant on primary production. Oscillations in prices and uncertainties resulting from them make the countries which produce the products in question less creditworthy than they would otherwise be, and thus hold up development in those countries.

The principal objection to buffer stocks, apart from all the multifarious technical problems involved, arises from the question who would pay for the initial purchases. If the formation of the buffer stock was indissolubly tied to the creation of international liquidity, no one would have to pay! The primary producer would receive in return for sales to the buffer stock drawing rights on the International Monetary Fund, which would be received by other nations in full and final discharge of indebtedness. Thus year by year, as buffer stocks were increased in proportion to the growth in the production and consumption of the commodities in question, the volume of international liquidity, generated by the creation of the credit instruments wherewith the stocks were purchased, would increase. This scheme would have a great advantage, as compared with open-market operations, in that the initial benefit of the credit creation would go to those who may be deemed to need it most, namely, the primary producers. Under the open-market operations scheme, the initial benefit would go to the rich countries. But again, any such plan as this will be confronted with powerful prejudices militating against its acceptance.

Accordingly it seems likely that no acceptable scheme will be found for increasing international liquidity on an adequate scale through the creation of new credit instruments. There may be prolonged discussions. But if no solution is found, balance-of-payments fluctuations will produce growing difficulties, as the ratio of means of payment to the value of world trade falls at an increasing rate. Let countries of continental Europe, which happen to be flush at the moment, make no mistake about this. They are part of a larger world, and currency crises elsewhere will hit back at them. There will inevitably be a trend toward tailoring imports year by year in accordance with the level of exports achieved. The multilateral system may easily break down, leading to renewed discrimination and, in the last resort, to barter. This would mean that the countries of the free world were moving toward the principles now adopted in communist countries. This would be a sadly retrograde movement.

As these problems and difficulties become more apparent, thinking may revert to the simpler solution of raising the currency price of gold.

11

The Two Functions of an International Monetary Standard: Stability and Liquidity

PER JACOBSSON

DIAGNOSIS

For an international monetary standard to function well, it must fulfill two functions: it must ensure stability among the various currencies, and it must also provide for expansion of liquidity as production and trade increase. This is elementary—but elementary things are often the most fundamental, and well worth rethinking.

By stability I understand maintenance of stable exchange rates as sustained by appropriate policies and monetary reserves strengthened in case of need by outside assistance. By liquidity I understand the supply of credit in national currencies as needed to finance and provide the means of payment for trade and production. As far as international trade is concerned, the availability of credits in the currencies of the major industrial countries is of paramount importance—and world liquidity problems will therefore be mostly a question of the capacity and readiness of those countries to provide credits and sustain the volume of means of payment. Their ability and readiness to do so is, of course, influenced by the size and movements of monetary reserves—which are important, therefore, for liquidity as well as stability.

While there is then a close connection between stability and liquidity, it is also important to distinguish between them.

Bearing this in mind, let me first cast a brief look back through the monetary history of the past hundred years. In the heyday of the gold standard before 1914, the industrial countries of the world enjoyed a high degree of stability of exchange rates. This was made possible by the link

This is the English version of an article published in *Bulletin d'Information et de Documentation*, the monthly bulletin of the National Bank of Belgium, in April 1962. It is reprinted with permission from the author and the publisher.

between gold and currencies, together with the free movement of gold between countries, which provided a strong currency structure for world trade and its financing. If there were an excessive credit expansion in a country and gold flowed out, the central bank in that country would normally increase its discount rate and in other ways apply any necessary credit restraint; the government might then heed the warning and be more cautious in its budget policy. But budget expenditure was not very high at that time. The amount collected in taxes, including local taxation, hardly ever reached a figure of 10 per cent in relation to the national income; it was what happened in the private sector that was the more decisive factor in monetary developments. If, on the other hand, a country received gold, it would register an expansion of credit, aided as a rule by a reduction of the discount rate. Thanks to such complementary policies, exchange rates were stabilized between the so-called "gold points," which were narrow enough to exclude really disturbing variations. It was useful—and I think it was important—to permit the small fluctuations between the gold points, for this helped to indicate the trend of the market, and often gave rise to equilibrating credit movements which reduced the actual shipment of gold. These fluctuations within the gold points can be compared to the amount of movement permitted in the structure by designers of skyscrapers. This flexibility in fact makes for greater strength, since rigidity is more often than not inimical to stability.

The pre-1914 gold standard also provided for an expansion in liquidity as the newly produced gold was distributed to various countries, spreading out fanwise from the London gold market. Some of the new gold was taken by industrial users, and some was hoarded (mostly in the East), but the greater part became available for monetary purposes. Some of it went into circulation as coins, but the rest found its way to the vaults of the central banks, which thereby increased their gold reserves held as backing for their liabilities in notes and deposits. The commercial banks, through which the gold usually passed to the central banks, were able, by the sale of the gold to the central banks, to increase their cash and thus were able in their turn to expand credit. The extent to which the credit volume could be increased in each particular country depended largely upon the institutional arrangements, such as the nature of legal cover requirements or traditionally accepted cash ratios.

The degree of expansion varied from one country to another. In the highly developed British banking system, credit was expanded on the basis of astonishingly small gold reserves; before 1914 the gold reserves were never more than £45 million (or about $350 million at the present dollar price of gold). In France, on the other hand, the possibilities of expansion were more restricted, and higher gold reserves therefore had to be accumulated. In the United States the means of payment appear to have increased more rapidly than the gold stock in the period up to 1914. Generally, however, the practices followed were fairly constant; in these circumstances it was the supply of new gold available for monetary purposes that was the decisive factor in determining the trend of credit expansion all around the world. The increase in the gold output after the discovery of the Transvaal Gold Fields around 1890 had a marked influence on the volume of credit, and the movement of prices up to 1914. In fact, there can be no doubt about the role that gold played in determining the trend of world liquidity in those years.

The gold standard, which was restored after World War I, in certain technical respects differed from the pre-1914 standard, for example—and this was a most important difference—in the increased practice of holding amounts of foreign exchange as part of the monetary reserves. What was perhaps equally important was that the whole milieu in which the restored standard operated had been materially changed; the London market, for instance, could no longer play the same role as before 1914. Also—and this point needs to be emphasized—the breakdown of the stabilization efforts of the 1920's was caused not by inflation but by deflation—by a decline in prices which began first in the raw material markets, then markedly in the United States, and eventually spread to Europe. What began as a typical cyclical decline in 1929–30 was aggravated by an insufficiency of liquidity once the decline had set in. Annual gold production in ounces was somewhat lower than before 1914 and the price remained the same, while money incomes rose considerably above the 1914 level. Moreover, most of the current output of gold went to replace the holdings of a few countries on the continent of Europe, especially France. The gold stock of the United States was no higher at the end of 1933 than it had been at the end of 1924. The impetus, therefore, that the gold output before 1914 had provided was this time lacking, certainly in the United States, and once the business decline set in, the policies followed were such that liquidity was not increased in any other way. For when the demand for commercial credits slowed down, central banks did not on their own initiative undertake any significant open-market operations to bring about an expansion of the credit volume, nor were interest rates in many fields adjusted sufficiently to lower and more appropriate levels. Not even an increase in the gold price saved the situation, for world trade kept on stagnating. If the more automatic methods tied closely to the current gold output employed before 1914 were thus found wanting, the task seems to fall on the monetary authorities to find, by their own actions, some way of increasing the liquidity required to make the monetary system function smoothly under modern conditions and without prejudice to stability.

PRESCRIPTIONS

Current Solution

This was briefly the background of the problems that faced the monetary authorities after World War II. That war left a legacy of problems, arising from discrepancies in the relative values of currencies. Great efforts were needed, including several alterations in par values of the principal European currencies, before a position of exchange stability was established between the main currencies. Evidence of the progress attained came by the end of 1958, when a number of countries, mainly European, felt strong enough to make their currencies convertible for nonresidents; subsequent increases in monetary reserves of those countries and of others have, of course, increased the chances of preserving exchange stability. But continued stability is not assured by itself; there must be, as in the time of the old gold standard, preparedness to pursue those policies, often complementary, in the different countries that will enable the exchange rates to remain realistic. Surplus countries must be prepared to expand credit, and countries that are exposed to strain must be ready to take the necessary corrective internal measures and must have sufficient resources at their disposal to meet the strain in the balance of payments while those measures take effect. Since, under conditions of convertibility, funds can be more easily moved from one country to another, the means for defense must be sufficiently large to prevent an impairment of the currency structure, and indeed must impress upon would-be speculators that they will not be able to control events by their operations.

In addition to the increased monetary reserves, there is now international assistance represented by credit arrangements between central banks and drawings and stand-bys which may be obtained from the International Monetary Fund. Credits between central banks as undertaken recently under the so-called "Basel Agreement" are essentially very short-term, while assistance from the International Monetary Fund is often for a longer period. Members are expected to repay the Fund when their position improves, with an outside limit of three to five years. Thus there is time for the authorities to take effective corrective measures—but this time is not time to waste! According to the established practices of the Fund, the greater the assistance given in relation to the quotas, the more exacting must be the standards which the corrective program must meet. Thus great safeguards have been built into the present system to ensure that the first of the two functions of the old gold standard—that of maintaining stability in exchange rates—may be adequately fulfilled. Very large sums of international resources are available to counteract pressures on the system. The Fund has resources of about $3 billion in gold assets which can be made available to its members and the equivalent of $6.5 billion in convertible currencies. The new borrowing arrangements recently negotiated will provide the equivalent of $6 billion of additional resources in convertible currencies which can be used in support of the currencies of any of the ten countries participating in those arrangements. These ten countries—the main industrial countries of the world—are most likely to be those exposed to any undue movements of short-term funds, so there is good reason for them to take steps to help each other in this way to avert any threat of impairment of the international monetary structure.

The Fund is thus in a position to assist all its members, large and small, and there is no reason to think that national and international defenses are inadequate to cope with the consequences of the practice of holding the key or reserve currencies (U.S. dollars and pounds sterling) as a part of the monetary reserves or on private account, particularly in view of the policies followed by the authorities in the United States and Great Britain to maintain the value of their currencies. Personally I agree with the statement of the President of the Deutsche Bundesbank, Mr. Karl Blessing, who in a speech to the Administration and Business Academy in Düsseldorf on November 10, 1961, said: "By the present convertibility system we have attained a degree of stability in relation to the dollar, and hence indirectly to gold, such as has not existed since 1914. It seems to me proper, in all fairness, to say this, since the Bretton Woods system has been so much criticized of late."

The prospect for exchange stability, therefore, appears to be good. How far, then, is the present-day system able to fulfill the second function of the pre-1914 gold standard, namely, the provision of sufficient liquidity to meet the growth needs of expanding economies?[1]

---

[1] The stability referred to above is in terms of stability of exchange rates and not in this context in terms of stability of prices (or purchasing power). Of course, stability in terms of prices is also important, but, as will be seen from the analysis attempted in this article, price stability should result from an appropriate liquidity policy aimed at the avoidance of both inflation and deflation.

One of the main features in almost every economy in the years following World War II was a high level of liquid assets in the hands of financial institutions and the public, in relation to the national income. There was, as a rule, no lack of credit available for financing production and trade in terms of national currencies. But only very few currencies, among them the U.S. dollar and the Swiss franc, were convertible at the time. Steady progress has been made since the end of the war to overcome the difficulties caused by the fact that most European currencies were not then strong enough to be made convertible. In the decade following the war constructive steps were taken, notably the Marshall Plan and the European Payments Union. Since the time of the Suez crisis, at the end of 1956 and the beginning of 1957, assistance from the International Monetary Fund has played a considerable role. Recognition of the services that the Fund can render found expression in the agreement in 1959 to increase by about 50 per cent the Fund's quotas, and more recently in the borrowing arrangements agreed to by ten major industrial countries. Since 1958, international liquid resources, not only in the hands of the monetary authorities but also in private hands, have been greatly increased outside the United States as a result of the over-all deficits in the U.S. balance of payments, which have been met by an outflow of gold of almost $6 billion and an increase in U.S. dollar liabilities to the extent of a further $6 billion. Indeed, in the present conditions of widespread convertibility, I doubt if anyone would characterize the present degree of international liquidity as inadequate. There have been no signs in recent years of lack either of resources to finance world trade for any creditworthy borrower or of the will among the leading nations to provide additional resources if and when changing world conditions made them necessary.

Outlook for the Future: Gold

But what about the future? The question has been asked, what might happen when there are no longer any large deficits in the U.S. balance of payments—and that day may come sooner than many expect. There is also the question whether or not the newly produced gold will be taken largely by hoarders, leaving little available for monetary purposes to back further credit expansion.

Taking the second question first, it is interesting to note that output in South Africa rose by 7 per cent in 1961, and in the Western world as a whole, that is, outside Russia and its associates, by 3 per cent, the total produced having a value equal to $1.2 billion. It seems that with modern techniques there is no risk of a decline in the output of gold. Sales from Russia may increase the amount to as much as $1.5 billion. If confidence in currencies continues to increase, less will be taken by hoarders, as has in fact been the case in recent months; and even after provision for industrial uses, amounts are likely to be available for monetary purposes that will surely not be insignificant. This does not mean that we shall be in a position to, or indeed wish to, return to a more or less automatic gold standard, as before 1914. Let us not forget that the monetary conditions even at that time were not altogether satisfactory. There was a deflationary period from 1873 to 1895, and after the discoveries of the Transvaal Gold Fields the general level of prices rose by some 25 per cent from 1895 to 1914. This rise, interrupted by some violent crises, created a great deal of unrest. Whether we like it or not, we shall for many reasons have to live under conditions of more managed currencies and we shall have to see to it that the currencies are well managed. For my own part, I think that the wish to restore an automatic gold standard is a dream, and I am not sure that it even is a beautiful dream. There is much in matters of discipline that we should remember from the old gold standard, but we cannot turn the clock back from the present, more managed gold exchange standard, in which gold is a useful auxiliary but no longer the master.

If this is so, the question that then becomes of great importance is the way in which liquidity can be created other than by additions in the gold supply.

Open-Market Operations

The outstanding example of this is in the United States. From the end of 1952 to the end of 1960, the U.S. gold stock declined by $6.5 billion, or over 25 per cent, but in the same period the money supply rose by $13.6 billion, or some 10 per cent. I am not going to consider here whether the increase that took place in the money supply was of the right order. But it cannot be said to have produced inflation in the U.S. economy: the wholesale price index in that country has not risen for over three years—a measure of price stability that has not been attained for a long time. No doubt the policies pursued were only made possible by the availability of large existing gold reserves, which are still substantial, but the authorities have employed a variety of techniques to help implement these policies— changes in interest rates, reduction of reserve requirments for commercial banks, and also open-market operations. Open-market operations particularly have become increasingly important and are now indeed at the very center of monetary management in the United States. In fact, the Open Market Committee of the Federal Reserve System, which was not part of the original structure of that system but was only set up in 1935, may perhaps now be regarded as the most important arm of the central banking authority of the United States, and certain of the techniques employed are still in the process of evolution.

In Great Britain, open-market operations by the Bank of England (and since 1932 also by the Exchange Equalization Account) were undertaken earlier than in the United States, and the practice has been spreading in recent years to the monetary authorities of an increasing number of countries. Now those responsible for these operations will always take into account what is happening in the balance of payments, as they have to do in all their monetary policy measures. For a number of countries, particularly the smaller ones, surpluses or deficits in the balance of payments will, I think, continue to exercise a predominant influence on their liquidity position, but in the major industrial countries the supply of domestic liquidity will not be slavishly tied to the movement of reserves. This needs emphasizing because I often discover an assumption (perhaps not always clearly expressed) that liquidity can only be enlarged if monetary reserves, either in the form of gold or in the form of foreign exchange, continue to increase. After all, such reserves are primarily needed to take care of temporary deficits in the balance of payments. If there is greater equilibrium in the balance-of-payments position, it would be possible to make do with smaller reserves in relation to the volume of credit, as Great Britain was able to do before 1914—even though at that time London was the world's clearing house for international financial transactions. After all, the liquidity the world needs to carry on its business is in dollars and sterling, French and Belgian francs, German marks, and other leading currencies, and if credit in the main currencies can expand together, the liquidity requirements of the world will be satisfied. Let me quote Mr. Blessing again, from the speech that I referred to earlier: "In a well-balanced world economy, smaller reserves are needed than in one that is badly balanced, and with sound balances of payments the monetary reserves will be better distributed among the various countries than they are now."

Provided present efforts of Britain to strengthen its monetary reserves continue to be successful, we are approaching a situation in which almost all the major industrial countries have considerable monetary reserves. It is on the policies pursued in these countries that the major responsibility for the trend in liquidity rests. If they act in close cooperation, they should be able to take the appropriate steps, by the employment of modern techniques, to prevent any insufficiency in world liquidity, and thus to withstand any tendency to either damaging inflation or deflation in the world economy.

This is, as I said, a problem primarily for the major industrial countries; it can never be too strongly emphasized that the underdeveloped countries need "genuine savings" for their development, which are long-term funds needed to finance investment.

Cooperation and the IMF

Fortunately, in the major industrial countries on both sides of the Atlantic, the monetary authorities have begun to work together much more closely. This is an improvement, the degree of which can perhaps only be appreciated by those who remember the interwar period, when the attempts to establish contacts between central banks seemed to give rise more to suspicion than to cooperation. What is even more important is that this cooperation is being established at a time when the problem of a lack of liquidity has not really arisen.

The principal task of the International Monetary Fund is to help currencies to keep in line with the general monetary trend, and in this way the Fund contributes to the stability and strength of the present exchange structure. But the Fund also, I think, makes an important contribution toward ensuring adequate liquidity for the world. By making resources available to those countries that are subject to strain, even though the assistance is repayable within a few years, the Fund will strengthen the weak spots in the monetary structure, and in that way help to prevent the emergence of cumulative effects (as was the case after the collapse of the Austrian Kreditanstalt in the spring of 1931). Furthermore, the technique of stand-by arrangements—credit lines from the Fund to member countries requiring assistance—can provide valuable support for a currency without having an actual drawing. It may thus be possible for the Fund to assist a country without other member countries having to part with any amounts of their own currencies.

Moreover, the very fact that the Fund's resources act as a second line of reserves means that the reserve positions of its member countries are strengthened, and they are thus more able to pursue, in cooperation with each other, the policies that at any given time are regarded as appropriate. While each country will have to be mindful of the relative strength of its own position and act accordingly, there may on occasion have to be a general concerted action to adjust the supply of liquidity to the over-all requirements of the world economy.

The Fund is one of the centers for cooperation where the task of formulating policies for such concerted action can be undertaken. It is not the only one; there are others, among them the Bank for International Settlements and the Organization for Economic Cooperation and Development.

In the last few pages I have tried to put down a few thoughts on what I consider to be the two principal aims of a monetary system—stability and liquidity. Now this is a very large subject, and I am well aware that I have only touched on a few main points and that there are many other problems which I have not been able to deal with in the framework of a single article.

But what conclusions can be drawn from those points that I have mentioned?

As far as exchange stability is concerned, great progress has already been made since the end of World War II. Convertibility has been restored in a great number of countries and a system developed under which substantial outside assistance can be made available to give countries the time required to take the appropriate measures to ensure enduring stability.

With regard to the liquidity problem, it is not possible to be quite so precise, mainly because the problem of a lack of international liquidity has not yet really presented itself in a form requiring concerted action among the monetary authorities—and there is no clear indication when it may do so. But we do know that if the problem were to arise, the monetary authorities could agree upon concerted action so as to increase liquidity in other ways than those that follow through an increase in their monetary reserves. A degree of freedom of action has been gained by the existence of primary monetary reserves, now of substantial size in most major countries, and a second line of reserves in the form of quickly available outside assistance.

These are, it seems to me, the lines along which future action may have to be taken. Decisions will have to be weighed and judgments balanced carefully, but there is no reason to believe that the Western world will be found deficient in this respect. If and when difficult problems arise, the monetary authorities will have to consider them in close contact with each other, and maybe then develop new techniques for which there has been little or no need to date. Such steps as have already been taken, for example, through the Fund's borrowing arrangements, do not close the door to any future developments that may in due course be found appropriate. I may say there is great flexibility in the Articles of Agreement of the Fund, as has already been illustrated by the borrowing arrangements. The strengthening of the monetary structure that has already been achieved and the degree of cooperation now existing among the various national monetary authorities must surely be regarded as auguring well for a solution of problems that may arise in the future.

12

The Problem of International Liquidity and the Multiple-Currency Standard

FRIEDRICH A. LUTZ

THE PROBLEM

The many plans that have been devised, in the last few years, for a more or less radical change in our international monetary system owe their existence to the fear of their authors that the international liquidity reserves will sooner or later become so scarce that the Western world will, unless appropriate measures are taken, be forced to follow a deflationary policy—with all the disastrous consequences which such a policy entails.

The argument—by now well known to every economist—is, in a nutshell, this: Gold production adds far less to the monetary gold stock than is required for the latter to keep pace with the expansion of international trade or Gross National Product of the Western world. Therefore, the dollar reserves of countries other than the United States must continuously expand in order to make up for the growing deficiency of gold reserves. An increase in dollar reserves, however, would require the United States to run a deficit in its balance of payments. Even if the surplus countries had, up to now, been taking the accretion to their foreign exchange reserves entirely in the form of dollar balances, they could not be expected to continue doing this once American dollar liabilities rose to an amount several times that of the American gold stock. As it is, the monetary authorities are even at present not willing to accumulate dollar balances to the extent of the whole of their countries' balance-of-payments surpluses, so that such surpluses cause, in part at least, a loss of gold for America. Clearly, then, the United States cannot afford to go on running a deficit indefinitely. But if it does not do so, there is bound sooner or later to be a scarcity of international reserves in the Western world.

This article appeared originally as No. 41 of the Essays in International Finance, March 1963, published by the International Finance Section of the Department of Economics, Princeton University.

For the purpose of the present discussion, I accept this diagnosis of the fundamental weakness of the present gold exchange standard; but I feel I must at least add that I do not think the scarcity of international reserves is a very imminent problem. Nonetheless, it is the economist's job to think in time about possible solutions for the dilemma to which I have referred. This sort of thinking has produced such a galaxy of proposals for fundamental changes in the present set-up that it may appear to many as a pleasant relief to find somebody advocating changes that do not involve radical departures from what we now have, and do not either require new international institutions or burden existing international institutions with new functions.

POSSIBLE SOLUTIONS

There are, in principle, only three solutions to the problem of a threatening shortage of international reserves.

The *first* consists in the adoption of a system of freely flexible exchange rates—a very neat solution inasmuch as it removes the problem of the adequacy of international reserves from the scene. However, I shall not discuss this method of dealing with the problem. I have been in the past, and still am, an advocate of flexibility of exchange rates at least within certain rather broad limits. But the resistance of the monetary authorities to flexible rates is, in almost all countries, so strong that this system has no chance of being adopted in the foreseeable future.

The *second* solution is an increase in the gold price. Again, I shall abstain from discussing this solution in detail. But I should like to make one or two remarks about it.

First of all, I feel pretty sure that the raising of the gold price by the United States would not lead to any change in exchange rates, since the European countries would follow suit. It would, therefore, not contribute to an improvement in the American balance of payments. But this does not mean that the measure would not make sense. If the price of gold were raised sufficiently, the United States could, with the consent of foreign monetary authorities, convert the latters' entire dollar balances—inclusive of the amount that might in the future be turned over to these authorities by commercial banks—into gold. If this happened the dollar would cease to be a part of international reserves. And if, with luck, gold production in the West (plus, possibly, sales of gold by Russia) were to rise high enough to cause the rate of growth of the monetary gold stock to match that of, say, international trade, it would not be necessary to use the dollar for reserve purposes even in the future. Now, since the monetary authorities consider gold the final and therefore most desirable international reserve medium, and since gold is the only medium that constitutes *net* international reserves—that is, reserves not matched by corresponding liabilities, as is the case with dollar balances—surely we should admit that this second solution is not as stupid as many economists would have us believe.

If nevertheless I do not advocate a rise in the gold price, it is mainly for two reasons.

The first is the scramble for gold, and the confusion in the foreign exchange markets, which will occur as soon as there is serious discussion of a move to a higher gold price. The intention to change the gold price cannot under present conditions be kept secret.

The second reason is the inflationary danger which the large increase in reserves of all countries with substantial gold stocks would entail. This danger need not arise in the case of the United States if its dollar liabilities were converted into gold so that its reserves increased very little or not at all. Elsewhere, however, the danger of inflation would undoubtedly be quite serious, because the balance of payments would, for a time, cease to act as a brake against inflationary policies, while at the same time the book profits obtained from the devaluation might tempt the authorities to engage in deficit financing which would in those circumstances be costless. Although the exercise of monetary discipline on the part of the countries concerned could undoubtedly prevent such inflationary consequences, I am not optimistic enough to believe that this is what would in practice occur. And if they were not prevented, the stimulating effect on gold production, which is a necessary part of the whole scheme, would sooner or later cease to make itself felt. The upward revaluation of gold might then have to be repeated. For reasons which are rather obvious, recurrent increases in the gold price would, however, make the gold or the gold exchange standard unworkable.

The *third* solution consists in widening the foreign borrowing potential of countries by making provisions for countries with surpluses in their balances of payments to lend to those with deficits. Strictly speaking, it need not be the countries with current surpluses that do the lending; it may be done by other countries possessing large international reserves, accumulated out of past surpluses. Nevertheless, I shall for simplicity's sake consider the lending countries as identical with countries having current balance-of-payments surpluses. The principle is best made clear by an extreme example:

Suppose an international institution were created similar to the defunct European Payments Union, but on a world-wide basis. All the surplus countries would "deposit" their surpluses with this institution, while all the deficit countries would run into debt with it to the extent of their deficits. Since the sum of the deficits always equals the sum of the surpluses, no balance-of-payments crisis and no shortage of international reserves could ever develop. This "system of unlimited credit" would, of course, be excessively inflationary, since each country would have an interest in drawing on the resources of other countries by running a deficit, and no country would be obliged to keep a strict watch on its balance-of-payments position. I do not, of course, advocate this system; I only mention it because it shows better than any other how the shortage of international reserves can be overcome by international borrowing and lending.

Now, all the plans that have been devised to solve our problem—except, of course, that of flexible rates and that of a rise in the gold price—are variations on this theme of increasing the borrowing potential of member countries by inducing or forcing those in strong foreign exchange positions to lend to those in weak ones. This is so, whether the IMF arranges for stand-by credits, or whether a world bank à la Triffin is set up with the power to create an international currency, or whether, à la Maudling, the IMF acts as a depository for the currencies which surplus countries do not wish to hold.

In case the IMF widens the borrowing potential in the way described, it is immediately evident that the solution of our problem consists in the readiness of the countries with strong foreign exchange positions to lend to those with weak ones. If a world bank à la Triffin is created, this is perhaps less obvious, but nevertheless true. If this world bank grants a credit to country A by creating a bancor deposit in its favor, and country A then turns this deposit over, in payment for its deficit, to country B, which then keeps the deposit, it is of course country B which is really giving the credit to country A. Or suppose that, under the Maudling scheme, a participant in the Mutual Currency Account decides not to convert the currency of another participant into dollars and then into gold, but deposits it—after notification of the debtor—with the Account in exchange for a deposit in some currency unit of fixed value in terms of gold. What really happens here is that the depositing country lends to the country whose currency is deposited in the Account.

From what has just been said it should be clear that the borrowing capacity of a country ought to be regarded as part of its international reserves. The IMF is following this principle when it adds a country's gross IMF position, i.e., its drawing potential, to its foreign exchange and gold reserves. But this is not sufficient. Consider the case of the United States. The willingness of other countries to lend to the United States by accumulating dollar balances is certainly an essential part of that country's international liquidity. Without it, the United States would have lost gold much more rapidly than it has and would therefore have been forced long before now to bring its balance of payments into order. And the fear that this willingness may not last indefinitely surely contributes to the feeling that the international liquidity position of this country is deteriorating.

Now it is important to realize that if a country makes use of this borrowing potential, the effects will be different according to which of two types of lending is involved. One type does not entail the creation of any international reserves for the lender, the other type does. And I suggest that a good way of grouping these plans is according to whether they provide merely for an increase in the borrowing potentials of deficit countries by inducing other countries to lend to them, or whether they go further than this and provide for a type of lending which creates reserves for the lender. To the first group belong such measures as the raising of IMF quotas and the granting of stand-by credits by countries in strong foreign exchange positions, as was done at the 1960 meeting of the IMF in Vienna. The Maudling plan and the extreme scheme outlined previously—the system of unlimited credit—also belong to this group. The second group comprises the Triffin and a number of similar plans. In the Triffin plan the emphasis is clearly not so much on the increase in the borrowing potential of the participating countries as on the creation of more units of international currency, consequent upon the borrowing countries' making use of this potential.

Looked at from the point of view of the above classification, the situation under the present gold exchange standard is this: Through the IMF the borrowing potential of all participating countries has been increased; and when any country borrows, the corresponding lending by other countries is of the "neutral" type, which does not create reserves for the lenders. The United States, however, has in addition a borrowing potential which others do not have. It consists in the willingness of other countries to acquire dollar balances; and the acquisition of such balances is representative of the second type of lending, namely, that which creates international reserves for the lender.

It is worth noting that those who have devised schemes to meet the danger of a future shortage of international reserves by expanding these reserves, rather than by merely widening each country's borrowing potential, do not wish to see an expansion of such reserves in the form of an accumulation of dollar balances such as might occur under the system we have at present. The reason is, as I pointed out before, that such an accumulation is, as a rule, accompanied by some loss of gold by America and leads in any case to a reduction in the United States' ratio of gold to short-term liabilities. Thus, as long as the present gold exchange standard exists and the American deficit continues, the "conservatives" are usually at one with the "reformers" in holding—paradoxically it may seem—that surplus countries should lend in a form that does not increase international reserves as a way of meeting the threatening shortage of such reserves. And pressure is brought to bear on countries with strong foreign exchange positions to "lend more," as the phrase goes. We may notice that in public discussions the acquisition of dollar balances is hardly ever considered lending. What those who ask for "more lending" really mean is that the surplus countries should lend in a manner which does not create dollar reserves; that is, they should either lend long to the United States or they should lend—whether long or short makes no difference here—to third countries. In both cases the surplus in the balance of payments of the lending countries and the deficit in the American balance of payments would be correspondingly reduced, compared with what they would have been if no such lending had taken place.

Now, this method of equilibrating balances of payments through "neutral" lending—or lending that does not create reserves—by the surplus countries, which in its extreme form is equivalent to the "unlimited-credit system" outlined before, is not any more sensible than the method of persuading, or compelling, surplus countries to lend to deficit countries in a manner that does create reserves.

The theory underlying both methods has its roots in mercantilism. It regards the countries with balance-of-payments surpluses as "natural" capital exporters, implying that such surpluses are a sign of wealth. People, who in any other context would have ridiculed the mercantilist view, are apt to talk in this fashion. The theory sounds especially strange coming, as it often does, from those who think of an accumulation of dollar balances not as "lending to the United States" but simply and solely as "addition to foreign exchange reserves." There are, however, others who do recognize that the acquisition of dollar balances reflects an excess of domestic savings over domestic investment and is a form of lending; and some of them are, I think, inclined to argue that there can be no harm in requesting a country which already has such an excess and is lending to change the form of this lending.

We should beware of accepting this point of view. For, while a surplus in the balance of payments does, it is true, signify an *ex post* excess of domestic savings over domestic investment, it does not necessarily signify an *ex ante* excess. An indication that the two things do not always coincide is the fact that interest rates are frequently higher in the surplus (lending) countries than in the deficit (borrowing) countries. Surely the explanation of the surpluses has to run in terms of the cost levels in the surplus countries being too low relatively to the cost levels in the others. And in such circumstances the right course of action is for the surplus countries to get rid of their surpluses not by long-term lending, but by measures which raise their imports and reduce their exports (and for the deficit countries to cooperate if possible by acting the other way round). This seems to me to be the proper cure for balance-of-payments troubles, and not the "unlimited-credit system."

One last point before I proceed to the more constructive part of this discussion. Once we realize the importance of a country's borrowing potential as part of its international liquidity, we cannot attach much significance to the customary calculation of the international liquidity reserves of the Western world which equates them to the sum of the various countries' gold stocks plus the dollar balances of countries other than the United States plus the sterling balances of the outer sterling area. For such a calculation makes no allowance for the borrowing potential of the various countries. It is, as I said before, not sufficient just to add their drawing rights on the IMF. On the other hand, there is no way of knowing the sum total of all the borrowing potentials. Moreover, we cannot ignore the fact that an increase in the dollar balances of foreign countries may reduce the remaining borrowing potential of the United States, or, that is, the willingness of foreign countries to accumulate further dollar balances, in which case international liquidity, for the world as a whole, has not risen to the extent indicated by the usual statistical measure. The point I am now making is not, it should be noticed, the same as the point made by many other critics of such statistics, namely, that these statistics neglect the fact that dollar and sterling balances are matched by corresponding liabilities of the United States and Great Britain, and therefore fail to give a true picture of net international liquidity which, they argue, should be taken as equivalent to the monetary gold stock alone.

Now if we do not accept, as a solution to the problem of international liquidity, the principle that countries should be compelled to lend, either in a way that creates reserves or in a way that does not, and if we are also of the opinion that the present system cannot last indefinitely, what way out is there?

THE MULTIPLE-CURRENCY STANDARD

In a series of lectures delivered in May 1961 in Amsterdam,[1] I proposed that the Western countries now holding dollar balances should in the future keep their international reserves not exclusively in one country's currency but in many, and that the United States too should follow a policy of holding other countries' currencies in addition to gold. Not every country, of course, would be eligible to serve as a key-currency country. No central bank would, I imagine, be prepared to hold the currencies of South American countries. The new key-currency countries would doubtless have to be chosen mostly from Western Europe.

The policy of holding reserves in a number of currencies rather than only one or two is acquiring a growing number of advocates, some of them in influential circles. Under Secretary of the Treasury Roosa supports the idea;[2] the London *Economist* favors it; and it is also part of the plan which Dr. Posthuma, one of the Directors of the Netherlands Central Bank, suggested a few months ago. Indeed there is little doubt that this is the direction in which the Western world is gradually moving. It was the United States that made the first move in this direction, following some experiments which the monetary authorities had carried out in the foreign exchange market with *borrowed* foreign currencies and which had convinced them of the desirability of acquiring, and holding, balances on their own account, once the country's balance-of-payments situation permitted it. From our present standpoint, the most important aspect of those foreign exchange operations—some carried out by the Treasury and others by the Federal Reserve System—is that they may prove to be a steppingstone on the way to the general adoption of the multiple-currency standard. But they merit attention also for their own sake, since they illustrate one of the advantages of holding balances in a number of different foreign currencies. However, since Mr. Charles A. Coombs of the New York Federal Reserve Bank has given a good account of them in the October issue

[1] Published under the title *The Problem of International Equilibrium*, by the North-Holland Publishing Company (Amsterdam, 1962).

[2] [See selection 14.]

of the *Bulletin of the New York Federal Reserve Bank*, I need not discuss them in great detail here. I shall illustrate the Treasury's operations by reference to its dealings in German marks following the appreciation of that currency.

After the revaluation of the mark in March 1961, anticipations of a second revaluation caused a speculative flow of funds from the United States to Germany. The funds came from three distinct sources: (1) from people buying marks with the intention of shifting back into dollars after the expected second revaluation of the mark had taken place; (2) from Americans who had future commitments in marks; and (3) from Germans who had dollars coming to them in the future and borrowed dollars now in order to change them into marks. It is not surprising that in this situation the premium on forward marks rose far above its normal level as determined by the difference between the short-term interest rates. It is in this forward market that the United States Treasury intervened with sales of marks, which the Bundesbank stood ready to supply. Through these sales it succeeded in sharply reducing the premium on the mark, thus making shifts of funds to Germany less attractive for all those who wanted to combine the purchase of spot marks with a sale of forward marks, as well as for Americans with mark commitments, and Germans with dollar receivables, who now found it preferable to buy forward marks instead of spot marks. In this way, the short-term capital flow from the United States to Germany in those crucial months was reduced; and—a further welcome effect—the gold loss which usually accompanies the acquisition of dollars by foreign central banks was kept smaller than it would otherwise have been.

The success of these operations encouraged the authorities to undertake others. Early in 1962 the Federal Open Market Committee authorized open-market transactions in foreign currencies. On the basis of this authorization the Special Manager of the Open Market Account for foreign currency operations negotiated a series of swap arrangements with foreign central banks. These are arrangements providing for reciprocal credit facilities between the Federal Reserve System and foreign central banks, allowing each partner to draw on the currency of the other up to a certain amount over a period ranging from three to six months. At the end of the specified term, the transactions are reversed at the same rate of exchange as that at which the original swap was arranged. This is a practice which amounts to giving a guarantee against the risk of an alteration in the exchange rate. The currencies which, through these swap arrangements, are put at the disposal of the Federal Reserve System can be used for making a variety of exchange operations aimed at influencing short-term capital flows. For instance, the use that was made of the swap arrangements with the Swiss National Bank and the Bank for International Settlements (BIS) —involving a rather complicated technical procedure—resulted in dollars (treasury bills) being held by the Swiss commercial banks and the BIS, instead of by the Swiss National Bank, which would have converted them into gold. It meant that the United States was spared a loss of gold, and that the Swiss National Bank was able to mop up some of the excess liquidity of the Swiss commercial-banking system.

Even more interesting, from my present point of view, than the actual operations carried out on the basis of the authorization given to the Special Manager of the Open Market Account to deal in foreign currencies is the statement, contained in this authorization, that one of its aims is "in the long run to provide a means whereby reciprocal holdings of foreign currencies may contribute to meeting needs for international liquidity as required in terms of the expanding world economy." In this statement, the adoption of the "multiple-currency standard" is envisaged as the means of overcoming the threatening shortage of international reserves. And it is this—the most important—aspect of this standard to which we must now turn.

Suppose the multiple-currency standard had existed for some time past and the balances held by monetary authorities in the various key-currency countries had reached an amount that was equal to the sum of the dollar and sterling balances held by these authorities at present. The officially held dollar balances amounted in September 1962 to $11.7 billion and the officially held sterling balances to $6.8 billion. The total of $18.5 billion was roughly equal to the gold stock of the two countries combined ($18.8 billion). If we include the nonofficial holdings of dollar and sterling balances, the short-term foreign liabilities of the two countries ($29.4 billion) amounted to 157 per cent of their gold stock. For the United Kingdom alone the ratio of official foreign holdings to gold was 244 per cent and of total foreign holdings to gold 353 per cent. The corresponding ratios for the United States were 73 per cent and 123 per cent. Let us now suppose that the key-currency countries consisted of the United States, the United Kingdom, France, West Germany, Italy, the Netherlands, and Switzerland. The total gold stock of these seven countries amounted in September 1962 to $31.3 billion. Balances of $18.5 billion (total of the officially held dollar and sterling balances) or of $29.4 billion (total of all dollar and sterling balances) thus amount to 60 and 95 per cent respectively of the combined gold stock of these countries. It is evident then that if these balances were spread over the seven countries, none of them would need to be in the position in which the United Kingdom (and also the United States, if all foreign-held dollar balances are taken into account) is at present of having short-term foreign liabilities bigger than the gold stock or, that is, having negative net reserves. Assuming it to be true that a rise in the ratio of foreign liabilities to the gold stock to the point where the former are a multiple of the latter undermines confidence in a key currency, it is surely an advantage of the multiple-currency standard that it keeps this ratio down.

The purpose of the above calculations is merely to illustrate a principle. I am, of course, aware that the ratio of foreign dollar balances to the American gold stock cannot be lowered by the owners of existing balances trying to buy other currencies with them. The only way in which the ratio can in fact be brought down is by America's making appropriate use of a future surplus in her balance of payments. In this country as in others the new policy would have to be applied to the foreign exchange reserves acquired in the future. For example, countries which in the future had balance-of-payments surpluses at a time when the United States itself was, let us suppose, approximately in balance-of-payments equilibrium, should not insist on gaining dollars or gold at the expense of the dollar and gold holdings of the deficit countries; they should instead be ready to acquire balances in any of the deficit countries that were members of the widened key-currency group. By so doing they would be adding to the total of international reserves instead of, as under the present system, merely shifting the existing reserves around. Similarly, if the United States itself moved into a surplus position, this need not entail any decline in the dollar balances or gold stock of other countries, were the United States prepared to hold foreign currencies and thus add to the total of international reserves. It is true that the United States might prefer to take the opportunity of reducing its dollar liabilities, and hence improving the ratio of the gold stock to them. Under the present system, this course would mean reducing the total of international reserves. But under the multiple-currency standard it need not mean this. For, so long as some other countries besides the United States had surpluses, these countries could build up balances in third countries, thus causing the decline in dollar balances to be offset by a simultaneous increase in other key-currency balances. In this way, America's ratio of foreign liabilities to gold could fall while other countries' ratios were rising. Indeed, these ratios might, in the longer run, be evened up as between the various key-currency countries.

To avoid a possible misunderstanding, I must stress that I am not advocating that countries which have surpluses in their balances of payments should *necessarily* accumulate balances in key currencies other than the dollar. I am not in favor of compelling some countries to lend to others against their will. If, for instance, a surplus of German marks came into the foreign-exchange markets, and no country wanted to hold additional marks, the mark would fall to the point where the German authorities had to support it by selling foreign exchange. But the foreign exchange they thus sold need not be dollars. It might just as well consist of other key currencies in their possession. In any case, however, it is Germany's balances abroad that would decline, and not other countries' balances in Germany that would increase. And this decline in her international reserves would be a salutary warning that other countries were not willing to finance her deficit.

THE QUESTION OF THE GOLD GUARANTEE

In the case that the multiple-currency standard were adopted, it would be desirable and, I think, necessary for all the key-currency countries to declare themselves ready to sell gold on request to foreign monetary authorities at a fixed price. In other words, central banks holding balances in foreign countries should be given direct access to gold in those countries instead of having to acquire first dollars and then gold, and the new key-currency countries should be in exactly the same position regarding gold sales as the United States was under the old system and would continue to be under the new.

This point may seem rather an obvious one. What is not so clear is whether the key-currency countries ought to give a guarantee against the exchange risk which foreign monetary authorities run when holding their currencies. The London *Economist* has repeatedly expressed the view that, without such guarantees, no country would be willing to hold balances in the new key-currency countries. This argument would, however, lose much of its force once those countries undertook to surrender gold on request in the same way as the United States. Balances in any of the new key currencies would then be on the same footing as dollar balances; and there is no reason why countries should be less willing to hold one rather than the other.

Nevertheless, the question of the gold guarantee deserves closer examination. (I assume that this guarantee would apply only in the case where the foreign exchange rates for the dollar were lowered, and not where the dollar price of gold was raised while exchange rates remained constant).

The best way of approaching the problem is to make sure what such a guarantee really implies. Suppose that the United States had given one in the past, and that now it contemplated devaluing the dollar in terms of foreign currencies, and raising the gold price correspondingly. Let us further assume that the other countries did not raise the gold price in their own currencies, so as in effect to counteract the American devaluation, but accepted the latter. (This reaction would, incidentally, be a more likely one if there were a gold guarantee than if there were not.) The United States would then have to add to the dollar balances held by the monetary authorities of other countries an amount of dollars corresponding to the degree of devaluation. For example, if the dollar were devalued by one-quarter, it would have to raise the existing dollar balances by one-third. In the case where the ratio of the gold stock to the original liabilities to foreign monetary authorities was unity or above, the profit obtained from the revaluation of the gold stock would suffice to provide the required sum. If the ratio were less than unity, the profit would not suffice; and the remainder of the funds needed would have to be raised by the Treasury, at the cost, most likely, of an increase in the public debt. If the devaluation had the desired effect of causing the United States' balance of payments to become positive, other countries would draw on their increased dollar balances to cover the deficits in their own balances of payments. By thus using up at once, or in the future, part, or all, of their additional balances, they could obtain a corresponding amount of goods as a free gift from the United States. This gift, if all of it were taken, would at present amount, in the case of a 10 per cent devaluation, to roughly $1.2 billion and, in the case of a 20 per cent devaluation, to double that sum. In other words, gold guarantees render devaluations very costly affairs. For this reason, they might well lead to a freezing of the exchange rates at the levels which they happened to have when the guarantees were introduced. Advocating gold guarantees may thus be tantamount in practice to advocating absolute rigidity of exchange rates.

In the absence of such gold guarantees, the London *Economist* asserts, no country (outside the sterling area) would be willing to hold balances in countries other than the United States. And this view seems to be shared by others. The essence of Professor Posthuma's proposal is that an understanding should be reached under which surplus countries would be obligated to take only a certain percentage—60 is the figure mentioned—of their surplus in gold and the rest in key currencies. The proposal thus compels countries to hold balances in addition to gold, but it does not make any specific contribution toward a solution of the problem we are now considering, namely, how the countries could be induced to hold balances in currencies other than dollars.

It would run against the general philosophy of my essay if I were to suggest a scheme that would compel countries to hold currencies which they do not want to hold. And I do not think that such compulsion is necessary. We should remember that the custom of holding only dollar balances as reserves originated at a time when the dollar was rightly considered as the only major currency that was safe. The dollar does not occupy this position at present, and if other key-currency countries besides the United States obligated themselves to surrender gold on request, dollar balances would no longer have an advantage over balances in other key-currency countries. In fact, the larger the dollar balances become in relation to the American gold stock, the more desirable must it appear to begin to hold balances in countries where this ratio is still zero, or at least small. The desire to spread the risk by distributing balances between several countries should be sufficient motive for adopting the multiple-currency standard. And if the United States were to lead the way by acquiring foreign balances as soon as it moved into a surplus position in its balance of payments, I feel sure that the present habit among countries outside the sterling area of using only dollars as reserves could, and would, be broken.

The fear that the system might lead to shifts of official balances between countries whenever rumors were afloat of an impending change in the exchange rate of a key currency is not, I think, warranted. Cooperation between central banks, and the "esprit de corps" among them, is so highly developed that they may be relied upon to keep quiet in such situations rather than add to the pressure on the country concerned. We have, at present, before us an example of such "cooperation" with the Federal Reserve System: foreign central banks are holding back from raising the ratio of their gold to dollar holdings when they receive additional dollars, and still more from converting existing dollar balances into gold. Two further points should be noticed. First, even if cooperation among the central banks were to break down on some particular occasion with respect to one key-currency country among many, the impact on the foreign exchange and gold markets would be much smaller than if the same thing happened with respect to a country that was the only one in which foreign balances were held. Second, the fact that a country is a depository of foreign balances makes for monetary discipline in that country and may thence render rumors of impending currency revaluations less frequent than they have been in the past.

A summary of the main advantages of the multiple-currency standard should focus on the following points:

1. The multiple-currency standard would remove the dilemma from which my discussion started, namely, that international currency reserves must grow at a certain pace, but can do so only at the cost of a deficit in the American balance of payments.

2. Since in the new key-currency countries the piling up of reserves would start from scratch, the ratio to their gold stock of their short-term liabilities toward the monetary authorities of foreign countries would not become alarmingly high for a long time to come. In other words, there would be room for a continuous growth in international reserves until a time so far distant in the future that no reasonable man would think it necessary to make preparations for it now.

3. The holding by one country of balances in others allows it to engage in operations in the spot and forward markets in foreign exchange in order to influence short-term capital movements, without its having to make special arrangements with foreign central banks for borrowing foreign currencies.

4. The introduction of the multiple-currency standard requires neither the creation of new international institutions nor the assumption of new functions by the existing ones.

5. The multiple-currency standard does not compel countries to lend in order to equilibrate balances of payments. If under it countries accumulate balances in others, this takes place of their free will.

6. It makes for monetary discipline instead of encouraging monetary laxity.

The advantages of the multiple-currency standard are indeed many. What it cannot, of course, do is to content those who expect from international currency reforms that they should permit countries with deficits in their balances of payments to continue in that position indefinitely. Neither the multiple-currency standard nor any other system, with the exception of what I have called the "system of unlimited credit," can achieve this miracle. Nor is it desirable that it should.

13

Reform of the International Monetary System

FRITZ MACHLUP

Every student of monetary economics remembers the bimetallism debate. When both gold and silver were international money, convertible into each other at a fixed rate, there was periodic trouble. Depending on the relative scarcity or abundance, people were always rushing from one money into the other. Students learned eventually that safety lies in having only *one* international money.

The world is now blessed with three international moneys: gold, dollars, and pounds sterling. There are periodic rushes, sometimes from sterling into dollars, sometimes from dollars into gold. This is to be expected in view of the faster increase in the supply of these currencies relative to the supply of gold. If three international moneys are convertible into each other at fixed rates, Gresham's Law will operate and the scarcest of the moneys will go into hoards.

MORE RESERVE CURRENCIES

Some money experts, instead of seeking safety in a return to a single international money, hope to find safety in larger numbers and urge that there be six or eight international moneys. Thus we are on our way to the multiple-currency-reserve standard. Let us hold our breath and hope it will work. I am afraid it can work only if all issuers of reserve currencies observe strict discipline and keep their currencies scarce.

Even this may not be enough. Assume that different central banks maintain different ratios in their reserve holdings; country A holds 40 per

Reprint of the statement made before the Subcommittee on International Exchange and Payments, Joint Economic Committee, December 14, 1962 (*Outlook for United States Balance of Payments*, Hearings, Washington, 1963), with permission from the author.

cent gold, 30 per cent dollars, 10 per cent sterling, 10 per cent francs, and 10 per cent DM, while country B holds 60 per cent gold, 20 per cent dollars, and 20 per cent francs. Any temporary flow of funds from A to B would change the demand for the various reserve moneys and, consequently, make some scarce and others abundant. Or assume that general elections are coming up in one of the reserve-currency countries, with a contending party promising to pursue an expansionary monetary policy. The resulting expectations may start hot-money movements out of this and into the other reserve currencies and into gold.

If we actually go into the multiple-currency-reserve system in a big way, I am bold enough to predict we shall end up eventually with a world central bank. I base this prediction on my understanding of monetary history. When in the past the banks of a country held their reserves in a multitude of separate reserve banks which pursued independent credit policies, a series of financial crises occurred which ultimately forced the country to establish a central banking system.

Perhaps, instead of indulging in prophecies, I had better proceed more systematically with a review of the various reform plans and the reasoning that underlies the proposals. The discussion of proposed reforms of the international monetary system suffers from a failure to distinguish clearly the objectives which the proposals are supposed to serve. Some of the plans may contribute to the solution of certain problems without doing anything to cope with other defects or dangers.

THE PROBLEMS

Three major problems should be distinguished: (1) fundamental balance-of-payments difficulties of individual countries, particularly the United States, (2) mass movements of short-term funds, induced by anticipations and fears, and (3) the long-run supply of monetary reserves, possibly required to sustain the growth of trade among nations.

Probably no reform can be fully satisfactory on all three scores. Some proponents of schemes for the improvement of the world payments system admit frankly that they can do little to help on the first problem—the imbalance of the U.S. foreign accounts—and do not intend to do anything about the third problem—the long-run supply of reserves. They hold that the imbalance of payments of the United States must be treated by policies not connected with the reform of the international monetary system. And they hold that, since the supply of monetary reserves is adequate at present and will remain adequate for the next few years, we should not concern ourselves with what may possibly become troublesome in only five or perhaps ten years from now. Hence they concentrate on the second problem, the speculative hot-money movements, and design systems to deal with it. There may be some danger in this because, fascinated by the fine schemes to cope with hot-money movements, we may get complacent regarding the other problems and put off too long the deliberations about their solution.

THE PLANS

I propose to present a quick survey of the five major types of reform plans and to indicate briefly what they could do with regard to the problems mentioned. I have discussed all five types . . . in a Special Paper, published by the International Finance Section of Princeton University.

These are the five types of reform plans:

A. *Extension of the gold exchange standard* from the present two reserve currencies to several additional reserve currencies.

B. *Mutual assistance among central banks* either through bilateral operations or through the IMF or other international financial institutions.

C. *Centralization of monetary reserves* either with or without specific provisions for the creation of additional reserves.

D. *Increases in the price of gold* either in one fell swoop or occasionally or in small quarterly raises.

E. *Freely flexible exchange rates* either without any official reserve-holding or with moderate open-market operations to smooth fluctuations in exchange rates.

THE U.S. IMBALANCE OF PAYMENTS

The first of our problems, the basic imbalance in the U.S. international accounts, is not touched at all by reform plans of types A and B. Plans of types C and D do not solve this problem either, but they provide more time for its solution; depending on the particular arrangements, they may allow several years of grace, if such a delay should be desired. Plans of type E remove this problem entirely or, more correctly, change its mode of appearance in that they replace troublesome payments imbalances with troublesome price movements.

LONG-RUN SUPPLY OF RESERVES

Skipping the second problem—hot-money flows—for the moment, let us see how the third problem—the growth of monetary reserves—is dealt with under the various plans.

Plans of type A—the extension of the gold exchange standard—may not be effective on this score. At first blush one might assume that the promotion of several more currencies to the status of reserve currencies would add considerably to the stock of international reserves. The question, however, is whether most of the central banks would actually be willing to carry significantly larger and ever-increasing balances in the new reserve currencies, and how the central banks of the reserve-currency countries would react to steady increases of their current liabilities.

It would be essential that the central banks whose liabilities become reserves of other central banks judge their own position by the "gross reserves," not by their "net reserves." It would also be essential that the reserve-currency countries as a group incur regular deficits in their aggregate balance of payments, since only in this way could the reserves of the "peripheral" countries increase. Thus, for a continuing growth in total monetary reserves the multiple-currency-reserve standard would depend on perennial deficits of reserve-currency countries. From 1950 on, it has been only the United States whose payments deficit created exchange reserves for the rest of the world. Now the world seems to be saturated with dollar reserves; but if it were willing to accumulate more reserves in the form of some other currencies, the payments deficits creating these reserves could be those of several countries, rather than of the United States alone, and this might be less disquieting. It still remains to be seen whether the countries whose currencies are eligible for reserve status, namely, the surplus countries of recent years—that is, chiefly, the members of the European Economic Community—would be willing to incur regular deficits of over a billion dollars a year. These deficits need not be on current account if the foreign loans and investments of the new banker countries increase sufficiently.

What has been the trouble with the dollar-reserve standard is likely to remain the trouble with the multiple-currency-reserve standard—and it represents a real paradox: The supply of reserve currencies to other nations depends on payments deficits incurred by the reserve countries; but the demand for these currencies will not endure if the reserve countries incur continual deficits. In a nutshell, the truth about reserve currencies is this: the more easily available, the less wanted.

What can plans of type B—mutual central-bank assistance—do toward a solution of the problem of the long-run supply of monetary reserves? At best they may reduce the demand for reserves, because stand-by arrangements for assistance make it unnecessary to hold reserves large enough to meet peak requirements of any size. But this does not dispose of the problem of long-run supply of reserves. If increasing reserves are needed for all countries together, arrangements under which one central bank can borrow from another are evidently inadequate.

The problem, assuming it is a real one, is effectively attacked by plans of types C, D, and E. They operate in quite different fashions: C by creating reserves in the form of increasing liabilities of a world institution; D by creating reserves in the form of gold (partly by putting a higher price tag on existing gold stocks, partly by paying more for new gold); and E by removing the need for monetary reserves altogether.

All three types of reform are viewed with great suspicion; it is hard to judge how they rank on the scale of rejection by conservative bankers. Their suspicions are quite understandable. Plans of type C create monetary reserves out of thin air, as it were; would it not be unsound, nay, irresponsible, to vest in any supranational agency the power to create international money at its discretion? Plans of type D create monetary reserves simply by announcing that gold is worth more than its present price; would this not be a mere trick, cheating those who have been willing to hold dollar balances rather than gold, and procuring windfall profits for the Soviet Union and South Africa, and for gold speculators and hoarders? Plans of type E do away with the need for monetary reserves by allowing exchange rates to make all the gyrations that would elicit or cut down the demand for foreign moneys so as to make it equal to whatever may be the supply at the moment; would it not be detrimental to commerce and industry if no one could ever be certain how much he would receive for his exports or how much he would have to pay for his imports?

Some of the objections to these reform plans are based on fears of inflation. Empowering a world central bank to create international money could undoubtedly result in world-wide inflation. Up-valuing the present gold stocks and paying higher prices for new gold would obviously invite credit inflation in many countries. Removing the central bankers' obligation to keep exchange rates stable, and freeing them of the concern about the size of their foreign reserves, would probably make them less cautious in their credit policies and more willing to yield to the constant pressures for easier credit and cheaper money.

The dilemma is that any scheme to avoid deflation may facilitate inflation. All plans that undertake to secure a "more adequate" supply of monetary reserves may be instrumental in providing an excessive supply. The question is whether this danger is uncontrollable and whether we should allow the fear of inflationary indulgence to condemn us to submit to deflation when it comes.

Economists often ask which is worse, inflation or deflation, and most of them conclude that *deflation* is worse. Perhaps we ought to ask instead which of the two is more likely to happen if we are not sufficiently vigilant, and one may have to conclude that it is *inflation*. If this is correct, we ought to have even more understanding for the suspicions of the men of practical wisdom, who resist any reform which facilitates the creation of new money, international or domestic. But stubborn resistance to any reform that deals with this problem is surely imprudent. If the problem is a real one, we must face it. Let us ask how the three types of reform rank in releasing the brakes against inflation.

CONDUCIVENESS TO INFLATION

A world central bank may be as prudently or as imprudently managed as a national central bank. It may be niggardly in creating monetary reserves or it may be free-hearted and full-handed. By granting credit to poor countries it may soak the rich ones, and by granting credit to countries with balance-of-payments problems it may bilk the frugal ones. By increasing the total of reserves it may induce inflation everywhere. But none of this is inevitable, and we may find ways of checking or avoiding excesses of this sort. We may succeed in installing proper safeguards and learn that our fears have been exaggerated.

An increase in the price of gold by a large percentage would not automatically induce inflation, but the temptations would be hard to resist, especially because the responsibilities would be decentralized. Many central banks or treasuries would have profits from the revaluation of their gold stocks, and surely not all of them could be trusted not to make use of these profits. In addition, the profits made by private hoarders of gold would not all stay unspent, and the spending of these profits would probably not be offset by monetary or fiscal restrictions. The inflationary potential of an appreciable increase in the price of gold is large indeed.

The abolition of fixed exchange rates and introduction of freely flexible rates would not *per se* induce inflationary tendencies, but it is possible that a potent cause for the central banker's self-restraint would be removed if he has no longer to worry about a loss of foreign reserves. That such worries can effectively curb monetary expansion is demonstrated by the example of U.S. policies during the last years. I have no doubt that only the concern and anxiety about continuing losses of gold have prevented our monetary authorities from pursuing more expansionary policies. But it should be possible to transfer the central bankers' sensitivities from the foreign reserve position to the foreign exchange level. This would be a matter of political education and of development of a new attitude in central bank management.

THE NEED FOR MORE DISCUSSION

All these possibilities and probabilities must be discussed with much more patience than many experts have been willing to bear. The bank managers and others with practical experience ought to stop regarding anything that has never been tried as impractical, and the theorists ought not to give up attempts to advance their favorite schemes just because the bankers refuse to listen. I admire the persistence of Professor Triffin in trying to sell his plan to an unwilling and sometimes disrespectful audience, and I applaud Professors Friedman, Halm, Sohmen, and many others for continuing their support of unpegged exchange rates despite the disdainful rejection by the traditionalists. I also want to pay my sincere respect to this Committee for providing the appropriate forum for this discussion and for inviting scholars of various persuasions to present their views on proposals for the solution of the problems before us.

THE GOLD PROBLEM

Let me conclude with some additional comments on the gold question. I started my statement with a reference to Gresham's Law and the recurrent or continuing rush into gold. From the U.S. point of view things seem to have improved: the rate at which we have been losing gold has diminished. This is due partly to the solemn promises made by President Kennedy, and partly to the fine cooperation given by the central banks of the leading countries. From a world point of view, however, the situation has not improved, but has deteriorated: the rate at which gold has been added to international reserves has dwindled to almost zero.

For the last ten years gold sales from new production have added on the average more than $600 million per year to the reserves of the monetary authorities. During 1962 no such increment has occurred; in the second and third quarters the gold reserves increased hardly at all. That is to say, all the gold from new production and from Soviet sales has been absorbed into private hoards. If this goes on and if the U.S. balance of payments is balanced, neither gold nor dollars will be available for monetary reserves. Then the problem which so many experts want to table for several years will become pressing much sooner.

Now, why does gold disappear into private hoards in increasing amounts? Obviously because people believe that it is a much better asset than any debt security expressed in any currency. Is this faith in the value of gold justified? Does gold have intrinsic value, independent of the will of the U.S. Congress? No, the value of gold rests on a myth which this Congress can destroy whenever it so chooses.

Gold is nothing but a price-supported commodity, widely demanded only because people believe that it has intrinsic value. If we decided to offer all our gold for sale, to throw our entire stock on the market, the value of gold would be reduced to the shadow of a shade. For a while, gold might become even a complete *non-valeur*. To be sure, I would never propose that we commit such a ruthless act. I would be against it, because I see no point in inflicting heavy losses on so many people for no good purpose. But I am not sure that we should not caution the people and make them realize that gold is worth just as much as the U.S. Congress determines it to be. Gold will be $35 an ounce, or $70, or only $30, or $20, or almost nothing, depending on your will.

If the hoarding of gold continues, the Congress should seriously consider teaching the world a lesson by lowering the value of gold a peg or two. The world ought to learn that gold is not always the safest bet. On the other hand, I fully realize that the gold myth may yet serve a useful purpose. It has often served as a chain or brake preventing reckless monetary policies, and we may still need this in the future. Good resolutions and moral precepts may not be satisfactory substitutes for firm superstitions. But when a superstition becomes a major nuisance to the world, we might decide to get rid of it. The golden calf is now a full-grown sacred cow, and perhaps the time to slaughter it is not far off.

14

Assuring the Free World's Liquidity

ROBERT V. ROOSA

DIAGNOSIS

In the present international financial climate, three familiar proposals are being widely discussed again on the grounds that they can assure the international liquidity that is necessary to absorb the shocks of any spreading disturbances:

Devaluation of the dollar by doubling or trebling the dollar price of gold.

"Guaranteeing" the dollar's present price so that other countries can readily go on accumulating more dollars to provide their needed increases in liquidity.

Immediate launching of plans for pooling all the international reserves of the Western world's monetary systems in a new supranational bank—usually visualized as one empowered to create additional supplies of a new international reserve currency that all subscribing countries would bind themselves to accept.

The latest expressions of support for these revolutionary approaches come at a time, perhaps surprisingly, when the United States, in cooperation with most of the other free industrial countries, is completing the groundwork for the most comprehensive restructuring of international liquidity arrangements since the founding of the International Monetary Fund at the end of World War II.

The paradox is understandable, for while the nature of practical monetary operations demands that they be established with the knowledge and the confidence of responsible financial officials in other countries, it is equally necessary that progress of this kind must initially evolve within a framework of confidential discussions and limited, step-by-step operations.

Reprinted from the *Business Review Supplement*, September 1962, published by the Federal Reserve Bank of Philadelphia.

There are grave risks of setting off disruptive speculation if there should be haphazard or uncoordinated release of information on any negotiations in process, or if new steps should be initiated or announced without preparation for cooperation by other affected countries.

That is why—although Treasury and Federal Reserve officials have been negotiating and designing and installing parts of the new structure for the past year and a half—it has not been possible in public discussion to make more than a few hinting references to the over-all pattern as a whole.

That is why some alert critics have, quite understandably, charged that those bits and pieces of the new machinery which were actually installed and publicly announced seemed to be only a patchwork improvisation of minor devices.

And that is also why, during the recent unsettlement over economic conditions here—coming before the United States had achieved the fundamental correction of its balance-of-payments position upon which the real strength of the dollar in the world depends—responsible observers have turned to the better-known, widely discussed proposals of earlier periods of unrest, instead of joining in an appraisal of the potentialities of the new design.

Fortunately, enough has now been accomplished to be able to put together a sketch, if not a blueprint, of the structure as a whole. Each of the pieces already in place has been reviewed and approved by President Kennedy; those which involved interpretations of existing legislative authority have been discussed in advance with the Chairmen of the respective Congressional Committees; some have required legislation, which either has been obtained or is now before the Congress. Other steps are ahead, but they will need to be shaped by critical public discussion, just as all of the measures already taken will be adapted on the basis of the experience now being gained.

Even the steps already taken would seem, however, to remove most of the premises on which cases have been built in the past for devaluation, or guarantees, or a heroic new supranational organization. Appraisals in the future will have to take into account all of the new developments, as well as the vast array of new dangers that any one of these three other approaches would create. But before turning to the sketch of what is new—a sketch that can be filled out more fully before the end of this year as other still-confidential efforts mature—it should be helpful to restate briefly the problems implied by the wide-ranging consideration of international li-

quidity and to take a look at the way devaluation, or guarantees, or a superbank might be expected to cope with such problems.

The Need for Liquidity

International liquidity is needed to service the regular flow of payments
among countries, to finance the shortfall when any particular country's
out-payments temporarily exceed its in-payments, and to meet large withdrawals caused by outflows of capital. The responsible financial officials
of virtually all countries are agreed that aggregate monetary reserves on
hand or mobilizable in the world today are adequate for regular payments
and for temporary swings in needs. The three debatable questions are:
(1) whether particular countries, notably the less developed, have access
to enough reserves for their regular needs, that is, whether the distribution
of existing reserves should be improved; (2) whether the emergency
sources of liquidity, particularly in the event of runs on any of the larger
countries, are adequate; and (3) whether existing facilities assure an adequate growth of total reserves for the future needs of an expanding world
economy.

Devaluation, guarantees, and a superbank are all proposed to answer,
in one way or another, these three questions. Yet each would, in providing
its answers, gravely alter important parts of the monetary system on which
the world depends, and which everyone takes for granted today. The new
convertible gold-dollar arrangements, however, build upon existing currencies and payments facilities; recognize the limitations upon monetary
devices as solutions for fundamental economic problems (including those
underlying the recent United States balance-of-payments deficits); and
avoid the hazards of despair and economic disruption so likely to result
from the displacement of the dollar as the universally recognized supplement and alternative to gold in meeting the international liquidity reserve
needs of the world.

Devaluation

Raising the price of gold by devaluing the dollar would certainly be
followed by similar action on the part of other countries. An increase in
the gold price would thus not help the United States balance of payments.
It would, however, mean writing up the gold reserves now held by any
country, presumably providing a "profit" which would permit all countries,
large and small, to start afresh with a feeling that, by the stroke of a pen
(or a legislative act), they had become richer. Any present maldistri-

bution would presumably seem less constricting with everyone suddenly better off; the greatest gainers might feel better able to lend reserves to those still in some need; total reserves would be so much greater that concern over future liquidity requirements would disappear; and the larger totals would provide fresh supplies of liquidity to meet any capital flight likely to occur—or so the argument goes.

But, in fact, devaluation of the dollar would, for practical purposes in the future, virtually destroy as much reserve liquidity as it might seem to create. For every holder of dollars before devaluation would have been tricked into heavy losses, losses as large as the gains would seem to be to those who had held gold instead. The possibility that the dollar could again serve, in any meaningful volume, as a usable part of general monetary reserves would disappear. In effect, the dollar holdings of other countries would thereafter be consumed, and the large part of world liquidity now represented by dollars would be gone. The world would be left without a major currency, generally acceptable as a supplement to gold. That is why most serious consideration of international monetary reform has long since dismissed devaluation of the dollar as a practical possibility, and has turned instead toward "guarantees," or the founding of a superbank, or both.

Dollar Guarantees

The appeal of a dollar "guarantee" is that it presumably assures the world that devaluation will not occur. For the key provision of any generalized guarantee must be that all dollars held as monetary reserves would receive full compensation for all losses in the event of devaluation. The aim of such contractual assurances is, of course, to persuade the other countries of the world that they can readily go on accumulating more dollars without any risk of loss. If guarantees were in this way able to assure all needed increases in liquidity without any offsetting consequences, it would seem that they could fit in very well as simply another feature of the new structure being erected for the convertible gold-dollar system.

In that event, so the argument goes, any existing maldistribution of liquidity could be met through assistance from the United States, with no risk that the further shifting about of such reserves, following their use by the needy countries, would bring them into the hands of unwilling holders. With everyone made absolutely certain that dollars held in monetary reserves would be revalued in the event of changes in the United States gold price, quick negotiations might ensue for effecting a uniformity in the ratio between gold and dollars in the reserves of other countries. Presumably there might even be a major move to turn in gold and acquire additional dollars, on which interest might be earned. There would seem to be no problem then of assuring ample liquidity for the indefinite future; an increasing supply of dollars would always be acceptable to fulfill such needs. Moreover, there would never be reason to fear the effects of any sustained balance-of-payments deficit, or to be concerned if domestic developments in the United States caused investors to move large blocks of capital out to other countries—in any such circumstances, the United States could simply take it for granted that the additional supplies of dollars thus created would end up in the monetary reserves of other countries, who would be content to hold them because of the guarantee.

But this recital of the gains to be expected from the use of guarantees itself suggests that perhaps the prescription is too good to be true. Those who have become enthusiastic proponents of guarantees seem sometimes to forget that the strength of the signature on any guarantee depends upon sustained confidence in the creditworthiness of the signer.

Moreover, the highest credit standing—and a currency capable of supplying the monetary reserves of the world should scarcely aim for less—is that of the debtor whose net worth is so great, and whose performance is so reassuring, that supporting guarantees would never be offered or required. What this means, translated into the position of the United States as supplier of reserves for the world, is that we cannot escape a fundamental interdependence between the strength of our economy, our balance of payments, and the dollar.

The case for guarantees rests upon a contradiction: in giving a guarantee, the United States would expect to release its domestic economic performance in some measure from the constraints imposed by the need for balance-of-payments equilibrium; in accepting a guarantee, other countries would expect the United States to maintain their confidence in its internal and external economic performance; otherwise, the guarantee would not be granted or renewed. Thus the United States would, in relying upon guarantees, incur an obligation initially or eventually to engage in recurrent negotiations with country after country. The end result would be either disciplines or constraints upon our own economic policy which, at the very best, could be no different from those already apparent, and which might, at the worst, become a complicated strait jacket of additional obligations, or the guarantee would be found unacceptable and all its supposed advantages would be lost.

Many countries today object to our balance-of-payments deficit, on the grounds that we are financing an aid and military effort which they could not afford, or would not willingly undertake, by foisting on them dollar deposits which they have no need to hold. Why should they, simply because they are offered a contractual guarantee, become implicit partners in underwriting programs that they themselves would reject? On the contrary, how much more likely may it be that one country after another will interpose conditions on its readiness to accept a guarantee—conditions that will at the least interpose their judgments more specifically into the determination of our military, aid, or investment activities abroad, or perhaps be made dependent upon our adopting their own formulas for achieving the needed further shrinkage of our over-all balance-of-payments deficit? And where would we find ourselves when the demands of one of our guaranteed creditors conflicted with those of another? How close might our position then seem to be to that of the debtor approaching receivership, with tier upon tier of first-, second-, and third-mortgage claimants to satisfy? Rather than negotiate the relative priorities of such contractual liens, the United States might be better advised (as Chairman Martin has recently intimated when asked about guarantees by the Joint Economic Committee) to give up altogether the obligations of maintaining a reserve currency for the rest of the free world.

There are many of the industrial countries, too, which fear any further substantial diversion of the resources of the International Monetary Fund into the financing of recurrent distress situations in many of the underdeveloped countries—distress situations which the affected countries customarily view in simple terms as a shortage of liquidity available to them. Can we expect these same critical industrial countries to accept more dollars, just because they carry a guarantee, if the dollars arise from continued or additional American effort to supplement the contributions being made by the International Monetary Fund toward these frequent "liquidity" requirements of the less developed countries?

Some part of the current movement of capital from the United States toward Europe is apparently induced by interest-rate differentials that are somewhat higher than normal relationships would otherwise bring about. Will the monetary authorities of other countries be content to go on acquiring more and more short-term dollar liabilities, as the by-product of these capital movements, simply because their gold value is underwritten by a contractual guarantee? Or will they take advantage of the negotiations relating to the introduction of guarantees to lay down their own conditions with an impact at least as severe, perhaps considerably more so, than that now exerted?

Surely any responsible financial official in this country would expect to negotiate in exactly that manner, and to exact much more precise and limiting conditions, if we were being expected to rely on a guarantee of the gold value of any one other currency to provide a major part of our own international reserve needs. The financial officials of the other countries are neither more modest nor more reluctant to exact conditions than we would be.

There is, in fact, no real escape, certainly not so long as we maintain a reserve currency for the world, from the kinds of limits upon our complete freedom of action which these various illustrations suggest. The one way to be assured of greater freedom is to achieve balance-of-payments equilibrium and, from time to time, a surplus in our own balance of payments. The effect of guarantees is, indeed, instead of creating greater freedom for us, to center all responsibility upon us. For those in the position of accepting guarantees are able to dictate their terms. If, instead, there can be a sharing, in some increasing degree, of the responsibilities now borne so largely by the dollar alone, the leeway remaining to us for independent action on our own initiative should broaden rather than shrink as expanding liquidity needs are met over the years ahead.

And in all of these reservations concerning the possible role of guarantees, there is another pervading theme which cannot be obscured. The United States abrogated a gold clause in contracts once; the action was supported by the Supreme Court and approved by joint resolution of Congress. What assurance can a mere guarantee provide again? Is not the real basis for any confidence to be found in the strength, performance, and credibility of the American economic and financial system, and only there?

Superbank

One great attraction of a super–central bank, or "an International Federal Reserve System," is that it would clearly provide for a mutual sharing of responsibilities by all of the countries of the world. Whether created out of the existing International Monetary Fund, or established as a completely new institution, its role would be to pool the reserve balances held by all countries, or at any rate all countries of the Free World. The deposits held in the superbank could be transferable on its books, so that the resulting differences between inflows and outflows of any given country could be settled through a central clearing house. The dollar would no longer have any special role to perform as a reserve currency; that role would instead be shifted to some newly christened monetary unit of account, representing the deposit balances held at the superbank.

While gold might still hold some attraction, and could be used as an alternative means of settling differences of accounts among countries, there would presumably be no essential role for gold in the system. Much of it might find its way into the vaults of the superbank itself, or gradually disappear in industrial uses.

On the assumption that the total supply of reserves available at the superbank could grow, and grow at a controlled rate that would preclude world-wide inflation and a reluctance to hold the reserve balances on deposit there, any long-run growth needs could be readily satisfied. The liquidity requirements of underdeveloped countries might be met through advances or loans extended to such countries by the superbank itself. And any serious pressures on a given country, because its balance of payments was in grave deficit on trade account, or because capital was leaving the country in heavy volume, could also be met through loans and overdrafts on the books of the superbank.

There are many variations and nuances and combinations of these several features which have been suggested in the writings of various proponents. But all such elaboration would represent a fruitless exercise if the basic premises on which the establishment of such a superbank rests should prove unsupportable. That, perhaps regrettably, is the inescapable conclusion dictated by the actual ways of the world—today and for any foreseeable future.

The money created by a superbank would be the most high-powered ever generated by a man-made institution, yet it would have no supporting supergovernment to make good on its debts or claims. Even with all the underlying resources of the richest nation on earth, the performance of the United States in providing additional reserves has been at times rather conspicuously called into question. And in our case, the world has the basic assurance that our performance will continue broadly to meet the tests of economic requirements because otherwise pressures can be exerted upon us through our own balance of payments. There will be no comparable assurance, and no comparable underlying strength in the new body. Instead reliance must be placed upon the conflicting interests represented in a multinational legislative body, to judge and resolve conflicting demands for larger or smaller increases in the supply of the new monetary unit, or for a greater or lesser shifting of its lending power toward one group of countries or another.

Even accomplishment of the first steps would be a heroic achievement. Simply to establish the superbank would require all countries of the world to give up their present reserves and accept instead the fiat issue of a super-authority existing without a superstate. But assuming that could be done, what would happen when differences of view begin to exercise conflicting pulls upon the central organization? So long as monetary systems within individual countries continue to be managed by men who think and act as bankers, one after another will begin to hedge his country's own position either by acquiring gold or by acquiring increasing holdings of one or more currencies of other countries in which he has confidence. And so long as trade continues among sovereign nations the opportunity to convert holdings of the superbank's monetary unit into holdings of one currency or another will be available.

Thus it would be inescapable, so long as major differences in economic policy arise among different countries, that those differences will prevent the systematic direction of the superbank on uniform and consistent lines. The outcome, if it is not utter chaos and impairment of normal payments transactions among nations, is likely instead to be a drifting back toward systems of reliance upon clusters of currencies, and dependence on the strength given to them by the economies which underlie them. The drift, if it is in that direction, will indeed be back toward a system of arrangements very similar to that now evolving as part of the structure of the new convertible gold-dollar system.

PRESCRIPTIONS

The claims for this evolving convertible gold-dollar system are necessarily modest. The experience gained as step-by-step innovations are being put in place is providing ample evidence that workable arrangements depend fundamentally upon confidence rather than upon binding compacts— and confidence in monetary affairs, as in political or business life, is not attained once-for-all in a single negotiation, or a single declaration or compact, but is gained through continuing performance. Moreover, it has become irrefutably clear, if there was ever any doubt, that major initiatives cannot succeed unless the leading countries are prepared to support them by working toward equilibrium in their balance-of-payments accounts, whenever internal disturbances, outside events, or ordinary economic developments create other pressures away from balance.

Nonetheless, it already seems reasonably certain that the new structure being erected around the established gold-dollar system can make possible important additions to the liquidity of underdeveloped countries; can provide ample resources for promptly meeting heavy drains or a run on the currency of any leading industrial country, including the United States; and can assure the flexibility and growth in total liquidity needed to serve the requirements of trade in an expanding world economy for some years ahead.

Further potentialities may come into view as and if the Common Market becomes a unified monetary system, and forward planning for that eventuality may soon introduce a new dimension into the consideration of arrangements for international liquidity. But at least until that greater fusion of the Common Market countries occurs, the essence of the monetary system of the free world will no doubt continue to be the fixed relationship between gold and the dollar, with the United States standing ready to buy or sell gold at its established price of $35 per ounce. The principal source of increases in liquidity will continue to be the annual increments of gold to the monetary reserves of the world, supplemented from time to time by controlled increases in the dollars held by other countries as a part of their monetary reserves.

Standing astride the gold and dollar reserves of most countries of the world will be the International Monetary Fund, into which all member countries have contributed working balances of gold and their own currencies, in amounts related to their own quotas (or conditional "drawing rights") in the Fund. Surrounding the dollar is a constellation of special bilateral relationships between the dollar and the separate currencies of most of the other leading industrial countries. Surrounding the gold reserves is a set of relationships now largely worked out through the London gold market, but representing participation by the leading European central banks, known colloquially as the "Basel group" which now also includes the United States.

The innovations of the past year and a half have centered upon the resources and usability of the International Monetary Fund, upon the direct relations between the dollar and other leading currencies highlighted by our initiation of activity in the foreign exchange markets, and upon the special arrangements for influencing the flow of gold into the world's monetary reserves. Virtually all of the changes have represented, and resulted from, a growing readiness on the part of the other leading industrial countries to begin to consider, and cautiously to undertake, some sharing of the responsibilities formerly carried so largely by the dollar.

Comprehending and reinforcing all of the new arrangements are the various activities of the OECD, and more particularly, its working party devoted to balance-of-payments and financial problems. Here, the opportunity for continuous interchange of information and criticism, among the leading industrial countries, provides the base of communications needed to carry forward operations that require mutual understanding of current developments and current policies. At the same time, it is conceivable that work can go forward through this and other organs of the OECD toward preparing the way for the next stage of practicable and foreseeable innovation in the area of international financial arrangements—the fusing of the United Kingdom into the Common Market; the evolution of a unified financial mechanism to serve the expanded Common Market; and the forging of appropriate operating and policy links between that organization, once it emerges, and our own financial institutions.

Meanwhile, it would be quixotic to hope, however, that the new arrangements will solve the liquidity needs of the underdeveloped countries; for in a full sense, nothing can. So long as these countries are energetically pursuing development programs, any international reserves not actually required as current working balances will be consumed in the purchase of more imports. Mere increases in reserves, therefore, will largely disappear. The need of these countries is for some greater assurance concerning the markets and prices of the raw materials they sell; for as much aid as can effectively be absorbed from whichever industrial countries are able to provide it; and for emergency facilities to provide needed foreign exchange to bridge unexpected seasonal or cyclical reverses. None of these needs can be met simply through broad global action; all are the object of energetic further effort by the United States and various international bodies at the present time.

So far as aid is concerned, the activities of already existing international institutions are being reinforced through the establishment of consortia to attract, into each of the underdeveloped countries as programs are developed, additional funds from the more prosperous countries of Western Europe. And with respect to emergency requirements, joint action by the International Monetary Fund and interested outside governments (often accompanied by leading commercial banks) provides practical possibilities for the kind of emergency assistance that can be used without abuse.

The most prominent question currently, however, is whether the new arrangements of the convertible gold-dollar system, once established and understood, can provide a mobilization of reserves to meet sudden and

heavy drains upon the dollar itself. So far as the precipitation of a run
through pressures on the London gold market may be concerned, the Basel
group has already achieved important results. Price changes are occur-
ring only over a range wide enough to make speculation costly, and there
is now a close, participating interest on the part of the principal European
countries, as well as the United Kingdom and the United States, in the
maintenance of orderly conditions there. To be sure, so long as nations
and individuals are free to exercise choices, and so long as changes occur
in the degree of confidence in the dollar or in other currencies, it will be
impossible to escape pressures. The gain has come in curbing capricious
or mere follow-the-leader raids upon the gold which serves the world's
monetary reserve needs, and in sharing the responsibility for required
action. Perhaps in an ideal world the interrelated monetary systems would
function even better if private individuals were not allowed to own gold
in any country, and if no London gold market existed. But for the world
that we have, the present arrangements represent a marked change and
improvement—a change which necessarily rests upon mutual and voluntary
action based upon confidence.

In a somewhat comparable way, through reciprocal holdings of currencies, through engaging in forward transactions in currencies, and
through the outright borrowing of dollars or of other currencies from foreign countries, the United States has developed arrangements to cushion
or offset a substantial part of any disruptive short-term capital outflows,
or to minimize the impact on our central gold reserve caused by shifts of
monetary reserves from countries whose gold ratios are low to those whose
gold ratios are high. To be sure, these arrangements, too, could not be
worked out if other countries felt that the credit risks were great; that is,
if their confidence should weaken in our ability and determination to regain
the initiative in controlling our own balance of payments, and to maintain
the freedom of our capital markets as well as the ready interchangeability
between dollars and gold. Nothing has been done which has not reflected
the combined judgment of both countries involved in every set of bilateral
relationships. Given that basic approach, and the mutual confidence it
implies, however, a new pattern of arrangements can provide an increasing
measure of protection for the dollar against incipient developments that
might otherwise grow into serious runs.

But for the eventuality that a run might actually occur, new arrangements have also been made. By providing additional stand-by resources
for the International Monetary Fund, the ten leading industrial countries,

whose actions will become effective as soon as the necessary legislation passes through the appropriations process in the American Congress, have made certain that adequate supplies of other currencies will be available to meet any needs that we might expect to face. So far as other countries are concerned, the recent mobilization of more than $1 billion within a forty-eight-hour period to stop a raid on the Canadian dollar provides striking evidence of the flexibility, the speed, and the magnitude of the facilities now available. And it is interesting evidence of the results that Canada has already, even before its longer-range program has been announced or implemented, regained within two months roughly two-thirds of all the reserves it had lost over the first six months of the year.

Looking further ahead, the new arrangements also are capable of providing for a steady growth in the monetary reserves needed to service the trade requirements of an expanding world. Dollars are still the currency to which all countries turn for a substantial part, if not the entire amount, of their international payments. Our financial institutions and our markets are increasingly well equipped to service the payments requirements of the world. It is a role which naturally accompanies our leading economic and political position. The only reason that the usefulness of the dollar has come into doubt is that, for some time, dollars have been added to the "money supply," i.e., the monetary reserves, of other countries at too fast a pace. That is because our balance-of-payments deficit was, in effect, creating reserve dollars for others, at a rate which outran the current requirements for liquidity in the world's monetary reserves. In these circumstances, just as occurs when money is created too rapidly inside any single country, renewal of the ready acceptability of the currency depends upon limiting further increases until the uses for that liquidity should have caught up.

Once the United States has its balance of payments fully under control, the rate of increase in the supply of dollars available to serve the international liquidity requirements in the world can also be managed. Whether or not there is a corresponding proportionate increase in the underlying supply of gold in the world's monetary reserves, additional increases in the supply of dollars can rest upon an accumulation by the United States of incremental amounts of the currencies of other leading countries. These other currencies, while not equally capable of serving the multitude of functions required of a reserve currency, can, as the United States acquires holdings of them, be brought into a further mutual sharing of some of the responsibilities which the international reserve system must itself carry.

What this may mean in the future in the way of additional consultation and negotiation with respect to the particular currencies so used, and the manner in which such currencies may cushion drains upon the dollar at particular times—serving in that respect as a substitute for drains upon the gold reserve itself—all remain to be worked out in the tests of day-by-day experience. But the structure of the new relationship has already been established. Its potential capabilities for meeting the world's longer-run liquidity requirements are clearly at least as promising as any of the more familiar proposals. And its possibilities for practicable operation in every-day affairs are clearly much enhanced by the fact that the new system builds directly upon the existing payments procedures to which governments and individuals are already well accustomed. This would seem to be not only the most promising, but also the most reliable, pattern for new developments to follow.

15

Cooperation to Solve the Gold Problem

HENRY C. WALLICH

. . .

DIAGNOSIS

The United States for a long time enjoyed among its many blessings that of not having to be concerned about its balance of payments. Our competitive position in international trade was very strong, our gold reserves seemingly impregnable. We could conduct our monetary and fiscal affairs to suit our domestic needs or fancies, could allow prices and wages to move as seemed right or convenient. The discipline of the balance of payments, which to other countries has always been a fact of daily life, was absent.

Now this idyll, which most of us did not even know enough about to enjoy, has come to an end. For three years, we have run annual balance-of-payments deficits of $3–$4 billion, to a total of over $11 billion. They have cost us $5 billion in gold and an increase of over $6 billion in foreign dollar holdings. Hereafter, living with our balance of payments will mean that we must (1) put an end to the steady drain, and (2) accept the discipline of the balance of payments as a potential limitation on our freedom of action.

The Deficits Crisis

We had deficits before the three big waves of 1958, 1959, and 1960 broke over us. In fact, as Exhibit I shows, we had moderate deficits in every year from 1950 on, with the sole exception of 1957. However, the significance of these earlier deficiencies was different. Balance-of-payments deficits are not a misfortune under all conditions, because the balance of payments is not an income account. It is more in the nature of a

Reprinted from the *Harvard Business Review*, May-June, 1961, through the courtesy of the author and publisher.

Exhibit I. United States Balance of Payments, 1949–1960

(In billions of dollars)

Type of Transaction	1949	1950	1951	1952	1953	1954	1955	1956	1957	1958	1959	1960*
Goods and services												
Merchandise exports	$12.1	$10.1	$14.1	$13.3	$12.3	$12.8	$14.3	$17.4	$19.4	$16.3	$16.2	$19.3
Merchandise imports	6.9	9.1	11.2	10.8	11.0	10.4	11.5	12.8	13.3	13.0	15.3	15.1
Balance	$ 5.3	$ 1.0	$ 3.0	$ 2.5	$ 1.3	$ 2.4	$ 2.8	$ 4.6	$ 6.1	$ 3.3	$ 1.0	$ 4.1
Income on investments, net	1.1	1.2	1.5	1.4	1.5	1.8	1.9	2.0	2.2	2.2	2.2	2.3
Services, including military expenditures, net	0.4	0.1	0.5	0.4	0.2	0.2	0.2	0.2	0.6	0.1	−0.1	−0.1
Total	6.7	2.3	5.0	4.3	2.9	4.5	4.9	6.9	9.0	5.7	3.0	6.3
Unilateral transfers, military expenditures, and capital, net†												
Remittances and pensions	−$0.6	−$0.5	−$0.5	−$0.5	−$0.6	−$0.6	−$0.6	−$0.7	−$0.7	−$0.7	−$0.8	−$0.8
Military expenditures	−0.6	−0.5	−1.3	−2.0	−2.5	−2.6	−2.8	−3.0	−3.2	−3.4	−3.1	−3.1
U.S. Government non-military grants	−5.0	−3.5	−3.0	−2.0	−1.8	−1.6	−2.0	−1.7	−1.6	−1.6	−1.6	−2.5
U.S. Government capital‡	−0.7	−0.2	−0.2	−0.4	−0.2	0.1	−0.3	−0.6	−1.0	−1.0	−0.4	
U.S. private capital—long-term	−0.7	−1.1	−1.0	−1.1	−0.5	−1.0	−1.0	−2.5	−2.9	−2.5	−2.2	−2.9
U.S. private capital—short-term	0.2	−0.1	−0.1	−0.1	0.2	−0.6	−0.2	−0.5	−0.3	−0.3	−0.1	
Foreign long-term capital, net§	0.1	0.1	0.2	0.1	0.2	0.2	0.3	0.5	0.4	‖	0.5	0.4
Total	−7.4	−5.9	−5.8	−6.0	−5.3	−6.1	−6.5	−8.5	−9.3	−9.6	−7.7	−8.9
Unrecorded transactions—errors and omissions†	$0.8	‖	$0.5	$0.5	$0.3	$0.2	$0.4	$0.6	$0.7	$0.4	$0.8	−$0.6
Over-all decrease (or increase) in U.S. gold holdings and increase in liquid liabilities‡	($0.2)	$3.6	$0.3	$1.1	$2.1	$1.5	$1.1	$1.0	($0.5)	$3.5	$3.8	$3.2
Memorandum item: sum of U.S. Government loans and grants, military expenditures, and U.S. private long-term capital exports	$7.0	$5.3	$5.5	$5.5	$5.0	$5.1	$6.1	$7.8	$8.7	$8.5	$7.3	#

* January–September seasonally adjusted annual rate.
‡ Excluding International Monetary Fund (IMF) subscription of $1,375 million in 1959. Decreases are shown in heavy print.
‖ Less than $50 million.
† Minus sign indicates outflow.
§ Excluding investment in government securities.
# Not available.
Note: This exhibit excludes military grants. Details will not necessarily add to totals because of rounding.

checking account, with the gold playing the role of the cash balance. A cash balance can be inconveniently large as well as too small.

Immediately after the war, our gold cash balance was very large, and the cash balances of many other countries were much too small. As a result, these countries were unable to maintain free currencies, and they had to control their trade tightly. Our deficits initially served the good purpose of increasing the gold and dollar reserves of the rest of the world. An almost universal return to free, convertible currencies and a rapid increase in world trade were the gratifying results.

Moreover, as long as the relatively modest pre-1957 deficit appeared to result from our foreign aid and military expenditures abroad, which were widely regarded as temporary, there seemed to be no reason for concern. The problem was, rather, how the rest of the world would get along when even one of these expenditures stopped. But some time during the early or middle 1950's it became increasingly apparent that both types of expenditures were very likely to become fixtures. This put another face on our deficits. It became clear that, even though the annual amounts averaged only about $1.5 billion at the time, something would have to be done about them once they had performed their function of restoring world liquidity.

In 1957, the deficit actually did disappear. This came about, though, as a result of temporary factors. The business boom abroad created a strong demand for our exports. That was overlaid, in turn, by the exceptional requirements for oil, coal, and other products generated by the Suez crisis at that time.

From the lofty heights of an annual rate of $20 billion (seasonally adjusted) in the first quarter of 1957, American exports plummeted to a low of $15.2 billion in the first quarter of 1959. This was the first act in what has been to date a three-act drama of the big payments deficit. The three acts coincide, very roughly, with the calendar years 1958–60. The magnitude of the deficit in each year was approximately the same, but the part of the villain seemed to shift in every act:

1. In 1958, *falling exports* were principally responsible for the deficit. The drop occurred in an environment that saw the ending of the Suez crisis and the beginning of a mild depression abroad. American imports declined moderately—broadly in line with declining business in this country.

2. In 1959, the principal immediate cause of the deficit was the rapid *rise in imports*. It started from a low in the third quarter of 1958 at an annual rate of $12.8 billion (seasonally adjusted) and went to $16.6 bil-

lion in the third quarter of 1959; its effect on the deficit was abetted by a stubborn failure of exports to advance until late in the year.

These circumstances seemed to reflect a difference in cyclical phase between the United States and the rest of the world. We emerged from the 1958 recession about nine months earlier than Europe, and some of the raw-material-producing countries of the world, especially our important customers in Latin America, did not really emerge from it at all. Hence American demand for foreign products revived earlier than foreign demand for our products. In addition, there were some special commodity situations that worked against us both on the export and on the import side. Underlying all the rest, there was the question of how far we had remained fully competitive.

3. In 1960, an important part of the deficit reflected an *outflow of short-term capital*. Exports revived very satisfactorily. Imports actually declined. This was the year in which Europe enjoyed once more a great expansion, while in the United States business began going downhill. Had it not been for the outflow of short-term capital that developed around the middle of the year, the deficit actually would have been quite moderate. But the two phenomena were related, of course. The capital outflow was brought about by the same circumstances that helped to reduce the rest of the deficit: The decline in business here and the boom abroad reduced our imports and increased our exports, but they also served to depress interest rates in this country while raising them abroad. As a result, as one gap began to close, another was opened up.

Causes of Deficits

In taking stock of our situation at the end of these three years, two facts become apparent.

First, although we improved our situation in 1960 as against 1958 and 1959, we have not yet solved our problem. It is quite possible, to be sure, that interest rates here and abroad may come into line as business conditions in the United States improve, and that a good part of the short-term capital may come back. Such a movement might even be sufficient to offset the remaining deficit in the basic balance of payments and perhaps to put us into over-all surplus. But an improvement in business may cause the basic balance to worsen, as our imports rise again. In that event we would make a great mistake to believe that we were out of the woods, since it is the basic balance, not the short-term capital flow, that we have to worry about in the long run.

Second, it seems clear that only part of the deficit in the basic balance arises from fortuitous combinations among cyclical phases and special commodity situations. Another part must result from more fundamental causes. For if a series of different circumstances in three successive years always produces the same result of a large deficit, one is justified in looking for some common and persistent cause.

There has been a good deal of talk about pricing ourselves out of and pricing foreigners into our markets. Prices for industrial products are hard to compare, particularly where quality and design differences are important. General indexes, too, are not completely helpful, because they tend to cover somewhat different products in different countries.

But taking the data for what they are worth, it would appear that increases in U.S. export prices have been significantly out of line with increases abroad *only in a limited range of products.* Using 1953 as a base for comparison, the data suggest that capital goods and particularly steel have advanced disproportionately. This is serious, because capital goods are among our most important exports. In *most* other types of products, however, increases in the United States have been at the high end of the international range, but on the whole do not appear to have become seriously uncompetitive.

Among particular products, automobiles have the most interesting story to tell:

The industry lost most of its market abroad in the 1950's, exports dropping sharply from 254,000 units in 1955 to 117,000 units in 1959. Meanwhile registration of imports advanced from 57,000 in 1955 to 668,000 units in 1959. But the industry fought back with the compacts, and while in export markets gains have not been spectacular, success in the domestic market has been very clearly demonstrated in the decline in foreign car registrations, which by December 1960 were 41 per cent below a year earlier. The experience seems to suggest both the import vulnerability of American markets and the capacity of a major American industry to meet this competition.

An alternative explanation of our balance-of-payments difficulties that has been put forward is the heavy burden the United States carries in the form of foreign aid, military expenditures abroad, and private capital exports. These special expenditures have averaged about $8 billion for several years, as the memorandum item at the bottom of Exhibit I shows. Undoubtedly they are a burden for the domestic economy and particularly for the balance of payments, where they must be offset by equivalent exports if a deficit is to be avoided.

It must be remembered, however, that such expenditures do furnish to other countries the means of buying American products (just as if we spent that money for imports which would increase their buying capacity). In a well-functioning international market, where all countries are fully competitive, a country's expenditures should automatically induce equivalent receipts. Only if these expenditures abroad advance very suddenly or very disproportionately, in relation to the spending country's own gross national product or in relation to world trade, would one expect receipts to lag.

Actually, however, United States expenditures for foreign aid, military development, and private capital exports have not in the aggregate advanced either sharply or disproportionately. They have gone to their recent level of about $8 billion from approximately $5 billion at the beginning of the decade. That is considerably less, percentagewise, than the growth of our own GNP over the period and probably much less than the growth of world trade. Therefore relative to the size of our own economy and to the channels of world trade, the special expenditures have in reality *declined*. Naturally it would be possible to reduce this burden still further. But it is an error to assign special responsibility for the deficit to these expenditures.

There is a still broader explanation which goes beyond a "single cause" diagnosis of our problem. That is the growing competitiveness of the industrial areas of the world, principally Europe and Japan. The effects of the war have been overcome; our allies and ex-enemies are now beginning to catch up with us in their techniques and scale of production. In many cases they enjoy the advantages of the late-comer: free use of the pioneers' know-how and the latest type of equipment. Their gains find expression in a whole range of competitive factors besides prices, from design and selling to delivery dates, credit, and servicing.

Most foreign countries take their exports very seriously. For them, exports constitute an important part of industrial output, without which they could not afford to build the plants and maintain the scale of operations they do. Their firms give preferential treatment to export business in the budgeting of promotional expenditures, in assigning of personnel and other facilities, and in general corporate thinking and planning. This is the source of the intense competition that the United States has encountered in our foreign as well as home markets.

Prescriptions for Deficits

This analysis of the roots of the payments deficit suggests that while there may have been temporary factors that made the years 1958–59 especially bad, there remain others that are more than temporary and that will require continuing counteraction. What lines of action are appropriate?

1. *Increased competitiveness.* We must continue our efforts to strengthen our competitiveness. In the past, this has been something of a holding operation, and to some extent it will have to continue that way. This applies particularly to the government's efforts to stem inflation by means of its fiscal and monetary policies. To avoid further price increases is essential, but one can hardly expect monetary and fiscal policies to bring prices down and make us more competitive. On the side of business and labor, however, opportunities exist not only to maintain but actually to in-increase our competitiveness. In some degree this is a matter of price and wage policies, in part it is a matter of meeting the foreign challenge in terms of design, quality, selling effort, credit terms, and service.

2. *Removal of trade restrictions.* We can strengthen the demand for American exports by continuing to press for removal of trade restrictions abroad. Many discriminatory restrictions have already been removed, partly in response to past representations. But particularly in our relations with the European Economic Community (EEC or Common Market) and the European Free Trade Association (EFTA) there is scope for negotiations that would improve access for American goods beyond what now seems probable.

3. *Exports.* We shall have to continue and intensify the export drive started in the spring of 1960. This drive combined intensified promotional efforts of the Department of Commerce with action of the business community to mobilize its resources more fully for exports. It has been supported by a new program of short-term export credit insurance and guarantees offered by the Export-Import Bank. This drive has not aroused as much attention as it might, perhaps for the very reason that exports expanded so rapidly during 1960. But the export drives waged by British manufacturers indicate that endeavors of this kind can be both patriotic and profitable.

4. *Sharing development burdens.* We shall have to pursue and go beyond past efforts at sharing international burdens in the fields of development assistance and defense. Steps already taken include the creation of the International Development Association (IDA) and the proposal for a reconstituted Organization for Economic Cooperation and Development. Other industrial countries will have to intensify their aid efforts.

Sharing of the development burden may not be enough, however. It helps the United States only rather indirectly by relieving it of possible future increases in such burdens and by adding moderately to demand for our exports. A sharing of military burdens, possibly in the context of NATO, must also be pushed.

These are the principal lines of approach that commend themselves, and of course there are lesser actions that could be readily taken. Among the latter are:

a) Reductions of duty-free imports by tourists.
b) Removal of tax-haven privileges for American subsidiaries abroad.
c) Removal of foreign restrictions on investment in the United States.
d) Encouragement of more tourism to the United States.

A wide range of additional measures exist that likewise could be adopted but that do not commend themselves except in grave emergency. These would include sharp cutbacks in foreign aid, in military expenditures, in private capital exports, in tourism, and in imports. Such restrictive measures are not in keeping with our international objectives or with our traditional liberal trade policies. And while they might be effective in reducing our outlays, they would boomerang in greater or lesser degree by way of foreign retaliation as well as reduction in demand for our products.

If a continued deficit compels recourse to measures like the latter, some painful choices would become necessary. My own reluctant preference would be, in that case, to make a start by restricting the flow of private American capital to the industrial, but not to the less developed, countries.

The Problem of Liquidity

If we are successful in bringing our balance of payments into reasonable equilibrium, we shall have dealt adequately with an important part of the problem confronting us. But, even then, we shall not have dealt with the whole of it. The balance of payments is inextricably tied up with the question of gold and foreign dollar balances. Our gold holdings have diminished, and foreign-owned dollar balances have increased as a result of past deficits. Merely stopping a further outflow will not settle the problems that exist in that area. At this point, therefore, it becomes necessary to turn from the balance of payments to gold.

Nature of the Difficulty

Our balance of payments primarily concerns us as traders. Our gold holdings concern us as bankers. "The United States is banker to the world" is a familiar phrase. Most people probably understand it in the sense that the United States and its citizens and institutions are great international lenders and investors. That is entirely accurate.

But the phrase has still another and perhaps more telling significance. The United States is also the depositary of much of the world's currency reserves, as well as of private international working balances. These are the famous foreign dollar holdings now totaling $21.3 billion at the end of 1960, of which $10.4 billion were official funds and $7.0 billion private funds, while $3.9 billion belonged to international institutions. The official balances are convertible into gold on demand, and while private balances are not, they could be turned over by their owners to foreign central banks or governments and thus become subject to conversion.

It is not farfetched to say that foreign dollar balances constitute the equivalent of demand deposits in a commercial bank. The United States economy therefore finds itself in the position of a regular bank: it has borrowed short and has lent long.

The United States gold holdings of $17.4 billion (January 1961) are the reserve that this bank carries to assure the prompt repayment of any depositor who wants his money back. They serve simultaneously as a reserve to tide the United States over periods of deficits in its balance of payments. For a nation whose total annual outlays abroad do not exceed $30 billion, and whose biggest recent deficits have been below $4 billion, a reserve of $17.4 billion seems more than ample. However, as backing for over $21 billion of foreign liabilities, which could be augmented by outflows of domestic funds, the same is not necessarily true. Accordingly, our gold is actually more important in connection with our banking function than with our trading function.

The countries whose central banks or governments hold official dollar balances use these balances as their international reserves. (The most important such country at present is Germany.) Usually the governments also hold greater or lesser amounts of gold. The whole arrangement sometimes is referred to as the gold exchange standard. The dollars held in official reserves constitute a kind of extension of gold. If they could not serve in that capacity, and if gold were the only accepted medium for international reserves, the total volume of world reserves would be that much smaller, and the world that much less "liquid."

In this way, the gold exchange standard has been a major convenience for the United States and for the rest of the world. It helped materially in restoring a free and stable world currency system after the war. Thanks to it, the deficits of the United States since 1950 have enabled other countries to increase their reserves without greatly reducing those of the United States. This, in turn, has made it possible for us to expand our financing of world reconstruction and development.

If the annual balance-of-payments deficits of the United States had remained small in recent years, the financing process might have gone on for a good many years more. Even so, it was not plausible that the United States could indefinitely increase its demand liabilities against an unchanging gold base (although the increasing vulnerability of our position might have dawned upon us much more gradually than it did when the three thumping deficits came in 1958–60). Given what happened, it is clear that the United States must act to protect the dollar. In other words, we must bring our balance of payments into reasonable equilibrium.

Yet success in that urgent endeavor will create a dilemma. If we no longer have deficits, the rest of the world will no longer have surpluses. It will have no source from which to increase its international reserves, except for new gold production and Russian gold sales. In that case, the rise in world trade may sooner or later make the world's reserves inadequate. That would raise the specter of a liquidity crisis. To put the matter in simplest terms:

The dollar, which is the basis of the world payments mechanism, is no longer invulnerable. To reduce its vulnerability, the United States must balance its international accounts. If the United States succeeds in doing that, however, it may be laying the groundwork for a world financial crisis at some future time.

We must face two different jobs: (1) to improve our balance of payments, and also (2) to improve the world payments mechanism.

It is important that these tasks be seen as two *different* jobs, albeit they are related. The tendency today, I fear, is to confuse them. It is tempting to think that there must be some financial mechanism that will help us solve the balance-of-payments problems. If such a device could be found, we would not then have to do the painful and disagreeable things that may still be needed to put right the balance of payments. There would then be no need to gear fiscal and monetary policy to balance-of-payments requirements, no need to cut tourists' duty-free imports, no need to struggle over military dependents abroad, no need to negotiate with Germany and other countries about help for the dollar.

In truth, of course, there is *no* such financial device. In fact, the basic condition for any financial device to function is that the United States first balance—or approximately balance—its international accounts. No mechanism could survive if it had to finance continuing heavy deficits of the largest trading country in the world.

The job to be done on the balance of payments not only is a separate job; it is also a more urgent job. One reason for its greater urgency is that its success is needed for the workability of a new mechanism.

A second reason is that world liquidity today is high, thanks to antecedent American deficits. It is ill-distributed around the world, to be sure, but that is a third and perhaps lesser problem. In the immediate future, there is no urgent need for an over-all increase in world liquidity.

I have said earlier what in my judgment remains to be done to strengthen our balance of payments. We are beginning to see daylight, but we are not yet out of the woods. Assuming success along those lines, we can turn our attention to the international monetary mechanism.

PRESCRIPTIONS

The approaches that have been suggested for developing an effective international monetary mechanism seem to fall into three groups:

1. The first and most modest approach, which could be implemented by a few of the leading countries pooling their wits and good efforts, may be called the "key-currency approach."

2. The second approach would expand the existing facilities of the International Monetary Fund, without substantially changing its structure.

3. The third, which would convert the Fund into a world central bank, is the most ambitious.

Key-Currency Approach

How would the key-currency approach work? The United States and some six or eight countries that are the principal holders of dollar balances would:

a) Agree on some coordination of policies in certain areas.

b) Align their interest rates within practicable limits so as to reduce arbitrage movements of short-term capital in search of higher interest rates elsewhere.

c) Cooperate in measures to reduce balance-of-payments deficits and surpluses due to other causes.

d) Perhaps limit the extent to which or circumstances under which they would draw gold from one another.

e) Possibly go into the question of gold guarantees for official foreign dollar and sterling balances, though I personally hesitate to recommend this device. If it were to be adopted, it should be limited to the protection of official dollar holders against a loss in terms of *their own currency*, not in terms of *gold*. Countries devaluing along with or somewhat less than the hypothetical move of the dollar would get no or only a correspondingly smaller compensation.

In this framework, further small deficits on the part of the United States might be tolerable. The danger of a world liquidity shortage would be pushed into the more remote future. Meanwhile, the habit of cooperation and coordination would be acquired and the groundwork laid for some more formal arrangements later on.

The key-currency approach is unspectacular, cautious, pragmatic, and tends to enlist the support of bankers more than of economists. It was proposed at the end of World War II, in competition with the more ambitious Bretton Woods Plans for a Monetary Fund and World Bank. The Bretton Woods institutions won the race, but it is perhaps not well remembered today that it took many years before the world's financial climate allowed those institutions to operate. For a number of years the Fund in particular remained inert, while the great needs of the times were met by the United States' direct loans to Britain and France, and later by the Marshall Plan. In other words, we practiced the key-currency approach, after first having invested much energy and money in institutions that were ahead of their times. That could happen again today.

Enlargement of IMF

The second approach, too, proceeds pragmatically and with a minimum of institutional superstructure. Its prototype is a proposal made by E. M. Bernstein, former research director of the International Monetary Fund.[1] Bernstein proposes to enlarge the resources of the Fund to meet possible large deficits and surpluses. Now, the resources of the Fund were in fact raised by 50 per cent in 1959, to the impressive total of $14 billion. Bernstein's proposal differs from this approach in that he wants to increase not just the general resources of the institution, but its resources in the currencies of those countries that may have large surpluses. He would let the Fund obtain the resources required by giving it the right to borrow, within specified limits, from the surplus countries. The working of this technique, which was considered as a possible alternative when the recent 50 per cent

---

[1] [See selection 9 of this volume, pp. 187–202.]

quota increase was being proposed, can be illustrated as follows:

If the currency needed were in Deutsche marks, the Fund would borrow them from Germany and turn them over to the country experiencing the deficit. That country could meet its payments to Germany with these marks. What it comes down to is that the creditor country would have to finance its own surplus within limits, by lending to the Fund.

The United States, after the war, did not look with favor upon such an arrangement. At that time we would have been the principal surplus country, and credit demands would have converged mainly on us. That objection was the reason why the IMF was set up with only limited access to the currency of any one country. The Bernstein proposal would reduce this original safeguard.

Aside from its mechanical simplicity, the proposal commends itself because it implies a realistic appraisal of the world's future liquidity needs. These liquidity needs, as Bernstein correctly sees, are not analogous to the need that businesses have for cash balances. While they are sometimes so construed, that is a false analogy. A business needs a working balance to handle the turnover of its receipts and payments. Anything in excess of that it can put into time deposits, treasury bills, or other "near-moneys." Of course these working balances must increase in proportion to the rising turnover. Hence it can reasonably be assumed that the money supply ought to rise in step with the rising volume of total business.

But the international reserves of a nation are not working balances—they are in the nature of rainy-day reserves. They need not increase in direct proportion to the nation's trade, if the prospects of a rainy day are receding as a result of a more stable world climate. Their place can be taken, to some extent, by international "near-reserves" in the form of more or less liquid foreign assets, including perhaps even direct foreign investments. Their place can be taken also by credit facilities, among them those of the IMF, which the present proposal would increase. The provision of stand-by facilities as proposed by Bernstein, in other words, seems more in line with the needs of the case than the supply of floating reserves.

International Central Bank

The third proposal is that for an international central bank. As contrasted with the preceding two, its principal distinguishing feature is that countries would carry part of their international reserves as deposits with the central institution; typically it is suggested that the IMF be expanded to perform that function. The analogy to the relation of commercial banks in the United States and the Federal Reserve is clear.

The outstanding proposal of this type is that made by Professor Robert Triffin of Yale.[2] Its principal merit rests on the fact that it not only provides a mechanically adequate international payments-and-credit mechanism, but incidentally also takes care of the existing dollar balances and so relieves the United States of the danger of runs on the dollar. It does this by requiring all countries holding dollars (and sterling) as part of their international reserves to transfer these currencies to the Fund. In lieu of having a claim on the United States or the United Kingdom, they would have a claim on the Fund. The United States and the United Kingdom, instead of owing a number of particular countries, would find their short-term liabilities consolidated in the hands of the IMF.

The Fund would implement its central bank function by providing liquidity for its members. It could do this by lending to countries that have balance-of-payments deficits, exactly as it does now. This would be analogous to a member bank borrowing from the Federal Reserve. Alternatively, it could make investments at its own initative in countries that in its judgment should have additional international resources available to them. That would be the counterpart of Federal Reserve open-market operations. In these ways, the Fund could keep world reserves rising in line with the expansion of world trade.

The advantages of the proposal appear tempting, but they are more than offset to my mind by its difficulties and drawbacks, particularly for the United States. The principal problems seem to be these:

1. *Strait-jacketing the U.S. balance of payments.* To avoid wildly inflationary reserve creation, the Fund would have to limit the amount of its annual lending. What would have happened if this arrangement had been in existence during the three years when the United States had an $11 billion deficit? As a properly functioning central bank, the Fund would have had to demand of the United States enough discipline to avoid such deficits. In default of rising exports, that would have meant to reduce foreign aid, capital exports, military expenditures, or imports.

Since we probably would not have been prepared to do this at the bidding of the Fund, other countries would still have continued to receive large amounts of dollars which they would have had to deposit with the Fund. The Fund, assuming it was not prepared to give the United States something like a $10 billion credit in three years, would have had to convert most, if not all, of these dollars into gold. Our gold losses would have been a good deal heavier than they have actually been.

---

[2] [See selection 1 of this volume, esp. pp. 38–54.]

Under this plan, therefore, the United States would find that it had deprived itself of the possibilities now existing for financing at least a part of a temporary balance-of-payments deficit through the accumulation of dollar holdings by other countries. While we must aim now, in any case, at a reasonable balance-of-payments equilibrium, for the reasons set forth earlier in this article, the permanent abandonment of this important source of financing would be a major sacrifice. It seems a high price to pay, on the part of the United States as well as of the rest of the world, for the advantage of consolidating our short-term dollar liabilities in the hands of the IMF.

2. *Burden of gold guarantee.* The Articles of Agreement of the Fund provide that countries must extend a gold clause guarantee to the Fund's holdings of their currencies. Should the currency of a given country be devalued, the country would have to appropriate a corresponding amount to indemnify the Fund for its loss. By being transferred to the IMF, United States official dollar liabilities would become subject to this guarantee.

This arrangement has the advantage of greatly strengthening other countries' confidence in the soundness of the Fund's assets. Hence it would increase their willingness to carry deposits with the Fund. But it would be a grave and burdensome decision for the United States, even though we felt morally confident that we would never devalue the dollar. At the very least, it might push us into policies of extreme caution to avoid having to make good. If the guarantee case should ever arise, the political implications of a commitment to indemnify "international bankers," while leaving unprotected domestic dollar holders, could be explosive.

3. *Technical and political difficulties.* In addition, a host of technical and political problems arise that need not be explored here. In an otherwise favorable environment, they could probably be solved. Under existing conditions, they add to the present impracticability of the proposal.

Looking toward the more distant future, an international central bank probably is a desirable goal toward which to work. Practically all national banking systems have evolved toward a central banking system, because it guarantees liquidity and can maintain financial discipline. This, of course, is part of the logic of the Triffin proposal.

But the world today does not give much indication of being ready for an international central bank. *If* such an institution could maintain enough discipline among the member countries to keep their financial policies in line and so avoid the emergence of large payments imbalances, it could operate successfully. But could it? The answer today is probably *no*. In that case, it would do little more than act as depositary of member countries' reserves, make loans to them, and maintain international liquidity.

These functions have in fact been carried out with reasonable proficiency by the United States under the existing gold exchange standard. As long as the proper environment for an international central bank does not exist, there is little to be accomplished by such an institution that could not be done within the present arrangements. The main difference of functional consequence that the central bank proposal would introduce is the automatic gold guarantee that the United States would have to give to its liabilities. If the United States were disposed to take this momentous step, it could do it independently of the IMF and so obtain the benefits of a greatly increased foreign willingness to hold dollars.

Historical experience shows that, at the time a national central bank is created, usually the biggest and strongest banks in the community are the ones that most resist this development. They lose certain advantages that appear not to be fully offset by the benefits to be derived from the new institution. It may well be that the United States, as the world's banker, is today experiencing a similar conflict. The United States should not stand in the way of progress once the time is ripe. But when the time comes, it is to be hoped that more attractive conditions can be worked out for the United States than apparently would result today if the IMF were expanded into an international central bank.

At the present time, our most advantageous choices seem to lie between they key-currency approach and the proposal for a moderate expansion of IMF functions. The first clearly is a temporary device that sooner or later should give way to a more highly organized arrangement. But it is more than a stopgap. It may be a necessary stage in developing the habit and techniques of international cooperation.

Whether the Bernstein proposal has more to offer at this point depends on what can be negotiated. If a formalized agreement concerning who is to lend how much under what conditions can be negotiated only at the cost of endless reservations, qualifications, and exceptions, its net value may not be great. Formalized agreements always set in motion centrifugal forces—everybody tries to protect himself against the unforeseeable consequences of his undertakings. By contrast, an informal approach tends to awaken centripetal forces; the participants try to make it work because they know that unless they do, they will have no instrument at all.

In the choice of approach, considerable emphasis should be given, in my judgment, to increasingly close cooperation and coordination in the formulation of national financial and economic policies. Our balance-of-payments problem has reminded us of a lesson that indeed we had learned and even practiced, but perhaps not as universally as needed. Balances of payments are, after all, two-sided affairs. The deficit of one country is the surplus of another. Out of this awareness there arose, after the war, the doctrine of the "good creditor country." The United States has acted as a good creditor since the war, even though finally it had to borrow the money to do it. It is now up to others to act as good creditors.

However, that alone is not enough. In addition, nations will have to learn to do the right thing not only independently and in isolation, with all others anxiously watching whether it will be done, but cooperatively, regularly, and reliably. Only then will all have the assurance they need to forgo protective measures now required by uncertainty.

This degree of policy cooperation is likely to develop only gradually. The United States, although probably acting as cooperatively as any other country, has understandably shied away more than any nation from formal commitments. But the recent balance-of-payments experience, in which we have come to be partly dependent on the cooperation of others, may serve as a lesson. As the world economy becomes more and more integrated, there is less room for independent action and more need for cooperation.

16

Toward a Reinforced
Gold Exchange Standard

XENOPHON ZOLOTAS

DIAGNOSIS OF THE PROBLEM

Present international monetary problems are closely connected with the peculiarities of the gold exchange standard under which recent developments and past experience are apt to give serious cause for concern. The heart of the matter in this respect is the acute twofold problem of the adequacy of the supply of international liquidity and of the vulnerability of reserve centers.

The inability of gold production to provide adequate finance for expanding world transactions, under conditions of free trade and currency convertibility, can hardly be made up by increasing foreign exchange balances; for these balances are subject to recursive shrinkages, as a result of precautionary and speculative conversions into gold. At the same time the reserve countries are thus being exposed to hazardous changes in speculative activity and in the state of confidence, which, in the short run, render the system prone to disintegration and give rise to serious doubt as to whether it can survive in the long run.

The problem is all the more serious because the adequacy and soundness of international reserves affects critically the process of development in the less advanced regions of the world. There is a connection between the problems of the international payments system and the rate of growth of developing countries; for, as Mr. Maxwell Stamp puts it, "the amount of help which the developed countries can give is limited by their own need to maintain healthy reserve positions."

If the reserve centers of the world are to continue performing ade-

This article is based on speeches made by Mr. Zolotas and in large part is taken from *Towards a Reinforced Gold Exchange Standard* and *International Monetary Order: Problems and Policies*, Bank of Greece Papers and Lectures, Nos. 7 and 12 (1961 and 1962). This printing is made possible through the courtesy of the Bank of Greece and Mr. Zolotas.

quately and soundly their liquidity-creating function it is urgently required to devise means and methods to correct the shortcomings of the gold exchange standard. The approach followed by the various proposals for reform stresses, quite rightly, the role of the International Monetary Fund in this respect and the necessity to expand its activities. The functions of the IMF in maintaining international monetary equilibrium, together with other international organizations, are of paramount importance.

It is, however, necessary to supplement any such reforms by operating directly on the gold exchange standard as it now works, in order to remove its inherent weaknesses and structural defects. The present paper aims to explore the possibilities of complementary reformative action in this direction.

While the gold exchange standard has practically freed the supply of international liquidity to the rest of the world from the limitations of gold production, it has nevertheless left gold as the sole medium to provide for the liquidity and secure the solvency of the key currency countries. Although it might appear rather inconsistent to talk of liquidity problems of the reserve countries, whose national currencies are supposed to be the very means of international payments, we are reminded, every time of crisis or near-crisis, that gold is the ultimate reserve medium, into which all countries stand ready to convert their foreign exchange balances in view of real or imaginary dangers. Furthermore there is evidence to suggest that several countries, including some important reserve holders, tend to increase both in absolute and percentage terms, the gold component of their total reserves. The inadequacy in these circumstances of the gold stock of the key currency countries, which constitutes their only means of defense, becomes apparent when account is taken of their net reserve position.

The gold exchange standard has recently been subject to a most timely reconsideration and critique, stressing its various defects and shortcomings. Joining this discussion, I would hasten to point out that although my attitude toward the gold exchange standard is no less critical than the views which eminent economists have expounded on that matter, I am at the same time more optimistic with respect to the viabiliy of the system, assuming, of course, that appropriate measures of reform will be taken in good time.

My basic contention is that the gold exchange standard does not and cannot provide for an increase in international liquidity on a global basis, beyond the margins set by the stock of monetary gold and its prospective increases. When account is taken of the net reserve position of the key currency countries together with the rest of the world, it is obvious that the gold exchange standard can only raise the reserves of the rest of the world at the expense of a corresponding decline in the net reserve position of the key currency countries. Consequently the level and the rate of increase of international liquidity depend, notwithstanding the gold exchange standard, on the stock of monetary gold and the flow of new gold production. It may be true that when we assess the liquidity of nonreserve countries, what is relevant is their gross reserve position, but it would be misleading to base our estimates of world liquidity on the gross reserve position of the key currency countries. Neglecting the international short-term liabilities of the reserve countries would be justified only if the gold exchange standard had established some kind of one-way convertibility, allowing for the conversion of gold into foreign exchange balances but not vice versa. This not being the case, the foreign exchange component of world monetary reserves has very precarious foundations since it depends on the benevolence of international speculation and on the factor of confidence, which determines the willingness of national monetary authorities to refrain from converting their foreign exchange balances into gold and from nervously shifting these balances from one reserve country to another. Given the stringency of the above conditions, it is obvious that the present gold exchange standard is a fair-weather system prone to disintegration at the appearance of a major hardship.

Furthermore the long-term prospects for the present gold exchange standard are either a continuous deterioration in the net reserve position of the key currency countries inevitably leading to the collapse of the system, or an inadequate supply of international liquidity with depressing effects on trade and eventually over-all economic activity. In this respect, given the inability of the gold exchange standard to increase world reserves as a whole, Triffin's contention that it may help in relieving a shortage of world monetary reserves, to the extent that the key currency countries are willing to let their net reserve position deteriorate, is rather overoptimistic. The gold exchange standard in its present form may only solve, conditionally and temporarily, the liquidity problem of the rest of the world.

PROPOSALS FOR CHANGE

I am firmly convinced that despite its structural weaknesses and defects the gold exchange standard can become a working, dependable mechanism capable of dealing with both the short- and long-term aspects of the international liquidity problem, without major institutional readjustments. The guiding principle for any reform plan should be the recognition that our efforts to maximize the potential effectiveness of international mechanisms and institutions are being subject to the side constraint of political feasibility and the traditional conservatism of monetary authorities, which must be taken into account if theoretical remedies are to be transformed into practicable solutions. In this respect, I believe that the following measures, while easily applicable within the existing institutional framework, will at the same time greatly contribute to the establishment of a stronger monetary order, i.e., of a genuine, multicurrency gold exchange standard, the main features of which are the following:

First, reciprocal accumulation of reserve balances among major trading countries in each other's currency, with the reserve centers leading the way.

Second, provisions of a gold (value) guarantee on foreign official reserve deposits by all major convertible currency countries.

Third, preferential interest rate and tax treatment for foreign official depositors of reserve balances, which possibly could also be extended to private foreign holders of short-term assets.

The above measures are complementary and not substitutes for each other, forming an integral policy device which should be implemented as a whole in order to be fully effective.

The over-all result of their application would be the establishment of a multicurrency standard, in which the responsibility of supplying international liquidity and defending the stability of the system would be shared among several leading countries. The mutual piling up of deposits in major convertible currencies—through the appropriate utilization of surpluses and the reciprocal extension of credit—would not only serve as the first line of defense for key currencies and as a means to economize on gold, but would also establish a multilateral monetary infrastructure, made up of a network of interdependent reserve currencies which would meet both the short- and the long-term aspects of the international monetary problem.

In such a context,, the simultaneous provision of the gold guarantee on foreign official reserve balances by all major trading countries would be indispensable. For it would be hardly possible otherwise to expect national monetary authorities to assume the responsibility of stockpiling each other's currency. The strengthening of confidence to this end appears necessary not only with respect to the present reserve currencies, but also and mainly with respect to those currencies that appear eligible to perform a key role in international transactions. On the other hand, as I have emphasized in several instances, if one reserve center were to adopt the measures alone, its efficacy would be limited. The gold guarantee, as I have proposed it, is an integral part of the above system of complementary measures, which would reduce our dependence on gold as a means of international payments, while maintaining it as the measure of value. As a matter of fact, it would hardly be necessary to bother about gold in the context of the above system, which would render a number of major currencies perfect substitutes for gold. Since the main responsibility of central banks, which determines the structure of their international assets, is to secure the gold value of their foreign exchange reserves, they should scarcely have a reason to prefer gold to interest-bearing holdings of guaranteed key currencies.

On the other hand, the provision of a multilateral gold guarantee would presently be the best answer to gold speculation and would definitely silence disturbing rumors and disequilibrating activities that exist in this respect. For the provision of the guarantee would serve as an indisputable proof of our firm commitment to maintain the present price of gold.

The current pressure on present reserve centers, due to the excessive recourse to their capital markets by the rest of the world, would be largely alleviated by the raising of several major currencies to the status of international monetary media. At the same time the proposed differentiation of interest rate and tax policies between the internal and external sectors would allow the existing and eventual reserve centers to secure the independence of their international position from internal policy requirements and to render the goal of external balance compatible with domestic high-employment equilibrium and increased rates of growth. It goes without saying that the regular coordination of interest rate policies among the financial centers of the world would be absolutely essential.

With the above system of interconnected policy measures we need neither transcend our present institutional framework nor limit our national responsibilities for discipline in order to cope effectively with the short- and long-run deficiencies of our present monetary system. We should not lose sight of its basic weakness as a result of recent improvements in the international monetary situation. On the contrary, it would be most timely and appropriate to undertake reformative action when it appears to be less urgently required rather than postpone it till the time of crisis, when it would be overdue and the least effective.

In the long run, there is always the well-known question mark on the ability of the present gold exchange standard to satisfy the liquidity requirements of free and growing world transactions. At present, the problem appears anything but urgent; conditions, however, may change rapidly in case of real or imaginary dangers causing a shrinkage in the foreign exchange component of world reserves, through the interplay of confidence and speculation effects. In a world of high political tensions and uncertain developments, both effects depend on volatile psychological factors and are bound to feed back on rumors. In view of the recursive character of the speculation and confidence effects, it would be unwise to overlook the necessity for reinforcing our defences against such unsettling occurrences.

Furthermore, a liquidity shortage may become evident faster than we think, if only because the reserve centers are too successful in restoring an over-all surplus in their balance of payments. Reconciling, therefore, the stability requirements of the gold exchange standard with the liquidity needs of the international economy would be one of the serious future problems.

It is only natural that a multicurrency gold exchange standard would be the effective and feasible answer to the threefold issue of liquidity adequacy, speculation effect, and confidence effect, since it has been designed in response to them. The proposed multilateral monetary infrastructure would provide an adequate and sound basis for the expansion of international liquidity, while the confidence and speculation effects would be minimized by the simultaneous provision of the gold guarantee and the coordinated manipulation of interest rate and tax policies.

The implementation of the proposed system should be a matter of international consultations and agreement, among the major trading countries, in which the role of the Fund would be of primary importance. In addition to the various ways in which the Fund could contribute to this end, the fact that the gold guarantee is an established practice in its transactions could probably provide a way out of the psychological barrier that appears to exist in this respect. Thus, it might prove useful that the gold guarantee be extended only on reserve deposits made either through the Fund, at the reserve centers, or with the Fund itself. In both instances the process would be completely voluntary for the countries concerned and the Fund would keep this type of activity outside the quota system. It goes without saying that the reserve balances deposited through or with the Fund would be as freely usable and transferable as ordinary reserve deposits.

It may be more expedient if in the initial stage the Fund limits itself to the role of an agent of depositor countries, following their instructions as to the form of their reserve deposits and the currencies in which they would like to hold them.

I believe that in this direction lies a valuable opportunity for the Fund to improve on its outstanding record of contributions to international monetary order.

We have come a long way since the days of the gold standard in attributing to international reserves a "buffer" role, but this should not carry us to the extreme of viewing an expansion of liqiudity as a panacea. As a matter of fact there are few problems which increased reserves alone could ultimately solve, without concurring domestic corrective measures and international coordination of policies.

In this respect the establishment and maintenance of realistic par values is of primary importance for the stability of exchanges and the safeguarding of free trade and currency convertibility.

It is also of crucial significance, as previously emphasized, to secure a systematic and adequate flow of developmental capital from the developed countries to the less advanced regions of the world. Neither a multicurrency gold exchange standard, nor any international monetary system for that matter, would be fully effective in maintaining over-all equilibrium in world transactions, unless appropriate action is taken to support the balance-of-payments position of primary producing countries and to promote rapid economic growth in developing nations. Continued expansion of world trade, as well as the stability of our monetary order will, in the final analysis, depend on the ability and willingness of major industrial countries to run deficits on capital account on a sufficient scale to sustain an adequate rate of growth in the countries in process of development. A reinforced gold exchange standard with an expanded monetary infrastructure would greatly enhance the ability of the developed countries of the Western world to meet these fundamental requirements of international economic order and growth.

Part III

**FLEXIBLE EXCHANGE RATES AND
RETURN TO THE GOLD STANDARD**

17

The Future of International Payments

JAMES E. MEADE

DIAGNOSIS

Present conditions call for a reconsideration by the highly developed, industrialized, wealthy countries of the Western world,[1] of the future of their arrangements for the conduct of their international payments. There are many reasons why such a review is now needed. The dollar has ceased to be a universally scarce currency and seems liable now, like other currencies, to recurrent periods of weakness; the Administration in the United States is in any case engaged in a review of the principles of U.S. economic policies at home and abroad; in Europe a solution is sought for the problem of reconciling the European Economic Community (the Six) with the European Free Trade Association (the Seven); and throughout the Western countries there is a growing realization of the need both to stimulate economic growth at home and to aid the economic development of the underdeveloped countries of Asia, Africa, and South America. Perhaps as important as any of these factors is the possibility of a far-reaching disarmament agreement between the communist and the Western countries; if this greatly desired event were to be realized, there would be many inevitable disturbances and strains in international payments as resources were, by one means or another, transferred from military to peaceful uses. It is of the first importance that there should be a system of international payments which would cope in a flexible manner with the very extensive readjustments that such a large disturbance would involve.

The purpose of this article is to suggest some improvements in the ma-

A revision of an article from the *Three Banks Review*, June 1961, published by the Royal Bank of Scotland, Glyn, Mills & Co., and reprinted from *Factors Affecting the United States Balance of Payments*, Joint Economic Committee, U.S. Congress (Washington, 1962).

[1] The countries which I have in mind are basically the countries of Western Europe and North America, though for some purposes we should add to the list some other countries like Australia and New Zealand—and possibly also Japan. Purely for the purposes of simple exposition I will call these "the Western countries."

chinery for international payments between the main national currencies of Western countries. But a financial system is only a means to an end; and in order to decide what principles one wants to adopt for a payments system one must first know what are the basic objectives which one wishes to achieve by means of it. Now in my view the basic objectives of a reformed system of payments between the Western countries fall into three main groups: freer trade; more liberal foreign aid; and a higher rate of domestic economic expansion.

In commercial policy the Western countries should now negotiate among themselves a substantial further reduction of all the obstacles which they place on imports from each other, and they should extend these reductions of barriers to imports on a most-favored-nation basis to their purchases from the underdeveloped countries of Asia, Africa, and South America without demanding any very substantial *quid pro quo* in the form of much freer access to the markets of these underdeveloped countries. President Kennedy's tariff bill which has now passed the House of Representatives would provide an ideal means to carry out this policy.

Such a policy is a necessary condition for the United Kingdom to join the European Common Market. For there are some real difficulties in the way of the United Kingdom simply joining the Six. One of the most important of these difficulties concerns the position of the underdeveloped countries in the British Commonwealth. At present there is free entry into the United Kingdom market for the products of such countries. At a time like the present, when there is increasing hope that the British Commonwealth can become more and more a real club of developd and underdeveloped countries from all parts of the world, it would be particularly unfortunate if the United Kingdom instead of letting in Indian manufactures free and taxing German manufactures had to let in Germany manufactures free and to impose the common European tariff and quotas on Indian manufactures. The best way of avoiding such a conflict is a general movement toward freer imports from all sources, as well as from each other, into all the developed countries of the West.

There is a need also for a substantially increased program of financial aid from the developed countries of the West to the underdeveloped countries of Asia, Africa, and South America. These countries are more and more determined to start a process of economic growth through industrialization and heavy investment in capital development. A large-scale flow of financial aid from the rich countries to these poorer and underdeveloped countries is the only way in which this process can be initiated without the rigid controls over private consumption and the grinding poverty which the finance of their own capital development solely out of their own domestic resources would involve.

It is important that such aid should be given in an untied form—the rich countries should provide financial aid to the poor countries, and the poor countries should be free to spend the aid on procuring the sort of capital equipment which they most need from whatever is the cheapest source. The country which should provide the aid because it is rich is not necessarily the country which can produce most cheaply the particular goods most needed by the country which receives the aid. Moreover, a system of tied aid may well cause the developing country to employ most wasteful forms of technique in its economic development. Machinery made in the United States, for example, is probably specially designed to save labor (which is scarce in the United States) even at the expense of employing much capital (which is relatively plentiful in the United States). Machinery to be used in India, for example, should be specially designed to save capital (which is scarce in India) even at the expense of requiring much labor for its operation (since labor is plentiful in India). Dollar aid which is tied to dollar machines may, therefore, be an inappropriate way to encourage capital development in India. It might, for example, be much better that a dollar loan to India should be spent on Japanese machinery, or should be used to finance the wages of Indian workers employed to produce by very labor-intensive methods a dam for irrigation purposes in India. In this latter case the dollar proceeds of the loan to India would be available to finance a general excess of India's imports over her exports during the process of capital development. Such Indian imports might well include some of the foodstuffs which the workers employed on constructing the dam would purchase with their wages.

There is one more basic requirement for a reformed system of international payments. In present-day conditions it is necessary that the national governments of the Western countries should feel free to use their domestic financial policies for the promotion of full employment, price stability, and economic growth in their economies without having to pay too much regard to their balances of international payments. The simultaneous achievement of the three domestic goals of full employment, price stability, and economic growth is difficult enough. The principles which must govern such action are now fairly well known. To maintain full employment the total level of money demand must be raised (by a cheap money policy, lower taxation, and higher government expenditure) so long as there is not sufficient demand to absorb the whole of the economy's potential output and must be lowered (by the opposite financial measures) if there tends to be too high a level of money expenditure relative to the available output of goods and services; to prevent a high level of demand from leading to a perpetual inflation of money prices and costs steps must be taken (perhaps the most difficult task of all) to prevent money wage rates rising more quickly than the general productivity of labor; and to set the financial background for economic growth monetary and fiscal measures must be taken to stimulate expenditure upon new capital development and to restrain expenditure upon goods and services for current consumption.

In all conscience this task is sufficiently difficult. It becomes impossible if the national governments have, in addition, to make it a primary objective of their banking and budgetary policies to maintain an equilibrium in their international balances of payments. According to the rules of the old-fashioned gold standard game, a country with a surplus on its international balance of payments should inflate its domestic money income, prices, and costs until its demand for imports had so grown and the availability of its exports so declined that its balance of payments was in equilibrium once more; and, conversely, a deficit country should deflate its domestic incomes, prices, and costs. But in fact this no longer happens. As the histories of the United States in the first ten years after the war and of Germany in the last five years show, a country which has a surplus on its balance of payments does not inflate domestically in order to get rid of this surplus; on the contrary, it uses its monetary and budgetary policies so as to achieve as far as possible domestic full employment, price stability, and economic growth. Germany, for example, in recent years has been very successful in achieving this combination of domestic objectives, and she has shown no signs of willingness to abandon these domestic objectives for a domestic inflation which would remove the surplus on her balance of payments. Deficit countries which are losing their reserves of gold and foreign exchange have not, of course, found it so easy merely to disregard their balance-of-payments situation. But they have in recent years been extremely unwilling to give up their domestic monetary and budgetary policies for full employment and economic growth. They have tried often to avoid the need for deflation by imposing restrictions on their imports, cutting down their obligations on foreign aid, tying the aid which they give to expenditures on their own products, borrowing from abroad themselves, and so on.

In my opinion it is right that the national governments of the Western countries should use their domestic monetary and budgetary policies primarily to achieve their domestic aims of full employment, price stability, and economic growth. These are outstandingly important objectives and their attainment requires the well-planned use of effective weapons. In the modern world these functions are the functions of *national* governments; there are no *supranational* governments or agencies designed for this purpose; even in the European Economic Community the objectives of full employment, price stability, and economic growth will remain primarily the responsibility of the national governments of the constituent countries; and until we have some form of supranational government for these countries with its own single currency, its own central bank, and its own system of taxes and public expenditure, these functions must remain primarily the responsibiilty of national authorities.

What is needed for the Western countries is a system of international payments that will allow the deficit as well as the surplus countries to devote their domestic monetary and budgetary policies primarily to the maintenance of domestic full employment, price stability, and economic growth. Moreover, the system must be such as to enable them to press ahead with the removal of tariffs and other obstacles to imports; they must not, that is to say, be driven to restrict imports simply in order to restore equilibrium to their balance of international payments. Finally, the system must be such as to enable them to develop an enlarged program of untied financial aid to the underdeveloped countries; they must not be under any compulsion to cut down their foreign aid, or to tie their foreign aid to their own national exports, as a means of putting their balance of payments into equilibrium and stopping a drain on their monetary reserves of gold and foreign currencies.

How far-reaching these requirements are can perhaps best be seen from the experience of the United States over the last year or so. The U.S. balance of payments has been in deficit. She has not increased her tariffs or intensified her restrictions on imports to put a stop to her loss of gold reserves; and she is much to be commended for not having done so. We must not return to the undiluted principle that deficit countries can restrict imports from surplus countries. This might well mean that the United States being in deficit could restrict imports from the underdeveloped countries. The United States has refrained from actually restricting her imports on balance-of-payments grounds; but it is most desirable that she should move in the opposite direction and lead the countries of the Western world in a general agreement to reduce trade barriers. President Kennedy's tariff bill marks a most notable step in this direction. But will the United States in fact be able to take such an initiative in reducing the barriers to her imports while she is engaged in putting right a serious deficit on her balance of payments?

Recently the United States has tended to tie the aid which she has given to underdeveloped countries more and more to U.S. products, as a method of reducing the strain on her balance of payments; and attempts have been made to persuade the Germans and other European countries with surpluses on their balances of payments that they should take over an increased share of the burden of the finance of aid to underdeveloped countries. No doubt a strong case can be made out for the view that the Germans and others should contribute more to the finance of foreign aid; but this case should rest on the fact that the Germans are rich and have a high standard of living and not on the fact that they have a surplus on their balance of payments. The principle that the countries with surpluses on their balances of payments should aid the countries with deficits on their balances of payments can lead to the ridiculous result that a poor territory (like Ghana) should aid a rich territory (like the United Kingdom) if the former happens to have a surplus on its balance of payments (due to a high world demand for cocoa) while the latter has a deficit (because the money cost of its manufactured exports is unduly inflated). United aid should be planned on an enlarged scale from the rich to the poor countries, and balances of payments should somehow be made to conform to these requirements. But can the United States with the present strain on its balance of payments be expected to take the lead in initiating such a reform, unless some alternative system for adjusting international payments can be found?

Finally, it is of the utmost importance that the U.S. Government should take early and effective monetary and budgetary measures to reflate demand inside the United States, to stimulate capital investment and economic growth, and generally to expand the domestic economy to absorb the quite appreciable amount of unemployed labor that has appeared recently. Such action is of central importance not only for the citizens of the United States themselves but also for the rest of the Western countries and of the underdeveloped countries. The maintenance and expansion of demand in the United States can greatly affect the exports of those other countries. In my view there is no doubt that the U.S. Government can organize a domestic economic expansion by means of its monetary and fiscal controls over the general level of demand. But may not the domestic expansion in the United States by expanding the U.S. demand for imports put a further strain on her balance of payments? Will the United States be in a position at the same time to give the necessary lead to the other Western countries in reducing their barriers to imports and in enlarging a program of untied aid to the underdeveloped countries?

PRESCRIPTIONS

The answer to this set of problems must, I think, be that the Western countries should make a freer use of alterations in the rates of exchange between their national currencies in order to preserve equilibrium in their balances of payments. Extreme advocates of this remedy would argue that if the rates of exchange between the main Western currencies—the dollar, the pound, the mark, the franc, and so on—were allowed to fluctuate completely freely in uncontrolled foreign exchange markets, the problem would be easily solved. I shall proceed in this article: first, by stating as convincingly as I can the case for holding this extreme view; second, by examining certain criticisms which have been made of this view; and, third, by proposing an actual scheme for international payments which attempts to take account of the many points made on both sides of this argument.

First, then, the case for freely fluctuating exchange rates: The statesmen of the Western countries, so it is argued, should concentrate their attention upon commercial negotiations for a general removal of their trade barriers against imports, upon a concerted program of untied foreign aid, and upon domestic financial policies to promote full employment, price stability, and economic growth. Let them forget their balance-of-payments problems. Of course, from time to time some of them will be in deficit and some in surplus on their balances of international payments. But in this case the currencies of the countries with strong balances of payments will appreciate in terms of the currencies of the countries with weak balances of payments. These alterations in exchange rates will look after the balance-of-payments problem by a double mechanism.

1. The appreciation of the strong currency and the depreciation of the weak currency will make the products of the former country relatively more expensive and the products of the latter country relatively cheaper to all purchasers. The products of the former will tend to give way to the products of the latter in all consuming markets, that is to say, in the do-

mestic markets of the two countries concerned and also in the markets of the other countries to which these two countries are exporting. In the end the consequential expansion of the exports of the country with the balance-of-payments deficit relatively to the exports of the country with the balance-of-payments surplus corrects the disequilibrium in international payments.

2. But this adjustment will not, of course, be immediate. It will take time for the exports of the country whose exchange rate has depreciated to expand at the expense of the products of the country whose currency has appreciated. Meanwhile the excess demand for the currency of the surplus country and the excess supply of the currency of the deficit country will cause the former currency to appreciate very markedly and the latter currency to depreciate very markedly in the foreign exchange markets. But this will induce the private speculator to move funds from the former into the latter currency. The excessive appreciation of the former currency in terms of the latter will be known to be only temporary; for, as soon as it begins to have its basic effect in stimulating the exports of the deficit country relatively to the exports of the surplus country, the change in the exchange rates will be in large measure reversed. The speculator, so the argument runs, in search of private profit will thus move funds out of the surplus (and excessively appreciated) currency into the deficit (and excessively depreciated) currency. This movement of private funds will serve to finance the temporary deficit on the balance of payments of the deficit country until the exchange rate variations have had time to carry out their basic role of adjusting the underlying elements in the balance of payments.

In fact any effective mechanism for adjustment of the balance of payments must perform a double function. The first function, which we may call the function of liquidity, is to provide a temporary support for the currencies of the deficit countries to meet short-run fluctuations in balances of payments or to finance temporarily a more fundamental disequilibrium in balances of payments, while a more permanent adjustment is being carried out. Freely fluctuating exchange rates provide such liquidity through the mechanism of private speculation, as funds are moved out of currencies which have appreciated unduly as the result of the immediate impact of a change and into currencies which for similar reasons have depreciated unduly. The second function, which we may call that of adjustment, is to bring about long-run basic changes in imports, exports, and other items in balances of international payments; and this is done by the effect upon imports and exports of permanent moderate alterations in rates of exchange.

Are there any snags in this argument? The weaknesses of the system can be examined under four heads.

1. The system will work only if the products of the countries concerned are competitive with each other. An appreciation of the German mark will reduce the surplus on the German balance of payments only if the resulting higher price of German products relative to British, American, French, and other products causes purchasers to buy considerably less German products and considerably more of the products of other countries. If this were not so, the change might do more harm than good; the higher prices of German products might cause the Germans to earn more, not less, foreign exchange for their exports; and if the Germans did not increase their imports of foreign products very appreciably, the result might be an increase rather than a decrease in the surplus on the German balance of payments. But the main industrialized countries of the West are in fact rather highly competitive in their manufactured exports; and if time is given for the adjustments to be made by the producers, traders, and consumers concerned in all the countries of the world, there is, I think, little doubt that exchange rate variations could cope with the long-run problem of adjustment between the Western countries. This would be even more certain if, as I have suggested, there were also freer trade between these countries and if the foreign aid which they gave were in an untied form. For both these reforms would make it easier for buyers of the products of these countries to shift their purchases from the more expensive to the cheaper suppliers; and this is what is needed in order to make a system of variable exchange rates work effectively.

2. An essential part of the mechanism is the movement of short-term speculative funds from a currency which has temporarily appreciated excessively into a currency which has temporarily depreciated excessively. Such speculation would, of course, turn out to be profitable to the speculator. But whether or not it actually occurs will depend upon the speculators having a good understanding of what is going to happen, that is to say, upon their being able to decide when a currency is "temporarily excessively" appreciated or depreciated and when it is not. In the absence of such well-informed speculation the system might be very unstable. Consider the following example. Suppose that there is a deficit on the U.S. balance of payments; the dollar depreciates; since it takes time for dollar exports to drive sterling and mark exports out of world markets, the dollar depreciates at first excessively; this gives an enormous price advantage to dollar products; producers, traders, and consumers after a time-lag shift

their demands very substantially away from sterling and mark products on to dollar products; this shift is so great as not merely to remove the deficit on the U.S. balance of payments but to cause a surplus; the dollar now appreciates excessively; this causes sterling and mark products to have an enormous price advantage over dollar products; after a time, therefore, there is a swing back in the opposite direction. The system might proceed by a series of ever-increasing excessive swings now in one direction and now in the other. The trouble could, of course, be prevented if there were a sufficient volume of well-informed speculative funds, which would mitigate the excessive swings in the exchange rates which lie at the root of the trouble.

3. The position might, however, be even worse if speculators not merely refrained from operating at the right time in the right direction, but actually operated in the wrong direction. Suppose once more that there is a deficit on the U.S. balance of payments and that the dollar depreciates in consequence. If speculators judge that simply because it has already depreciated a lot, it is likely to depreciate still further, they may themselves sell dollars and buy other currencies long after the dollar has depreciated sufficiently to put the U.S. balance of payments into equilibrium in the long run. They may, if they operate on a sufficiently great scale, make the position even more unstable than it would have been in the absence of all speculation. If speculators act in this way, they are liable in the end to make very considerable financial losses, because they will be left in the end in the position of holding no dollars but only marks and pounds when at last the excessive depreciation of the dollar comes to an end so that it regains value in terms of other currencies. But not all speculators will necessarily lose—only those who are in the end left carrying the baby. Some persons may speculate against the dollar when they know it is already depreciated below its true long-term value, simply because they think that others are going to continue to speculate against the dollar and that they themselves will be able to get out of dollars before the downward movement comes to an end.

4. But there is one further danger which may intensify the instability of uncontrolled fluctuating exchange rates. Suppose that the United Kingdom has a deficit on its balance of payments, so that sterling depreciates in terms of other currencies. Suppose that the depreciation is at first rather excessive. The depreciation of the pound will cause the price of imports to go up in terms of pounds; this will cause the cost of living to go up; and this may in turn cause the money wage rate to go up. If all this

happens sufficiently quickly and on a sufficiently large scale, the result may be to cause a rise in money costs of production in the United Kingdom which largely or wholly offsets the competitive advantage gained by the depreciation of the pound itself. In this case the strain on the United Kingdom balance of payments would cause a further round of currency depreciation, followed by a further round of internal cost inflation, and so on. And in this case the speculators who speculated against the pound, while they would intensify the trouble, would not lose money, because their own speculation would help to cause the internal cost inflation and thus to justify the speculation itself. This danger can, I believe, very easily be exaggerated; for even in the United Kingdom the price of imports accounts for only a small part of the cost of living, and the effects of the rise in the price of imports upon the cost of living and of the cost of living upon the wage rate are both likely to be delayed.

However great or small these dangers may in fact be, they are real possibilities. For this reason the authorities of the Western countries are extremely unlikely to adopt an uncontrolled system of freely fluctuating exchange rates. It may be, as I personally greatly hope, that exchange-rate variations will be used more readily and frequently than in the past as a means of maintaining equilibrium in balances of payments; but if so, these variations will certainly be controlled to a greater or lesser degree by the authorities. The normal instrument for such control is the national exchange equalization account; the national monetary authority holds a fund made up partly of its own national currency and partly of a reserve of gold and of other foreign currencies; if it wishes to prevent an appreciation in the value of its own currency it buys gold or foreign currencies in order to sell its own currency, and vice versa.

In the bad old days of mass unemployment in the 1930's, before the governments of the Western countries had learned by financial policies to maintain their internal domestic demands at adequate levels, this system led to complaints of competitive exchange depreciation. The authorities in one country would purchase gold and foreign currencies with their national currencies simply in order to make their national currencies depreciate (even though there was no deficit on their balance of payments), in order to cheapen their exports in foreign markets, in order to undercut the products of their competitors, in order to give employment to their own workers at the expense of foreign workers.

This danger is now little more than a bogy. National governments now know how to control total demand and there are so many useful things that each can do with unemployed resources that they are exceedingly unlikely to try to depreciate their currencies competitively against each other simply to find employment for their workers in export markets. But it was largely to fight against this danger that the rules of the International Monetary Fund were devised, whereby national governments undertook to peg their currencies in terms of gold and only to alter the peg from time to time in order to remove a fundamental disequilibrium in their balance of payments. This system is, in my opinion, a bad one. It means that if, for example, a deficit appears on the United Kingdom's balance of payments, the British authorities are under an obligation to maintain the value of the pound (by selling gold and dollars and buying pounds in the exchange equalization account) until some once-for-all cataclysmic depreciation of the pound by 20, 30, or 40 per cent takes place to remove a fundamental disequilibrium. This provides a golden opportunity for useless antisocial speculation. During this period of support of the pound all speculators can see that the pound will certainly not be appreciated and may be very substantially depreciated. They sell pounds and buy dollars, knowing that at the worst they will not lose and at the best may make a quick profit of 20, 30, or 40 per cent. And such speculation serves no useful purpose; on the contrary, it merely piles an extra unnecessary strain on the pound.

This sort of danger is particularly great in the case of currencies like sterling and dollars which are held as international reserve currencies by other countries. The amount of sterling balances held as liquid reserves by foreigners is, as is well known, greatly in excess of the total gold and dollar reserves held by the United Kingdom authorities. If overseas holders of sterling lose confidence in the pound and try to move their funds out of sterling into gold and dollars, this can put a quite intolerable strain on sterling. The dollar is more and more reaching a similar position. In recent years international liquidity has been increased largely by other countries holding more and more of their reserves not in gold, but in dollars. The consequence is that against the gold reserves of the United States there is now a large liquid debt of dollar balances held by other countries. Lack of confidence in the dollar which caused these foreign holders to shift from dollars into gold or sterling can now put a very great strain on the U.S. gold reserves.

A SPECIFIC PLAN

In my opinion, then, the Western countries need a reformed system for international payments in which (1) much greater use is made of variations in exchange rates than has been the case in recent years, (2) exchange rate variations are, however, subject to some public control to avoid the dangers of misguided speculation, and (3) the special problem of potential instability of the great international currencies like the pound and the dollar are met. I will close this article by making some proposals which would meet these points. I shall put my proposals forward in the form of a precise "ideal" scheme in order to be able to explain the principles briefly and clearly. In the real world it would, of course, be capable of many modifications.

I suggest, then, the following scheme:

1. All the national monetary authorities of the Western countries would agree to pay all their monetary reserves (gold, dollars, sterling, etc.) into a reformed International Monetary Fund. They would receive in exchange gold certificates at the current gold value of their reserves which they had paid into the IMF. They would agree in the future to hold only gold certificates as their reserves, and all newly mined gold which was not taken up by the private market (for industrial purposes or for private hoarding) would be paid into the IMF.

2. The national monetary authorities would then let the value of their national currencies fluctuate in value in terms of gold certificates according to changes in supply and demand in the foreign exchange markets. Each national monetary authority would now possess a national exchange equalization account made up partly by holding of its own currency and partly by a holding of the gold certificates which it had acquired from the IMF in exchange for its foreign exchange reserves. It could, therefore, if it so decided, moderate the fluctuations in the value of its national currency in terms of gold certificates by buying or selling its own currency for gold certificates in its exchange equalization account. But it would no longer be in a position to shift its foreign exchange reserves from one form of foreign exchange to another (e.g., to sell pounds in order to buy dollars or to reduce its dollar balances in order to hold gold).

3. The IMF would now hold an enormous additional fund of gold and national currencies (in particular pounds and dollars) which were paid into it from the reserves of the national monetary authorities. These would be an addition to its present holding of the gold and national currencies which were paid into it on its inception. It could now act as a most important supranational exchange equalization account. If in its opinion, for example, the pound was temporarily unduly depreciated in terms of dollars, the IMF could sell dollars and purchase pounds out of its holdings of these currencies.

4. Moreover, the IMF could now purchase (or sell) national currencies such as pounds, dollars, marks, francs, etc.) for gold certificates. Gold certificates would be held by the national monetary authorities as their sole form of monetary reserve and private operators might also hold gold certificates as a convenient form of reserve of external currency. The IMF by issuing new gold certificates to purchase national currencies (or by buying up existing gold certificates with some of the national currencies which it held) could thus control the total issue of gold certificates. By doing so it could ensure that the total amount of international liquid reserves was kept in line with the needs of international trade and payments.

How might such a system work in practice? Let me give a short account of how I personally would hope that it might be made to work. The national governments of the Western countries would concentrate on national policies for the maintenance of full employment, price stability, and economic growth and on reaching international arrangements for agreed reductions in their trade barriers and for agreed programs of untied aid to the underdeveloped countries. They would not concern themselves too much with the consequences upon their balances of international payments, but would rely upon variations in the rates of exchange between their national currencies (under the control and guidance of a reformed International Monetary Fund) to bring about the necessary adjustments.

The reformed IMF would in this case become a real supranational exchange equalization fund. It could use its large fund of various national currencies to give temporary support to one currency in terms of another if such temporary support was desirable. It would itself have to judge, no doubt in close consultation with the national monetary authorities, whether private speculation should be supplemented or offset in order to prevent an excessive temporary depreciation or appreciation of particular currencies.

These operations of the reformed IMF could always be supplemented by the operations of the national exchange equalization accounts which could buy (or sell) gold certificates with their own national currencies in their own national exchange equalization accounts, if they wished to prevent an excessive temporary appreciation (or depreciation) of their national currency. But it would be greatly to be hoped that national exchange equalization accounts would be used less and less frequently. In modern conditions it would be a most appropriate division of functions between national governments and a supranational monetary authority, if the former concentrated on policies for economic expansion, foreign aid, and the removal of trade barriers while the latter concerned itself with the control of foreign exchange rates. Such a system could be made to work efficiently and would remove any possibility that the national governments might use their national exchange equalization accounts for purposes of competitive exchange depreciation in order to obtain national advantages for their trade.

In addition to its functions of offsetting temporary excessive fluctuations in exchange rates by buying one national currency and selling another, the reformed IMF would also be able by buying (or selling) national currencies for gold certificates to increase (or to decrease) the total amount of liquid international funds available in the form of gold certificates. The IMF could buy and sell national currencies for gold certificates with the aim of keeping the value of gold certificates constant, not in terms of any single national currency (for the national currencies would be varying in terms of each other), but in terms of national currencies in general. Such stability of the value of gold certificates in terms of a composite index of national currencies would make it an admirable form of international liquid asset. Insofar as national monetary authorities operated their national exchange equalization accounts, gold certificates, having a more or less constant value in terms of national currencies in general, would be an admirable form for holding their reserves of foreign exchange.

Even if, as is to be hoped, the operations of the national exchange equalization accounts withered away as the system developed, the controlled provision by the IMF of international liquid reserves in the form of gold certificates would still remain of major importance. For gold certificates could be held by commercial banks and by other private institutions and individuals who, because their business involved them in international transactions, needed to hold their own reserves of foreign exchange.[2] Indeed, there would be no reason why those who wished to do so should not express their business contracts in terms, not of any single national currency, but of gold certificates. In particular, this possibility

---

[2] National monetary authorities would have undertaken to hold gold certificates and no gold, but private individuals and institutions would be free to demand from the IMF the redemption of gold certificates with actual gold. But against this liability the IMF would now hold the whole of the present gold reserves of the monetary authorities of the Western countries. In the unlikely event that such reserves proved insufficient for this purpose, the IMF would have to restrict the supply of gold certificates and to allow the price of gold certificates and of gold to rise in terms of national currencies in general. But this is a very remote possibility. One of the advantages of the scheme which I propose is that it would provide adequate liquidity without a rise in the price of gold in terms of national currencies in general.

might greatly ease the flow of international loan capital in a regime of fluctuating rates of exchange between national currencies.

There is nothing absurd in modern conditions in having an international currency of this kind, controlled by a truly supranational authority, and at the same time having a number of national currencies whose values may fluctuate in terms of each other and in terms of the international currency. As long as we entrust to the national governments the main functions of public finance and of policies concerned with the maintenance of full employment, the control of inflation, and the stimulation of economic growth, we cannot preserve *both* a liberal cooperative system of international trade and of foreign aid *and also* fixed exchange rates between national currencies. But this does not mean that there is no proper function for a really powerful supranational monetary authority. Those who, like myself, wish to move in the direction of effective world government will welcome this fact. All federal or confederal arrangements rest upon a sensible division of functions between the "central" and the "local" governments, suitable to the practical problems of the real situation. I suggest that for the Western countries the division of functions in monetary matters should be of the kind which I have outlined in this article.

Such proposals raise, of course, the most far-reaching questions of the proper nature for the management and governing body of an IMF that was transformed into so powerful a supranational instrument. It would be inevitable that it should be operated, in its day-to-day decisions about the purchase and sale of national currencies, by a small body of expert international servants, recruited no doubt largely from the treasuries and central banks of the constituent countries; but at the same time the principles of its operations should be supervised by a governing body of ministers or high officials from the governments of the member countries. But these matters cannot be discussed in this article.

COMMENT[3]

My paper was frankly utopian in form in the sense that it contained an outline of a perfect or ideal system of international payments regardless of existing political or other practical difficulties. Such an academic exercise has its practical uses because it helps one to determine what are the

---

[3] Reprinted from Appendix, *Outlook for United States Balance of Payments*, Hearings (December 14, 1962), Joint Economic Committee, Subcommittee on International Exchange and Payments (Washington, 1963).

general forms which one would like the more immediate and practical improvements to take. As far as international payments are concerned my ideal solution is based upon a combination of two principles:

1. That there should be some agreed system, under the auspices of the IMF, for adjusting the amount of international liquidity to the increased needs for international monetary reserves arising from the natural growth of international trade and payments; and

2. That greater use should be made of variations in the exchange rates between national currencies for the adjustment of balances of international payments.

I recognize, of course, that the immediate application of these two principles in the ideal form presented in my paper is not practical politics. But I would urge most strongly that some practical steps should now be taken in both these directions. I do not want to comment in detail on the form which any immediate reforms in the provision of international liquidity should take. I have personally a preference for the method advocated by Professor Triffin. But the essential point is to make adequate arrangements of a flexible kind which will ensure that the countries of the free world (in particular the United States, the United Kingdom, and the EEC) should not be hindered in their policies for domestic economic expansion and for freeing their international trade and payments by fears of stringencies of means of international payment due to the fact that international monetary reserves are growing less quickly than their international payments for trade and other purposes.

But I would very much like to comment on a practical immediate step which might be taken to give a small degree of flexibility to exchange rates. But, first of all, I would like to repeat very briefly why, in my view, some move in this direction is essential. It is greatly to be hoped that (1) the new U.S. trade legislation together with current negotiations between the United Kingdom and the EEC will result in a substantial removal on a nondiscriminatory basis of restrictions on imports from all sources by the highly developed countries of the free world; (2) all these countries (and not only the United States) will provide economic aid and capital for the development of the underdeveloped countries on an extended scale in accordance with their own national wealth and resources; and (3) all these countries will adopt domestic policies for stimulating the growth and expansion of their economies, while avoiding domestic wage, cost, and price inflations.

If effective steps are taken in these three directions, there can be no doubt at all that disequilibriums in international payments will develop from time to time.

For many years to come, however great is the extension of international consultation and cooperation between these countries, it will be the national governments and not a single supranational authority who will be responsible for national policies for wages, taxation, monetary supplies, and so on. Consider only one possible example. Suppose that as a result of national policies in "Surplusia" labor productivity rises at 3 per cent per annum and the wage rate rises at 2 per cent per annum, while in "Deficitia" labor productivity rises at only 2 per cent per annum but the wage rate rises at 3 per cent per annum. By all recent experience both countries would be adopting very successful domestic wage policies; but the cost-price structure will be falling by 1 per cent per annum in "Surplusia" and rising by 1 per cent per annum in "Deficitia." There will be an ever-growing strain on "Deficitia's" international payments; and by the end of five years "Deficitia's" costs will be 10 per cent too high relatively to "Surplusia's."

Changes of this order of magnitude are quite unavoidable in modern conditions. Yet if "Deficitia" is not to be forced either to restrict her imports or to cut down her foreign aid below the level which is appropriate to her real wealth and national resources or to abandon her domestic policies for economic expansion, there must be an adjustment in the rate of exchange between the two national currencies. By no other means can liberal international policies for trade and payments be reconciled with national policies for wages, full employment, and economic growth.

Many persons are—quite rightly—alarmed at the prospect of large and frequent variations in exchange rates, with the threat of competitive exchange depreciations and of extensive speculative movements of hot money. But to meet the essential needs outlined in the previous paragraph all that is rquired are extremely moderate changes in rates which would, moreover, occur only in response to basic structural needs. I would propose, therefore, for earnest and immediate consideration a change in the rules of the International Monetary Fund on the following lines:

1. Each member would as at present fix a gold parity for its national currency.

2. Each member would be allowed in any year to raise (or lower) this par rate by 2 per cent above (or below) the parity fixed in the preceding year.

3. Each member would undertake never to raise the price of gold in

terms of its own currency by the permitted 2 per cent unless it was at the time incurring a substantial loss of monetary reserves.

4. Each member would undertake never to lower the price of gold in terms of its own currency by the permitted 2 per cent unless it was at the time incurring a substantial accumulation of monetary reserves.

These provisions would have the following effects:

1. No country would be called upon to alter the exchange value of its currency unless it chose to do so.

2. No country would depreciate its currency unless it was in international deficit.

3. No country could appreciate its currency unless it was in international surplus.

4. The maximum rate at which a country's exchange rate could vary in either direction would be 2 per cent per annum. This should be sufficient over a period of years to make a very substantial contribution to the removal of the inevitable structural cost-price disequilibriums.

5. Since there would be a firm guarantee that no country's national currency would change in value at a greater rate than 2 per cent per annum, the incentives for the speculative movements of funds would be very limited. They could be offset by the monetary authorities in the country whose currency was expected to depreciate (or appreciate) by setting short-term money rates of interest at the most 2 per cent above (or below) the rates ruling in the other countries.

Reform on these general lines has in recent years been suggested by a number of people. I would like to give them all possible support in the sincere belief that some greater flexibility of exchange rates is, for the reasons given above, an essential feature of any practicable scheme for the liberalization of trade and payments in modern conditions.

18

Gold Exchange Standard a Danger to the West

JACQUES RUEFF

DIAGNOSIS

In all countries where the currency is connected with the dollar the situation each day becomes more and more similar to that which turned the recession of 1929 into a "great depression." The instability of the monetary structure is such that the merest incident in international relations on the economical or financial plane would be enough to provoke a world disaster. Yet the remedies proposed during current negotiations will not get down to the root of the trouble but instead will prolong for months or years the mistakes which have led to the present situation. Indeed, for the West, the most urgent duty is to recognize the danger which menaces it, and, in preventing it, to re-establish in the free world a monetary system, generating (or a generator of) balance and duration.

From 1926 to 1929 the world of monetary convertibility was carried on a wave of exceptional expansion. If one analyzes the elements of the monetary situation at that time, one will see that it was characterized by a massive influx of capital, coming from England and the United States, first toward Germany, as a consequence of the financial cleansing realized by the Dawes plan (1924), and, second, toward France after the Poincaré cleaning-up (1926–28).

But these transfers of capital were of an entirely new character and apparently very unusual. In fact, the liquid funds, although entering into the economy of the countries which received them, essentially Germany and France, where they were generators of extra credit—did not leave the countries of origin overseas. This paradoxical situation was the effect of a profound modification insidiously brought about in the monetary systems

Reprinted from *The Times* (London), June 27–29, 1961, through the courtesy of the author.

of countries with convertible exchange, the application of a recommendation formulated by the international monetary conference which took place at Geneva in April–May, 1922. The Resolution No. 9 of this conference asked for "the conclusion of an international convention tending to economy in the use of gold through the maintenance of reserves under the form of balances in foreign countries." It is in the application of this recommendation that the conditions known only under the Anglo-Saxon name of "gold exchange standard" replaced the old gold standard after World War I—mainly in France and Germany and in all countries where the exchange had been restored by the financial committee of the League of Nations.

According to the statutes of these conditions, the banks of issue are authorized to create an exchange not only against credits in national exchange and against gold which they hold, but also against foreign currencies payable in gold, that is to say, after the World War, payable in pounds sterling and dollars. As a result of this large influx of sterling and dollars from overseas to the countries which had recently recovered, the Continental banks of issue, instead of asking for payment in gold, which they would have been obliged to do under the gold standard, left these pounds and dollars in deposit at their place of origin, where they were usually lent to national borrowers. The banks of issue viewed this new system with all the more favor because it substituted productive credits of revenues to ingots or gold pieces which were entirely unproductive.

The functioning of the international monetary system thus became reduced to a mere children's game in which one party had agreed to give back their investments, after each game of marbles, to the party who had lost the game.

To verify that the same situation exists in 1960, *mutatis mutandis*, one has only to read the message of President Kennedy on the stability of the dollar on February 6, 1961. He indicates with an admirable objectivity that from January 1, 1951, to December 31, 1960, the deficit of the balance of payments of the United States had attained a total of $18,100 million. One could have expected that during this period the gold reserve would have diminished by the same amount. Amounting to $22,800 million on December 31, 1950, it was, against all expectations, $17,500 million on December 31, 1960. The reason for this was that during the said period the banks of issue of the creditor countries, while creating a counterpart in dollars which they obtained through the settlement of the American deficits, the national currency which they remitted to the holders of credits on the United States, had replaced about two-thirds of these same dollars on the American market. In doing so during 1951 and 1961 the banks had increased by about $13,000 million the amount of their credits in dollars.

Thus, to reach this amount, the deficit in the balance of payments of the United States did not necessitate any settlement in foreign countries. Everything took place on the monetary plane just as if the deficit had not existed. This is how the gold exchange standard brought about an immense revolution and produced the secret of a deficit without tears, to the countries in possession of a currency benefiting from international prestige allowing them to give without taking, to lend without borrowing, and to get without paying. The discovery of this secret profoundly modified the psychology of nations, for it allowed countries who were benefiting from it to disregard the internal consequences that the gold standard normally attached to a deficit in the balance of payments, leaving the donator the joy of giving and to the receiver the joy of receiving. It had only one consequence: the monetary situation of which President Kennedy traced out the principal lines, and of which it is now necessary to define the effects.

In presenting these facts I shall certainly not forget that the deficits of the balances of payments of the United States have been more than compensated by the donations and loans which have been given with a generosity without precedent in history, to peoples who after the war were without foreign currencies. But the method through which one gives is not less important than the object of the gift, especially when it is of a nature profoundly affecting the stability, even the existence of the giver and the receiver. Added to that is the fact that the situation that I am going to analyze was neither established nor wanted by the United States; it is the product of a prodigious collective error which will remain in history and will eventually be recognized as an object of astonishment and scandal.

In a paper which I gave on March 17, 1932, at the Ecole Libre des Sciences Politiques I spoke lengthily of the question of the gold exchange standard and drew attention to what would be the inevitable consequences. This speech is reproduced in *Les Doctrines Monétaires à l'Epreuve des Faits* (Alcan, 1932) and will shortly be re-edited.

The substitution of the gold exchange standard for the gold standard entails three essential consequences. The first result is that while under the conditions of the gold standard any deficit in the balance of payments caused a reduction in the purchasing power in the deficit country, under conditions of the gold exchange standard the total volume of buying power is in no way affected by deficits in balance of payments no matter what their amount.

Undoubtedly internal buying power is affected by other influences, especially by credit policy. It is at all times the result of a great number of factors, more or less independent of each other. In particular, internal inflation can check and even reverse the restriction of buying power which, under gold standard conditions, is caused by any deficit of the balance of payments.

But with this reservation, one must note that even in a case where the national income is identical to the national product (that is to say, providing there is no inflation), the gold exchange standard removes the regulating influence of the monetary mechanism which would have existed under the gold standard. Thus under the gold exchange standard a country's payments can only be in balance under the most favorable conditions, and this balance depends entirely on a systematic credit policy or on the direct, authoritative regulation of the foreign exchanges.

But the experience has shown time and again that if it were not impossible it was certainly very difficult for the monetary authorities to carry out systematically by way of policy the credit restrictions from which in effect the gold exchange standard had liberated them. As to the official manipulation of the balance of payments by such means as the restriction of purchases from abroad or by restricted currency allowances to tourists, or even by the prohibition of movements of short-term capital, in my opinion this has always been a fiasco.

The layman is often surprised to see the decisive effect which variations in purchasing buying power have on the debits of payments. There is no point here in elaborating the theory of this phenomenon. It will be sufficient for me to say that every excess in the internal demand for the national product tends to hold it back at home, whereas any difference in the opposite direction tends to free for export a fraction of the riches offered on the market.

In the second place, under the gold exchange standard system any deficit in the balance of payments of a country whose currency is returned to it—the United States and, in the sterling area, England—produces a duplication of the world's credit base. In effect the claims transferred for the settlement of the deficit are bought against the creation of money, by the banking system of the creditor country. The cash balances thus created are handed over to the debtor countries. But at the same time, these claims against which the creditor country has created money are replaced on the market of the debtor country. Thus everything happens as if these currencies had never been exported in the first place. Entering the credit system of the creditor country, but remaining in the debtor country, the claims representing the deficit are thus doubled.

It is through this mechanism that the substitution of the gold exchange standard for the gold standard, which in a period when payments were roughly in balance would not have much effect on the total buying power, becomes a powerful instrument of world-wide inflation as soon as big migrations of international capital intervene.

The above analysis has been proved absolutely but tragically true by the events that preceded and followed the 1929 slump.

As already stated, the financial cleansing of Germany and France in 1925 and 1929 had led to a massive influx of capital from overseas to these two countries. But both of these countries were practicing a system of gold exchange standard which by the duplication of credit gave an exceptional expansion to the boom of early 1929.

The movements of capital which have taken place from the United States to Germany and France during the years 1958–60 have caused, through the same mechanism, an abnormal rise in the price of shares on the financial markets.

In a period when capital is returning to its old home from a country to which it had been moved for safety, this coincidence can be inflationary in one without being deflationary in others. The first drag along the others—where there is nothing to restrain the boom—and thus all the countries that have adopted the gold exchange standard system find themselves carried away on a powerful wave of inflationary expansion, either economic or financial.

The preceding statements are in no manner incompatible with those theories which see in increases in salaries which do not correspond to a rise in productivity the origin of the process of inflation, and oppose demand inflation to cost inflation. Although it is difficult in such a case to separate cause from effect, there is no doubt that the constant increase of total purchasing power causes and makes legitimate the demands for higher salaries, at the same time removing every obstacle to this end.

But the third and most grave consequence of the gold exchange standard system is the fallacious character of the structure of credit which it engenders. In the message mentioned earlier, President Kennedy noted that at the end of 1960 the $17,500 million gold reserve of the United

States was the backing on the one hand of $20 million of foreign short-term or demand credits and, on the other hand, of the $11,500 million of internal monetary supply in the United States.

I do not presume to state that the existing gold stocks are not sufficient in present circumstances to assure the security of the currency of the United States. Moreover, President Kennedy has stated his intention to reduce, through a modification of the present regulations, the amount of gold required as a backing for the note issue. In addition the dollar could draw for support on several assets not yet used—especially its drawing rights on the International Monetary Fund, as well as large credits abroad.

It is not the value of the dollar that the above statements put to doubt. They are only made to establish the fact that the application of the gold exchange standard, in a period of large movements of capital, has established a double mortgage, mounting to a very big sum, on an important part of the gold stock of the United States. If the holders of foreign credits in dollars asked for the payment in gold of an appreciable amount of their debts they could really provoke a collapse of the pyramid of credit of the United States.

Assuredly they will not do so. But the simple fact that they have the right to do it obliges us to recall that it was the collapse of the house of cards built on the gold exchange standard in Europe which turned the recession of 1929 into a "great depression."

In 1960, keeping all one's sense of proportion, the same circumstances are present. If care is not taken the same causes could produce the same effects. Therefore it is absolutely necessary, before it is too late, to correct the situation arising from the duplication of the pyramid of credit founded on the world gold stock.

PRESCRIPTION

The way out of a system of gold exchange standard, which has functioned between a large number of countries during a prolonged period of time, creates two problems: (1) the substitution for the monetary system existing in these countries of a system which will not favor or maintain the deficit of countries whose currency is considered as equal to gold by the banks of issue which receive it; and (2) the removal of a situation rendered dangerously vulnerable by the duplication of the edifice of credit built up on the gold stock of countries with a currency which is taken as being equal to gold. In future, any system established should prevent creditor countries from receiving, in settlement of their claims, a buying power which the debtor countries would not have lost. To this end, no bank of issue should be able to lend a foreign creditor the currencies against which it had already created a buying power in its own monetary field.

The system of the gold standard, even limited as in the United States to exterior payments—a system which obliges the banks of issue to give currency only against gold or against credits drawn up in national currency—fulfills this condition. It would therefore be acceptable in every way and satisfy the above-mentioned claim. However, other systems of multilateral compensation could fill the bill, on condition that the balances drawn from the settlement of the deficits should not be at the disposal of the deficit country, as for example by a short-term loan on its money market.

Such a sterilization, because of its voluntary and onerous character, would always border on the precarious, whereas one resulting from the gold standard would have the unconditional and inevitable consequences of the rules which characterize it. The evolution of the European union of payments, through the progressive "hardening" of its conditions of settlement—that is to say, by the augmentation of the fraction paid in gold in the settlements implied—gives the example of a steady advance toward a system based on the gold standard.

To suppress the danger of risks which have been the heritage of fifteen years of gold exchange standard, there is unfortunately no other solution for the West than to repay in gold the greater part of credits in dollars accumulated in the assets of the banks of issue. Only such a reimbursement can remove the risks of a collapse or sudden deflation, which the duplication of the edifice of credit built up on the gold reserve of the United States involves.

The difficulty of the operation lies in the sudden reduction which such repayment would inflict on the gold reserves of the Federal Reserve System. However, the situation is less grave than it appears to be, President Kennedy having enumerated the resources available for such a reimbursement if the need arose. In any case, the removal of the gold exchange standard, if it is not the effect of panic (which is precisely what must be avoided), can be organized progressively.

The suppression of the characteristic duplication of the gold exchange standard (causing the disappearance of cash in the banks which issue the dollar credits) would, however, diminish the total volume of the monetary liquidation and could reduce it to less than the minimum required for the execution of daily settlements. Such a consequence should not be tolerated, and to prevent it several proposals have been put forward, the most important being that of Professor Triffin.

This plan, very similar to the one presented by Lord Keynes in 1943, is ingenious as it would certainly considerably diminish the needs of liquidity of the central banks, because of the concentration of cash on hand. But in the complex system envisaged by Professor Triffin the new currency of settlement would only be partially convertible and under certain circumstances could be bound to a forced rate. Also, the issuing authority, because of the rights of issue, would be provided with the right to draw on the savings of member states.

It was the fear of inflation which caused the rejection of the Keynes plan in 1943. These reasons seem valid again today and, indeed, also hold good against several other plans of the same inspiration. The rejection of an inflationary solution has led certain commentators to reseek in the overvaluation of the price of gold, the augmentation of the nominal value of metal money. They observe that this price has remained static at its 1933 level of $35 per ounce, in spite of the fact that since then the prices in dollars have doubled.

There is no doubt that the increase of the price of gold in dollars, and at the same time the price of gold in all currencies whose rate had been fixed in dollars, would augment the nominal value of the currency reserves, and in so doing, facilitate the liquidation of incidental cash in hand, the result of the functioning of the gold exchange standard. It would, however, be rather imprudent to deduct by simple calculation the estimate of the necessary rise or even to affirm that a rise could not be avoided.

First, the methods of settlement which would render possible the extension and perfection of the institutions of compensation already in existence would greatly diminish the volume of indispensable liquid money. It is untrue that the production of gold is not as much affected by the price assigned to it as by the movements of the general price levels.

The above remarks indicate that the necessary liquidation of the gold exchange standard sets difficult problems—of a political kind on the one hand and of a monetary technique on the other. This necessitates deep study and discussion, and for the preparation of such a discussion it is essential to realize that the problems are neither exclusively, nor even essentially, American. Their solution can only be found in a thorough modification of the system now in use for the settlement of the balance of international exchanges, and thus of the rules of the national banks of issue.

Whether the gold exchange standard is principally responsible for the deficit of the balance of payments of the United States, it was not of their making, but that of the international monetary conference of 1922.

What has been done by an international conference can only be undone by an international conference. But it is essential that it should be undone quickly. A monetary crisis would compromise the financial cleansing now being carried out at last in all states of the West. It would expose their economies to a grave recession, which in its turn would carry with it all the dangers of a "great depression."

In any case, be it through the "hot" or the "cold" method, the problem of the gold exchange standard will be settled presently. It is essential that it should be settled in the "cold" method. To this end government initiative is urgent and indispensable. If it comes in time it will save the populations of the West from disorder and from the sufferings of a new world crisis.

19

The Case for Going Back to Gold

MICHAEL A. HEILPERIN

During the summer of 1962 the gathering doubts about the strength of the U.S. economy, reflected in the stock market plunge and the flagging of business enthusiasm, were accompanied—and indeed reinforced—by renewed uneasiness about the strength of the dollar. To be sure, as Washington spokesmen have been emphasizing, the balance-of-payments deficit has been running at a lower rate than last year. But there is still a considerable deficit, and the cumulative effect of deficits in ten out of the last eleven years has given foreigners a $16.9 billion claim against U.S. gold reserves. And although the outflow of gold itself has somewhat abated, memories of the frightening 1960 run on gold are still fresh, and its causes are still with us.

Politicians as well as monetary authorities seem deeply impressed with the perils of the situation. The Kennedy Administration professes its determination to bring the balance-of-payments deficit to an end, and in considering ways to speed up the domestic economy it is painfully aware of the need to keep up the appearance of fiscal integrity. The Federal Reserve and the central banks of Western Europe have taken steps to cooperate in meeting any speculative movement that might threaten the dollar.

Such defensive measures are reassuring, but the fear of crisis will persist and can be banished only by a positive policy that leads to a profound reform of the international monetary system. The aim of such reform must be to establish order in the monetary relations of the U.S. and its trading partners in the Atlantic family of nations.

The essentials of monetary order can be summed up in three conditions:

First, the guarantee of unqualified freedom in international payments —i.e., no controls or threat of controls on the exchange of one currency for another.

Second, a fixed relationship among the various currencies so that businessmen can plan their trade and investment operations ahead without fear that their money will suddenly change in value.

Third, a means of bringing the balance of payments of every country quickly into equilibrium so that some countries do not go on suffering chronic deficits while others keep building up embarrassing surpluses.

My contention is that these conditions of order can be brought about only by a restoration of the gold standard—in its classic sense, with currencies unconditionally redeemable in gold at home and abroad, and with the settlements of international accounts made in gold and gold only. In my judgment, this move will have to be accompanied by a revaluation of gold.

The return of gold to its once pre-eminent position as the base of money and credit is the only way of insuring against wide fluctuations in the values of currencies and restrictions on free exchange. And the sensitive response of the money supply to the flow of gold in and out of a country would be the most effective discipline on national economic policies.

The steps back to the gold standard should be taken in unison by all the advanced industrial nations of the West, but it is fitting and proper that the initiative should come from the U.S. A bold and imaginative approach to monetary order would be a natural companion policy to President Kennedy's trade program, for free trade cannot flourish on weak and uncertain financial underpinnings.

I am aware that this proposal is highly controversial, and that it will strike some readers as preposterously anachronistic: *"Go back* to the gold standard? Haven't you noticed that Queen Victoria has been dead for a long time?" An eminent New York banker has gone so far as to suggest that restoring the gold standard would be "like repealing the twentieth century." I am tempted to reply that the twentieth century, with its record of wars, tyrannies, and depressions, might be well worth repealing. But a more serious answer is to paraphrase a remark Winston Churchill once made about democracy: "It has been said that democracy is the worst form of government except all those other forms that have been tried from time to time." So it might be said that the gold standard is the worst form of monetary system—except all other forms.

The monetary arrangement under which the Western world has been transacting its business for most of the past half-century is intrinsically unstable and disorderly. Monetary experts call this arrangement the gold exchange standard; it is, in fact, an adulterated version of the gold standard. Its main characteristic is that only two major currencies, the British pound sterling and the U.S. dollar, are backed by gold. Other countries base their currencies partly on the reserves they hold in pounds or dollars —on the assumption that these "key currencies" are "as good as gold." The deficiencies of this arrangement were admirably described in *Fortune* a year ago by the eminent French economist Jacques Rueff.[1]

As Rueff pointed out, the fact that other countries use dollars as reserves for their money means that they are ready to accept dollars, in lieu of gold, in settlement of U.S. balance-of-payments deficits. This in turn allows the U.S. to go on running deficits without losing a commensurate amount of gold; thus the deficits do not have the effect they should have in diminishing the U.S.'s own money supply and setting in train the retrenchment that would bring its international accounts back into balance. Moreover, foreign central banks have been basing an ever expanding supply of money and credit on the ever expanding dollar reserves they are accepting as payment from the U.S. In effect, two pyramids of money and credit have been built on the straining back of the U.S. gold reserve.

The great danger is that a crisis of confidence—a sudden fear that the dollar was no longer "as good as gold"—would cause a disastrous credit collapse not only in the U.S. but throughout the noncommunist world. The precautions taken by central bankers to avert speculative movements would be of little avail against such a general crisis of confidence. The very countermeasures governments would be likely to take in an emergency—for example, stringent exchange controls—would only worsen the catastrophe.

Even if the situation is viewed in less dire terms, the danger is still apparent. Essentially, the gold exchange standard introduces a volatile component into monetary reserves. The dollar is volatile because it can be converted into gold at any time (not by American citizens, but by foreigners); that is why dollars are held as reserves in the first place. Once dollar reserves are so converted, they disappear. But the rate at which foreigners exchange their dollars for gold is not based on any tangible, predictable economic circumstance; it depends on confidence. As we have seen in the past couple of years, the U.S. gold loss comes in flurries, each creating waves of anxiety that build into long-term uncertainty. By reducing the volume of currency reserves available to finance world trade, any sustained conversion of large amounts of dollars into gold could lead

---

[1] "The West Is Risking a Credit Collapse," *Fortune*, July 1961.

to a sudden and acute shortage of international liquidity, with deflationary effects on trade and business activity generally.

The gold standard would, above all, take this volatile component out
of money. Once mined, gold remains in being, even if it is occasionally
hoarded. It would provide a firm, secure reserve for money and credit
and give international trade and investment much greater protection from
the vagaries of confidence.

GOLD STANDARD HISTORY

Over the years, an economic mythology, built of misrepresentation and
oversimplification, has grown up around the gold standard. To begin with,
it was an interlocking system of national managed currencies: the price
of gold was fixed by statute, bank notes were fully convertible into gold,
and there was absolute freedom of gold imports and exports. Central banks
had a far greater management function than is usually admitted by text-
book writers; much judgment had to be exercised, and errors were not
infrequent. There were, however, certain important limitations on the freedom of action of monetary managers; these were imposed by the obligation to keep notes fully convertible into gold. Thus the gold standard made
it impossible, in practice, for the various countries to carry on "independent" national policies of either inflation or deflation. As an empirical
fact, prices "moved in step" throughout the whole gold-standard area.

The gold standard also contained within it a mechanism to keep international payments in balance, operating through an international "signaling system." When a country had a deficit in its external payments, it lost
gold, which caused its economy to contract. When it had a surplus it gained
gold, which caused an expansion. This loss or gain of gold acted as a signal for monetary authorities to undertake measures to bring external payments into balance: generally these measures amounted to changes in the
official discount rate (*up* in deficit countries, *down* in surplus countries),
accompanied by open-market operations that would lead, in deficit countries, to credit contraction, and, in surplus countries, to credit expansion.

The timing and extent of these measures were the major responsibility
of central banks (and it is here that we find management and exercise of
judgment). The important thing is that the signals were followed by appropriate policies—i.e., those that would reinforce the effect of gold movements. In practice, international payments were kept in balance by movements of short-term capital from surplus to deficit countries, induced by
the differential in interest rates.

It should be noted that under the old gold standard there was *full* convertibility—i.e., convertibility into gold coin. The merit of this was well put in an essay by Oxford economist Sir Roy Harrod, who comments from the vantage point of British experience (Britain, as is well known, was the center of the nineteenth-century gold-standard system). Wrote Harrod: "The British doctrine, held with great emphasis and often repeated, was that if you wanted to discourage individuals from hoarding gold as a store of value, the sovereign recipe was to make sterling absolutely freely convertible by individuals . . . into gold. By establishing free convertibility, you caused gold hoarding propensity to wither and die."

Though it did not prevent occasional local panics and depressions, the gold standard satisfied the requirements of long-term international monetary order. For about two hundred years, ending in 1914—i.e., during the entire period that Britain was *de facto* or legally on the gold standard— the "secular trend" of prices, expressed in sterling, was level: this means that such price movements as took place over that long stretch of years were invariably reversed, thus preserving the value of money for the saver and investor.

George Bernard Shaw, who could be very shrewd, especially where money was concerned, wrote in *The Intelligent Woman's Guide to Socialism, Capitalism, Sovietism and Fascism*:

> The most important thing about money is to maintain its stability, so that a pound will buy as much a year hence or ten years hence or fifty years hence as today, and no more. With paper money this stability has to be maintained by the government. With a gold currency it tends to maintain itself even when the natural supply of gold is increased by discoveries of new deposits, because of the curious fact that the demand for gold in the world is practically infinite. You have to choose (as a voter) between trusting to the natural stability of gold and the natural stability of the honesty and intelligence of the members of the Government. And, with due respect for these gentlemen, I advise you, as long as the capitalist system lasts, to vote for gold.

In the heyday of the gold standard, most people would have considered this advice beyond argument, and only a shrill minority of American Greenbackers and Free Silverites would have raised their voices in dissent. Why then did a monetary system that worked so well for so long fall into such wide disrepute?

World War I, by disrupting the sensitive network of finance, trade, and investment in Europe, dealt the gold standard a blow from which it really never recovered. During the war, with all fiscal and monetary disciplines necessarily cast to the winds, the gold standard was honored only in the breach. By the early 1920's the price level as expressed in currencies at their prewar parity had risen 60 to 100 per cent. But the price of gold itself remained the same, and since the cost of producing the metal had increased along with other prices, production of new gold declined. Consequently, monetary authorities began to worry about a shortage of gold.

It was then that they came up with an arrangement that would, in the language of the 1922 Genoa Economic Agreement, "economize on the monetary uses of gold." The Genoa Conference originated the gold exchange standard as we know it today. The theory was that gold could be "economized" if countries were not required to base their currencies on gold itself but could use as reserves those few "key" currencies that were backed by gold. The adoption of the gold exchange standard wrought an unwholesome change in the monetary rules of the game, for it weakened the signaling system and the whole delicate mechanism that had brought equilibrium under the gold standard. Yet the experts of that time (and even most experts today) failed to make a sharp enough contrast between the two systems. The old system came to be blamed for the faulty functioning of the new one—wrong economic diagnosis, compounded by bad semantics.

At the time of the Genoa Conference, the only nation that was actually on gold was the U.S. In 1925, Britain went back to the gold standard in a modified form called the "gold bullion standard"—i.e., anyone could convert pounds into gold bullion but there was no gold coinage. Thus the pound joined the dollar as a "key" currency. But the mistake the British made was to re-establish the 1914 sterling price of gold. This automatically put the pound back to its pre-World War I parity with the dollar (4.86 dollars to the pound). In terms of the price levels in the two countries, this was unrealistic; the pound was overhauled by about 10 per cent.

As a result, British exports became, at least in part, noncompetitive, and there ensued a period of high and chronic unemployment, aggravated in 1929 by the onset of the world-wide depression. The gold standard was blamed *as a system* for what amounted to two wrong decisions: (1) a mistake in fixing the parity of the pound, and (2) a mistaken belief that gold could be held at its prewar value.

As financial chaos spread throughout Europe, central banks began converting their sterling reserves, causing a run on Britain's gold when, in September 1931, the gold standard was suspended. The pound was devalued in relation both to gold and to the dollar, British exports expanded, and unemployment declined. The abandonment of the gold standard was given credit for what was, in effect, a long-needed correction of the currency's overvaluation.

The crisis spread in 1932 to the dollar. U.S. bank failures undermined international confidence in the dollar, and there were large, though by no means dangerous, withdrawals of gold from the country, just as Franklin D. Roosevelt took office. One of his first steps was to suspend gold shipment abroad and to order private owners of gold in the U.S. to deliver up their gold coin or bullion against bank notes. Thereupon, from the end of October 1933 until January 1934, Roosevelt progressively raised the dollar price of gold (which had long been fixed at $20.67 an ounce) as a matter of policy, because he was assured by his economic adviser, Professor George F. Warren, a Cornell agricultural economist, that this was the way to raise the general price level. In *The Coming of the New Deal*, Arthur Schlesinger, Jr., recalls the capriciousness with which this policy was carried out:

> Starting on October 25, Henry Morgenthau and Jesse Jones met in the President's bedroom every morning to set the price of gold. Jones was there as head of the RFC, which did the buying; Morgenthau, because of his recent experience in helping maintain wheat prices through a government purchase program . . . While Roosevelt ate his eggs and drank his coffee, the group discussed what the day's price was to be . . . One day Morgenthau came in, more worried than usual, and suggested an increase from 19 to 22 cents. Roosevelt took one look at Morgenthau's anxious face and proposed 21 cents. "It's a lucky number," he said with a laugh, "because it's three times seven" . . .

Little wonder that "tinkering with the price of gold" today makes bankers shudder.

In January 1934, the price of gold was finally stabilized at $35 an ounce of fine gold. It has stayed there ever since. The Gold Reserve Act ruled out gold coinage and declared that "no currency of the United States shall be redeemed in gold." No private individual or bank in the U.S. is permitted to own gold except for industrial, professional, or artistic use (in 1961 the prohibition was extended to American citizens residing abroad). The Treasury, using the Federal Reserve as its banker, was authorized to sell gold to foreign governments and central banks in settlement of U.S. balances abroad. The dollar at home became an inconvertible paper currency, though backed by gold to the extent of 25 per cent of outstanding Federal Reserve notes and demand liabilities. This "anchorage to gold" is the last safeguard against "printing press" inflation.

The coup de grâce to the gold standard, so far as the U.S. was concerned, was delivered by the U.S. Supreme Court's celebrated "gold clause" verdicts on February 18, 1935. The gold clause, written into certain contracts, specified payment in gold dollars. The purpose was to protect lenders against currency devaluation, and it was obviously incompatible with New Deal monetary policy. In two five-to-four decisions the Court ruled that the authority of Congress to regulate the value of money was paramount and the gold clause was therefore void in private contracts. The effect of this ruling by the highest court of the land was to make people wonder how much any tie to gold was worth in practice.

DIAGNOSIS OF PRESENT CONDITIONS

World War II threw the international monetary system once again into chaos. The U.S. came out of the war with most of the world's effective productive capacity—and about 60 per cent of its gold. During this period of "dollar shortage," most nations struggled to conserve foreign exchange by imposing strict controls on monetary transactions. But the effort to restore normal conditions began early, with the Bretton Woods agreement in 1944, which provided that the currencies of participating nations should be given a fixed gold value; it allowed gold a minor role in the settlement of international accounts. Essentially, Bretton Woods revived the gold exchange standard as it had originated at Genoa twenty-two years before—i.e., currencies could be backed not only by gold itself but by reserves of "key" currencies that were fully backed by gold. Once again, the pound and the dollar became the "key" currencies.

The great innovation of Bretton Woods was the establishment of the International Monetary Fund as a sort of first-aid station for temporarily disabled currencies. By drawing on the Fund, countries confronted by drains on their reserves could gain a breathing spell and put their houses in order before panic developed. Eventually, under the firm and expert guidance of Dr. Per Jacobsson, the Swedish economist who was appointed managing director in 1956, the IMF became an important influence for monetary stability. Gradually, the nations of Europe were emboldened to begin dismantling their exchange controls. In 1954 the London gold market was reopened, and in 1958, by formal agreement, European authorities adopted "nonresident convertibility"—i.e., a person who does not officially reside in a country has the unrestricted right to convert the currency of that country into any other. By then, the dollar shortage had passed into history, and, ironically, it was the U.S. that was beginning to worry about its gold reserves.

Many leading monetary authorities, Dr. Jacobsson included, insist that there is nothing wrong with the present situation that cannot be corrected by more effective use of the IMF and the exercise of stronger self-discipline by individual governments. Their assumption is that the dollar and other vulnerable currencies can be defended, in the short run, by the deployment of IMF resources to curb speculation, and, in the long run, by voluntary efforts to end balance-of-payments deficits. This optimistic reliance on voluntary policies seems to me delusory. It is precisely because the U.S. and other nations have felt insufficient compulsion to put their houses in order that we are in our present fix. And the reason why this compulsion is lacking is that the gold exchange standard actually encourages procrastination.

A number of American and European experts agree that improvisation and stopgap measures won't work. But a brief look at some of their recommendations for monetary reform shows that they differ as sharply in their diagnosis as they do in the cures they offer.

One widely publicized group of money doctors considers the problem to be entirely one of insufficient liquidity, by which they mean that insufficient means of payment are available for settling international accounts. The contention is that there is sufficient liquidity only so long as the U.S. has a payments deficit and keeps pouring out dollars; if the U.S. deficit were to disappear, liquidity would dry up. The cure this group proposes is to establish an entirely new international currency, to be issued by the IMF against reserves of gold and key currencies that the Fund would acquire from national central banks. The latter would be required to deposit a set fraction (say 20 per cent) of their own reserves with the IMF, in exchange for an equivalent amount of the international currency. In addition, the IMF would engage in credit and open-market operations that would enable it to issue more of its currency as growing international trade created the need for it.

THE TRIFFIN PLAN AND OTHERS

The best-known advocate of this approach is Professor Robert Triffin of Yale, whose "Triffin plan" has been making the international rounds since 1959.[2] The grandfather of the idea was Lord Keynes, who proposed

[2] [See selection 1 of this volume, esp. pp. 38–54.]

an international currency and "clearing union" in 1943, a year before the IMF was born.[3] Keynes called the international currency unit "bancor," a concept used, with variations, by Triffin.

Logically, this scheme, which would erect a vast structure of IMF credit on a very inadequate gold base, would lead eventually to the demonetization of gold. This is hardly surprising, considering that Keynes called gold "a barbarous relic," and Triffin makes no bones about referring to the monetary uses of gold as "absurd." If gold ceased to be of any importance, what would keep the international currency from expanding indefinitely into a runaway inflation? In Triffin's view, the board of directors of the IMF would have the sole power to issue "bancor," and this power would be strictly limited so as to avoid inflation. But it is not clear how this safeguard would work in practice, or how the vaguely defined open-market and credit operations of the IMF would affect monetary conditions in individual countries. Perhaps the most telling criticism of the Triffin plan was made not long ago by Under Secretary of the Treasury Robert V. Roosa, when he derided "the often proposed types of action that basically involve an oath of allegiance by all governments and central banks to a synthetic currency device, created by an extranational authority bearing neither the responsibilities nor the disciplines of sovereignty."[4]

A second school of monetary reformers shares the Keynes-Triffin disrespect for gold but comes to very different conclusions. The so-called "floating rates" approach, advocated by Professor Milton Friedman of Chicago University, among others, would abandon gold reserves and fixed exchange rates and allow the market place to determine what a currency was worth. Currencies would be fully convertible with each other, and would fluctuate the way stocks do in response to the play of supply and demand. If a country were running a balance-of-payments deficit, the "market" for its currency would be poor and its rate of exchange would fall. This would have the effect of boosting exports and eventually erasing the payments deficit. Conversely, a country running a payments surplus would find its currency in great demand and quoted at a high exchange rate; its exports would decrease, and the surplus would disappear. The great appeal of the "floating rates" system is that, in theory, it would automatically keep the balance of payments of all nations in equilibrium and thus remove that problem from the realm of practical preoccupation. In practice, however, movements of exchange rates would not have a corrective effect on the

---

[3] [Keynes's proposal is reproduced as selection 2 of this volume.]
[4] [See also selection 14 of this volume, esp. p. 268.]

balance of payments unless accompanied by appropriate government fiscal and credit policy. A country bent on inflating its economy would feel far less restraint than at present. Moreover, floating rates would cause intolerable confusion. World business is made up of thousands of individual decisions that must be based on the ability to anticipate future conditions. The absence of fixed exchange rates would remove the stability that is an essential of monetary order.

OWN REMEDIES PROPOSED

Only a return to the gold standard can satisfy the need for monetary order. I do not pretend that the path to this fundamental reform will be easy. It will require the closest international cooperation, the sure hand of monetary authorities, and the most enlightened and courageous statesmanship.

There is an organization already in being through which the advanced nations of the West can work together to construct a new monetary framework. Its mouth-twisting title is the Monetary Subcommittee of the Economic Planning Committee of the Organization for Economic Cooperation and Development. Represented on it are the U.S., Canada, Britain, France, West Germany, Italy, the Netherlands, Sweden (as delegate for the Scandinavian countries), Switzerland, and Austria. The chairman is Emile van Lennep, the able Treasurer General of the Netherlands. The van Lennep group is already engaged in creating a more favorable monetary environment for durable monetary order. It is exploring, in particular, ways of coordinating national fiscal and credit policies for countering cyclical recessions. At present its scope is limited to encouraging voluntary cooperation, but it could easily be converted into an instrument for formal commitments.

As I envision it, the return to the gold standard would be accomplished in two phases. Phase I would be an agreement by all the nations in the van Lennep group—meaning, in effect, the whole Atlantic Community—henceforth to pay off all balance-of-payments deficits in gold and gold only. Countries that based their currencies in part on reserves of dollars or sterling would continue to do so for the time being, but further accumulation of such reserves would be halted. This step would bring to a halt the perniciously deceptive spread of dollar holdings abroad under the gold exchange standard. The U.S. would be compelled to get its payments into balance in a hurry—or face immediate and continuing losses of gold. This transition would give the participating nations a chance to get used to the new discipline, and to begin synchronizing their monetary and interest-rate policies.

Phase II would comprise three separate but simultaneous moves:

1. A decision by the U.S. to pay off in gold all short-term dollar obligations held by foreigners. This would finally get rid of the gold exchange standard and put the dollar once again on firm footing. No longer would an uncertain threat hang over U.S. gold, encouraging speculation and threatening financial crisis.

2. An agreement by the nations in the van Lennep group to make all their currencies fully convertible into gold. Convertibility is, of course, the essence of the gold standard. The U.S. would have to repeal the New Deal monetary legislation and restore private ownership of gold. Quite apart from other considerations, this would be a welcome reaffirmation of a property right that has been denied Americans for a quarter of a century.[5]

3. Joint action, again by the van Lennep group, to double the price of gold in terms of all currencies. For the U.S., this would mean raising the price from $35 to $70 an ounce. My motive is not, I must emphasize, to get the U.S. out of its present scrape. Nor do I share the view of economists such as Sir Roy Harrod that a rise in the gold price, by itself, would solve our monetary problems by increasing international liquidity; the root of these problems is not shortage of liquidity but disorder. My reason for revaluing gold is that, otherwise, the transition to a true gold standard would be impossible. For one thing, if the U.S. were to pay off immediately its dollar debts abroad at $35 an ounce, it would lose so much of its reserve that none would be left to support the domestic currency.

For another thing, though there is no real liquidity shortage in the world today, one might eventually develop when the expansion of money and credit became tightly linked to gold. Just as it did after World War I, the price of gold has remained unchanged while the prices of everything else has risen sharply. As a result, gold production has been discouraged, and additions to the world gold supply have lagged far behind the expansion in world trade. Over the past decade, newly mined gold provided only about one-third—and since 1958 one-fourth—of the annual increase in currency reserves (not including those of the U.S.). The difference was

---

[5] A number of advocates of the gold standard, notably Professor Walter Spahr of New York University, urge a return to gold coinage. Gold-bullion convertibility—i.e., the right of individuals to exchange sizable sums of money for gold-bullion bars—would serve the purpose of the gold standard without introducing the complications that the issue of coins might entail.

made up by gold from U.S. reserves (which dwindled from $23.2 billion worth in 1952 to $16.4 billion worth this year) and by increased dollar holdings abroad.

When the gold standard is re-established, nations will no longer be able to augment their reserves by increasing their dollar holdings. When gold becomes the exclusive means of international payment and the exclusive backing for currency, therefore, it will become crucially important that the supply of new metal keep pace with the growth of trade. The present price of gold is inadequate to ensure such a supply.

The proposal to revalue gold will provoke a number of objections. Some people will see it merely as a devaluation of the dollar. This is such an explosive issue that hardly anyone in a responsible government position will even admit that it is being considered. But a careful distinction must be made between a unilateral devaluation of the dollar, undertaken in panic, and a readjustment of the gold price, accomplished by international agreement as part of a plan to restore monetary order.

A second objection that will be raised is that revaluation will have a great inflationary effect because, rightly or wrongly, people associate any jiggering of the gold price with inflationary finance. But this danger will be averted under my proposal because revaluation will be accompanied by full gold convertibility of the dollar, the best possible safeguard for stable money.

Finally, critics will point out that any change in the gold price will have to be approved by Congress, which might spend many months in debating the matter; meanwhile there would be such a mighty run on U.S. gold reserves as to precipitate the very crisis of confidence we have been so fearful of. This is a telling objection, but it is not insurmountable. If all the countries in the Atlantic Community undertake these reforms in the proper international spirit, it should be possible for central banks to take the joint action needed to stem a run on gold during the time revaluation is under public discussion. This will require considerable ingenuity and skill, but the stakes of lasting monetary reform surely justify the effort.

The most serious objection to the whole idea of reviving the gold standard is that it would deprive governments of their freedom of action in dealing with cyclical unemployment and recession. In fact, however, the gold standard would allow governments considerable leeway in fiscal policy. For example, the U.S. could run a deficit to counter a recession if it met the deficit by borrowing at high enough rates of interest to tap genuine savings—and not, as has been the case in the past, at such low rates that it was in effect pumping inflation into the economy. The gold-standard discipline would not prevent the U.S. from coping efficiently with domestic problems; it would merely narrow the choice of methods used.

Those who believe that the U.S. should be free to inflate its way out of recessions will doubtless feel frustrated; perhaps it is high time they were. Americans still suffer, as a nation, from a hangover of economic nationalism from the days when we were a much less important economic and political influence on the world scene. We have learned a great deal about our international role in the past forty years. This is one more lesson.

Once these reforms have been carried out, the great edifice of free trade can at last be completed—on a foundation of stable money. The U.S. will play its role as the world's greatest creditor nation with a currency that inspires universal confidence. The whole noncommunist community of nations will take on greater political and economic strength with which to protect its freedom and assist the backward countries to improve their lot. By reinstating gold as the heart of the international monetary system we shall be drawing upon successful past experiences, rather than taking a hazardous flight into the unknown. We shall have built a bridge over the half-century of disorder.

20

International Reserves and Liquidity

THOMAS BALOGH

The abrupt return to "nonresident convertibility"[1] by most Western European countries at the turn of 1958–59, and the doubts which have crept in about the ultimate strength of the dollar since, increase rather than diminish the importance and economic-political actuality of the two documents reviewed in this paper. The first of these was prepared by the staff of the International Monetary Fund, at the request of several member governments, for the meeting of the Fund at New Delhi in the autumn of 1958. It formed the basis of the discussion on the adequacy of international liquidity available at present, and led to the resolution instructing the Executive Directors to consider the increase in the Fund's quotas, an instruction which was carried out and forms part of the second document.[2] Both thus achieved their purpose in the narrow sense of the word—the increase in the lending capacity of the two Bretton Woods institutions.

In the present review I shall try to demonstrate that self-imposed limitations have vitiated the attempt to offer a serious contribution to a debate of great importance on the monetary needs of the non-Soviet orbit, faced as it is with an increasingly effective communist challenge. The problems discussed are far more complicated than they seem, and the solution recommended and adopted does not offer a lasting basis for the steady growth of the noncommunist world.

Reprinted from *The Economic Journal*, June 1960, through the courtesy of the author and the Royal Economic Society. The article is a review of *International Reserves and Liquidity* (A Study by the Staff of the International Monetary Fund, Washington, 1958), and *Proposals for Increasing the Resources of the International Monetary Fund and the International Bank for Reconstruction and Development* (Cmnd. 652, London, February 1959).

[1] In some countries, of which Germany is perhaps the most important, the degree of convertibility was greater. *De facto* all controls over the export of capital have been abandoned.

[2] The second part concerns the increase in the borrowing powers of the International Bank simultaneously proposed and agreed upon.

BACK TO THE QUANTITY THEORY

The Staff Report of the IMF does not provide a solid theoretical foundation for an evaluation of policy for international reserves. It is based on the double axiom that the supply of money has a direct and simple relationship to business activity and the balance of payments, and that reserves have a similar role in determining money supply. The following *obiter dictum* (p. 68) is typical:

> The link between the amount of reserves and the amount of domestic money has been weakened in all countries that have not made a stable fixed rate of exchange an overriding objective of monetary policy. *An increase in the supply of domestic money may not lead to a loss of reserves if the exchange rate is allowed to depreciate* [my italics, T.B.].

This implies that international reserves and their maintenance are not merely ends in themselves but are also something which could by themselves (without some conscious policy decision involving outlay) have a direct and immediate influence on economic activity—"increased reserves failed to stimulate trade" (p. 25). "It is indeed questionable in retrospect whether any amount of reserves would have been large enough" (in 1931) to "stave off the troubles in the existing exchange structure" (p. 23).

The Keynesian analysis, which showed clearly that it is *outlay* and *not its monetary image* that matters, has been completely thrown overboard. Even odder seems the treatment of capital movements. It is implied that the need for reserves will depend on the "degree of efficiency of the prevailing international credit system" (p. 9), and "day-to-day disturbances, and even seasonal movements, of international payments need make no great demands upon reserves when credits of various kinds can be arranged."

No doubt international capital movements and a well-working international credit system might, in certain circumstances, help to bridge gaps between imports and exports. But it is illegitimate to imply (pp. 2, 3, 6, 10) that the movements of international short- and long-term capital are necessarily of a "balancing" character.[3]

The vital question is totally neglected, whether the need for reserves is determined not merely by the *size of foreign trade* (or rather international

---

[3] The Radcliffe Committee (*Report on the Working of the Monetary System* [Cmd. 827, 1959] has accepted the view (§ 727), though they also admit that in an open system restrictive measures must become necessary to restore confidence in the currency (§§ 402 and 436).

payments) but also by its *instability*.[4] The question is not discussed whether such instability could be dealt with more quickly and at less cost in terms of income forgone, by policies which embrace not merely "the realism of the existing pattern of exchange rates" and "the appropriateness of domestic and monetary fiscal policies" (p. 9), but the whole armory of countermeasures, including quotas, which have been tried with great success in countries such as Australia.

Few people who lived through the last international liquidity crisis of 1929–34 will recognize their memories of those past events in the interpretation of history offered in this document (p. 23). It is not astonishing, therefore, that the analysis of the current situation is somewhat less than balanced. It is flatly asserted that the increase in the granting of private international credits (p. 27) has decreased the risk of foreign exchange "tensions." The fact that the public sector has grown since before the war seems to be regarded as a *destabilizing* factor, as it often makes countries' economies "less flexible" (p. 28). One would have thought that the growth of the public sector (and welfare transfer payments), especially in America, and the consequent strength of the built-in stabilizers of budget surpluses and deficits, had made the monetary system safer and far more flexible, and therefore had stabilized the economies. The fact that the 1953–54 and 1957–58 United States recessions were rather quickly reversed and did not result in vast export surpluses is demonstrably connected with this development. Surely the Fund cannot prefer a greater flexibility—downward.

Accordingly, a somewhat narrow view is taken of the functions of the Fund. "The financial assistance of the Fund is of course of a short-term character, mainly intended to bridge the gap while the countries *themselves* [my italics, T.B.] take whatever measures may be necessary to restore equilibrium" (p. 76). Not a word is said about the assistance of the Fund being required for so long as a major creditor country suffers a deflationary bout. The implication is that the assistance must be used to give time to the *debtor* country to take restrictive measures and cut back ambitious development programs, irrespective of what the *depressed creditor* may be doing in his turn. This must give a deflationary bias to the world economy.

---

[4] This is also true of Professor Triffin's essay "The Return to Convertibility: 1929–1931 and 1958—? or Convertibility and the Morning After" (*Banca Nazionale del Lavoro Quarterly Review*, No. 48, March 1959), however welcome his support for increased liquidity. [See also selection 1 of this volume.]

So long as the United States was continuously fully employed there might have been some excuse for refusing to create additional international liquidity out of thin air, on the argument that it might merely fan the inflationary excess in the United States. But was there any justification for this policy in 1957–58? Are poor countries to cut their development expenditure because there is a recession in the United States or the United Kingdom? Will that not aggravate the recession in the fully developed areas? Will that further fall not create a cry for more "flexibility"? Where is this cumulative process to end? One wonders why, for instance, nothing is said of the so-called scarce-currency clause, which was to have been the great safeguard against persistent creditors by enforcing reasonable creditor policies, and on the basis of which such eminent economists as Keynes and Harrod recommended the acceptance of the Bretton Woods Final Act.[5]

The document is not clear on this point (p. 55):

> There is now greater understanding of the conditions necessary for an improvement in the reserve position. For example, a recent statement by the Monetary Committee of the International Chamber of Commerce recommended that countries gradually reduce their debts to central banks, and thus strengthen not only their internal conditions but also their reserve holdings.[6]

A combined deflationary action on the lines suggested by all countries would obviously not merely fail to strengthen anybody's "internal condition" but also lead to severe unemployment. If the process is ruthlessly pursued by *all*, even their foreign reserves cannot increase. The deflationary policy of any single country will, oligopolistically, be matched by countervailing efforts at deflation of others, all descending in a spiral without any change in their reserves.

The tantalizing problem whether high investment and faster development might not in the longer run enable a balancing of international payments of weaker countries without import cuts, and on the basis of a steadily increasing standard of life, is not even considered.

This attitude necessarily aggravates the deflationary bias inherent in the Bretton Woods arrangements, and it is only slightly mitigated by the existence and activity of the Bank. The latter has certainly performed an

---

[5] Significantly the Radcliffe *Report* completely repudiates these romantic claims (§ 690).

[6] Semantic philosophers might be tempted to use this passage as an examination question, asking how many tacit and inconsistent assumptions lurk in the latter part of the second sentence.

important task in easing the flow of funds toward underdeveloped areas. But two factors stand out, both sobering to optimism. The rate of lending, while increasing, has yet to reach the rate of $1 billion per annum. It remains less than 1 per cent of world imports. The worsening of the terms of trade of primary producers by 2½ per cent would wipe out the effect of this lending.[7] In actual fact these terms moved 7–8 per cent against the primary producers between 1957 and 1958.[8] Thus the sort of policy advocated by the spokesmen of the International Monetary Fund is likely to harm the poorer countries more than any aid that is or can at the moment be contemplated.

Perhaps the most important conclusion of the Staff Report is the continuous fall[9] recorded since 1948 in the rate of expansion of both international trade[10] and manufacturing production.[11] The Report complacently states (p. 71):

> Past experience seems to show that periods of very rapid expansion are generally followed by periods of more moderate growth. It is of course impossible to forecast what the rate of growth will be in the years immediately ahead, but it would probably not be overoptimistic to retain the conventional "normal" annual rate of about 3 per cent for the growth of world trade.

Considering that the latter rate is less than half that achieved in the period 1948–56, when the reconstruction of war damage in large parts of the non-Soviet world was far advanced, this view is indeed not "overoptimistic." It is less than a half, probably nearer a third, of the rate achieved by the Soviet bloc, according to United States intelligence reports. Inasmuch as "past experience" is based on the absence of any coherent attempt to control cyclical fluctuations, this estimate of the future implies a dismal reflection by the staff of IMF on the skill which is likely to be evinced in the management of the international economic destinies of the non-Soviet orbit.

[7] Cf. National Institute of Economic and Social Research, *Economic Review*, No. 1, January 1959, p. 15.

[8] This has at last been pointed out by the U.N. World Economic Survey for 1958, especially pp. 3–11. In the previous year the U.N. still seemed to be worried by world inflation.

[9] Table 17, p. 70.

[10] From 7.5 per cent per annum in 1948–56 to 5.4 per cent between 1951 and 1957. Since 1957 world trade has fallen about 10 per cent (*International Financial Statistics* [IMF], August 1959, pp. 22–23).

[11] From 6.1 per cent per annum in 1948–56 to 5 per cent in 1951–57. Between 1957 and 1958 world industrial production fell 3 per cent, and even in the first quarter of 1959, despite the American recovery, it stood only fractionally higher than in 1957 (U.N. *Monthly Bulletin of Statistics*, August 1959, Special Table A, p. viii).

The Report fails to discuss these further implications of its own analysis in terms of loss of growth of output or equality. The implication is that monetary policy not merely works but works with great ease and subtlety —and achieves as good results as can be expected. The bookkeeping identity between the foreign balance and the difference between domestic output and national expenditure is (as seems to be the fashion these days) used in a schedule sense to demonstrate that cuts in home outlay, through monetary policy alone, will optimally and smoothly readjust the balance of payments.[12]

The Report seems to show conclusively that most governments and central banks "tried to achieve ratios" between imports and reserves "in the sense that if reserves rose beyond some such level, they saw fit to adopt a more expansionist policy" (p. 48). They do not seem to realize that this demands arrangements for a continuous supplementation of the increase in international liquidity if this (depending mainly on the increase in monetary gold) falls short of the desired rate of expansion of production and trade. But there is no discussion of such policy aims, and after a lengthy statistical exercise which aims at showing that the rate of increase in monetary reserves need not be as high as that of the (rather modest) estimate of economic growth of the free world, the Report comes to the conclusion:[13] "It is doubtful whether, in the circumstances of the world today, with world trade greatly expanded in volume and value, the Fund's resources are sufficient to enable it fully to perform its duties under the Articles of Agreement." On this basis the Executive Directors recommended a 50 per cent increase in quotas.[14] This was accepted and carried out.

AN ECONOMIC THEORY OF RESERVE HOLDING

Judgment on the adequacy of international reserves will depend on the aims of economic policy and the role which these reserves can play in the execution of that policy in relation to other means of policy.

a) The policy followed by the (dominant) members of an open system, their willingness and ability to limit surpluses and deficits on inter-

[12] Cf. Sir Robert Hall, "Reflections on the Practical Applications of Economics" (*Economic Journal*, December 1959, p. 651).

[13] *International Reserves and Liquidity*, p. 99.

[14] "Enlargement of the Fund Resources through Increases in Quotas," a report by the Executive Directors, IMF (Washington, December 1958), p. 16.

national payments, the rapidity with which single countries can, under the prevalent rules of the game, legitimately take steps directly to limit the consequences of a loss of balance, these are some of the factors which will decide on the adequacy of monetary reserves. *The need for liquidity is a combined function of the size of likely balances, i.e., of the volume of international payments and the magnitude and duration of their instability. Fundamentally this is determined by the policy framework (in particular the range of "admissible" means of readjustment) and the ends of policy,* especially how much unemployment and slowing down of growth countries will tolerate.

b) It should be noted that a very large proportion of total trade and payments is concentrated among a few major powers. The number of these effectively independent units is further reduced by groupings based in international monetary affairs on key banking centers and key currencies.[15] These groupings are often regional, and sometimes, as was the case with the Sterling Area until convertibility was introduced, their coherence is buttressed by explicit institutional arrangements. The more complementary the regional grouping, the freer it is in its choice. The more circumscribed its policy aims, the smaller is its need for reserves, because the smaller the proportion of trade to national income, the quicker it can adjust any adverse balance and the less likelihood there is that such balances would arise. Shared policy goals, whatever their nature, whether avoidance of unemployment or of gold losses, will in any case reduce this need for the world as a whole. Thus the assumption of the Staff Report that the following of "sound" policies all round reduces the need for reserves is accurate. It amounts to the basic assumption that countries will not attempt to maintain employment if some powerful ones refuse to do so.

If, on the other hand, full employment is a universally declared policy, and governments are able and willing to intervene promptly in case of a deflationary or inflationary shock by all appropriate means, including controls and fiscal policy, the minimum safe levels of reserves will be far smaller than in a system in which prolonged unemployment is tolerated (or even induced, in order to ensure price stability) in dominant countries while others try to avoid competitive deflationary policies. In the former case the imports of the dominant country will be steady, while in the

[15] Economically the United States itself is a regional (rather than national) unit, whose high complementarity, which automatically reduces dependence on foreign supplies, is further backed by tariff and quota regulation.

latter they might suffer from an attempt to maintain stability through cutting demand. Thus the import capacity of peripheral countries would be damaged and only the possession of large reserves would enable them to continue their development. A system which freely permits capital movements, even if they are of a speculative nature, will, under modern conditions, require far higher reserves than a system where speculative capital movements are severely discouraged.[16] It is the volume of *payments* and its instability, and not merely that of *visible trade*, which is the rational determinant of reserve requirements.

The relationship of the member countries of the world economy to one another is therefore one of oligopoly. Countries will trim their behavior to one another. The discouraging feature of this relationship is that, so long as international reserves are scarce, behavior which will induce gains of gold will be at a premium, because severe losses of gold must induce others to follow suit in such policies (the recent behavior of European countries when the United States was embarrassed by gold losses is an excellent example). Thus scarcity of reserves is likely to aggravate itself; and uncertainty about strong countries' monetary strategy would have the same result. Safety-first would counsel deflation.

There is a further reason why it is only too likely that the system will have a bias against full growth and employment and in favor of avoiding gold losses at whatever cost in terms of expansion. Under modern conditions[17] adherence to the "classic" rules which demand symmetrical expansion as well as contraction might seem incompatible with domestic stability, especially price stability.[18] If the problem of domestic inflation cannot be solved by policies not impinging on the balance of payments (by their employment effects), a balanced functioning of the world payments system will not prove possible. Any increase in reserves will then repre-

[16] This has been accepted by the Bretton Woods Conference (Articles of Agreement, Art. VI, Sec. 2/3), which prohibited the use of borrowing power at the Fund to sustain capital exports. The IMF seems to regard all capital movements as "balancing" and does not discuss the need to encourage the application of its own charter. The spirit of the charter contrasts sharply with the attitude of the Bank of England as characterized by one of its ex-Directors, Mr. Siepman (letter to *The Times*, August 31, 1959). This regards control of capital movements as "futile and mischievous" or worse. The Radcliffe Committee (*Report*, par. 728) is skeptical of the effectiveness of control, but did not discuss this (possibly dominant) reason for its failure in Britain. It nevertheless advocates its retention.

[17] This reluctance to expand was already the case in the 1920's. When Mr. Montagu Norman persuaded Governor Strong in 1927 (Sir H. Clay, *Lord Norman* [London, 1957], p. 237) to lower the discount rate in order to ease London's difficulties, the drift toward the stock market crash of 1929 started.

[18] Cf. *Oxford Economic Papers*, June 1958.

sent a deflationary impact abroad because it originates in a cut in demand.[19]

c) The acquisition of international reserves by any one country as a result of export surpluses or borrowing represents a real sacrifice in terms of forgoing investment (or for that matter consumption). This sacrifice can be justified by using such reserves to pay for imports only if it enables the holder to increase over time the growth of its economic activity and investment, despite disturbances in its balance of international payments, in comparison to the level which would have been possible without such reserves. Inasmuch as the initial level of investment would be higher if export surpluses were not used to accumulate reserves, this means that the reserves enable the avoiding of a more than proportional toll over time as a result of these disturbances and the restrictions which they make inevitable. These disturbances can originate either abroad, i.e., a fall in the demand for exports (or a flight of capital), or internally, e.g., through crop failures. "Free" reserves are therefore one of the means by which the necessity of interrupting the growth of the economy might be obviated and optimum growth over time might be secured.[20] Only by fulfilling this role can the sacrifice incurred by keeping resources uninvested be justified. It should be noted that the use of reserves is a once-for-all gain. Only if the consequential increase in national income results in an increase in investment would it have continuing beneficial effects.

The forgoing of the increase in the level of investment implied in a cumulative increase in the reserves reduces the potential maximum rate of growth. If an increase of the rate of growth enhances the possibility of accelerating the increase of income without imperiling the balance of payments (and enables the country, eventually, to acquire reserves without slowing down growth), the accumulation of reserves is not justified. It should be noted that policy measures (e.g., exchange or import control) which obviate cuts in investment in case of balance-of-payments difficulties would reduce the rational need for reserves.

Borrowing could be the other alternative. The choice between borrowing and reserve holding will depend on the terms on which borrowing can be done (and thus on the character of international financial organizations)

[19] This is especially true if one of the international banking centers whose liabilities constitute the reserve of other countries were to start trying to "increase its liquidity" by "repaying liabilities." The thoughtless advocacy of increased liquidity for London has been one of the danger points in the last recession. The warning of the Radcliffe Committee (*Report,* par. 663) against thoughtless forcing of repayments is welcome.

[20] An alternative would be to hold reserve productive capacity or stocks of commodities.

in comparison to the loss of real income due to the holding of reserves (which might themselves yield some income).

We might conclude:

(i) The poorer the country, i.e., the smaller its capital supply, the greater probably the real sacrifice implied in the holding of reserves in terms of the potential income forgone.

(ii) This sacrifice by poorer countries might be reduced by keeping their reserves in freely marketable, income-earning assets,[21] though the maximum rate of income earned in this way must be well below the increase in domestic output and income forgone.

(iii) Poor countries will probably have greater need for holding reserves than richer ones, and this for two reasons. On the one hand, the instability of primary products markets and of harvests is notorious, and such countries mostly depend on a few products of this type, which increases their risk. On the other hand, their capacity to obtain credits on reasonable terms is much less than that of richer countries, unless purposive international institutional arrangements are made.

(iv) The limitations on the choice of policy (e.g., the prohibition of direct controls over imports and exports) impose disproportionate burdens on poor countries. Their acceptance of such burdens is rational only if international arrangements are made to offset this burden by special grants or credit arrangements.

None of these points have been considered by the Staff Report.

d) If reserves are kept in assets of another country, total international liquidity is increased, as the accumulation of gold exchange is the alternative of acquiring gold. This introduces a further complication because the acquisition of these assets (instead of gold) has a (relatively) inflationary impact, their repayment a deflationary impact. If the former happened in a situation of all-round full employment, and if the financial center disregarded in its policy making the increase of its liabilities, the process might facilitate general inflation. This danger has been much emphasized. Less

---

[21] This is the justification, from the "lending," colonial territories' point of view, of the British colonial currency and banking system. Unfortunately the investment policy of the Crown Agents for the Colonies (latterly for Overseas Territories) was so unthinkingly mechanical that the dear money caused considerable capital losses to these relatively poor territories. The emotional reaction to this admitted mismanagement might well be a liquidation of the sterling reserve system (the number of new "Commonwealth countries" accumulating gold reserves is steadily increasing). This, as we shall see, inevitably imposes a strain on the world reserve situation.

attention was paid to postwar[22] waves of liquidation of gold exchange reserves. This happened at almost regular two-yearly intervals in the case of Britain, and contributed much to the severity of the balance-of-payments crises which caused interruptions of expansion in this country. There has also been at times some liquidation of dollar balances.[23] If this process were to gather momentum, it might well result in a general deflationary pressure.[24]

e) An over-all shortage of liquidity will make itself felt by simultaneous pressures on the reserve position of a number of countries while no major country deems it advisable to permit the loss of gold reserves in accordance with the "classic" rules of the gold standard.[25]

This might force deflation on a number of others to prevent their losing gold. An oligopolistic struggle might arise: attempts at increasing reserves would cancel each other. The reserve position of individual countries would not improve. But the general deflationary pressures would leave all worse off in terms of increased unemployment and fallen national incomes. The costless provision of *additional* reserves, e.g., by increases in the price of gold or the creation of additional internationally accepted means of payment, would then be the proper response, which should be contrasted with efforts of single countries to raise their reserves by attempts at redistributing *existing* reserves. On the other hand, no amount of additional reserve can be "sufficient" if the losing countries continue policies which lead to deficits in the balance of payments.

f) If the rate of increase in international liquidity permits the achievement of full employment, any further increase of reserves must be sterilized to avoid inflation. At this point some rules of discipline will have to be evolved stabilizing the rate of investment and consumption in the poorer

[22] And of course in the period after 1929. Indeed, the severity of that depression can, to a considerable extent, be explained by the financial crisis which began in 1931 and finally disrupted even the United States banking system and currency.

[23] Since 1956 the more rapid expansion of *exchange* as contrasted with *gold* reserves has come to an end. Total world gold reserves have increased by almost $2 billion between 1956 and 1959, and the gold reserves outside the United States at the end of 1956 by almost $3.5 billion. Official foreign exchange holdings, however, have been slightly drawn down, from $17.015 to $16.540 billion at the end of 1957. This was mainly due to a liquidation of sterling liabilities, but balances in America have also been reduced by almost $300 million.

[24] Cf. the United States Secretary of the Treasury's declaration to the 1959 meeting of the Governors of the Bretton Woods institutions as reported in *The Economist*, October 3, 1959, p. 63.

[25] This is exemplified by the perverse reaction in Europe to United States gold losses. Cf. below (pp. 356–57).

areas of the world. Inasmuch as these areas will have to rely more and more on stand-by credits for meeting exceptional strains (having used their low-yielding assets to speed up development), it should not be impossible to maintain such discipline.

g) The holding of reserves might then be confined to richer countries. Development in poor areas might be speeded up by enabling the poor to use their existing reserves to accelerate investment by arranging stand-by credits to them. Thus reserves which do not yield income would be concentrated in the hands of rich countries alone. Thus an international cooperative reform of reserve policy would have contributed to the equalization of the rate of investment and growth,[26] while minimizing the over-all need for reserve-holding.

THE ELEMENTS OF A SOLUTION

A satisfactory solution of the problem of international reserves must, in my opinion, be able to provide the basis of stable and rapid growth in the non-Soviet orbit. It must purposefully eliminate purely financial obstacles in the way of continued growth.

It should be noted that such a solution is intimately bound up with the diagnosis of the cause of inflation. No government will, or can afford to, tolerate the emergence of a strong upward trend in prices. This is still automatically identified with the existence of excess demand. It follows that inflation is fought mainly, if not exclusively, by restrictive monetary policies. The experience of the 1957–58 recession, when the rise in manufactured prices continued despite large unemployment, has been completely disregarded. This failure of diagnosis has made rational and balanced international economic policy impossible in the non-Soviet orbit. Large and persistent creditor countries (such as Germany) may well refuse to use the increase in their reserves because of the fear of aggravating the international rise in prices. Thus deficit countries must redouble their effort at restriction. The oligopolistic game described in the previous section will then become unavoidable. Good international behavior demands that stable prices—a perfectly legitimate and politically vital policy goal— should be secured without increasing the imbalance in international pay-

---

[26] These problems were treated exhaustively in two publications of the Oxford University Institute of Statistics: *New Plans for International Trade* (M. Kalecki, E. F. Schumacher, and T. Balogh, Oxford, 1943) and *The Economics of Full Employment* (F. A. Burchardt and others, Oxford, 1944).

ments through one-sided deflationary action. A rational solution should therefore include:

(i) a mechanism by which internationally acceptable means of payment (i.e., liquidity) can be created when necessary, sufficient to prevent a scarcity of reserves causing a general deflationary pressure. While it is not certain that scarcity in this sense in fact has arisen, a combination of American fears of further gold losses, at a time when Americans are far from fully employed, with a situation in which no other country feels sufficiently comfortable to expand vigorously, suggests that the time may not be too distant when such shortage will become obvious.[27]

(ii) rules by which the need for such additional international liquidity could be minimized, or at least kept within limits; the creation of vast amounts of cash (e.g., to counteract a persistent deflationary pressure) itself might result in a loss of confidence and painful attempts to liquidate the system.

I shall deal with these two aspects of the problem one by one, though the acuteness of the first problem will be determined by the success with which the second is tackled. As we have seen, the problem of liquidity is a question partly of the relation of "stocks" (international reserves) to "flows" (the balances arising out of international payments) which will be determined by policy and partly (but in some sense more acutely) by the consistency of the "stock" itself. It might be as well to get this latter problem out of the way.

a) The Effectiveness of Reserves

The Geneva Conference in 1922 advocated (i) the restriction of the circulation of gold, (ii) the use of the gold exchange standard, and (iii) a redistribution of gold reserves; these were to be the main ways in which the "effectiveness" of insufficient gold reserves (so to speak, their velocity of circulation) could be increased.

(i) The hoarding of gold has been increasing since the war, and so has the industrial demand. While the French stabilization and the return to "normality" in Europe might reduce the former, this is not a factor which ought to be regarded too optimistically. It is not likely that the addition to the monetary gold stock will be at a rate higher than $700

---

[27] If we define scarcity of liquidity as a reluctance to embark on expansion while there is unemployment in a major country, the winter of 1962–63 definitely saw the emergence of such scarcity. [Added 1963, T.B.]

million per annum. This is equivalent to less than 1½ per cent of total world reserves (including foreign exchange) and about 2 per cent of gold reserves.[28] This rate is rather low, especially if (as seems likely) the policy trend toward greater "liberalization" continues. The latter trend inevitably results in larger potential balances, i.e., increased need for reserves because of the rather slow effectiveness of monetary measures (as against direct controls) in readjusting trade and payments; and the likelihood of increasingly acute speculative capital movements.

(ii) The transfer of gold reserves from the United States to the "middle-income-class" countries (mainly Europe) has increased the "effectiveness" of gold-holding. In these countries "free gold" is a larger portion of the total reserve. But (as seems certain)[29] this process of redistributing world reserves has exhausted the limit of comfort and tolerance of losses in the United States. Thus, no further gains can be expected from this source.

(iii) The trend in gold exchange holdings has shown marked instability since 1956. Between the end of 1957 and June 1958 almost $0.7 billion liabilities were liquidated. Most of this was due to the penury in primary producing countries; there is no evidence of liquidation of balances due to nervousness about the dollar.[30] A number of central banks, however, might have decided as a matter of policy to hold a larger portion of their reserves in gold. Sterling liabilities have been at times (e.g., 1957) under violent pressures. Their recent recovery need not be more stable than in 1950.

It would be foolish to think that an increase in gold exchange balances will contribute significantly to the problem of international reserves. Both in the case of England and in the case of America the very accumulation of exchange reserves by other countries has been regarded as a growing national weakness instead of being viewed as a vital contribution to main-

[28] The argument that hoarded gold represents a much larger portion of gold reserves outside the United States (about 3 per cent as at the beginning of 1959) does not mean much. The reaction of the United States Government to recent gold losses shows that the point at which defensive action is going to be taken has been reached. The "free gold" (i.e., gold available for balance-of-payments purposes and not absorbed by reserve requirements) accommodated only $8.2 billion out of a total of $20.6 billion reserve at the end of 1958. The free gold was just over $8 billion. The short-term liabilities of the United States amounted to $14.6 billion and foreign portfolio investments in the United States (which are liable to liquidation in bull markets) to $9 billion. Of the short-term debt $8.7 billion represented the holdings of foreign governments and central banks. Thus the possibility of embarrassment is not inconsiderable unless international cooperation is forthcoming.

[29] See above (p. 353).

[30] Unofficial holdings rose. So much for the claim that foreigners need be "reassured" by deflationary measures of the U.S. dollar!

taining the liquidity of the world economy as a whole. Indeed, it is all but certain that more formal arrangements would be needed if the fact that international liquidity is provided by liabilities of the United States or the United Kingdom is to be prevented from increasing instability. The liquidation of gold exchange reserves, as at the end of the 1920's, took place at the most awkward moment from the point of view of the domestic monetary policy of the "banking centers" and led to the prolongation and aggravation of the depression.

To obviate any repetition, rules for good-neighborly conduct between treasuries and central banks should be worked out. This might take the form of an agreement between the members of the IMF not to demand the conversion of existing foreign exchange balances into either gold or other currencies (e.g., from sterling to dollars) unless it is needed for payment of genuine current transactions and nonspeculative lending operations. Countries which have no exchange control even on capital movements would have to pledge themselves to discourage such transfers between the currencies of member countries, and at any rate refrain themselves from such transactions in respect to their own holdings. There is acute prejudice against such undertakings for fear of "exchange losses." But such losses are unlikely unless a large-scale conversion of foreign exchange liabilities is attempted. A gold clause might obviate unjustified fears, and thus prevent its having to be implemented.

On the whole, the elaboration and acceptance of such rules of good-neighborly conduct seem (at any rate in the short run) more conducive to preventing international economic difficulties arising purely out of financial reasons than do more ambitious plans—put forward by Professor Triffin—providing for the absorption of existing foreign exchange assets (and liabilities) by the International Monetary Fund and their liquidation.[31] The liberal attitude of the United States Government in permitting the loss of some $4 billion in two years without severe restrictive action, which enabled the replenishment of European reserves through an improvement in the balance of payments, contrasts painfully with the sluggishness with which the Western European countries responded to the need to ease the problem of the United States. The strengthening of the Common Market will further increase this trend. This emphasizes the need for more conscious institutional safeguards internationally.

[31] The liquidation of these assets would be undertaken safely only if the resultant increase in the liabilities of the IMF could be counted as part of the reserves of member countries. Cf. below (pp. 364–65).

b) Reducing the Need for Reserves

The need for reserves would be reduced if a mechanism existed which would impart alternating bias to international adjustments so as to preserve or restore the balance in international payments at a high and stable level of employment. The bias would have to alternate according to whether employment was rising or falling.

At, or nearing, full employment it would be as necessary to exert an increasing deflationary pressure as it is to ensure that adjustments are made mainly by creditor countries expanding demand and economic activity, so long as there is unemployed or underemployed productive capacity. We have already pointed out that this problem is complicated by the fact that prices might be rising irrespective of the fluctuations in employment. Neither the Staff Report nor the Report of the Executive Directors[32] recognizes this double requirement because of their failure to diagnose correctly the process of price inflation.

(*i*) *Automatic credits: regional or universal clearing.* One way to reduce the need for liquidity, and at the same time to apply some pressure on persistent creditors (to which debtors automatically are subject), is by obliging them to provide credit to carry the part or the whole of their surplus.[33] In this way the creditor will share in the inconvenience of the imbalance, and will, within reason, i.e., within the limits imposed by the general world economic position, have to contribute to the readjustment— thus he will have to promote an increase in income, demand, and imports to "clear" the credit balance. This method has severe limitations. It cannot offset a persistent deflationary bias in the world economy, and it might promote inflation when all participants are fully employed.

Such clearing systems were not difficult to organize on a bilateral or (like EPU) multilateral basis, so long as convertibility was limited and payments had to be made through central banks. They were restricted to regions within which differential liberalization of trade and payments had been promoted and did not extend to transactions with countries beyond the regions. These were dealt with on a different (though not necessarily bilateral) basis.

The introduction of full convertibility has made the task more difficult. The consequences of the rise of the so-called free market in "transferable

---

[32] "Enlargement of the Fund Resources through Increases in Quotas," Cmnd. 612.

[33] This is, in my opinion, a more illuminating way of regarding clearing arrangements than defining them as increasing international liquidity.

sterling" in Zürich and New York exemplify these difficulties,[34] which stem from the possibility that debtors within the region might be creditors outside, or vice versa. So long as *all* countries in the region are in balance with the *outside* countries and this balance is not the consequence of special discriminatory restrictions, no special problem arises. But if the region as such, or important parts, are in disequilibrium with the rest of the world, convertibility and nondiscrimination cause a conflict of interest. Direct settlement, short-circuiting central banks, becomes advantageous for the creditors within the region; the currency of the ultimate largest outside creditors will be desired by all. Thus the need for *universally* acceptable liquidity increases. The automatic credit mechanism between members can no longer function at the moment it is most required, or rather it will force the creditors within the region to finance the deficits of the debtors with outside countries. At that point the interest of the creditors in the clearing could be maintained only if they were able to obtain discriminating favorable conditions for their exports within the region. It would otherwise suit them more to use their surpluses in the most advantageous market. Thus a regional clearing would not really work in a regime of full convertibility—unless it involved reciprocal commercial discrimination in favor of the participants' exports. The proposal of creating a quasi-multilateral clearing in Europe without retracing the liberalization in convertibility and commercial policy will founder on this obstacle.

It would, of course, be possible to provide for compulsory deposits by creditor countries,[35] and thus for forced multilateral credits. As soon as there is complete convertibility, however, regional creditors cannot possibly be required to adopt an expansionist policy—for their balance with the countries outside the clearing agreement might then deteriorate and the regional clearing does not help them to meet their obligations. In a multilateral world, as the Americans now have an opportunity of seeing for themselves, the most sluggish major creditor (at present the Common Market countries) determines the basic monetary situation. Without discrimination in favor of each other's products, self-interest drives all members of a region toward complete convertibility and the by-passing of clearings, which would reduce capability of purchasing in the cheaper market.

In a universally convertible world the answer might be sought in a *uni-*

---

[34] Cf. my paper in *The Banker*, 1954, and Sir Donald MacDougall's evidence to the Radcliffe Committee. The Germans, in particular, made full use of this possibility of reducing their credit balances in EPU while receiving 100 per cent gold payment.

[35] This has been suggested by Professor Triffin ("The Return to Convertibility").

versal compulsory clearing. The aim of forcing the central banks of the creditors to do part of the "readjustment" by providing automatic credits might be achieved by obliging the central banks of the "strong" currency countries to undertake all supporting operations of the "weaker" currencies in the "free" markets, and by providing that only part of these balances would have to be repurchased by the debtor countries against gold (or equivalent convertible currency). Credit would be provided automatically to sustain trade and payments and reduce the extent of the immediate readjustment, permitting the creditor country to expand, rather than the deficit country to contract. While this system is advantageous in a world threatened with a secular shortage of international liquidity, it would hamper efforts to impose a brake on expansion once full employment has been attained. If the present system is markedly deflationist in its bias, this would be one-sidedly expansionist.

(*ii*) *Purposive creation of equilibrating demand.* It seems unlikely that such a universal clearing agreement would be more easily negotiable than a more purposive and, therefore, more satisfactory arrangement.

The most logical and effective of such schemes was evolved at the Oxford Institute of Statistics during the war,[36] and completely lost sight of. It merits resuscitation. It provides for the automatic use of persistent surpluses of "mature" creditor countries whose creditor status is due to their less-than-full employment, for loans on a medium-long-term basis to be used for the acceleration of the economic development of "underdeveloped" countries. These loans would be additional to loans and grants provided for on a noncyclical basis to promote development in order to reduce international inequality. The demand would be canalized toward the "mature" deficit countries, i.e., countries in balance-of-payments difficulties to the benefit of those underdeveloped countries which need them most.

In times of general full employment the mechanism would necessitate restrictions on the part of the fully employed mature deficit countries. At the same time the extent of this readjustment would be limited to the minimum.

c) *Creating Additional Liquidity*

It is unlikely that any of these "balancing" schemes could become fully operative for a considerable time or that they would work so perfectly as to obviate all increase in the demand for international liquidity beyond

---

[36] *New Plans for International Trade.*

likely availabilities. The possibility of a scarcity of international liquidity has been accepted, as we have seen, even by the Staff and executive Directors of the IMF. Their recommendation was (*a*) to increase the quotas of the IMF and the capital available to the IBDR. I shall try to show that this scheme is unlikely to fulfill the requirements. Alternative steps to increase liquidity would be (*b*) to increase the price of gold, and (*c*) to enlarge the conceptions of Bretton Woods. Of the two, the latter is by far the better because it is the more flexible.

(*i*) *The increase of IMF quotas.* The raising by 50 per cent of IMF quotas was recommended last year and carried through as a full solution to the need for increased international liquidity. It can undoubtedly palliate a really grave liquidity crisis, and is therefore welcome. It is hardly likely, however, that it will prove an effective solution for preventing less spectacular long-run deflationary pressures, especially if the Staff Report is right in stating that most countries wish to preserve a stable ratio of reserves to imports. In any case, quotas in the IMF do not formally form part of the reserves of the country, and their enlargement, therefore, does not represent an automatic increase in reserves. They can only be used with the consent of the Fund, and consent has not hitherto been given unconditionally. Inasmuch as even that part of the quota which has to be paid in gold is not absolutely at the disposal of the country, one can argue that the increase in quotas actually diminishes the fully available reserves of member countries; they certainly diminish the reserves visibly available. The Fund in 1959 rightly undertook open-market operations, i.e., bought United States Government securities to offset the diminution of the United States gold reserves that would have followed the payment by the United States of the increase in its International Monetary Fund quota. As the United States was already losing gold, this further loss might have upset confidence. The whole incident clearly demonstrates the fact, strongly denied by the authorities of the IMF, that an increase in IMF quotas is not equivalent to an increase in world reserves in the minds of the banking world. While this has been a most interesting and hopeful precedent, it does not solve the problem which must be solved, i.e., the *securing of a net increase of visible reserves parallel with the expansion of production, trade, and payments.*

Now it is impossible to establish an internal credit mechanism without giving some discretion to its management. And these discretionary powers must include authority to impose conditions on would-be borrowers to prevent inflationary excesses. The criticism which can be leveled against the

Bretton Woods Act, and even more against its interpretation by the management of the IMF, is that it is entirely one-sided, imposing readjustment on the debtors only, irrespective of the general world situation. The use of quotas was made conditional on the imposition of stringent general deflationary policies going far beyond the original (and already one-sided) obligation to pay an increasingly penal rate of interest and the pressure for early repayments. Thus the utilization of these quotas will in all probability result in restrictive action, even if the world position cries out for expansion. It is completely different from countries using their own gold reserves. There is a further important drawback. IMF quotas will not increase automatically with the increase in the need for liquid reserves, i.e., with the expansion of output, world trade, and payment. Their expansion must be specially arranged. This will take time. Moreover, *in each subsequent period the need for borrowing will increase because the ratio of "own" reserves to payments will decrease if the rate of growth of gold reserves remains below that of output and payments.* Recovery will, therefore, be increasingly burdened with repayments. A deflationary bias will be imparted to the world economy. However helpful it might be to stem exceptional crises, the increase in the IMF quotas will not safeguard stable expansion.

(*ii*) *An increase in gold prices.* An increase in gold prices could give a full (if inordinately expensive) answer to the problem of increasing international liquidity and increasing demand. It has consistently been advocated by Sir Roy Harrod, apart from interested parties. A doubling of the price, for instance, would add some $40 billion to gold reserves; this would substantially help to restore the "liquidity" of the two great "banking centers" and thus reduce the risk of a wholesale liquidation of sterling or dollar balances, a risk which conjures up the picture of a liquidity crisis. An increase of the gold price would also accelerate the expansion of the volume of gold production (apart from the increase in its unit value); it might well reduce the tendency to hoarding, which has been estimated at about $1 billion in the last three years alone.[37] The yearly addition to monetary gold might then increase toward $3 billion, thus sensibly diminishing the gap between the expansion of reserves and trade or output. It would increase the purchasing power of the producing areas and thus tend to maintain world demand.

The arguments against an increase in gold prices are so well known that

---

[37] Bank for International Settlements, *Twenty-ninth Annual Report*, 1958–59, p. 117.

they need not be repeated at length. It would benefit mainly South Africa and the Soviet Union, in no way high-priority claimants for extraordinary international largesse. Moreover, the rate of increase of reserves would not be adequate unless a quite exceptional amount of resources is devoted to gold mining—surely a rather wasteful method. Finally, in the once-for-all gain due to the revaluation of existing reserves, those countries most in need would benefit least, because though the distribution of gold reserves has improved, it was the rather rich European countries which benefited. In any case no Republican administration in the United States would countenance it for a moment. It has been, and must remain, ruled out in practical politics.

d) The Enlargement of the Bretton Woods Conception

We can now draw together these various suggestions into what I think might be considered a consistent scheme. In its totality such a scheme would seem quite unattainable at the moment politically. It has, however, the great advantage that it can be achieved progressively. Such a solution should ideally combine the "liquidity approach" (i.e., the capacity to create new liquidity) with the "equilibrium approach" (i.e., arrangements to reduce the need for liquidity) in an organic way without mixing them, i.e., without making one institution responsible for these two tasks, which might be incompatible. One single authority should be responsible for *short-term* aspects of the problem of maintaining balance between countries (including, however, that of imposing on persistent creditor countries the obligation to take action to help in eliminating the surplus). A second should be in charge of *long-term* measures mitigating the tendency to imbalance while coordinating these with the endeavor, now accepted by all highly developed areas, toward diminishing international economic inequality, i.e., channeling capital and technical and administrative ability toward the underdeveloped areas.

It should be noted that this dichotomy of tasks has been recognized by the leading spirits of the Bretton Woods Conference in the creation of two institutions. It is unfortunate that at no time does there seem to have been a coordination between them to minimize deficits caused by recessions in economic activity in leading countries. But, as we have seen, the postwar obsession with inflation was overruling a rational approach to the problem.

(*i*) *Toward an international central bank.* The transformation of the IMF into an international central bank would be the least costly and most effective way of dealing with the problem. This would necessitate a reshaping of the Charter on an essential point. The present system of quotas treats borrowing as "sales" to the Fund of the borrowing country's "weak" currency against the purchase from the Fund of "strong" currency. Thus there is no relationship between the changes in the reserves of a country and its position at the Fund. In fact, the *increase* of a country's "quotas" (i.e., in its borrowing capacity) results, as we have seen, in a *fall* in its visible reserves because of the gold payment of 25 per cent of the quota, and the existence of stand-by arrangements does not visibly increase the liquidity of the central bank. This might be regarded as basically unimportant and merely a question of bookkeeping. Unfortunately confidence depends on such irrational factors, and the present arrangements are symbolic of the incapacity of the Fund to relieve a shortage of international liquidity in such a way as positively to strengthen national reserves.

Several methods are available to ensure that borrowing from and repayment to the Fund should systematically affect the level of reserves and thereby the policy of the member central banks.

a) It would depart least from the present constitution if the first (gold) tranche of the quota were treated as *part of the reserve of a member country*. This solution would not increase the Fund's capacity to create liquidity. It might therefore be acceptable to the majority at present. It would represent a notable step forward.

b) The next possible step would be to *increase the first tranche* of the quota from the present 25 per cent to a higher percentage *without additional gold payments* and continue to include it in the reserves of member countries.

c) Finally, *all deposits of countries with the Fund might be treated as part of the member countries' reserve*. If these remained, however, convertible into gold or other "scarcer" or "stronger" currencies, the danger would remain that the Fund might be denuded of "acceptable" means of payment. Thus this final step would have to be linked *with an undertaking not to withdraw or convert deposits with the Fund*. At this point the Fund would become a central bank and the center of a universal clearing capable of creating an adequate volume of international liquidity.

Borrowing from an international central bank would, of course, have the same effect as using the quotas of IMF. It would be invidious, and would force the country in question to restrictive measures. This would be perfectly justified at times when employment is high and discipline must be enforced to prevent inflation. It would not be sufficient when there is a danger of cumulative deflation. If "rediscounting" were all an international central bank could do, there would be no reason to establish one.

A central bank, however, could undertake *active open-market operations*, increasing the liquidity of those countries which legitimately need it.[38] Such an occasion would arise if countries came under pressure because of depression elsewhere (as was the case in most primary producing countries last year).

d) An elaborate new disciplinary code would have to accompany the establishment of such an institution so that the possibility of creating internationally acceptable liquid resources should not be misused. In this manner a middle way between uncontrollable inflation and undesired deflation might be found.

e) Two methods are available to give creditors further safeguards as an inducement to accept such a solution. The first is to increase a country's vote as its deposits increase and stipulate that further creation of international liquidity would be subject to an affirmative vote by an increasingly qualified majority. If, e.g., Germany's basic deposits represented x per cent of the total and this increased to, say, y per cent, its vote might be increased by a given percentage which is in relation to x/y and so on. Expression of total liquidity by over 5, 10, 15, 25 per cent per annum might be subject to the affirmative vote of a qualified majority, e.g., three-fifths, two-thirds, three-fourths, seven-eighths, etc., of all votes. This would enable large creditors to veto further expansion.

Alternatively,[39] the central bank's maximum lending power might be limited by some formula (e.g., a certain percentage of growth or a certain relationship to aggregate foreign payments).

All these are points of detail. The important thing is that means should be found by which changes in deposits or drawing rights at the IMF should make themselves automatically felt (as is the case in the gold exchange standard) *as an equivalent change in international liquidity* of the countries concerned and thus *automatically influence policy*. Without this the required balance in the reaction of the system cannot be achieved and it will remain biased against debtors. I think the foregoing scheme achieves such balance because the central bank in its lending and open-market oper-

[38] The IMF, by buying United States securities against gold, in fact inaugurated such international open-market operations (cf. above).

[39] This would be less desirable, as *mechanical* percentage increases in the *stock* of reserves might not be able to deal successfully with unexpected fluctuations in *flows* (i.e., in the balance of payments). This is the real weakness of Professor Triffin's proposals as against the original Oxford Institute scheme.

ations can insist that "autonomous" or persistent debtors take effective remedial action.

(*ii*) *Toward an international development fund.* When the two Bretton Woods institutions were created, a wit remarked that the Fund ought to have been a Bank and the Bank a (continuously alimented) Fund. The fifteen or so years of peacetime experience confirms the prescience of this joke. The point on which the Bank's activities have least achieved the desired effect is that its lending has had no relation (and under its present dispensation could not have any relation) to the ebb and flow of economic activity in highly developed areas. Yet it could have exercised a doubly beneficial effect if its aim of lessening international inequality through stimulating investment had been pursued so as to help in taking up the slack in international productive capacity.

I am not here concerned with the question of whether a decisive increase in the allocation of resources by highly developed countries for aid to poor areas is desirable, though it would obviously in itself contribute to the maintenance of demand. What would, in this context, be desirable is the automatic use of an increasing portion of persistent creditor balances for long-term investment in underdeveloped areas. Such a link between the central bank and a Fund to which longer-term lending activities are entrusted would decrease the need for international liquidity by reducing the credit (and debit) balances of persistent surplus countries and thus help in limiting the need for the expansion of international liquidity.

In the past year the dollar has been under some pressure, and the awkward narrowing in the gap between United States "free gold" and potential demands on it has shown the weakness of the existing arrangements. A further liquidation of the gold exchange standard and the reduction of dollar and sterling balances could hardly help, resulting in several cuts in foreign aid and starting a deflationary spiral. Britain and Western Europe have mainly benefited by the discomfiture of the United States. But their monetary strength would be undermined by an active American policy reducing the deficit. It would therefore be no more than prudent if they took the initiative in buttressing the international credit mechanism. As a first step they might sponsor the calling of an international financial conference, to work out, as a first priority, rules of good-neighborly behavior which will prevent or reduce the dangers of those sudden gusts of hot money, by refusing to convert gold exchange balances in their possession into gold. Hot money must not be allowed to endanger the stable expansion of the non-Soviet world as it did before the war. Such an international financial conference should, second, also set in motion reforms needed for the gradual transformation of the two Bretton Woods institutions into an effective force to stabilize growth in the non-Soviet orbit.

Institutional reform cannot accomplish much if there is no determination in using the instrument created. But at the moment there are unnecessary legal constrictions which would prevent the best intentions from succeeding.

POSTSCRIPT[40]

Several plans aimed at remedying a possible shortage of international liquidity have been presented since the writing of the article reprinted above. In this postscript I shall briefly comment on the limitations inherent in all of these plans by using the concepts which I have developed in the preceding pages.

a) Those plans which provide a sudden arbitrary increase in reserves[41] might meet the secular increase of the demand for liquidity *for a time*. They obviously *could* deal with panics and depressions *if* the increases were sufficiently large, but as the secular increase in demand is continuous and the addition is once-for-all, these plans do not provide a long-term solution. Conversely, large-scale addition to reserves might prove inflationary if there is substantial full employment in large parts of the world economy or if the addition to liquidity enables some countries to increase their demand for imports beyond the level of current demand for additional reserves by the "creditor" countries.

b) Alternative schemes[42] provide reciprocal (stand-by) credits from creditors to debtors. They might be able to deal with confidence crises and with demand by liquidity arising out of depressions, provided the character of the sudden demand is correctly diagnosed at an early date. They cannot deal with the secular increase of demand because the stand-by credit

---

[40] Reprinted from Thomas Balogh, *Unequal Partners* (Blackwell, Oxford, 1963), II, 256–57.

[41] E. Bernstein, "The Adequacy of U.S. Gold Reserves," *American Economic Review*, 1961, and "Reserve Centers and the International Monetary Fund," *Irish Banking Review*, 1961.

[42] E.g., Dr. Blessing's scheme operated through BIS, Basel (the so-called Basel Agreement) ; and Mr. Bernstein's first proposals. The increase in quotas of the Fund and the strengthening of the International Bank, the former reinforced by the so-called Paris Club Agreement, providing for discretionary extension of credits by surplus countries, are of the same kind. The discretionary element has been strengthened and with it the power of, and attraction of being, creditors (cf. IMF, *International Financial News Survey*, September 29, 1961, and January 12, 1962). The Keynesian revolution of attitudes which originally bore more heavily on creditors has been frustrated.

is not counted (for policy purposes and from the viewpoint of treating confidence) into total reserves. They cannot provide an answer to the need for international reserves arising out of a structural (long-term) failure of creditor countries to increase demand, probably the most important of the threats to stability and growth.

c) Plans based on the creation of new liquidity in prescribed proportions and based on the willingness of central banks to keep part of the funds thus created at an international institution (IMF)[43] represent a solution of the problem of the secular increase of demand. They are likely to be insufficient for dealing with any of the other disturbances that demand a sudden and massive increase in liquidity; moreover, they offer insufficient safeguards against inflationism in periods of exhilaration.

d) Plans which link the creation of liquidity rigidly with grants to underdeveloped areas[44] might solve the problem of secular demand and depression but could not deal with a confidence crisis or with long-term structural defects of the world monetary system. They might, moreover, be far too inflationary in times of full employment.

Thus the proposals put forward at Oxford during the war, providing for two institutions with some discretionary powers, seem still the best. They would have to be followed by coordination policies that would prevent a wholesale liquidation of gold exchange reserves and would harmonize policy in both creditor and debtor countries in order to minimize the need for readjustment. Finally, any remaining imbalance might be dealt with by using the productive capacity of (mature) debtor countries to help the development of backward countries. The recurrence of a persistent deflationary bias in the non-Soviet part of the world economy and its eventual defeat might thus be avoided.

The actual position is somber: the use of IMF funds is now conditional upon the pursuit of "sound" policies, and it is probable that the French and German bankers will be even less prepared for a balanced coordination of the policies of debtors and creditors so as to prevent a one-sided deflationary readjustment. From this viewpoint my essays were far too optimistic, as I thought that the policy of Dr. Jacobsson and the Americans was the worst we could expect. In comparison to the European bankers they now seem less unreasonable. The outlook is therefore troubled, unless the European "planners" achieve an unexpected victory.

---

[43] E.g., Robert Triffin, *Gold and the Dollar Crisis*. [See selection 1 of this volume.]

[44] E.g., A. M. Stamp, *Manchester Guardian*, February 10 and 13, 1961, and *Lloyds Bank Review*, October 1958. [See selection 3 of this volume.]

21

International Liquidity–
Problems and Plans

HARRY G. JOHNSON

PROBLEMS OF THE INTERNATIONAL MONETARY SYSTEM

The problem of the adequacy of international liquidity has been dramatized by the balance-of-payments problem from which the United States has
suffered since 1958, and particularly by the speculation against the dollar
in late 1960 which culminated in the sharp rise in the price of gold on the
London market to over $40 an ounce. The United States deficit and the
speculation against the dollar called attention to the extent to which the
United States has assumed (without the deliberate intention of so doing)
the position of an international reserve currency country in the postwar
period, and have showed both the vulnerability of a reserve currency center
and the precariousness of the reserve currency system as a means of meeting growing international needs for liquidity.

The central fact underlying current international monetary problems
is that the growth of the supply of monetary gold in the postwar period has
not kept pace with the growth of international trade and the need for international reserves; the gap has been made good by a reduction in United
States gold holdings, and (quantitatively more significant) a growth of
foreign holdings of U.S. dollar balances. . . . Of the increase in these
reserves from 1950 to 1960, 36 per cent was provided by increases in the
stock of monetary gold and 64 per cent by increases in foreign exchange
holdings, of which almost all consisted of increases in dollar holdings. Of
the increase in reserves held by countries outside the United States, moreover, slightly under a third was accounted for by the increase in the world
stock of monetary gold, about a third by reduction of U.S. gold holdings,

Reprinted from the April 1962 issue of the *Malayan Economic Review* through the courtesy
of the author and publisher.

and slightly more than a third by increases in foreign holdings of U.S. dollar balances.

Both the reduction of United States gold holdings and the growth of foreign holdings of U.S. dollar balances were the result of United States balance-of-payments deficits, and have been accompanied by a steady weakening of the United States net reserve position. . . . Both the U.S. deficit and the U.S. reserve position suddenly became a source of serious concern after 1957, when the U.S. began to run a much larger balance-of-payments deficit, and a larger proportion of this deficit began to be taken out in gold rather than accumulation of dollar balances.[1] But a deficit and the associated weakening of the reserve position of the United States have been characteristic of the postwar period. During the period 1950–56 the United States ran an average deficit of $1.4 billion, of which $0.4 billion took the form of a gold loss, and $1.0 billion the form of an increase in foreign dollar balances; in this period, the deficit and gold loss were regarded as desirable, part of the contribution of the United States to the reconstruction of a multilateral world trading system. In 1957, largely as an indirect consequence of Suez, the United States had a surplus of $0.4 billion, and as foreign dollar balances increased by $0.4 billion, the U.S. gained $0.8 billion of gold. In 1958–60, however, the average U.S. deficit was $3.7 billion, over two and a half times the 1950–56 average, financed by an average gold loss of $1.6 billion and increase in dollar balances of $2.1 billion, the proportion of gold loss to deficit increasing from 29 per cent to 43 per cent between the two periods. In consequence, the gross liquid assets of the United States are now about equal to its gross liquid liabilities—slightly larger or slightly smaller, according to how these terms are defined . . .—as contrasted with the position at the beginning of the postwar period, when assets were roughly triple liabilities.

The counterpart of this balance-of-payments history of the United States, and particularly of the accumulation of dollar balances by other countries, is that about two-fifths of world international reserves consist of foreign exchange, of which dollars constitute the larger part. (Moreover, dollars and not sterling have accounted for the increase in foreign exchange holdings since 1949.) In fact, since the war the noncommunist world has got onto a gold exchange standard, based primarily on the dollar and secondarily on sterling. This development was not consciously planned, but

---

[1] In 1959, the deficit was largely accounted for by a sharply adverse movement of the U.S. current account; in 1958 and 1960, it was mainly due to outflows of U.S. and foreign capital prompted by higher interest rates abroad and, especially in late 1960, by speculation against the dollar.

has been the result of a natural evolution strongly influenced by certain features of war and postwar economic history: the accumulation of sterling balances in the course of sterling area wartime finance and the failure to fund these balances at the end of the war; the inadequacy of the International Monetary Fund as a means of providing liquidity, especially in face of postwar inflation, and the decision that the Fund should be inactive during the Marshall Plan; and the dollar shortage and the resulting central position of the United States as a provider of scarce goods and reconstruction capital. Nevertheless, it bears a close parallel to the efforts that were consciously made after World War I to establish a gold exchange standard so as to economize on the use of gold as a monetary reserve—an effort which broke down disastrously in the 1930's.[2]

The experience of the breakdown of the gold exchange standard in the 1930's, and the recent balance-of-payments difficulties of the United States, show that the gold exchange standard is a precarious system of international monetary organization. Two main problems are inherent in it. The first is associated with the reliance of the system on the use of national currencies to provide international reserves, and arises from the fact that liquidity can be destroyed by the conversion of national currencies into gold. Such conversions may be the result of speculation against a reserve currency, based on suspicion of the reserve currency country's ability to maintain convertibility of its currency into gold; or of capital outflows prompted by interest rate differentials resulting from the different requirements of domestic policies and not offset by counteracting changes in forward exchange rates. Both types of causation will result in the destruction of liquidity insofar as countries gaining reserves as a result of them are not prepared to hold the currency of the reserve-losing country (indeed, the central banks of reserve-gaining countries may themselves contribute to the speculative pressure by converting currency reserve holdings into gold). The possibility of such conversions poses an especially acute problem for the reserve currency countries, since the domestic policies required to avert them may be in sharp conflict with the policies indicated by do-

---

[2] The parallelism, the dangers of the system, and the need for reform have been argued most forcefully by Robert Triffin in *Gold and the Dollar Crisis* (New Haven: Yale University Press, 1960) and "The International Monetary Position of the United States" (Summary of Robert Triffin's Statement before the Joint Economic Committee, October 28, 1959, in *Employment, Growth, and Price Levels*, Hearings); unfortunately Triffin's own plan is an uneasy compromise between the realization that an effective solution requires the replacement of gold by an international credit currency and the desire to produce a negotiable scheme, which requires the retention of gold as the ultimate reserve. I criticize the Triffin plan below; at this point I would like to acknowledge the stimulus and provocativeness of his writings. [See above, selection 1, esp. pp. 15–37.]

mestic considerations; but it also involves the danger that the whole system will break down (as in the 1930's) in a scramble to convert foreign exchange holdings into their nonexistent gold equivalent.

The second major problem is associated with the system's reliance on increases in monetary gold stocks and increases in reserve currency holdings to provide the increase in international reserves needed to support the expansion of international trade and commercial transactions, and arises from the fact that insofar as the stock of monetary gold grows more slowly than reserve needs, reserve currency holdings must expand more rapidly than reserve needs. This poses two problems. First, the nonreserve currency countries must be induced to accumulate holdings of reserve currencies rather than gold, which requires both adequate confidence in the reserve currencies and the attraction of adequate interest earnings. Second, the reserve currency countries must increase the supply of reserve currency to the rest of the world by running a balance-of-payments deficit; this inevitably involves increasing its liabilities faster than its assets, so weakening its reserve position and its capacity to command international confidence.[3] A third problem is that the supply of new monetary gold may itself be reduced by private gold hoarding prompted by lack of confidence in the system, which hoarding may occur (and has occurred) despite the expressed confidence of official monetary authorities in the system.

Before proceeding to discuss the contemporary manifestation of these problems, it is worth while to comment on one puzzling aspect of the gold exchange standard. On the face of it, this system involves a net benefit for the nonreserve currency countries, which receive interest payments from the reserve currency countries in return for allowing the latter to hold their gold reserves for them, and a corresponding loss (the interest paid) together with the assumption of a certain risk (the subordination of domestic policy to the performance of reserve currency obligations) by the reserve currency countries. Why are the latter nevertheless satisfied to operate the system? In general terms, the answer is that the system contributes, or is thought to contribute, to the national economic power of the

---

[3] Even if the reserve currency countries absorbed all the new monetary gold, their gold reserve ratio against liabilities held by other countries would have to fall for total international reserves to increase faster than the monetary gold stock; to maintain a given gold reserve ratio, the reserve currency countries would have to draw gold from nonreserve countries. For a more extensive and formal treatment of the theory of a reserve currency system, see Peter B. Kenen, "International Liquidity and the Balance of Payments of a Reserve-Currency Country," *Quarterly Journal of Economics*, LXXIV, no. 4 (November 1960), 572–86.

reserve currency country in the world economy. In the first place, the use of a country's currency in international transactions gives direct and indirect advantages to its banking, financial, and commercial community, in the form of commissions, commercial contacts, and so forth; these advantages can easily be (and have been argued to be) illusory, since the obvious profits from an international banking business can easily be more than offset by the indirect disadvantages that policies governed by the obligations of international banking impose on other sectors of the economy. Second, the growth of foreign holdings of a country's currency means that foreigners are lending to the reserve currency country real resources which can be used by that country either to raise its domestic expenditure or for international lending, foreign aid, military assistance, and so forth, which enhance its international influence.[4] Thus, of the $61.2 billion of foreign aid of various kinds extended to the rest of the world by the United States in the period 1950–60, $20.4 billion—one-third—was indirectly provided by other countries through the United States deficit (of this amount, $6.7 billion was provided in return for gold, and $13.7 billion in return for dollar assets). The system therefore in effect channels command over real resources to the reserve currency countries, so enhancing their international influence.

The influence so acquired makes the reserve currency countries reluctant to consider abandonment of the system, while at the same time it provokes envy and resentment on the part of the economic and political rivals of these countries, so creating strains within the system facilitating its breakdown and inhibiting the adoption of measures for strengthening it.

The present international monetary system confronts two, and possibly three, major problems. The first is the vulnerability of the reserve currency countries to international short-term capital movements. The second, and most debatable, concerns the adequacy of present international reserves. Sir Roy Harrod has argued that there is a serious shortage of reserves, and stated that "in my own judgment the shortage is already so great as to be the primary cause of the free world having shown inadequate growth rates in recent years,"[5] since the shortage leads countries to meet balance-of-payment oscillations by deflationary policies and import restrictions rather

---

[4] This feature of reserve currency holding has frequently been commented on in criticisms of the British colonial currency system, which has the automatic effect of making the colonies lend to the mother country the real resources represented by any increase in their domestic currency circulation.

[5] Sir Roy Harrod, "A Plan for Increasing Liquidity: A Critique," *Economica*, XXVIII, no. 110 (May 1961), 200 [reprinted as selection 5 of this volume].

than ride them out. This view, however, seems to be based mainly on an overgeneralization of British experience. Most writers on the subject, and the International Monetary Fund, do not regard the present level of international reserves as seriously inadequate, and are primarily concerned with the third problem, the adequacy of the prospective growth of reserves.

The measurement of the adequacy of international reserves raises extremely difficult conceptual problems, which have so far not been satisfactorily solved. For most countries, the primary purpose of reserves is to finance adverse swings in the current account, and the desirable level of reserves presumably depends on the probable magnitude of such swings. But for countries where currencies are widely used in international financial transactions, the reserves serve the same function as the reserves of a bank in a banking system lacking a central bank, that is, the rather nebulous function of ensuring the confidence of the depositors that they can obtain cash on demand. While the desirable level of reserves is presumably related to the quantity of short-term debt outstanding, the function provides no firm guide to what the relationship should be—both Britain, with a reserve ratio of about one-third, and the United States, with a reserve ratio of about 100 per cent, have been subjected to speculative capital outflows in recent years. Practical discussions of reserve adequacy ignore these complexities, and generally take as their key figure the ratio of reserves to annual imports—a practice the logic of which is more relevant to the immediate postwar context of economic planning in the face of dollar shortage than to contemporary conditions of international competition and convertibility.

On this basis the International Monetary Fund Staff study on *World Reserves and Liquidity*, published in 1958, estimated that over the period 1958 to 1967 the excess of the growth of reserves needed to support the expansion of world trade over the increase in the supply of monetary gold would be small enough to be filled easily by a modest growth of reserve currency holdings. This optimistic conclusion depended, however, as Triffin points out,[6] on two crucial assumptions: that the countries holding relatively large ratios of gold would not wish to increase their holdings further, while those holding relatively small ratios would not wish to build up their ratios; and that the volume of trade would increase by 3 per cent per annum. Triffin strongly questions both assumptions, particularly the latter, and produces revised estimates showing that if Britain and France

---

[6] *Gold and the Dollar Crisis*, Part I, chap. 5. [See also above, p. 27.]

were to build up their reserves to a normal (40 per cent) level, the increase in monetary gold supplies over the period would provide only 55 per cent of additional reserve needs even at a 3 per cent growth rate of trade, and only 35 per cent at a 5 per cent growth rate.[7] Thus, on Triffin's analysis, there is a substantial prospective shortage of reserves; and this shortage is unlikely to be overcome by further expansion of the gold exchange standard, especially as American policy is likely to be directed in the future against running the sustained balance-of-payments deficits required to provide a flow of dollar balances to the rest of the world, and in any case other countries are likely to become less willing to accumulate such balances.

The discussion of these problems of the contemporary international monetary system, and the advocacy of proposals for solving them, have been carried on in two different contexts—as part of the discussion of national economic policy in the reserve currency countries, where most attention has been given to the problem of dealing with international short-term capital movements, and in the specific context of international monetary organization, where both the short-term capital movement problem and the long-run problem of reserve adequacy have been subjects of concern. This article is concerned with proposals for modifying the international monetary system, but it may be useful to mention briefly some of the proposals for national action to mitigate the threat of disruption by international short-term capital movements that have been advanced. These include the offer of gold guarantees to official holders of the reserve country's currency to prevent withdrawals prompted by loss of confidence; the offer to official or to all foreign holders of securities bearing special high-interest rates, to prevent withdrawals when domestic conditions require domestic interest rates lower than foreign interest rates; and official intervention in the forward markets for foreign exchange, aimed at creating a forward premium on the currency sufficient to offset any interest rate differential favoring investment in foreign money markets.[8] Another set of proposals calls for a more comprehensive presentation of the reserve currency country's international capital position, designed to elucidate the causes and significance of changes and discourage undue emphasis on changes in gold

---

[7] *Ibid.*, Part I, chap. 5, Table 8. [Reproduced as Table 6, above, p. 29.]

[8] This theoretically appealing device was strongly advocated to the Radcliffe Committee by various British economists, but rejected by the Committee mainly on practical grounds. For a recent analysis of it, together with the main references, see John H. Auten, "Counter-Speculation and the Forward Exchange Market," *Journal of Political Economy*, LXIX, no. 1 (February 1961), 49–56.

reserves as such. Finally, it has been argued that the United States should abolish the requirement of a 25 per cent reserve of gold against Federal Reserve notes and deposits, to dispel any lingering misapprehensions about the availability of the whole gold reserve of the United States to finance international deficits.

PROPOSALS AND PLANS FOR IMPROVING THE
INTERNATIONAL MONETARY SYSTEM

The proposals that have been put forward for improving the international monetary system can be classified in a variety of ways—by the degree of international cooperation required, by the extent of the institutional changes involved, and so forth. For present purposes, the most convenient classification is according to the type of international monetary system that would result. Three alternatives have been proposed in recent discussions—the abandonment of the system of fixed exchange rates and international reserve holdings entirely, in favor of a system of floating exchange rates; restoration of a predominantly gold standard system, by means of a substantial increase in the price of gold; and a strengthening of the present system of using credit for international reserves by one means or another—the last alternative being the subject of those proposals that can properly be described as "plans." To this list should be added a fourth alternative that has been lurking in the background of the discussion, demonetization of gold and replacement of it by international credit currency provided by an international central bank.[9]

Floating Exchange Rates

The theoretical case in favor of floating exchange rates is, in my opinion, virtually incontestable.[10] The main theoretical objections to it concentrate on the possibility of destabilizing speculation, a possibility the

[9] The items in this list are not mutually exclusive, since the proposal to raise the price of gold could be regarded as one means of strengthening the gold exchange standard, while, as will be seen, some of the proposals for strengthening the gold exchange standard amount to taking steps toward the establishment of a world central bank. Moreover, not all the alternatives require international cooperation to put them into effect: any individual country can adopt a floating rate, and some of the plans for strengthening the gold exchange standard, such as the Zolotas plan, merely call for widespread adoption of measures that a nation could undertake on its own.

[10] See Milton Friedman, "The Case for Flexible Exchange Rates," pp. 157–203 in Milton Friedman, *Essays in Positive Economics* (Chicago: University of Chicago Press, 1953), and Egon Sohmen, *Flexible Exchange Rates: Theory and Controversy* (Chicago: University of Chicago Press, 1961).

empirical evidence for which is very difficult to assess;[11] and in any case it is doubtful whether the probability of such speculation could be greater under a floating rate than under the present system, which provides a one-way option for exchange speculation. The practical objection that the international financial and merchanting community prefers fixed exchange rates raises the question of the weight to be given to the opinions of interested parties, particularly as insistence on the maintenance of fixed exchange rates indirectly entails a demand for the pursuit of conservative domestic economic policies. There may, however, be some substance in the view implicit in the strong attachment to fixed exchange rates that fixed rates between national currencies, like the use of a common currency within national boundaries, contribute significantly to the efficient working of a liberal economic system by removing one element of uncertainty. Until recently, the Canadian dollar provided the most important counterexample; but the Canadian dollar is for many reasons a special case. Be that as it may, the strongest obstacle to the adoption of a floating rate system is the commitment of the leading trading countries, especially the United States, to a fixed exchange rate system, and the institutionalization of that system in the International Monetary Fund. Abandonment of the fixed rate system in favor of floating rates between the major currencies would involve a greater degree of institutional change than any of the alternatives.

An Increase in the Price of Gold

This solution has been most cogently argued, among professional economists, by Sir Roy Harrod.[12] A substantial increase in the price of gold, say a doubling of it, would contribute to a solution of all three problems of the present international monetary system simultaneously: it would immediately increase the amount of world liquid reserves, both by increasing the value of existing stocks of monetary gold and by inducing dishoarding (an effect which might, in the light of 1930's experience, be substantial);

---

[11] Triffin's argument (*Gold and the Dollar Crisis*, Part II, chap. 1) that speculation on a depreciation will prove self-justifying, by inducing an inflation of internal wages and prices, so that the system will contain a "depreciation bias," assumes without adequate justification that wages and prices are initially in some sort of neutral equilibrium, or else that the monetary authorities follow a permissive policy with respect to wage and price increases. The experience of the European countries in the immediate post–World War I period to which he refers is consistent with the interpretation that speculators correctly appreciated the inflationary character of the domestic policies these countries were pursuing.

[12] For his most recent statement, see "A Plan for Increasing Liquidity" [reprinted as selection 5 of this volume; see also selection 10 by the same author].

by increasing the value of gold reserves it would reduce the danger of disruption by a scramble to convert foreign exchange holdings into gold; and it would increase the long-run growth of the world gold supply by both its direct effects on the value of new gold production and the indirect effects via stimulating production and discouraging hoarding.

The objections to raising the world price of gold are of widely varying merit, some of them amounting to little more than rationalizations of irrational opposition to the proposal. One objection, advanced by Triffin, is that the measure would be a temporary expedient that would have to be repeated. This is not necessarily so, owing to the effects on the value of annual new supplies of monetary gold; but the fact that the increase in price would have an immediate, once-for-all effect on the value of the existing stock would entail the disadvantage of an immediate excess of liquidity with possible inflationary consequences unless the profits were sterilized and then gradually desterilized, and there is no reason to expect that the resulting rate of growth of the supply of monetary gold would match the growth of liquidity needs. A second, politically important, objection is that revaluation of gold would entail a handsome gift to the Russians and South Africans in their capacity as gold producers, and so lend support to communism and apartheid respectively. As to the Russians, it can be argued that the resulting strengthening of the free world economy would far outweigh the gift to their welfare, though to be relevant this argument must assume that an increase in the gold price is the only feasible solution to the liquidity problem. As to apartheid, there is no reason for thinking that an increase in the profitability of gold mining would weaken the position of the Africans rather than strengthen it.[13] A third objection is to the inequitable distribution of the gains from gold revaluation, which will accrue to existing holders rather than to countries needing additional reserves most; this objection raises some knotty questions about the definition of "need," given that individual countries can by policy determine the size of their own reserves, and also ignores the fact that the purpose of the proposal is to increase the total stock of reserves, not to influence its allocation. The objection does have some force, however, insofar as the countries that have cooperated most in extending the supply of reserves by holding currencies rather than gold would be relative losers. The most cogent objection is that the proposal would reaffirm the faith in gold as the only "real" inter-

[13] Sir Roy Harrod's contention that employment in gold mining has a desirable civilizing influence on the Bantu ("A Plan for Increasing Liquidity," p. 202 [reprinted above, p. 119]) does, however, seem to carry the argument too far.

national money, and the principle of tying the quantity of money to the stock of a commodity costing real resources to produce, a principle that has been abandoned in the domestic monetary affairs of most states with the realization that money can be created without cost and yet be managed sensibly. In addition, the implementation of the proposal would at bottom be inconsistent with the principle of the gold standard system. If gold were revalued on the basis that Harrod and others have suggested, restoration of the purchasing power of gold on terms of commodities in some base year, and that procedure were accepted as conforming to sound principles, the resulting "gold standard" could amount to a parity policy for gold producers, not a monetary standard tying the quantity of international money to the quantity of gold in existence.

Strengthening the Gold Exchange Standard

Proposals for strengthening the present system of using national credit money as international reserves have taken a wide variety of forms, depending largely on the extent of institutional change which their authors have thought practicable. I shall discuss them in order of increasing institutional change, which is not the chronological order in which they have been presented to the public.

Increased central bank collaboration. This is the mildest approach to strengthening the present international monetary system, and in fact represents no more than an explicit advocacy of a more determined pursuit of a direction which the leading central banks have already begun to take, notably in the Basel Agreement that followed the appreciation of the German mark early in 1960. The proposal is that central banks should collaborate to avoid the disruptive effects of international short-term capital movements, by coordinating their domestic policies so far as possible to avoid creating interest rate differentials stimulating international short-term capital movements, and by agreeing to hold acquisitions of each other's currencies resulting from such capital movements rather than convert them into gold. Undoubtedly such collaboration can prove helpful, as in the case of the Basel Agreement, but its usefulness is likely to be very limited, both because a central bank's first duty is to its own government and because it involves negotiations among autonomous powers each with its own views of the contemporary situation, views probably of a conservative nature and likely to be conflicting. (The Basel Agreement was actually a group of bilateral agreements, whose main effect was to enable Britain to postpone by a few months her appeal to the International Monetary Fund.)

Reliance on central bank collaboration is therefore likely to result in break-down in a crisis—the eventual failure of the efforts of Montagu Norman and Benjamin Strong to manage the gold exchange standard by central bank collaboration in the interwar period is relevant here. Such reliance is especially risky in a reserve currency system, owing to the interrelation between the reserve currency role and national power in the world econ-omy: to ask a nonreserve currency central bank to support the reserve cur-rency is to ask it to support the policies of the reserve currency country and strengthen the international influence its reserve center position gives it, and this it may be reluctant or unwilling to do.

The Stamp plan. Under the plan proposed by Maxwell Stamp, former United Kingdom Director of the International Monetary Fund,[14] the Inter-national Monetary Fund would be authorized to issue gold certificates up to a certain value ($3 billion was suggested), which members would agree to accept from the Fund or a member's central bank in return for their own currencies. These certificates would be given to an aid-coordinating agency which would allocate them to underdeveloped countries, which in turn would use them to buy capital equipment from the industrialized countries, the certificates eventually finding their way to the surplus countries.

The Stamp plan ingeniously attempts to combine aid to underdeveloped countries with a once-for-all increase in international reserves; it does nothing to solve the capital movements problem or the long-run reserve problem, though the latter could presumably be dealt with by repeated applications of it. As a scheme for increasing international reserves, it is critically defective. At the outset, it is not clear whether the certificates are to be exchangeable for gold or convertible currencies at the Fund itself, or not. If they are not, the result would be the creation of a fictional kind of international reserve currency, transferable between Fund members but not convertible into gold, a currency which members might well try to pass off onto one another; if they did not do so, or were somehow debarred from doing so, the certificates would not in fact serve the function of reserves, and the aid to which they were attached could be provided as well by grants from the surplus countries to the underdeveloped countries. If the cer-tificates are to be exchangeable at the Fund, as the term "gold certificate" seems to imply, the effect would be the same as if the Fund made an open-market purchase of irredeemable non-interest-bearing securities from the aid-coordinating agency in return for a sight claim on its own reserves of

---

[14] See *The Guardian*, February 10 and 13, 1961, and the Spring 1961 issue of *Moorgate and Wall Street*. [See also selection 3 of this volume.]

gold and convertible currencies: even if the certificates were not in fact cashed their existence would seriously diminish the Fund's freedom of action, and encashment of them would drastically reduce the resources the Fund could place at the disposal of its members. In short, if the certificates are not intended to be convertible into gold at the Fund, their issue would amount to the creation of a special kind of international credit currency with restricted acceptability; if they are intended to be convertible, their issue would amount to disposal of part of the Fund's liquid assets.

The Zolotas plan.[15] The Zolotas plan for reforming the international monetary system has as its guiding principle recognition of "the side constraint of political feasibility and the traditional conservatism of monetary authorities"; its intent is to be practicable. The plan is aimed primarily at removing the dangers of disruption of the system by short-term capital movements, but its long-run purpose is to permit continued expansion of the gold exchange standard. It consists of three recommendations:

1. The reserve countries should hold sufficient balances of the major convertible currencies ("compensating reserve deposits") to provide a first line of defense for their currencies;

2. All convertible currency countries should provide a gold guarantee on all balances held in their respective currencies by foreign treasuries and central banks;

3. All major trading countries should establish differential interest rate and tax treatment for official foreign depositors of short-term balances.

The aim of the third recommendation is to insulate a country's domestic policy from its international position and eliminate destabilizing profit-induced capital movements; the aim of the second is to inspire confidence and permit the first recommendation to be implemented safely. The first recommendation, for the building up of compensating reserve deposits by reserve currency countries, is the novel element in the plan. Its purpose is to strengthen the currencies of these countries against speculative attack.

Zolotas argues that the accumulation of compensating reserve deposits would not impair the net liquidity position of the trading countries whose currencies were accumulated, since these accumulations would be used purely for defensive purposes and not for transmitting disturbances from one part of the world to another—that is, balances of a trading country's

[15] Xenophon Zolotas, Governor of the Bank of Greece, *Towards a Reinforced Gold Exchange Standard*, Bank of Greece Papers and Lectures, no. 7 (Athens, 1961). [Reprinted as selection 16 of this volume.]

currency would only be drawn on to finance capital outflows to that country, which otherwise would be gaining reserves. To make this part of the plan operational, he acknowledges, the reserve currency countries would have to accumulate enough of *each* of the major trading countries' currencies to meet any likely capital outflow to them. This requirement, however, suggests one major weakness of the scheme: there is nothing to prevent holders of a reserve currency in a number of countries from attempting to convert their holdings into the currency of one country, so that to ensure adequate supplies of all the currencies that might be demanded the reserve currency country might have to hold a total stock of foreign currencies larger than its own deposit liabilities—in short, to be perfectly safe the reserve currency country might have to be a substantial creditor, rather than a debtor, in relation to the other major countries! And if it did not hold sufficient compensating reserve deposits in each major trading country's currency, the net liquidity positions of the latter countries would be impaired by the risk that compensating reserve deposits in their currencies might be drawn on to finance capital outflows from the reserve currency country to some other country. Quite apart from this problem, the fact that holdings of reserve currencies would be partially offset by compensating reserve deposits in the holder's currency would reduce the incentive to both parties to operate the gold exchange standard—the reserve currency country would lose some of its freedom to dispose of funds deposited with it, since a part of these funds would have to be reinvested in compensating reserve deposits, and the depositing country would be likely to have to pay out some of its interest receipts on its reserve currency holdings in interest on compensating reserve deposits in its currency.

The process of building up compensating reserve deposits would also be likely to create problems, since to finance these accumulations the reserve countries would have to run smaller deficits, or surpluses, on their other international transactions. Zolotas is particularly concerned about the possibility that the accumulations might be financed at the expense of aid to the underdeveloped nations, and argues that the requisite balance-of-payments adjustments can be achieved in other ways than by a reduction of such aid. This is true, but the alternative adjustments might be indirectly harmful to the underdeveloped countries, since they could easily entail deflationary pressure on the world economy. More important, the outcome of an effort to accumulate other countries' currencies might be a reduction in the latter's holdings of reserve currencies and a loss of gold reserves by the reserve countries, rather than a net accumulation of gold and exchange holdings by the reserve countries. In other words, the effect might be a strengthening of the liquidity position of the reserve currencies via contraction of their liabilities rather than expansion of their assets.

These considerations suggest that the Zolotas plan relies for success much more on collaboration between central banks than is apparent at first sight. The accumulation of holdings of other countries' currencies is after all simply a more reliable alternative to obtaining their agreement to lend their currencies when desired, and if they are reluctant to lend, they can take steps to avoid being put in the position of being obliged to do so. To bring the plan into operation would require the active collaboration of the central banks of the major trading countries; and this would raise the problems already discussed under that heading.

The Bernstein plan. The two most carefully worked-out, longest-standing, and consequently most discussed plans for the reform of the international monetary system are those advocated respectively by Dr. Edward Bernstein, former Director of Research at the International Monetary Fund, and Professor Robert Triffin, of Yale University. Dr. Bernstein's plan[16] consists of three proposals, aimed at the three aspects of the liquidity problem discussed above:

1. Integration of members' quotas at the International Monetary Fund into their working balances: this would increase the available total of international reserves, since quotas are not currently treated as first-line reserves because their use is subject to obtaining the approval of the Fund. (Dr. Bernstein does not, however, believe that there is currently a general shortage of international reserves, so that the intention of the proposal is primarily to strengthen the position of the reserve centers.)

2. Creation of a special lending arrangement as an adjunct to the Fund, in the form of a Reserve Settlement Account: under this arrangement, the leading trading countries—the United States, Britain, the Common Market countries, Canada, and Japan—would undertake to lend to the Reserve Settlement Account by subscribing for International Monetary Fund notes up to a stated amount on request, the national currencies so subscribed being lent by the Fund to a member undergoing an outflow of capital; the notes would be of relatively short maturity, carry a gold guarantee, and be redeemable before maturity by a holder suffering a balance-of-payments deficit, and both notes and loans would bear interest at rates negotiated

---

[16] For recent statements of the plan, see Edward M. Bernstein, "The Adequacy of United States Gold Reserves," *American Economic Review, Papers and Proceedings*, LI, no. 2 (May 1961), 439–46, and Bernstein, "The Reserve Centres and the International Monetary Fund," *The Irish Banking Review*, June 1961, pp. 17–22. [See also selection 9 of this volume, written by the same author.]

between the Fund and the lending or borrowing country. This proposal is the central feature of the Bernstein plan, aimed at remedying the vulnerability of the system to international short-term capital movements.

3. Provision of additional reserves at intervals as required, by increases in members' quotas in the International Monetary Fund; this proposal is aimed at providing for the long-run growth of liquidity needs.

The Bernstein plan has a number of important practical advantages. In the first place, it builds on the established role of the existing international monetary institution, the International Monetary Fund, and seeks to supplement it by a method not requiring a radical change in the constitution of the International Monetary Fund itself. Second, it recognizes the fact that what really counts in international monetary affairs is the behavior of the handful of large trading and reserve-holding countries. Third, the proposed special lending arrangement, in contrast to reliance on informal collaboration between central banks, would make the reserve currency country's problem in borrowing to offset a capital outflow one of a single negotiation with the International Monetary Fund, rather than of separate negotiations with other national central banks, thereby minimizing the possibility of obstructiveness prompted by national jealousies or excessive conservatism and enabling an international view of the situation to be brought to bear.

On the other hand, the plan has potentially serious defects. In the first place, the integration of members' quotas in their international reserves, to be effective, would require removal of present limitations on the use of these for meeting balance-of-payments deficits. At present members have automatic access to the first 25 per cent of their quotas (their gold subscriptions to the Fund) and virtually automatic access to the second 25 per cent; thereafter drawings are subject to increasingly stringent conditions of Fund approval. These conditions enable the Fund to exercise control over "undisciplined" countries, a control which in the past has proved beneficial. Second, the Reserve Settlement Account plan raises some problems. One concerns the interest rates paid and charged by the Account, in the possible case in which interest rates in the lenders' markets exceed interest rates in the borrowers' market: if rates paid and charged by the Account are related to national interest rates, the Account will in this case run at a loss; if the rate charged is fixed above the rate paid to avoid this, then either the lenders must lend to the Account at below their own market rates—a subsidy to the borrowers—or the borrowers must pay a rate above their own market rate, in which case the Reserve Settlement Account arrangement amounts to offering the lenders a gold guarantee and a special high interest rate, an offer which could equally well be made by the borrowing country on its own initiative (though not, of course, with the same certainty of response). Another problem concerns the incidence of loss in the event of a devaluation by a borrower: presumably the borrower's obligation would be expressed in terms of gold. Finally, the provision for prematurity redemption of rates held by a country undergoing a deficit might cause trouble: if the amount the holder wanted to cash exceeded the unused lending commitment of the country whose currency it wanted to acquire, the Fund would have to make good the difference by drawing on its own gold and exchange assets—in short, it might not be possible to keep the business of the Reserve Settlement Account separate from that of the Fund.

The most serious weakness of the plan, however, is its reliance on increases in Fund quotas to meet future needs for increased liquidity. One major objection to this is that the timing and amount of such increases will depend on the will of the major reserve-holding countries, with the probability that increases will be little and late because the pressure to make out the case for them will be felt mostly by the deficit countries, and their arguments will tend to appear as a demand for special assistance. Also, like periodic revaluations of gold, this method would tend to involve sequences of excessive and deficient amounts of reserves. Moreover, equal all-round increases in quotas would not be a very efficient way of increasing reserves, since quotas are not related at all closely to reserve needs; and the requirement that a proportion of the quota increase be subscribed in gold would create problems, either by putting pressure on poor countries short of international reserves or by inducing countries holding reserves in reserve currencies to draw gold from the reserve currency countries for deposit in the International Monetary Fund. The most fundamental objection, however, is that Fund quotas, even if they were to be counted with first-line reserves as Bernstein recommends, would remain an adjunct of an international monetary system based on gold as its ultimate reserve.

The Triffin plan. The Bernstein plan seeks primarily to strengthen the gold exchange standard by providing an international lending arrangement that can be used to counteract capital outflows from a reserve center country. The Triffin plan[17] involves a more radical attack on the gold exchange standard itself, its aim being to replace the use of national cur-

---

[17] Triffin, *Gold and the Dollar Crisis*, Part II [reprinted in part as selection 1 of this volume; see esp. pp. 38–54]. For a searching criticism of the Triffin plan, see Harrod, "A Plan for Increasing Liquidity," on which parts of the following argument draw heavily [reprinted as selection 5 of this volume].

rencies as international reserves by the use of international credit money. Its central proposals are:

1. To convert the International Monetary Fund into a genuine international central bank in which members would keep part of their international reserves on deposit. These deposits, which would be obtained initially by transfers of existing reserve assets to the Fund, would have the attractions of earning interest equal to the average rate of return on Fund assets, and of carrying a guarantee of convertibility into gold; but in case these attractions are insufficient to overcome inertia, Triffin suggests that members should be required to hold a minimum of 20 per cent of their reserves on deposit with the Fund.

2. To transfer the remaining reserve holdings of sterling and dollars to deposit with the Fund, the Fund to have the option of liquidating the assets acquired by this and the previous proposal subject to a maximum rate per annum which Triffin puts at 5 per cent.

3. To empower the Fund to conduct open-market operations to assist members in balance-of-payments deficit and to increase the stock of international reserves. With respect to the latter, Triffin suggests that Fund open-market purchases should be designed to increase world reserves at an internationally agreed rate of 3 per cent, or possibly 4 per cent or 5 per cent per annum.

The Triffin plan aims at solving the problems of the gold exchange standard system by replacing it with an international central banking institution—the reformed International Monetary Fund—which would deal with the two major problems of short-term capital movements and long-run liquidity growth by open-market operations. As Sir Roy Harrod has stressed in his criticism of the plan, Triffin does not provide for an increase in the current stock of international reserves, presumably because (like Bernstein) he differs with Harrod in not considering this a serious problem.

A number of objections may be, and have been, made to the Triffin plan. One is that the transfer of part of reserves to the Fund would in fact initially reduce world liquidity, since countries would regard Fund deposits as being less reliable in emergencies (particularly war) than gold; this objection would seem to rest on the assumed prevalence of anachronistic views about the likely nature of future wars. More serious objections relate to the possible consequences of the transfer of the remaining sterling and dollar balances to the Fund. One such, voiced rather bitterly by Harrod, stresses the inequity of the loss to the reserve countries (specifically, to the United Kingdom) of the commercial advantages accruing from use of their currencies in international transactions; but, as argued above, the indirect costs to a reserve country of the policies required to maintain confidence in its currency may well outweigh the direct and obvious advantages—one suspects that this is especially likely in the British case—and in any event the nub of the problem is that the use of national currencies as international reserves is a dangerous system of international monetary organization. A more fundamental difficulty is that the countries obliged to exchange the excess sterling and dollar holdings for Fund deposits may not wish, and will not be obliged by the 20 per cent requirement, to hold the resulting Fund deposits, and if they demand gold instead, while the Fund is obliged to hold onto the sterling and dollar deposits it has acquired, the result would be a serious drain of gold out of the Fund, one which could exceed the quantity of gold in the Fund's possession, and in any case could seriously weaken the Fund's capacity to conduct open-market operations freely.

A third set of objections relates to the proposal to expand world reserves by Fund open-market purchases of securities and loans. These would have to be large and continually increasing, in consequence of both growing needs and the necessity of offsetting the maturation of past loans or purchases and the destruction of liquidity by the gradual disposition of the initial acquisition of sterling and dollar balances; and in the nature of things they would tend to be concentrated in the securities markets of the advanced countries, so that these countries rather than the underdeveloped nations would enjoy the benefit of the credit by which increasing international reserves are created. To meet this objection, Triffin and other supporters of his plan have been suggesting (a variant of the Stamp plan) that the credit should be channeled into loans to the underdeveloped countries through the medium of loans to the International Bank; but there are definite limits to the possibility of implementing this suggestion, both because the annual amounts of money involved would be very large in relation to the present turnover of the Bank and would strain its capacities to administer and its customers' capacities to absorb loans of its usual type, and because the result would be to load the Fund with relatively illiquid assets. A more fundamental difficulty is that already mentioned in connection with the transfer to the Fund of excess sterling and dollar balances: since recipients of the additional Fund deposits created by open-market operations would be obliged to hold only 20 per cent of them with the Fund, and free to convert the rest into gold, the Fund might suffer a steady loss of its own gold reserves, and eventually prove unable to maintain confidence in its ability to furnish gold on demand to its depositors.

This is indeed the most fundamental objection to the Triffin plan: that it does not in fact remove the central weakness of the gold exchange standard, which is inherent in the freedom of holders of reserve currency to demand conversion of their holdings into gold, but instead internationalizes the problem by transferring it to the International Monetary Fund. Just as the liquidity of a reserve currency country is inevitably weakened by allowing foreign holdings of its currency to expand more rapidly than new supplies of monetary gold, so the International Monetary Fund, if it undertook to provide additional international reserves by open-market purchases or lending at a rate sufficiently great to increase international reserves more rapidly than the world supply of monetary gold increased, would inevitably lose gold or at least suffer a steady reduction of its gold reserve ratio *unless* its members held an increasing proportion of their total reserves on deposit with it. In other words, under the Triffin plan *either* the problems of the gold exchange standard would eventually re-emerge, in the form of diminishing liquidity of the Fund and increasing doubts about the Fund's ability to deliver gold to countries gaining reserves and unwilling to hold more than the required minimum of deposits—in which case there would be an increasing need for central bank collaboration or some sort of Bernstein plan to provide credit to the Fund itself—*or* countries would have increasingly to economize on gold by holding increasing proportions of their reserves in the form of Fund deposits—in other words, they would have to move toward the gradual international demonetization of gold in favor of the use of Fund deposits as the ultimate international reserve money.

The Triffin plan is therefore something of a halfway house between the gold exchange standard and the establishment of a genuine international credit currency entailing the demonetization of gold. Its outlines are apparently the result of a compromise between a clear appreciation of the basic defect of the gold exchange standard—relying on the expansion of credit money to provide increments to international reserves while retaining gold as the ultimate international medium of exchange—and the desire for a negotiable scheme, the prerequisite for which at present is the retention of gold as the ultimate standard of value. The compromise runs the risk of reproducing the problems of the gold exchange standard in another form, before the trading countries of the world are ready and willing to take the next logical step of abandoning gold altogether and replacing it by an international credit currency provided by a world central bank.

An International Central Bank?

Although it has not been recommended by any participant in the discussion of the contemporary international liquidity problem, presumably because it is far removed from the realm of practical negotiability, the replacement of gold by an international credit currency seems the ultimate logical solution to the problem of providing adequate liquidity in a system of fixed exchange rates. Such an international monetary system, which could be established by having all countries deposit their reserves in the International Monetary Fund and then demonetizing gold, would not be vulnerable to liquidity crises resulting from efforts to convert credit money into scarce gold, since this would not be possible; nor would the provision of the increasing reserves required to support the growth of world trade be tied to the vagaries of new gold production and private gold hoarding, as modified by ingenuity in finding ways of substituting for the use of gold.

The main objection to this system would evidently be the sacrifice of monetary sovereignty it would demand of the major countries, which would be obliged to submit their domestic affairs to scrutiny by the international central bank before obtaining special assistance in meeting balance-of-payments deficits. Such scrutiny of a country's affairs by other countries or by international agencies has fast been becoming established practice in the postwar period, so that the change in fact would not be all that novel; and while conforming with the recommendations of an international institution may involve some surrender of sovereignty, the need to do so may also on occasion provide useful supporting pressure for policies that a country's government ought to pursue but is reluctant to adopt for internal political reasons. The strongest opposition to the establishment of the system would be likely to come from the reserve currency countries, prompted by fear of loss of the advantages the present system gives them; but these advantages may well be illusory, nor is it clear that a substantial part of the profits earned by an efficient banking and commercial organization would be lost by the transfer of reserve holdings in the national currency to an international institution—the international central bank would be likely to hold a major part of its assets in the form of liabilities of the advanced countries.[18]

---

[18] Sir Roy Harrod's arguments against the Triffin plan seem rather inconsistent on this subject. At one point he argues against the destruction of liquidity by the liquidation of sterling and dollar assets transferred to the Fund, at another against the likelihood that the Fund's open-market purchases would be carried on mainly in the advanced countries. Since Britain and the United States bulk large among the latter, the "liquidation" would probably consist mostly in giving the Fund freedom to vary the composition of its dollar and sterling portfolios.

The operation of an international central bank would, however, raise some problems for which solutions would be necessary. One would be provision for the absorption of losses incurred on assets held in the currency of a country that devalued: this could be solved by obliging the devaluing country to contribute sufficient additional units to the international central bank to compensate it for the devaluation loss on its portfolio. Another would be the problem mentioned above, that the open-market purchases required to create credit to meet growing reserve needs would tend to be concentrated on the securities markets of the advanced countries, favoring them at the expense of the underdeveloped countries; this could be solved partly, by channeling part of the credit into direct or indirect loans to the underdeveloped countries, but more suitably by directing open-market security purchases toward the countries contributing most to the underdeveloped countries by loans and especially by grants and other forms of assistance not giving rise to debt. A final and potentially serious problem is that, like national central bankers, the managers of the international central bank might fall victim to ill-founded fits of inflationary or deflationary sentiment. This danger could be avoided, at least partially, by following the Triffin plan in binding the international central bank to increase the quantity of international reserves at a steady rate calculated to support steady growth of world trade at stable prices.

POSTSCRIPT

After this article was accepted for publication, the International Monetary Fund announced arrangements for supplementing its resources of convertible currencies by borrowing from its ten leading industrial members.[19] Under the arrangements, the participating members agree to lend their own currencies to the International Monetary Fund up to stated limits, as follows: United States, $2 billion; Britain and Germany, $1 billion; France and Italy, $550 million; Japan, $250 million; Canada and the Netherlands, $200 million; Belgium, $150 million; Sweden, $100 million. The Fund will pay interest on these borrowings under a formula which currently yields a rate of 1½ per cent per annum, plus a borrowing charge of ½ of 1 per cent. The use of them by Fund members will be governed by established Fund policies and practices with respect to the use of its resources. These arrangements, initially sponsored by Per Jacobsson, Managing Di-

[19] *International Financial News Survey*, XIV, no. 1 (January 12, 1962), 1–2, and *Supplement*, pp. 9–12.

rector of the International Monetary Fund, are very similar to Bernstein's proposed Reserve Settlement Account, except that the loans are to be made directly to the Fund. They are designed solely to deal with the short-run liquidity problem, in effect providing additional stand-by credit of up to $3 billion for the United States and Britain to draw on in case of a capital flight. These arrangements could easily prove insufficient, because the participants have the final word in determining how much of their currencies they will in fact make available to the Fund in any particular case, and there is provision for an elaborate and possibly time-consuming process of consultation and voting on this question.

22

Three Experts on the Reform Plans

Mr. Bernstein: . . . The Posthuma plan would in fact give a prescribed amount of credit to each country through the holding of these foreign reserves. Incidentally, they would have to carry with them an automatic exchange guarantee for this reason.

Suppose this was set up in the International Monetary Fund. Each of these countries would deposit with the International Monetary Fund certain amounts of its own currency and get credit in these reserve units. They would then pass the reserve units to each other along with gold as a composite standard. As these would be held by the International Monetary Standard, they would carry an exchange guarantee. I do not think anyone can talk of a Posthuma plan without it.

Mr. Johnson: I did not gather that from your statement.

Mr. Bernstein: I did not mention it there.

Representative Reuss: The hitch in the Posthuma plan is that it too has limits, and those limits are whatever they agree on as the holding.

Mr. Bernstein: The first thing you want to bear in mind is that we are not trying to solve the whole reserve plan with the Posthuma plan. The Posthuma plan in my opinion is specifically useful for stopping the attempt by the big financial centers to get themselves more secure and more liquid by raising the proportion of their reserves in gold. They attempt to escape from a currency which may be temporarily weak, you see, by selling out.

The Posthuma plan would end that. It would provide actually for the holding of $11 billion more of foreign exchange reserves—foreign exchange as reserves—than are held now. All these countries together hold

This discussion took place between Representative Henry S. Reuss of Wisconsin; Edward M. Bernstein, research economist, Washington, D.C.; Harry G. Johnson, University of Chicago; and Fritz Machlup, Princeton University, on December 14, 1962, and is reprinted from *Outlook for United States Balance of Payments*, Hearings, Joint Economic Committee, Subcommittee on International Exchange and Payments (Washington, 1963). It brings out well some of the critical assumptions and implications of several of the plans for reorganization of the international monetary system reprinted in this volume. Among those is the Posthuma plan, which has not been made available to the public. This plan is mentioned in the paper by Mr. Bernstein, and its contents are brought out more clearly in the discussion below.

around $10 billion of each other's currencies. They could hold $21 billion under the Posthuma plan, based on their $33 billion of gold.

Representative Reuss: Let me say this about the Posthuma plan, and I have not studied its details. If the arithmetic of the Posthuma plan is sufficient to take care of washing out any foreseeable hot money flow or short-term capital flow, then it would seem to me, to achieve the goal that you have in the half sentence we are talking about, necessary to provide reciprocal credits to finance such capital movements as do occur. But it has to be adequate——

Mr. Bernstein: Certainly along with the $6 billion of special reserves under the Paris agreement there is plenty there.

Representative Reuss: The trouble with the Paris agreement, with all due respect to that agreement, is that it is a long ways from being automatic. While it is said that they can convene these gentlemen quite rapidly, they still have to be convened at various levels.

Mr. Bernstein: I do not think that would be the real difficulty with it. There are difficulties with the Paris agreement, but I do not believe the fact that it is not automatic is of great consequence. The truth of the matter is that when there are crises you do get the money.

The trouble in fact with all such arrangements is that they require a present condition of crisis. Now, I would like systems that do not require a condition of crisis before they become effective.

Representative Reuss: But avoid the crisis by being automatic.

Mr. Bernstein: It is not that you cannot get the money when there is a crisis. The history of central bank cooperation on giving aid to each other goes back a very long time.

In 1837 the Bank of France lent money to the Bank of England. In 1871 or 1872, the German Government was very cautious about withdrawing gold when the indemnity of the Franco-Prussian War was paid by drawing bills on London. The German Government was very cautious in withdrawing gold, and got a pat on the back from Walter Bagehot. The United States and the French both helped the British with resources during the 1920's.

There is no difficulty about this. The trouble is that they require a present condition of crisis. That is what I do not like. And that is what I prefer about a reserve system that would get rid of it. That is one thing I want to do with the International Monetary Fund too, get rid of the crisis condition that precedes some drawings.

Representative Reuss: I think you have phrased in very simple language the essential element in any plan for dealing with short-term capital outflows, namely, that it has to try to obviate a crisis rather than merely patch it up after it has occurred. And whether it be an adequately funded Posthuma plan, or a neopayments agreement fixed up for the circumstances of the 1960's, or some other plan, it does seem to be your view in your testimony that this country should promptly take steps to negotiate and put such a plan into agreement.

Mr. Bernstein: Yes, I think we ought to go ahead and try to get such arrangements for meeting these problems, not just the hot-money business, because after all, most of the outflow of funds in the last two years of short-term money was bank money, and hardly hot; it was something else. I am also disturbed, Congressman, about the danger that when funds move out there will be a call for gold.

Representative Reuss: Thank you for the moment. Now, Mr. Machlup, . . . I have got a question or two to ask you.

. . .

You point out three types of reform plans which in one way or another address themselves to the general question of increasing the long-run supply of reserves. You point out that in general the establishment has been much too complacent about the supplier of reserves. In your opinion, it is not just something for the sweet by-and-by, but it is something that has to be faced right now or in the next year or two.

Mr. Machlup: At least we ought to think about it now.

Representative Reuss: You throw away the first two types of reform plans you mentioned as not, whatever their other merits, addressing themselves to the long-term problem of reserves, which leaves you with centralization of monetary reserves, that by and large is the kind of IMF plan that Mr. Bernstein was on the verge of discussing—a little different, perhaps.

Mr. Bernstein: Plus Triffin.

Mr. Machlup: That is right. For I think you would need a bit of centralized creation of reserves.

Representative Reuss: Second, increasing the price of gold. Third, flexible exchange rates. Then you addressed yourself to the inflationary potential of these three plans. And I think your conclusion was that the least inflationary probably, if properly safeguarded, was this centralization of monetary reserves. Increasing the price of gold by decentralizing matters led to considerable dangers of inflation, and likewise until philosophers become central bankers, freely flexible exchange rates, you felt, had an inflationary potential.

Mr. Machlup: On this last one I am not so sure. I think it should be possible to change the attitude of central bankers even faster. So I would not be so gloomy regarding the effects of freely flexible rates . . . It is not necessary that this third plan is really inflationary.

Representative Reuss: The second one——

Mr. Machlup: The second one is outright inflationary.

Representative Reuss: It seems to me that has more inflationary danger.

Mr. Johnson: I think the point is that the second plan is a once-over big increase, that is, really the inflationary aspect of it, whereas the centralization could create reserves at a relatively slow rate, and the floating rate system does not require reserves.

Mr. Bernstein: I might add, too, that in my opinion any of these schemes depending upon the creation of reserves, as distinguished from the plan in which quotas are made automatically a part of the reserves, is distinctly deflationary.

I do not believe it is possible to operate the Triffin plan in the present world without deflation. It would deflate the reserves of the world.

Mr. Johnson: Is it a once-over deflation or is it chronic?

Mr. Bernstein: It is a bias. Part of it is once for all. For example, the elimination of present quotas in the Fund and the eradication of dollar and sterling balances held by other countries are deflationary. Countries would get a deposit in the Triffin bank for their dollars and sterling. But in turn the United States and the United Kingdom would have to maintain an over-all payments surplus to liquidate that obligation to the world central bank.

That is a part of the bias. That is a once-for-all deflation, though stretched out.

But inherently it is impossible in the Triffin scheme to make loans to countries to become part of world reserves. The large industrial countries would not be borrowers. It is very easy for them in fact to earn reserves if the others will borrow. The smaller countries would not in fact qualify as borrowers.

The truth of the matter is that even in the Federal Reserve System, depending upon loans, as they once thought they would, has become impractical. In the Federal Reserve System as we have it today—I think less than one-half of 1 per cent of the ousanding Federal Reserve bank credit last Wednesday was in the form of borrowings by member banks. Ninety-four per cent consisted of the holding of securities. So you would have to get around to a system really of open-market operations.

Mr. Machlup: Which is the basis of the Triffin plan.

Mr. Bernstein: This is now part of the Triffin plan, but I want to get to lending too. . . .

[Mr. Bernstein then presented the Note on the Triffin plan reprinted in this book, on pp. 198–202.]

Representative Reuss: . . . Mr. Machlup, in your analysis of these various plans you asked but did not answer questions. For example, as to plan D, to increase the price of gold, you asked: "Would this not be a mere trick, cheating those who have been willing to hold dollar balances rather than gold, procuring windfall profits for the Soviet Union and South Africa, and for gold speculators and hoarders?" Well, it would, in fact, whatever its advantage, have those disadvantages, would it not?

Mr. Machlup: Yes, I formulated questions regarding all three types of reform that tackle the long-run problem, questions reflecting the doubts and suspicions in the minds of the bankers. But in this case—regarding the gold price increase—I share their doubts and suspicions, which I do not necessarily do with respect to the other two plans.

Representative Reuss: You then asked a question concerning plan E, the flexible exchange rate plan. Would not this plan be detrimental to commerce and industry if no one could ever be certain how much he would receive for his exports or how much he would have to pay for his imports?

Mr. Machlup: I do not believe that it would be detrimental, because there are two institutions which would avoid that detriment. The one is the institution of the forward market, in which people could at least for current transactions secure a hedge, and therefore know full well what they will get for their exports and what they will have to pay for their imports.

And the second factor is that built into the new system would be the new mentality of the central bankers, that they must not carry on a policy which would lead to intolerable gyrations of the exchange rates.

In other words, this is the transfer of sensitivity of the central banker from watching the reserves to watching the exchange rates. And they would have to carry on a policy that would avoid undue gyrations.

Representative Reuss: I have a question for you, Mr. Johnson. But did you want to comment first?

Mr. Johnson: I want to comment on that. It is usually argued that a fixed rate system with variable reserves puts a great deal of pressure on policy, whereas a floating rate system does not.

I would maintain, on the basis of the Canadian experience, that a floating rate system probably puts more pressure on in the sense that many more people are aware of the exchange rate and fluctuations in it than are aware of fluctuations in the gold reserve. In fact, Canadian experience can be interpreted as an example of monetary mismanagement consisting in the first place of being too pleased when the value of the currency went up, and then panicking when the currency went down.

So the moderation of opinion would have to go the other way rather than the one Professor Machlup is asking.

Representative Reuss: Let me ask your views on a couple of other proposals that have been made. First, is my understanding correct that you share with Mr. Machlup a feeling that the free world is or will shortly be faced with an insufficiency of reserves, and that something ought to be done about it?

Mr. Johnson: Yes, I do.

Representative Reuss: As to that something, I would like your comment on Mr. Bernstein's proposal for integrating IMF quotas in national reserves. Do you favor that? And would it, in your opinion, be adequate to meet future reserve needs?

Mr. Johnson: As to the first part of it, I do favor it, and have favored it since Mr. Bernstein began to suggest it, because it seems to me that if we have this institution, and given that it is easier to develop an existing institution than it is to replace it, this is a logical step to take. I think it does raise some problems concerning the nature of the Fund itself. The Fund was designed to have certain limitations in it which would have to be dropped to achieve this reform, but I think that would be manageable, particularly if Mr. Bernstein is prepared to go around the world saying that it is manageable.

How far this would be adequate, I think, depends very much on his proposal that you should meet reserve needs by increasing quotas. Now this, I think, raises some problems, because if you are really going to meet future reserve needs, you must be prepared to change the relative sizes of the quotas.

I think, also, that because increases in the quotas have to be agreed among the members, you may have the difficulty that you won't get large enough increases or that you will get discontinuous increases of the same sort as you would get if you changed the price of gold, because, if you remember, the last time there was a very large increase in the quotas after the world had had to be convinced that the quotas were not big enough. In that respect, changing the quotas has the same sort of disadvantage as changing the price of gold; it is a discontinuous operation.

I would prefer to see the IMF evolve gradually into a Triffin-type world central bank. It may be that this is the best step toward that. I would have my doubts whether it would be a permanent solution, but as a way of educating world opinion toward the idea of a more rational system of providing reserves than the gold standard, I would be in favor of it.

Representative Reuss: Your proposal, Mr. Bernstein, at least in the streamlined form in which you presented it today, and previously to this committee, does not include the use of any IMF reserve deposit or other piece of paper, negotiable or nonnegotiable, which might, in time, grow into an additional reserve currency—or does it?

Mr. Bernstein: No; it does not. It would, in fact, involve the simple proposition that the quotas in the Fund are reserves. A country that wants dollars, instead of selling a certificate to the Federal Reserve Bank of New York, merely asks the Fund to have the Federal Reserve Bank of New York put dollars into its central bank account. There would be no deposits. The quotas themselves would be the reserves. As they draw them down it would be the same as drawing down deposits, but we would not call them deposits.

The country that draws down the quota would find it has less reserves just as when it draws down a deposit. A country that, so to speak, provides the means for the Fund to meet a drawing quota by another country would have a larger unused quota in the Fund the same as an increase in its reserves. You simply would not call it "deposits."

Representative Reuss: The use of a quota would not be evidenced by any new type of negotiable instrument; it would simply be an open book, a contract.

Mr. Bernstein: It could be carried in a country's own accounts and in the Fund accounts, as is done in any case.

Representative Reuss: And since it could get any currencies it wanted from the Fund, it would not need a note from the Fund to buy them elsewhere, because it would already have them?

Mr. Bernstein: That is right.

Mr. Machlup: May I ask a question of Mr. Bernstein? How would this increase the reserves? Assume quotas have been raised, and each country counts these quotas into its reserves. But now as a country uses its quota, this merely leads to bookkeeping transfers, but not to a regular increase in reserves.

Mr. Bernstein: Integrating the quotas with the working reserves of members—if you did this gradually—would mean that at the end of some time, five years from now, all of the reserves of the world would be equal to gold plus foreign exchange holdings plus quotas of the Fund.

Now, these quotas are transferred from one country to another as they are used. Aggregate reserves are not changed by that; they are not diminished by it; they are not changed.

Representative Reuss: This increases the service of existing reserves through increased mobility.

Mr. Bernstein: First it increases the present reserves you have for payments. But as to the future growth of the reserves, what you would have to do is use the power the Fund has for revising quotas at any time, and a compulsory quinquennial review.

Mr. Johnson is right; the last big increase in quotas was imposed on a reluctant management of the Fund by the demands of a few important members. As a practical matter, it would have been much better not to have increased the quotas at that time so much, but to have moved promptly toward including the existing quotas as part of the working reserves.

If the quotas were now included in the reserves, they would certainly make the reserves very adequate. But in time this pressure will again arise, and you can have much more moderate increases much more frequently.

Representative Reuss: So the real question between three people like yourself, [each one believing] that reserves need in the immediate future to become more readily available, . . . is as to whether it is enough, as Mr. Bernstein suggests, to count IMF quotas and then marshal and mobilize them more efficiently, or whether you actually need an additional source of new reserves over and beyond the national reserves which are created by countries running a deficit.

And I gather that Mr. Bernstein feels that at least his proposal should be tried first before you get into the question of whether you need new sources of reserves.

Mr. Bernstein: If you are going to have a Triffin plan at all, you have to wipe out the quotas in the Fund. I know you can change the Triffin plan all along to meet all objections, and I am all for making these changes, but that does not get rid of the notion that until these changes are accepted there is a deficiency in the plan.

Now, the big deficiency of the Triffin plan, apart from all of its operational deficiencies, which I think would be in practice insoluble, is that it would wipe out all the quotas as they exist today. These quotas do have reserve meaning. You would then have to find the equivalence of it through an enormous increase in credit in the very first few years under the Triffin plan.

In good faith it is going to be very hard to find borrowers under the Triffin plan in any case. The use of open-market operations actually is a device for throwing back on the United States and the United Kingdom, the reserve centers, the creation of reserves for the rest of the world.

I am not sure how much they would want it, particularly if they are under obligation then to repay the new institutions. The Triffin plan does have big deflationary features which would have to be eliminated before you can depend upon the creation of credit as a device for adding reserves for the future.

Representative Reuss: Without getting into details of plans—and as you say, they change before the human eye, so it is sometimes difficult to keep up with them—why could not your plan accommodate itself to a rather prompt next phase in which the IMF does accept deposits from members and issue negotiable instruments? This would be a way of creating new international reserves against the possibility that the reserves created by national methods, by running a balance-of-payments deficit, may not be adequate, because the payments deficits of the key currency countries may not be large enough.

Mr. Bernstein: Congressman, if it makes the thinking easier for anyone on earth, I am perfectly willing to stop using the word "quotas" and say that we will have initial deposits of the International Monetary Fund credited to each country equivalent to its quota, and therefore we will transfer these deposits. There is not any difference.

Representative Reuss: That, however, does not produce any new reserves.

Mr. Bernstein: If the quotas are counted as reserves, the world would have a large increase in reserves over the few years during which the new policy is gradually put into effect. Thereafter, new reserves could only come into being by an increase in these quotas. The Fund would credit each country's account as it increased the quotas. At any given time the use of the quota would not affect aggregate reserves. It would merely transfer quota rights from one country to another.

Now, under any credit scheme, you can increase reserves only if you increase lending more than the repayments. Loans are not made once to stand out forever. In any system in which reserves must grow a billion dollars a year, for example, through loans, there would have to be a vast turnover of these loans. Otherwise the credit given by the institution would be a permanent grant to the initial recipient.

I figure that if the Triffin plan had the same test as the International Monetary Fund, that a credit should be repaid in three years, or five years at the outside, the institution would have to turn over $4 or $5 billion a year in loans, after a few years, to get an annual growth of $1 billion in reserves. And the turnover would have to be much larger the longer the institution operates. That is why we would have to move away from the loan concept altogether to open-market operations. And that would not be easier either.

Representative Reuss: One of your main difficulties with the Triffin proposal, in addition to some of its administrative complexities, is that you fear it is deflationary. Now, let me ask you this question.

What additional features need to be grafted on your proposal presented here this afternoon, your two- or three-step proposal with respect to the IMF, in order to create new reserves?

Mr. Bernstein: No features, except that I have not emphasized that the Fund should from time to time and more frequently than in the past have a review of quotas and increasing them. That is the only feature you would have to add to have a growth of reserves in this form.

Representative Reuss: And if it did review and did find that the free world reserves were inadequate, these additional reserves would be created by methods other than by the countries incurring a balance-of-payments deficit.

Mr. Bernstein: That is right.

Representative Reuss: They would be created in effect by a stroke of the pen, would they not; that is to say, countries would not have even to put in their own currency in the full amount of the new quota?

Mr. Bernstein: It would not matter whether they did or not. The fact is, the statement you made is that the reserves would be created by mutual credit. You would be giving credit not to one borrower, but everybody would get simultaneously a mutual credit. And this would be a permanent mutual credit.

The only condition would be that the country must in fact use this as a reserve, drawing it down and replenishing it, and not use it as a source of capital. It would be a creation of credit in a sense, certainly. That is the only way you could define it in economical terms.

Representative Reuss: Why is this not a very simple way of proceeding, your plan plus this paragraph? Why does not this have within it the capability of supplying the free world with the reserves that are needed irrespective of how much gold is mined?

Mr. Bernstein: I am not an unbiased witness on this. You had better ask a witness who finds that this does not do the job.

Representative Reuss: Yes; really I will. I will ask Mr. Machlup.

Mr. Machlup: Well, I am delighted that Mr. Bernstein clarified his plan now to make it quite certain that these increased quotas are really a creation of credit. I think these words do not appear as clearly in his previous writings, and indeed the use of the old terminology—quotas rather than deposits—lends support to a misinterpretation of his plan.

Representative Reuss: But as we now have it—and we all heard it very clearly——

Mr. Bernstein: There is nothing in the statement, by the way, that you have today which has not appeared in any number of the papers I have written.

Mr. Machlup: Don't be so modest.

Representative Reuss: Gentlemen, we should not bog down on who said what when. I think the question is—the proposal enunciated here by Mr. Bernstein with the added paragraph that we have just discussed—why does that not do what needs to be done?

Mr. Machlup: If it is to be a feasible proposal, I would like to make the reserve increase a year-by-year proposition, not a quinquennial or even biennial one.

Representative Reuss: As needed?

Mr. Machlup: No, not as needed. This would be difficult to decide, because who knows what is needed?

The question is whether we should use some rule of thumb, or whether we should use discretion. I do not think we can solve it this afternoon. But if you say "as needed," there is again the danger that we wait for a crisis.

Mr. Bernstein: We can do both things, we can do what Professor Machlup said, do it a little bit steadily, and then if you have a crisis, do an extra little bit at that time.

Representative Reuss: Mr. Johnson.

Mr. Johnson: I think it is becoming clear, Congressman, that there is some difficulty in understanding Mr. Bernstein's proposal because it has two separate elements in it.

One is simply to make the present IMF arrangement more acceptable. At present it is a borrowing right that is subject to restrictions. He wants to remove those restrictions so that the borrowing rights can be freely used. That part of his plan, I think, corresponds with other suggestions to the effect that the arrangements by which central banks will lend to each other should be made more automatic, so that the credit should be available on demand rather than subject to approval. As long as it is subject to approval, then countries will not count the asset as equivalent to reserves they actually have in their own hands. Now, that is a change in the nature of the Fund.

The second part of it is the provision of extra reserves by increasing quotas. And here I think the objection that Professor Machlup and I have is that as the Fund now operates, quotas are increased at widespread intervals and by large amounts. And they are increased by amounts which are determined by how the major countries feel at that particular time. He and I would both like to see the reserves increased gradually rather than at widespread intervals, and in a fashion which depends less on whether there is a crisis situation or lack of it and more on some concept of what the world needs to support an expanding trade and payments structure.

In his last statement I think Mr. Bernstein has come very close to our position.

Mr. Bernstein: Yes.

Representative Reuss: I think on this——

Mr. Humphrey: Do you want to ask a question about the feasibility of this composite currency, where the relations are tied? We have had no discussions as to that. And I think if some of the panel can comment on it we would be glad to have it. We had the suggestion of a composite currency in which the various parts of it have to be rigidly tied. Is this a feasible——

Mr. Machlup: I will take the question, if you would like me to. I would say it is a feasible plan, provided that the participating countries observe an unusual degree of discipline, which will deprive them of as much sovereignty in the use of monetary policy for internal affairs as the old gold standard did, if not more so. And I cannot see why any nation that has in the past resisted the fetters of the gold standard would accept the fetters of this multicurrency-bound scheme.

Mr. Bernstein: Excuse me. I may not have been clear. Is it understood that these funds would be transferable only among the eleven countries?

We are not proposing—these eleven countries are not proposing to impose on, say, Brazil, the acceptance of the multicurrency units. Suppose Brazil has dollars it wants to convert. It would not get the gold plus these currency units; it would get gold if it wants it. It is only these eleven countries. So no country has to accept a standard under which it ties its currency, so to speak, to these units. These eleven countries would do it by themselves.

Mr. Johnson: We can put Professor Machlup's point another way which I think is more graphic.

We have two problems: One is that there is not enough gold to enable all countries to hold the amount of gold they want. And the other is that they are not really prepared to trust each other's currencies as substitutes for gold, and probably quite rightly, given that every country has the freedom to change its exchange rates.

What this proposal amounts to is a piece of gadgetry designed (*a*) to reduce the demand for gold, and (*b*) to make countries hold each other's currency, hold it in bundles containing some of everything. It is like buying a unit in an investment trust, or something like that.

And I think Professor Machlup and I both feel that you cannot really solve these basic difficulties of too little gold and distrust of each other's currencies by this kind of gadgetry unless you have got enough agreement to enable you to adopt a simpler solution such as a world currency, or a new credit reserve currency acceptable by these countries.

Representative Reuss: Why is that simpler? It seems to be equally good, but no better.

Mr. Johnson: Well, if you were smart enough to realize that this is what you had to do, you would be smart enough to accept the simple solution instead of a piece of gadgetry of this kind. That is our contention.

Mr. Bernstein: Mr. Johnson may well be speaking for both of them, and in that case my reply would go to both equally. May I make this point: The concept—first, calling it gadgetry seems to me —

Mr. Johnson: I said I was going to be graphic.

Mr. Bernstein: Seems to me to be a very graphic way of describing a very modest change, really, in the institutional arrangements that exist. But my question is this: If any country is going to be hesitant among these eleven in holding as a reserve these composite currency units of the eleven richest countries in the world, what makes you think that you could ever persuade these countries to hold as reserves, for which they give real resources, deposits in an international unit, a central bank whose assets, corresponding to the reserve liabilities, consist of credits that it has given to any number of countries, none of which is likely to be as good as these eleven, and which holds bonds originating from loans to countries in perpetual financial trouble?

This is one of the difficulties of our present institutional arrangement. We live in a world in which countries hesitate to hold dollars and sterling as reserves—and maybe properly; I do not think so, but maybe properly.

Now we have proposed to these countries, "You have difficulty in swallowing more dollars and sterling as reserves; we are going to give you an easier pill to swallow." It is an international unit whose real assets consist of loans to any number of countries, and of bonds purchased so that they can simultaneously develop and in the course of spending provide reserves for the rich countries.

It is my feeling that if Mr. Johnson and Mr. Machlup think it will be hard for any countries to accept the holding of these eleven currencies, I cannot see how it will be possible to get them to accept the international currency unit based on operations of such an international institution.

Representative Reuss: Mr. Johnson, do you want to comment on that?

Mr. Johnson: If this argument of Mr. Bernstein's were all this convincing, then everyone in this country would never hold a deposit in an individual bank, but would instead insist on having a deposit distributed among all the different banks, because that would save them from the risk involved in the assets chosen by any particular bank. In other words, if you are going to use credit money, you will have to start by accepting that you are depending on the trust and the capacity of those who create the credit to do it wisely. And I do not think you can get around that need by parceling things up in bundles and saying, "There you are, there is a bundle that saves us from risk."

It will not save you from risk unless the fundamental conditions are present. And if you are prepared to assume that they are, you might as well have what I consider a more efficient way of doing it.

Representative Reuss: Perhaps I should have adjourned the hearing about five minutes ago when there was complete harmony prevailing between the members of the panel. But I think we did pretty well, and I am very grateful to you all for the distinct contribution that you have made to our deliberations. . . .

23

Recommendations of Six Brookings Experts

· · ·

THE PRESENT DILEMMA

The balance-of-payments deficit . . . is not the major source of the international financial problem of the United States. That problem consists of the constraints imposed on the United States in its efforts to attain the more basic objectives of policy. It is the changed position of the dollar —the loss of foreigners' desire to continue accumulating dollars—which imposes these constraints. While balance-of-payments deficits have undoubtedly accentuated this change in the last few years, they are not its sole cause, and their elimination would not restore the dollar's position as virtually the only hard currency in a soft-currency world.

When a country performs a banking and depositary role, the relation between its balance-of-payments position and the strength of its currency is not so direct as is commonly assumed. The Swiss franc continues to be a strong currency, although the deficit in the Swiss balance of payments is much larger in relation to gross national product than that of the United States. Similarly, the dollar was strong during the early and middle 1950's despite U.S. deficits. Its recent weakness, as we have explained, reflects the growing strength of European economies and other irreversible changes, as well as the impact of larger U.S. deficits. While a prolonged period of surpluses would strengthen the dollar, it would not restore the dollar to the unique position it enjoyed in the first postwar decade. Unless U.S. surpluses are so large and persistent that they undermine confidence in other currencies, the special demand for dollars that reflected lack of confidence in other currencies will not reappear, and the dollar will continue to be only one among several strong national currencies.

Reprinted in slightly condensed form from *The United States Balance of Payments in 1968* (The Brookings Institution, Washington, D.C., 1963) by Walter S. Salant and Emile Despres, Lawrence B. Krause, Alice M. Rivlin, William A. Salant, Lorie Tarshis. This volume is a revised version of a report submitted to the Council of Economic Advisers and is reprinted through the courtesy of The Brookings Institution. The findings and conclusions of the study are those of the authors and do not purport to represent the views of the other staff members, officers, or trustees of The Brookings Institution.

Moreover, under present international monetary arrangements, a U.S. surplus may be difficult, if not impossible, to attain. The forces making for improvement in the U.S. balance of payments will cause a deterioration in Western Europe's payment position. At the same time, with decreasing deficits, the United States will be contributing decreasing amounts to the growth of Western European international reserves. Faced with increasing balance-of-payments pressures and reserves which they are reluctant to see reduced, Western European countries probably would take measures to cut their imports and to restrain demand—even at the cost of slower growth— and to restrict foreign aid. Such measures might succeed in preventing the development of a U.S. surplus. More important, however, is the fact that neither large Western European deficits nor the measures of retrenchment which the deficit countries might take to forestall or correct them are in the basic interest of the United States.

The United States thus faces a dilemma. On the one hand, U.S. balance-of-payments deficits make the rest of the world increasingly reluctant to go on accumulating liquid dollar claims, and they hamper pursuit by the United States of vital domestic and international objectives. On the other hand, large and sustained surpluses may not be attainable; even if attained, they would not be desirable since they might not free the United States from undesirable constraints and they would impose constraints on other Free World countries.

Nor would a continuing state of approximate balance in U.S. payments be satisfactory. Even if the United States could maintain a balanced position, the effort to do so would not free it from constraints in pursuing other objectives. At the same time, the expansion of international liquidity would not keep up with the world's needs, so that constraints and pressures on other countries would increase. The most that can be said for such a delicate state of balance, even if it could be achieved, is that it probably would be less unsatisfactory than either substantial U.S. deficits or substantial U.S. surpluses.

Thus, no position of the balance of payments—whether surplus, deficit, or balance—would simultaneously free the United States from undesirable constraints and provide for needed expansion of international monetary reserves. It is clear, therefore, that the present problem is not primarily a balance-of-payments problem. More fundamentally, the problem is the basic inadequacy of the international monetary mechanism in relation to requirements of the Free World.

This inadequacy stems from a combination of two circumstances. First, the major advanced countries are not likely to be faced with persistent imbalances arising from deficiencies or excesses of aggregate demand. Their imbalances are more likely to result from structural factors, such as changes in technology, competitive position, relative productivity (sometimes in an important individual industry), or the structure of world demand for a country's products. When deficits or surpluses in international payments result from such factors, the affected countries have no means of eliminating the imbalance quickly without jeopardizing domestic economic growth, price stability, or other vital objectives.

Second, the existing monetary mechanism does not provide enough liquidity to enable countries to finance deficits over periods long enough to reach equilibrium by using the much slower means that do not jeopardize vital objectives. Since 1950, the greater part of the increase in international reserves has taken the form of liquid dollar claims. This method of increasing reserves can no longer be depended on, because neither the United States nor any other country willing to allow its currency to be used as international reserves can be confident that the holders will keep their reserves in the form of its currency over a long period; they are likely to fear conversion into gold or other currencies.

Countries whose currencies are held by others, therefore, tend to regard increases in liquid liabilities as almost equivalent to losses of gold. The result is an excessive preoccupation in the advanced countries with balance-of-payments objectives to the exclusion of far more important goals of national and international policy. As the volume of international transactions expands, this problem is likely to become worse. If the U.S. deficit is eliminated and the growth of reserves becomes dependent solely on the increase of monetary gold stocks, the inadequacy of international liquidity will become increasingly acute; the preoccupation with balances of payments probably will override considerations that are fundamentally more important.

. . .

THE NEED TO IMPROVE THE INTERNATIONAL
MONETARY MECHANISM

The present international monetary system is essentially a system of quasi-fixed exchange rates with international reserves held in gold and national currencies (principally dollars and sterling). The price of gold in terms of dollars is fixed, and other currencies are pegged to the dollar, thereby providing a fixed structure of exchange rates among various currencies. The pegs are adjustable, however. Adjustments have been made with sufficient frequency in the postwar period to keep the possibilities of further changes alive in the minds of central banks and private owners of capital.

In our view, fixity of exchange rates is a virtue. Fixed rates remove much of the uncertainty which would otherwise be inherent in international movements of goods, services, and capital. They tend to increase the volume of trade and productive international investment, thus contributing to efficient use of world resources and to economic welfare. The more certain it is that the rates will be maintained, the greater are these advantages. If confidence in the maintenance of exchange rates becomes firmly established, it is likely that the process of adjusting balances between countries will begin to resemble more closely adjustment among different regions of a single country, in which equilibrating movements of capital induced by small differences in interest rates play a major role. Such a development, although involving some loss of national autonomy in monetary policy, would ease the adjustment process. In addition, by increasing the economic interdependence of the Free World countries, it may tend to increase their political cohesion. We believe, therefore, that the present system of fixed exchange rates should be strengthened so as to preserve and enhance its advantages and mitigate its disadvantages.

The main disadvantage of the fixed rate system as it now exists is that it requires countries whose payments are not in balance to restore balance more rapidly than may be consistent with important domestic and international objectives. The speed at which a payments imbalance can be eliminated without endangering such objectives depends on its cause. One class of imbalances results from excesses or deficiencies of demand induced by inflation or deflation in individual countries. Although imbalances of this class call for prompt adjustment, they no longer occur frequently in the advanced industrial countries. Contracyclical policies are reasonably effective in preventing deflation; the internal objective of price stability is, in most of these countries, an effective restraint on inflation caused by excess demand.

The other class—and the most frequent cause of serious imbalances in these countries—is structural change. Under liberal trading conditions and freedom of international capital movements, and with increasing similarity in the patterns of demand and output in the large countries, structural changes must be expected to cause larger imbalances than they formerly did. Moreover, in an increasingly dynamic world, the pace of structural change must be expected to increase. Under these conditions, it will be quite unwarranted to assume that large deficits necessarily call for drastic action designed to restore payments equilibrium quickly. Imbalances caused by structural changes call for structural adjustments—shifts in the use of capital and labor with a view to changing the pattern of production, expansion, or modernization of the capital stock in particular industries, or other measures which require several years to be effective. They require time, not drastic action aimed at achieving an immediate result.

The great danger of a system of fixed exchange rates operated with the existing and foreseeable level of reserves is that it does not permit deficits to be financed long enough to make the kind of adjustments that are most often neded. Deflationary measures, the classical means of improving the balance of payments, cut employment and real incomes—effects which are neither politically feasible nor economically desirable in a modern industrial country. In the United States, large absolute reductions in real income cause only small decreases in imports, and these decreases are partly offset by decreases in exports, so that very substantial declines in total production and income are necessary to induce relatively small improvements in the net balance of payments. Furthermore, higher interest rates, while discouraging domestic investment, may not be effective in attracting capital to a weak currency when strong currencies are available.

Measures to reduce imports by raising tariffs or imposing other trade restrictions are equally undesirable for reasons which hardly need to be re-emphasized. So are direct controls on capital movements and cuts in foreign aid and government spending abroad for defense and other purposes. Nor is it desirable for advanced creditor countries which are having balance-of-payments difficulties to transfer to primary producing countries their burden of payments adjustment by curtailing lending to those countries.

The combination of the normal fixity of exchange rates with the possibility that they will be changed when an imbalance has persisted long enough to be judged fundamental makes rapid adjustment especially difficult. The possibility that a weak currency will be devalued discourages equilibrating capital movements and fosters disequilibrating movements, and does so at all times, not merely in times of crisis. By doing so, it reinforces the basic factors originally responsible for the currency's weakness. Disequilibrating capital movements cannot be counteracted by small differences in interest rates, because such differences have no effect when there is no confidence that the parity will be maintained. Moreover, when the authorities decide to devalue—either because they wish to or because they can no longer withstand the pressure on the currency—they are usually eager to convince the market that the new exchange rate can be held. One way to accomplish this purpose is to make the devaluation so great that no one will doubt that the new rate can be maintained. As a result, currencies which have been overvalued before their parities are altered are likely to be undervalued afterward. Thus, the adjustable peg system has these disadvantages: the efforts to defend an exchange rate are complicated by speculation; devaluations are likely to be too long delayed; and devaluations are likely to be excessive when they are finally made.

If an international payments system is to provide the benefits of fixed parities without these disadvantages, it must generate confidence in the fixity of the parities. Given greater liquidity, confidence in the fixity of parities would probably develop, because it would gradually be recognized that enough time was available to restore equilibrium in the payments of the major countries without revaluation of their currencies.

The belief that balance-of-payments adjustments at fixed parities are possible if enough time is available rests on several considerations. First, some imbalances are caused by random or cyclical developments which are likely to average out over sufficiently long periods, even in the absence of corrective governmental policies.

Second, some imbalances result from shifts in the competitive position of major national industries, resulting in losses of exports or increases in imports. These competitive challenges often induce competitive responses, although these responses may take several years to affect the balance of payments. The response of the U.S. automobile industry to the challenge of foreign cars is an example.

Third, these competitive responses can be supplemented by government policies to stimulate investment in export and import-competing industries and thus to improve a country's competitive position. Substantial increases of investment in such industries, whether induced by competition or by government policy, often take several years to be effective. In fact, if they are not offset by reductions in other forms of expenditure on goods and services, they may temporarily increase deficits and require several years to be effective in reducing them.

Fourth, the international transactions of governments are now a large component of total international transactions. Given a reasonable degree of international cooperation, without which any system is in danger of breaking down, it should be possible to adjust some of these transactions gradually in ways that reduce imbalances.

Fifth, although money wage rates can be reduced in industrial countries only at the cost of increased unemployment and slower growth, a country with a deficit can reduce the general level of money costs per unit of output slowly over time by preventing the general level of its money wage rates from increasing as fast as output per man-hour. If these reductions in money costs are not completely offset by increases in profits, a country can improve its competitive position, provided that prices in competitor countries do not fall as rapidly. This proviso suggests the desirability of international cooperation regarding cost and price policies.

Sixth, after the fixity of exchange rates is assured, countries that can pursue flexible fiscal policies can correct imbalances without reducing domestic output or inflating the domestic price level. They can do so by changing interest rates relative to those abroad and offsetting the domestic effect of such changes by fiscal policy.

It is to be noted, however, that nearly all these forms of adjustment require time to be effective. In a world in which internal adjustments cannot be made quickly without sacrificing objectives more important than balance in international payments, a system of fixed exchange rates can work only if long periods are allowed for the adjustments to take place.

THE CHARACTERISTICS OF A SATISFACTORY INTERNATIONAL MONETARY MECHANISM

An international monetary system which enables countries to restore balance-of-payments equilibrium slowly over periods of several years must have the following characteristics:

1. *It must provide enough liquidity at the outset to finance substantial imbalances while adjustments are taking place, and it must provide for increases in liquidity as the need for liquidity grows.* Liquidity need not take the form entirely of reserves owned by the countries to whom it is available. It can be provided wholly or partly in the form of drawing rights, support extended to deficit countries by surplus countries, or other credit facilities extended either directly or through international institutions. In any case, because imbalances arising both from persistent and stubborn shifts in basic transactions and from short-term capital movements are potentially quite large and are likely to grow, the increases in international reserves and other forms of liquidity must be substantial.

2. *Additional liquidity which takes the form of credit should be available readily and promptly, and for a period long enough to permit elimination of the deficit.* Substantial amounts should be obtainable automatically by deficit countries. By agreement, additional amounts should be made available to countries with particularly intractable balance-of-payments problems if appropriate measures for dealing with these problems are being taken. Preferably, the amounts available automatically should take the form of open-account facilities with ceilings, within which there should be no fixed repayment dates. The discretionary amounts should be repayable on terms that reflect a realistic assessment of the time required to bring the balance of payments into adjustment.

3. *The possibility of shifting reserves from weak to strong currencies must be prevented.* If additional reserves were held in national currencies, this possibility would be a continuing source of instability and would impose constraints on the countries whose currencies were used as reserves. Avoiding these constraints would require an agreement under which countries with strong currencies would support weak currencies by maintaining or, if necessary, increasing their holdings of the weak currencies. Such an agreement would have to be accompanied by guaranties of the values of the reserve currencies. Even then, any deficit country that avoided reserve losses by incurring increased liquid liabilities to others would be likely to regard the increases in these liabilities in the same way that it now regards reserve losses. It would thus feel the very constraints which an improved system should seek to eliminate. These problems would be avoided if industrial countries committed themselves to hold a substantial fraction of their reserves in an international institution, with creditor countries accumulating credits denominated in an international unit of account and debtor countries accumulating similarly denominated debits or reducing previously acquired credits.

4. *For such a system—or indeed for any system—to work, it is probably necessary that the principal financial and industrial countries consult fully and frequently and coordinate policies that have substantial effects on international payments.* This consultation and coordination is likely to be particularly necessary in view of the magnitude of imbalances that are likely to develop. It should include wage and price and commercial policies as well as monetary and fiscal policies.

The main objection often made to providing additional liquidity, especially if it is available unconditionally, is that countries may use the resulting leeway to indulge in inflationary excesses without fear of running into payments difficulties. This danger cannot be completely discounted. Nevertheless, the advanced industrial countries have increasingly recognized the dislocations caused by rising prices and have developed a disposition to curb inflationary developments on purely domestic grounds. The additional discipline provided by the balance of payments is indiscriminate in its application; it induces restraint without regard to whether internal conditions call for restraint or expansion. While it adds something to the disposition of advanced countries to curb internal inflation, its benefits in such situations are far less than the social costs it imposes when domestic expansion is needed.

A second objection to the provision of additional liquidity is that it would permit countries to continue misallocation of resources and deprive them of the stimulus to improve productivity. To the extent that deficits result from the loss of export markets, however, the decline of profits resulting from their loss gives business firms ample incentive to develop new products and to increase efficiency, whether or not more liquidity is provided. In fact, countries that seek to eliminate deficits quickly without incurring the social costs of otherwise undesired monetary and fiscal restriction usually resort to import restrictions, exchange controls, and similar devices. Such measures worsen, rather than improve, the allocation of resources and reduce incentives to increase productivity. Deflationary measures also restrict investment and hamper modernization and innovation. Indeed, since efforts to improve resource allocation and increase efficiency usually require several years to be effective, and are more likely to be made in an atmosphere of general expansion and unrestricted foreign competition, they are remedies that argue in favor of, rather than against, the provision of additional liquidity.

We do not suggest that the developing countries be included in any arrangements for additional reserves or automatic access to credit facilities. Their balance-of-payments problems are very real and pressing, but they are of a long-term character and cannot be solved by mere increases in liquidity. In these countries, import demand chronically outruns ability to import, either for monetary and fiscal or for structural reasons. Thus, the key problem is the amount of aid which the advanced countries should provide to finance imports of goods and services by these countries, since the financing they provide will be used to purchase imports rather than to accumulate reserves.

If an adequate system of international liquidity is developed, it should be possible to dispense with changes in exchange parities, and to replace the adjustable peg system with permanently fixed parities. It will take a number of years, of course, to demonstrate the effectiveness of the system and to build up confidence in the permanence of the parities.

When that confidence has been established, a further useful step would be a widening of the limits around the par values within which the actual market rates are allowed to fluctuate. The limited fluctuations of exchange rates permitted by such a widening of the support points would have a number of advantages. First, they would give rise to capital movements which, under the conditions specified, would be stabilizing rather than destabilizing and would reduce the need for using official reserves and credit facilities. Second, they would permit greater variability in short-term interest rates among countries than would be possible with absolutely fixed market exchange rates, thus permitting somewhat greater national autonomy in monetary policies. Finally, even the limited variation in exchange rates possible with support points of 2 per cent to 3 per cent on either side of parity would be helpful in promoting balance-of-payments adjustment. Among industrial countries producing similar products, price elasticities in international trade over periods of several years can be expected to be high, so that small changes in exchange rates would have considerable influence on trade balances.

. . .

MEASURES TO IMPROVE THE ARRANGEMENTS FOR INTERNATIONAL LIQUIDITY

A major effort of the U.S. government in the next two or three years should be directed toward achieving an adequate international liquidity mechanism. The immediate task is to formulate a plan which meets the criteria for a satisfactory system. The next task is to seek international agreement on such a plan. While early agreement is desirable, it must be recognized that it may be difficult to obtain. The major Free World countries will have to relinquish part of their freedom to choose the form in which their international reserves are held.

The freedom of choice provided by the present system is more apparent than real, however, and that fact may make agreement on a new system easier. Under today's conditions, Western European countries are maintaining or expanding their dollar holdings not because of their own preferences, but rather to provide support to the dollar and avoid destroying the dollar exchange standard. The case for replacing this type of stopgap international cooperation with more solid institutional arrangements for expanding liquidity is strong. Western European countries, however, are not likely to be receptive to U.S. proposals which seem to be little more than an invitation to commit themselves more irrevocably and firmly to propping up the present dollar exchange standard. They no longer desire to keep accumulating dollars unless guaranteed against exchange losses. If the United States wishes to gain European support for an expanded international liquidity arrangement, therefore, its proposals must take this attitude into account. Institutional arrangements should be proposed that will permit the liquid claims of surplus countries and the liabilities of deficit countries to be denominated in an international unit of account, either with the IMF or with a new international payments union associated with it.

Thus, to obtain agreement on an international liquidity system may well require curtailing the role of the dollar as a reserve currency and transferring part of this function to an international organization. Such an outcome should not be unwelcome to the United States. It is true that the United States as well as other countries benefited from the use of the dollar as a reserve currency in the early postwar period. By supplementing the world's limited supplies of gold, dollar reserves facilitated the growth of world trade and payments. In the 1950's, the willingness of other countries to increase their dollar holdings enabled the United States to finance deficits with relatively small gold losses. Now that the dollar is no longer the only strong currency, however, the United States feels acutely constrained by the possibility that countries holding their reserves in dollars may switch to other currencies or gold. On balance, the reserve-currency function has become a burden, rather than a benefit, to the United States. If the reserve-holding function can be performed in some other way, the United States should be glad to lay down the burden.

The creation of an international payments union would not mean the end of the role of the dollar as a reserve currency in areas where this role is still appropriate. Canada, Japan, and most Latin American countries would undoubtedly wish to hold their reserves largely in dollars because of the closeness of their commercial and financial ties with the United States. Indeed, since these countries look chiefly to the United States for external financial support, the United States should seek commitments from them to hold the bulk of their reserves in dollar balances. Thus, a clearly definable dollar area would be established, with the United States performing the depositary function as well as the lending function for this group

of countries. The financial relationship between the United States and
Western Europe is different; it is not a relationship of one-way dependence,
but of reciprocal interdependence. It would be inappropriate, therefore,
for the United States to seek the same commitments from these countries.
It is burdensome, however, for the United States to continue performing
the depositary role for Western European reserves without such commitments. For this reason, the United States should welcome the conversion
of European reserve holdings of dollars into balances with an international
institution.

The United States should persist in its efforts to obtain agreement as
long as necessary. In particular, it must resist any tendency to lose interest
as its balance of payments improves and the dollar becomes stronger. Since
agreement may be difficult to reach while the United States is in substantial
deficit, hope of agreement should not be given up while there is a prospect
that the U.S. deficit will disappear.

AN ALTERNATIVE INTERNATIONAL MONETARY MECHANISM

If it becomes clear that agreement on a satisfactory liquidity mechanism cannot be obtained, the United States must seek an alternative.

We have already stated why a one-step devaluation of the dollar is not
desirable as a means of dealing with the balance-of-payments deficit. Also
it is not a desirable way of improving the international monetary mechanism. While such a devaluation, if accompanied by corresponding devaluations of other currencies, would result in a one-step increase in the money
value of the world's gold stock, it might add little to total world liquidity,
even in the short run. Some gold might be released from private hoards as
holders took steps to realize their capital gains. But, on balance, it seems
likely that devaluation would make individuals and central banks more
reluctant than they are now to hold liquid assets in the form of dollars and
other national currencies and more inclined to hold gold. In any case,
although devaluation would probably give some stimulus to gold production, this would not provide continuing growth in liquidity commensurate
with world needs. Moreover, the benefits of devaluation would be distributed unequally and capriciously among countries. In sum, devaluation
might seriously impair the operation of the existing monetary mechanism
and would not put anything better in its place.

We also reject the alternative of using comprehensive controls over
imports of goods and services and over capital movements in order to

maintain a fixed exchange rate, although this does not exclude the possibility of informal restraints on U.S. purchases of new issues of Western European securities. The substantial economic and political costs involved in such a reversal of postwar policy would exceed any gains it could yield.

The best alternative to a system of fixed rates with provision for increasing liquidity, in our view, would be a modified system of flexible exchange rates consisting of a dollar-sterling bloc and an EEC bloc. There would be relatively fixed rates within each bloc and flexible rates between them. Adoption of this system would imply cutting the tie between gold and the dollar.

In contrast to a fixed-rate system, a system of flexible rates has the advantage that both the short-run competitive position can be changed and the longer-run structural adjustments can be made without general deflation of money costs in deficit countries and general inflation in surplus countries. A reduction in the value of a deficit country's currency reduces the prices of its exportable goods in foreign currencies, thereby encouraging foreign demand for them and raising their prices in its own currency. The rise in the domestic price reduces the domestic market for them, releasing more of existing supplies for export. It also raises the prices of imported goods in the national currency, discouraging their importation and shifting domestic demand toward domestically produced goods and services. Thus the competitive position of the deficit country can be improved rapidly without deflation. The reverse changes occur in surplus countries without inflation.

The changes in demand and prices which occur under flexible rates also facilitate the necessary longer-run structural adjustments. In a deficit country, resources are attracted to production of exportable goods and import-competing goods because their prices rise more than those of domestic goods. Under fixed rates this incentive to shift resources occurs only through deflation of the general price level, with smaller downward pressure on the absolute prices of internationally traded and import-competing goods and services than on other goods and services. A flexible rate program avoids the adverse effects that downward pressures on prices have on output in all sectors. So long as the country whose currency declines in value maintains fiscal and monetary policies that prevent prices from rising as much as its exchange rate falls, it can make the necessary structural adjustments without the destructive consequences of general deflation.

Since there appears to be little need to adjust the exchange rate between the dollar and the pound, it should be possible for the United Kingdom and the United States to agree on arrangements for mutual currency support. With such arrangements, the present rate between their currencies could be maintained indefinitely, the present restrictions on the outflow of British and sterling area capital could be removed, and the British and U.S. capital markets could be integrated. Such cooperation would be in the interests of both countries. Countries whose economies are closely aligned to the United States and the United Kingdom—those in the Western Hemisphere and Scandinavia, most of those in Asia and the Middle East, and some in Africa—would probably want to peg their currencies to the dollar-pound.

Within Western Europe, the logic of economic integration demands that fixed parities be maintained among the members of the European Economic Community, a fixity which they could easily effectuate. Countries whose economies are closely aligned to the EEC—such as Austria, Greece, Switzerland, North Africa, and the French Community—would presumably wish to tie their currencies to those of the EEC, which could be done through cooperation of the appropriate monetary authorities. The only significant fluctuations, therefore, would be in the rates between the dollar-sterling bloc on the one hand and the Western European bloc on the other. Violent changes in these exchange rates would be prevented by intervention of the stabilization authorities in the foreign exchange markets. In practice, we would expect the range of these fluctuations to be limited.

There are many advantages to recommend this modified flexible exchange rate system. Primarily, it would allow the United States to pursue most of its national objectives without undesirable balance-of-payments constraints. The United States would enjoy greater national autonomy in the use of fiscal policy, since the external consequences of such policies would be offset by movements in the exchange rate. The fluctuations in themselves would provide a mechanism through which basic imbalance between currency blocs could be corrected.

Such a flexible exchange rate system would also reduce the need for international reserves. A deficit country would no longer need substantial reserves to relieve pressures on its exchange rate. Support for its currency would automatically be provided by the surplus countries of its own bloc. If a whole bloc were in deficit, the surplus countries of the other bloc would be induced to enter the market in support of the weak currencies to prevent unwanted appreciation of their own currencies. Although this system could be adversely affected by destabilizing speculation, such speculation would probably be smaller than under the present system of adjustable pegs with inadequate liquidity. With flexible rates, speculation would involve the risk of substantial loss as well as the prospect of substantial gain. Moreover, the central banks of the major countries, acting in cooperation, could easily counter the pressure of destabilizing speculation. Cooperation would be forthcoming because both appreciating and depreciating countries have an interest in preventing the exchange rate from reflecting destabilizing speculative forces.

One objection sometimes made to a flexible exchange rate for the dollar is that the maintenance of the present gold parity and the present exchange rates between the dollar and other currencies are essential to U.S. national power or prestige. We think this view mistaken. The power and prestige of the United States derive in large degree from its economic strength and vigor, which in turn depend on its high productive potential and its success in using that potential. Failure to maintain the present gold parity would do far less to damage U.S. prestige than continued failure of the economy to operate at or near capacity. One of the most striking lessons of international currency experience since World War I is that countries which have sacrificed basic national objectives in order to maintain overvalued parities have suffered major economic losses and in the end have failed to maintain the rates. If the United States sacrificed needed domestic production in an effort to maintain the dollar exchange rate in the face of continuing balance-of-payments deficits and inadequate provision for international liquidity, it would lose power and prestige, as well as the output that it could otherwise have produced.

Nevertheless, there are some true costs in adopting our second-best two-bloc proposal. The volume of international trade and capital movements between the members of the two blocs would probably be smaller than under a system of fixed parities with adequate provision for international liquidity. While the costs to traders of fluctuation in exchange rates would be tolerable as long as there was an active forward exchange market, the discouraging effects might still be substantial. Some unity and cohesion of the Free World might therefore be sacrificed. That is why we regard the two-bloc system as inferior to a system of fixed parities with adequate provision for liquidity. We believe its cost to be less, however, than that of any alternative that would be available if the improved fixed parity system could not be attained. The two-bloc system would eliminate the deflationary bias inherent in fixed rates with inadequate liquidity. It would contribute to fuller use of productive capacity and more rapid economic growth so that, despite the impediment of rate flexibility, world trade might be larger than under the present system.

CONCLUSIONS

The major policy recommendation of this report is that the United States seek agreement on an international payments mechanism that permits the achievement of the important goals of national and international policy. If the balance of payments is not to be a perverse constraint, the nation needs a means whereby the balance-of-payments disturbances can be adjusted without compromising these goals. We believe that, given sufficient time, adjustments can be brought about under a fixed rate system without sacrifice of high priority objectives through the normal working of market forces, supplemented, where necessary, by governmental policies consistent with a free society. The lack of an adequate international liquidity mechanism unduly limits the time available for making such adjustments. To overcome this deficiency, we advocate that the United States seek an adequate liquidity mechanism.

If such a mechanism should prove to be unobtainable, we recommend as the best alternative the adoption of a modified flexible exchange rate system. This would be the least harmful means of obtaining international balance if it were not possible to develop a fixed exchange rate system with adequate provision for liquidity.

24

After the Gold Exchange Standard?

ROBERT TRIFFIN

One of the most persistent challenges that confront mankind is that of readjusting outworn institutions and modes of thought to ever-changing needs and conditions. The failure to do so in time is responsible for many of the economic disasters, internal revolutions, and international wars that litter its long history. In the political and military fields, it threatens us today with an atomic war which might provide indeed for all our problems a "final solution" disturbingly reminiscent of another "final solution" for which Mr. Eichmann is now standing trial in Tel-Aviv.

BACKGROUND

Vain Attempts to Resurrect the 1914 Gold Standard

The same anachronisms and absurdities extend to an area in which traditional wizardry should not be lightly equated with wisdom: the area of our international monetary institutions and policies. It would seem somewhat paradoxical and ludicrous to claim that the most rational and economic system of international settlements conceivable in this second half of the twentieth century consists in digging holes, at immense cost, in distant corners of the earth for the sole purpose of extracting gold from them, transporting it across the oceans and reburying it immediately afterwards in other deep holes, especially excavated to receive it and heavily guarded to protect it. Yet, we have, ever since 1914, devoted our best efforts to resurrecting the corpse of the old gold standard as the only realistic alternative to the international monetary chaos that marked most of the last half-century.

The first restoration of convertibility, in the late 1920's, collapsed after

This article is reprinted from the *Weltwirtschaftliches Archiv*, Band 87, 1961, Heft 2, through the courtesy of the author and the publisher.

a few fitful years only, under the first onslaught of the world depression. The second restoration of convertibility is less than two and a half years old. And already the gold panic of last October, the dollar crisis of last fall and winter, the still developing sterling crisis have brought out into the open the fragility and vulnerability of an international monetary structure totally unadjusted to present-day needs and conditions.

The Forgotten Flexibility and Adaptability of the Nineteenth-Century Monetary System

Indeed, what we tried to resurrect in 1928 and in 1958 was not even a corpse. It was a myth: the myth of a monetary system regulated by automatic market forces, protecting it against both the blessings and the curses of human decisions, and particularly against the inflationary proclivities of national governments.

According to this myth, the creation of money, in the nineteenth century, was strictly regulated by the gold standard. That is to say, fluctuations in the money supply were automatically controlled, for the world as a whole, by fluctuations in gold production, and for any individual country, by fluctuations in its gold assets, controlled themselves by the fluctuations of its balance of payments.

Let us admit, at the outset, that the maintenance of free and stable exchange rates is, and will always be, inseparable from long-term equilibrium in each country's balance of payments, and that such equilibrium is itself dependent upon the harmonization of monetary policies among the countries concerned. There is no doubt that the nineteenth-century gold standard imposed in this respect an ultimate brake on national monetary expansion in any single country, keeping it roughly in pace with monetary expansion in other gold standard countries.

There were, however, two elements of flexibility in the system, the importance of which is not sufficiently appreciated by the apostles of monetary automaticity.

The first is the crucial role of large-scale and persistent international capital movements financing substantial and persistent disequilibria in balances of payments on current account, and facilitating the acceptance of the ultimate discipline exercised by residual gold settlements upon national monetary policies.

The second is that the international pace of monetary expansion for the world as a whole was far from being automatically determined by fluctuations in gold production. Even the unprecedented expansion of gold mining after 1848 would have been insufficient to satisfy the monetary requirements of an expanding world economy. These requirements were met, to a far greater extent, by the enormous development of credit money, in the form of paper currency and bank deposits. At the very heyday of the gold standard—from 1880 to 1910—the latter alone increased by about ten times the country's total gold stock in the United States, and by about thirty times in the United Kingdom.

It is indeed this extraordinary flexibility and adaptability, rather than its supposed subordination to gold automaticity, that constitute the major characteristics of the nineteenth-century monetary system and the main explanation of its long survival and undoubted success.

They involved a constant evolution of monetary and banking institutions, marked not only by the gradual transfer of monetary functions from metallic money to credit money, but also by the growing underwriting and regulation of the latter by national central banks, endowed with a monopoly of paper currency issues, acting as a depository for commercial bank reserves and lender of last resort, and concentrating gradually in their coffers the bulk of each country's international gold reserves so as to enable them to preserve the international stability of the country's currency against temporary fluctuations in its balance of payments.

The Emergence of the Gold Shortage

This slow and gradual evolution was abruptly arrested by the collapse of the system at the outbreak of World War I, and its later resumption was heavily handicapped by the steady increase in credit money and price levels consequent upon the war itself. Monetary gold stocks, calculated at prewar parities, could not but fall drastically in proportion to money supply, production, and trade. Moreover, the average increase both in total and in monetary gold stocks was also declining from about 3 per cent a year in prewar days to 2 per cent or less after the war. This rate of increase was far below the minimum requirements for the growth of international monetary reserves in an expanding world economy.

The international monetary conferences of Brussels and Genoa and, later on, the Gold Delegation of the League of Nations debated endlessly and fruitlessly throughout the 1920's the problem of the international gold shortage, until it was temporarily, but disastrously, resolved for them outside the conference room by the collapse of world trade and production and the cascade of currency devaluations of the early 1930's, not to mention the spiraling of trade and exchange restrictions that marked the utter breakdown of the international monetary system in the 1930's and 1940's.

The unholy conjunction between the nostalgic disciples of gold automaticity and the new apostles of monetary nationalism was to rule out for many years the further evolution of international monetary institutions necessary to foster a rational adjustment of the supply of world reserves to the monetary requirements of an expanding world economy. The growth of world reserves was left dependent therefore upon a bundle of highly haphazard and erratic factors, the interplay of which could only result in a seesawing succession of deflationary and inflationary pressures upon the international monetary system.

Palliatives and Stopgaps

Gold production remained, in principle, the basic source of increase in world reserves, but accounted in fact for less than half of the increase of world reserves over the last half-century. Its actual contribution to reserve increases varied widely, from about 12 per cent of the total over the years 1929–33 to about 90 per cent in the period 1934–38, and a bare third in the last ten years.

A succession of stopgaps and makeshifts supplemented the gold in short supply.

The first lay in the continuation and acceleration of a nineteenth-century trend, i.e., the withdrawal of gold from actual public circulation, and its concentration in the coffers of central banks and treasuries. This accounted for no less than 30 per cent of the total reserve increases over the period 1914–28, and 44 per cent of the increase in gold reserves alone. This source of supply was not inexhaustible, however, and was in fact exhausted in the early 1930's with the withdrawal of gold coins from active circulation in all countries, including finally the United States of America.

A second expedient lay in the revaluation of gold in terms of national currencies. Over the years 1914–60, gold prices increased by 69 per cent in the United States, 194 per cent in the United Kingdom, and more than 15,000 per cent in France. If world reserves are expressed and calculated uniformly in terms of the U.S. dollar, however, only the dollar devaluation enters into account. It contributed more than 100 per cent of the increase in world reserves over the period 1929–33, other sources of increase being offset during these years by the simultaneous liquidation of sterling and dollar balances previously acquired and retained as monetary reserves by the central banks of other countries.

A third and growing source of world reserves has been, in recent years, from Russian gold sales in Western markets. These sales accounted for more than a fifth of total increases in Western gold reserves over the years 1950–59, and well over a third of such increases in the two years 1958 and 1959. Their abrupt suspension last summer helped pave the way for the October break in the London gold market and the dollar crisis that ensued. Their resumption since then has also played a role in the subsequent decline of gold prices on the markets.

Finally, the fourth and major source of world reserve increases has been the over-all balance-of-payments deficits of the United Kingdom and the United States, and the acceptance of sterling and dollar I.O.U.'s as supplementary means of reserve accumulation, alongside insufficient gold supplies, by the central banks of other countries. Sterling and dollar balances are, by far, the major component of foreign exchange reserves whose increase, for the world as a whole, accounts for more than a third of total reserve increases since 1914, and nearly 60 per cent of such increases over the decade of the 1950's. The wildly erratic nature of this component of world reserves is amply demonstrated by recent movements in official sterling and dollar holdings:

a) officially held sterling balances *declined* by more than $870 million between December 1956 and September 1958, but *increased* by $625 million in the following two years;

b) officially held dollar balances *declined* by $500 million in the first three months of 1957, but have *risen* since then by about $2,500 million, including an increase of more than $1,200 million in 1960 alone. This latter increase, let it be said in passing, was three to four times as large as the total growth of world gold reserves during that year.

Such is, in brief, the system which determines today the creation of international monetary reserves:

a) for a small, but rising fraction—9 per cent over the last ten years, but more than a third in the last three years—the whims or, worse, the strategy of Mr. Khrushchev's gold sales to the West;

b) for a larger, but still minor, fraction—34 per cent over the last decade—the hazards of mining production, much of which could be paralyzed tomorrow by the eruption of racial warfare in South Africa;

c) finally—and for well over half of total reserve increases in the last ten years—the wild and unpredictable fluctuations in the balance of payments of the United States and the United Kingdom, and in central bankers' willingness to finance part of these countries' over-all deficits through the continued accumulation and retention of dollar and sterling I.O.U.'s as a component part of their countries' monetary reserves.

Can anyone seriously argue that such a system—if indeed it can be dignified by that name—can safely be relied upon tomorrow, any more than in yesteryears, to adjust world reserves to actual requirements in an expanding world economy and to serve as a basis for a stable and viable system of international settlements? The point to be kept in mind is not that these various sources of reserve supply taken together have failed to provide enough liquidity. They may well, on the contrary, have provided too much, particularly in recent years owing to the enormous growth of dollar balances—official and private—associated with the $10 billion deficits incurred by the United States since the end of 1957.

The indictment of the present, unorganized gold exchange, or key-currencies, standard is that it can only operate—and has indeed operated for nearly half a century—in an utterly haphazard fashion, creating far too little liquidity at times, and at other times far too much, but then only through generalized currency devaluations or through a persistent piling up of sterling or dollar I.O.U.'s bound to undermine in the end the acceptability of these so-called key currencies as safe reserve media for other countries' central banks.

The Twilight of the Key-Currencies System

This danger has long been recognized in the United Kingdom, after the dire experiences of 1931, of 1947, of 1949, and of the recurrent sterling crises of the following decade. Neither the United Kingdom nor the other countries have shown any inclination, over the last ten years, to meet international reserve requirements through any continued piling up of sterling balances. The U.S. dollar substituted for sterling in this role in the years following World War II. But, after a long period of complacency, and the huge gold outflows of the last three years, the United States also have proclaimed their determination, and demonstrated their capacity, to stop their balance-of-payments deficits and the persistent piling up of dollar balances abroad.

This threatens, however, to eliminate the source from which two-thirds of the rest of the world's monetary reserves have been fed in the 1950's, and about three-fourths over the last three years. The build-up of world liquidity may well have been too rapid over this period, but a reduction of the rate of reserve increases by three-fourths or even two-thirds certainly could not fail to bring to an end the spectacular development of world trade and production which has marked the postwar years.

This, admittedly, is a long-run problem to which it is very difficult to elicit any early reaction from bureaucrats always anxious "not to cross any bridge before they come to it." More immediate, and indeed actual, is the Damocles sword suspended over British and American monetary policies by enormous sterling and dollar balances, legally convertible on short notice or on sight, under present convertibility arrangements, into gold or foreign currencies. Foreign-held dollar balances have passed over the last ten years from 38 per cent only of the United States gold reserves to more than 105 per cent as of last December. As for sterling balances, they have long been a multiple of British monetary reserves, and were about four times as high as the latter at the end of last year.

The dangers of such a situation have long been evident. They have repeatedly interfered with the proper conduct of monetary policy in the United Kingdom and, more recently, in the United States. Restrictive credit and interest rate policies had to be resorted to, not only when necessary to correct domestic inflationary developments and basic deficits in the balance of payments, but merely in order to protect the countries' reserves against excessive outflows of short-term funds, even at times when low interest rate and expansionary policies, fully compatible with long-run stability in external payments, were clearly called for to fight economic stagnation, recession, and unemployment.

On the other hand, the ease with which balance-of-payments deficits could, at other times, be financed by foreign accumulation of sterling or dollar balances tended, on such occasions, to postpone unduly remedial measures clearly called for by the deterioration in the two countries' basic position on external account. The much vaunted discipline of the gold standard has indeed been replaced, under the new gold exchange or key-currencies standard, by long periods of overindulgence, to be paid for later by a sudden and violent crisis in the international position of the key currencies.

The recurrent sterling crises of the last thirty years and the dollar crisis of the winter of 1960 have finally awakened even the most obdurate and conservative central bankers to the fragility of the present key-currencies standard. They realize the dangers which it involves not only for the reserve currencies themselves, but also for a world monetary system which has become more and more dependent upon them. Foreign exchange reserves—mostly dollar and sterling—constitute today no less than 55 per cent of the monetary reserves of countries other than the United States and the United Kingdom. A collapse of the key currencies would therefore entail inevitably a collapse of the world monetary system itself, not to mention the sharp reversal of the liberal commercial and foreign aid policies which have contributed so powerfully to the unprecedented expansion of world trade and production of the last decade.

PERSPECTIVE

Current Reform Plans

The need for international currency reforms, strongly denied as recently as last September by the monetary pundits assembled in Washington for the annual meeting of the International Monetary Fund, is now universally recognized. The Fund itself has opened consultations on the problem with its members, and similar explorations have been going on for several months now among the countries of the European Economic Community and, more recently, in the Economic Policy Committee of OEEC.

Among the various plans which have been openly advocated to meet the problem, three have received so far a disproportionate share of publicity: the Bernstein plan, the Stamp plan, and—if I am not mistaken—the Triffin plan.[1] Let me summarize, very briefly, the main outline of each of them.

a) The Bernstein plan. The Bernstein plan aims primarily, or even exclusively, at enabling the Fund to prevent large-scale capital movements among major countries from inducing excessive gold flows susceptible of endangering the stability of the main currencies used in world trade and payments. In order to achieve this purpose, it proposes that the Fund negotiate with these countries a series of stand-by commitments or lines of credit which could be drawn upon by the Fund whenever necessary to finance, through Fund lending to members in deficit, payments due by them to members accumulating large surpluses in their balance of payments.

b) The Stamp plan. The Stamp plan has an entirely different purpose. Concerned with the long-run problem of international liquidity, it would

---

[1] Edward M. Bernstein, "The Adequacy of United States Gold Reserves," *American Economic Review*, LI (1961), 439; Maxwell Stamp, "The Shortage of World Reserves" and "Ending the World's Gold Shortages," *Manchester Guardian*, February 10 and 13, 1961; Robert Triffin, *Gold and the Dollar Crisis, The Future of Convertibility* (New Haven, 1960). [See also selections 1, 3, and 9 of this volume.]

authorize the Fund to issue debentures, up to $3 billion, to finance lending to underdeveloped countries. All member countries of the Fund would agree to accept such debentures, apparently without any limit whatsoever, in payment for their surpluses, but would also be able to use them at any time to settle their deficits in international payments.

c) The Triffin plan. The Triffin plan is more ambitious. In its mildest version, it would merely authorize the Fund to accept, from member countries which wish to take advantage of this facility, international reserve deposits guaranteed against the dangers of currency devaluation or inconvertibility inseparable from the present accumulation of monetary reserves in the form of national currencies. Reserve deposits with the Fund would be as exempt from exchange risks as gold itself, but would also—as opposed to gold reserves—pay interest to the depositor. They should normally be extremely attractive to central bankers and displace gradually, without the need for any compulsion whatsoever, the use of foreign exchange, and even gold itself, as monetary reserves by member countries. A more ambitious version of the Triffin plan, however, would introduce compulsory reserve requirements with the Fund, in proportion to each country's level of total international reserves, so as to consolidate the system against any sudden conversion of deposits into gold by members. Even these minimum deposits with the Fund would nevertheless remain as fully liquid and usable as gold itself to meet all and any deficits in a country's international payments, but they could not be converted needlessly and capriciously into independent gold hoards.

Finally, the Triffin plan advocates as highly desirable the elimination of national currencies as a means of international reserve accumulation by central banks. This third feature of the plan would almost certainly be the most difficult to negotiate, particularly with the United States and the United Kingdom. It would, in particular, meet strenuous objections from all the Colonel Blimps, who confuse the use of dollar and sterling as international reserves with the prestige of the American or British flag, and who remember nostalgically the added resources derived in the past by both countries from the growth in their foreign short-term indebtedness, but close their eyes to the far more actual danger of withdrawals and liquidation of sterling and dollar balances in future years.

The resources derived by the Fund from the constitution of such deposits would enable it:

1. to adjust future levels of liquidity to the requirements of an expanding world economy;

2. to finance through its lending and investment operations any balance-of-payments deficits of a purely temporary character, and to support agreed stabilization programs designed to correct more permanent deficits in a country's international transactions;

3. to offset in particular, through corresponding shifts in its own investments portfolio, the impact of undesirable movements of short-term funds among the major financial markets of the world;

4. to do away, whenever the opportunity arises for a broad reform of the Fund's Articles of Agreement, with the absurdly rigid, cumbersome, and wasteful system of capital subscriptions from which the Fund has derived up to now useful assets in gold and a handful of currencies, but also vast amounts of bolivianos, cruzeiros, rupees, rupiahs, bahts, kyats, and other currencies totally useless for Fund lending.

Tentative Appraisal of the Three Plans

It will be no surprise to you to hear that my own preferences go to the Triffin plan, which would meet at one stroke all these various objectives, rather than the more limited objectives of either the Bernstein or the Stamp plan, valuable as these may be.

a) *The Bernstein plan.* The Bernstein plan makes no pretense of meeting the long-run liquidity requirements of an expanding world economy. This would continue to depend on future and recurrent increases in the Fund's capital, requiring each time cumbersome negotiations with several scores of countries, new international agreements among their governments, and—in most cases—legislative approval by their congress or parliament. Under the mechanism of the Fund, three-fourths of these additional capital subscriptions would be in the national currency of member countries and would—except for a handful of them—merely result in flooding the Fund with currencies with which it is already overflowing and for which it will have no earthly use in the foreseeable future. What point is there in complicating in this senseless fashion the already overburdened process of international negotiations for the mere pleasure of increasing even further the already bloated Fund holdings of cruzeiros, bolivianos, rupees, rupiahs, bahts, kyats, etc.? One is forcibly reminded of the old saying: "The mountain labors, and brings forth . . . a mouse!"

Mr. Bernstein's plan to meet short-term capital movements is not entirely devoid of the same absurdities. Its main claim to negotiability is indeed that it preserves intact the traditional procedures of operation of the IMF, no matter how absurd these have proved to be in the dire light of experience. The $6 billion lines of credit which he proposes are indeed tantamount to an increase in the national currency—but not in the gold—subscriptions of a limited number of Fund members. It is likely indeed that *some* of these lines of credit may prove useful in adding to the Fund's holdings of currencies of which its present supplies *may* prove inadequate in the future. But this is most unlikely with respect to the $3.5 billion dollar and sterling contributions which are contemplated in the Bernstein plan. Both countries are more likely to experience further over-all deficits, rather than surpluses, in their balance of payments, at least for some time to come. The Fund, moreover, already holds disproportionately large stocks of both currencies ($1.5 billion in sterling, and more than $3.3 billion in dollars). Of the other $2.5 billion to be raised from Germany, France, Italy, etc., a good portion may be unavailing also, since some of these countries may also run surpluses far short of their subscriptions—or even be in deficit—while the subscription of one or a few others may fall far short of their own surpluses. Once again, the "mountain" of paper commitments to be negotiated may turn out in the end to yield a mere "molehill" of lending power actually usable by the Fund.

I certainly agree that Mr. Bernstein's plan would be better than nothing. I am afraid, however, that it may distract attention from the basic defects in our international monetary system which I have stressed above, and that by leaving untouched the Fund's machinery itself, it would perpetuate the obvious flaws in that machinery which experience has brought to light.

The amounts of currency at the disposal of the Fund would remain dependent on advance, and necessarily haphazard, guesses about the future evolution of each country's balance of payments and on *ad hoc* negotiations with prospective creditors. Specific action by the Fund would also remain necessary in each case to thwart—or offset—the normal tendency of members to concentrate their borrowings on the so-called "reserve currencies" or "key currencies," rather than on the currencies of the countries with over-all balance-of-payments surpluses.[2] If and when sufficient support can be gathered for amending the Fund's statutes, it would seem to me far preferable to seize upon this opportunity to simplify, streamline, and rationalize the whole Agreement in such a way as to minimize the need

---

[2] Mr. Bernstein suggests that the reserve currency countries whose currency has been regrettably requested from, and improperly sold by, the Fund can always *offset this destabilizing action* of the Fund by subsequent drawings of the surplus countries' currencies. This is true, but remains nevertheless an unnecessarily roundabout and ludicrous procedure of achieving the Fund's stabilizing objectives.

for future revisions or makeshifts and for periodic renegotiation of the capital subscriptions of members. This could be done, most simply and rationally, by substituting for the present capital subscriptions of the Fund a system of minimum deposit requirements adjusting continually and automatically to future fluctuations in each country's monetary reserves, i.e., to its balance-of-payments surpluses or deficits and, therefore, both to its lending capacity and to the Fund's legitimate needs for its currency.

b) *The Stamp plan.* Mr. Stamp's proposals attack directly the problem of international liquidity left unsolved by Mr. Bernstein, but they seem to me insufficiently developed and precise, particularly as to the obligation of members to retain—as well as to accept—Fund debentures as part of their reserves. No clear criterion is offered in this respect, and the possibility seems to be left open to members to try to pass back such debentures from one to another as fast as they can if, for any reason, they prefer gold to claims on the Fund. Moreover, the over-all amount of debentures would in any case have to be increased periodically over time, and each of these increases would presumably require a new round of international negotiations and parliamentary approvals.

Finally, Mr. Stamp's plan, just as Mr. Bernstein's plan, leaves untouched the basic flaws in the Fund's machinery discussed above, and fails to control the haphazard creation or destruction of international liquidity associated with the use of *national* currencies as *international* reserves by central banks.

c) *The Triffin plan.* I would be less than candid, however, if I left unmentioned the major objections raised against my own plan. They come, as I have already mentioned, from opposite ends of the political spectrum. Conservative central bankers are afraid of the inflationary potentialities of a system which would, in fact, endow the Fund with money-creating power. Inflationists and monetary nationalists, on the other hand, denounce the harsh discipline which the Fund might impose upon prospective borrowers and the loss of national sovereignties to a world central bank, which they read into my plan.

I have tried to forestall the first objection by a very simple proposal. Any expansion in Fund lending and investments, susceptible of increasing world reserves at more than an admittedly modest and noninflationary rate of, say, 3 or 4 per cent a year, would require special majorities of three-fifths, two-thirds, three-fourths, or even more, of the total voting power of members.

As for the second, and opposite objection, it should be obvious that there is nothing in my proposals that would make the discipline of the Fund on prospective borrowers any harsher than it is now, or than the Executive Board of the Fund wishes it to be. Nor would they limit the national sovereignty of any member any more than it already is. On the contrary, they would offer all Fund members an additional outlet for the investment of their reserves, which they do not have at present, and which would combine the attractions of both gold and foreign exchange holdings, i.e., safety against exchange risks together with earning power. The United States and the United Kingdom might, it is true, be requested by the Fund to repay some of the outstanding dollar and sterling balances turned over by members in exchange for Fund deposits. But they are now exposed to sudden, unpredictable, and massive liquidation of such balances by their present owners, for speculative or other reasons, while the Fund's requests for repayment would be limited to some moderate pre-agreed annual ceiling and should be presented only insofar as useful for the discharge of its over-all objectives of international monetary stabilization. On the contrary, the more flexible investment techniques open to a reformed Fund for the placement of its vastly expanded resources would be of particular benefit to the United States and the United Kingdom, since they would be less likely to trigger dangerous psychological market reactions than the current lending procedures of the Fund.

Let me note, in passing, that international agreements are not the only way in which a country can lose its real sovereignty. On the contrary, they may often strengthen a country's effective sovereignty by protecting it against unilateral action by others. In the present case, the transfer of outstanding dollar and sterling balances to the Fund would precisely restore to the United States and the United Kingdom a freedom of monetary and credit policies which both countries have lost through the previous accumulation of dangerous levels of short-term indebtedness abroad in the form of highly liquid dollar and sterling balances.

Nor do my proposals really contemplate the establishment of the full-fledged world-wide central bank or super–central bank, which some commentators have read into them. All they would do is create a central depository for central bank reserves, now dispersed among national money markets—primarily London and New York—in the form of foreign exchange holdings, and to organize a clearing house for settlements among national central banks. The reformed Fund would in no way control or assume responsibility for national monetary issue functions, which would remain entirely, as they are now, at the discretion of national monetary authorities in each of the participating countries. Inflationary abuses of these functions would inevitably continue to be sanctioned in the end by price rises and reserve losses and currency devaluation. There is a far cry, therefore, between my proposals and the creation of a world central bank.

What is true is that the Fund would be enabled to intervene more actively than at present to adjust the creation of international liquidity to the legitimate needs of an expanding world economy, to offset through appropriate shifts in its investments the dangerous impact of destabilizing capital movements, and to give more adequate support to members whose deficits either are recognized as purely temporary in character or are in the process of being corrected through the implementation of mutually agreed stabilization policies. Properly used, these functions could not fail to develop in time habits of international consultation, cooperation, and even integration of national monetary policies which would greatly strengthen the chances for the long-run maintenance of both exchange freedom and exchange stability among the participating countries.

Allowing ourselves to dream, or to peer into a more distant future, we might finally note that the modest functions which I have ascribed above to a reformed IMF—i.e., to act as a clearing house for its members and a central depository for their reserves—are precisely the crucial functions universally assumed by national central banks at the origin of their development, and from which their other functions grew up gradually through some internal, but compelling, logic. I would myself welcome, rather than deplore, the perspectives for future evolution of the international monetary system which might be suggested by this analogy with the past evolution of national monetary and banking systems the world over. Yet, I cannot, as of now, attach too much weight to such idle speculations.

The Case for a Regional Approach

There exist, on the other hand, much more solid grounds for hoping that the adoption of similar reforms in a regional, rather than in a worldwide, framework, might assist powerfully the development of an increasingly closer monetary integration—even up to and including a full monetary unification—among countries which are pursuing, with sufficient determination and good luck, long-run objectives of economic integration and political federation. The European Economic Community clearly comes to mind as a possible candidate for an evolution of this sort.

On the other hand, I must admit to some skepticism as to the possibility of implementing at this stage through the International Monetary Fund even the modest steps which I have described as necessary and possible in the short run to consolidate the present international monetary structure against obvious sources of vulnerability and eventual collapse. Something will undoubtedly be done within the next few months to increase the resources of the Fund, but I am afraid it will remain far short of the mark. The large number of participating countries—about seventy today—imposes upon the Fund an administrative organization extremely heavy and complex, making next to impossible the secrecy of deliberation and the rapidity of decision often indispensable in this field. The lack of close contacts and mutual understanding and trust among such a heterogeneous group of countries is a further handicap palliated, but not eliminated, by the adoption of rigid and legalistic rules of operation and of a voting system which gives relatively little weight to some countries—particularly in continental Europe—which would become major contributors to the deposit system contemplated above.

These difficulties are not insurmountable, but they require, in my opinion, a more realistic organization of international monetary cooperation, and particularly a drastic decentralization of the International Monetary Fund's machinery. Such decentralization is universally accepted as necessary for the effective organization of policy-making decisions in a national community. All power is not vested in the national government. Some of it is left to provincial or state governments, and even to smaller administrative units such as counties, cities, townships, etc. If this be necessary even within a historically integrated community, how much more necessary must it be in the initial building stages of an international monetary administration encompassing widely heterogeneous areas, with vastly different problems arising from a variegated history, and at greatly uneven stages of political, economic, and financial development. To ignore these realities, to insist on concentrating all power in a world-wide body—be it the International Monetary Fund or the United Nations—risks making of this body a mere debating club, rather than a true administration in constant contact with the problems to be resolved, and with effective leverage to carry out the decisions arrived at.

My own feeling, therefore, is that instead of being implemented through the IMF alone, the reforms which I have advocated should be inserted in very large part within the framework of existing, or future, regional organizations such as the European Economic Community, the Organization for Economic Cooperation and Development (OECD), the Latin American Free Trade Area, etc.

Toward an Atlantic Monetary Organization?

The most important and immediately feasible step in this direction could be taken on the occasion of the creation of OECD. An Atlantic Monetary Organization among all OECD countries should be set up along the lines described above. The members of OECD could distribute their international deposits between the IMF and the Atlantic Monetary Organization in rough proportion to their pattern of international trade and payments outside and within the OECD area. This would help solve, or bypass, the voting power hurdle in IMF by keeping a substantial portion of the deposits under the more closely knit and more workable management of OECD.

These possibilities should retain the attention of the working group recently set up in Paris by the Economic Policy Committee to determine the future lines of international monetary cooperation among the OECD countries. President Kennedy, in his Message of February 6 on the balance of payments and gold, specifically called for international monetary reforms designed to reduce the present dependence of an expanding world economy on "increased gold production and continued growth in holdings of dollars and pounds sterling. In the future, it may not always be desirable or appropriate to rely entirely on these sources." And after referring to the necessary strengthening of international monetary institutions—especially the IMF—he continued:

> The United States must take the lead in harmonizing the financial and economic policies for growth and stability of those industrialized nations of the world whose economic behavior significantly influences the course of the world economy and the trend of international payments. . . . The OECD is of vital importance for assisting, on a cooperative basis, the developing countries of the free world. It will also provide a solid framework within which we can carry out intensive and frequent international consultations on the financial and monetary policies which must be pursued in order to achieve and maintain better balance in the international payments position.[3]

The same note was struck in a *United States Aide-Mémoire on the Balance of Payments*, released on February 20:[4]

> Sustained accumulation of gold and other international reserves by any one country is disruptive to the international community. Especially now, when

[3] "President Kennedy's Message on Balance of Payments and Gold Outflow," *New York Times*, International Ed., Paris, February 7, 1961.
[4] "U.S. Note on Payments," *ibid.*, February 21, 1961.

trade is expanding faster than gold production, we must learn to use our reserves on a communal basis, recognizing that one nation's gains can only be another nation's loss . . . Our common task is to design a reserves policy for the alliance which will recognize the responsibilities to the common interest of surplus and deficit nations alike.

Finally, Britain's Prime Minister, Mr. Macmillan, stressed during his visit to Washington last April the political as well as the economic considerations which make it imperative for the Western nations to adjust their monetary, as well as their commercial, institutions to the common policies which they are bound to pursue if they wish to survive. He spoke forcefully about the "unsatisfactory" nature of present monetary arrangements, noting that world trade had expanded fourfold in money terms since the war, against only a doubling of the international credit base.

All sorts of remedies are being suggested. The main difficulty about many of them is what I might call the mental hurdles which they present . . . there seems to be something immoral in increasing the credit base by mutual agreement. It is done often enough in our internal economies; but the extension to the international field is hard to swallow. . . . Just as each individual country painfully acquired a central banking system, so there ought—ideally—to be a central banking system for all the countries of the free world.[5]

Equal emphasis was also placed by the Prime Minister on immediately feasible steps in this direction, and particularly on "the urgent need of bringing together the Six and the Seven" and of thinking "not so much nationally or even in terms of greater economic cooperation between nations but in terms of wider groupings . . . of large areas transcending national boundaries."[6]

Current Prospects

The fulfillment of these lofty objectives and calls for action can only be achieved, however, by overcoming the enormous inertia of timorous, tradition-bound bureaucrats, who have always opposed such revolutionary changes in the institutional framework and modes of thought to which they are accustomed. I don't doubt that some progress toward international monetary consolidation will emerge from the current debate, but we still

[5] "Speech by the Prime Minister, the Rt. Hon. Harold Macmillan, M.P., at the Massachusetts Institute of Technology, on Friday, 7th April, 1961," released by Admiralty House, pp. 8–9.

[6] *Ibid.*, pp. 6–7.

run the risk, President Kennedy and Prime Minister Macmillan notwith-standing, of yielding once more to the almost irresistible temptation of confining this progress to halfway measures and stopgaps that would close, rather than open, the door to the further adjustments and historical evolution of our international monetary system indispensable to its survival in a fast-changing world.

The explorations and negotiations now under way may well uncover other, and better, means of dealing with the problems which I have raised. Anybody who has ever participated in negotiations of this sort cannot but be keenly aware of the need to prune, amplify, and readjust initial proposals in the light of the unforeseen difficulties, but also of the unsuspected opportunities, which only the actual process of negotiation can bring to light. This applies to the Triffin plan as well as to the Bernstein plan and the Stamp plan. The greatest obstacle to the maximum achievement that should be hoped for and striven for would be a premature freezing of discussion in some predetermined channel, a barring of the door to a full exploration of all feasible techniques for strengthening the international monetary structure of the West, and indeed of the world itself.

Index